J. A. Dehner sj

Theology and Sexuality

Blackwell Readings in Modern Theology

General Editors: L. Gregory Jones and James J. Buckley

Duke University, North Carolina; Loyola College, Maryland

Blackwell Readings in Modern Theology is a series of constructive anthologies on important topics in modern theology. Each volume brings together both classic and newly commissioned essays on a particular theme. These essays will provide students and teachers in colleges, universities and seminaries with a critical entry to key debates.

For a full contents listing or for more information visit our website at http://www.blackwellpublishers.co.uk/religion

Published works

The Theological Interpretation of Scripture
Classic and Contemporary Readings
Edited by Stephen E. Fowl

The Postmodern God
A Theological Reader
Edited by Graham Ward

Inquiring after God
Classic and Contemporary Readings
Edited by Ellen T. Charry

Theology after Liberalism
A Reader
Edited by John Webster and George P. Schner

Theology and Sexuality
Classic and Contemporary Readings
Edited by Eugene F. Rogers, Jr.

Theology and Sexuality

Classic and Contemporary Readings

Edited by

Eugene F. Rogers, Jr.

BLACKWELL
Publishers

First published 2002

2 4 6 8 10 9 7 5 3 1

Blackwell Publishers Ltd
108 Cowley Road
Oxford OX4 1JF
UK

Blackwell Publishers Inc.
350 Main Street
Malden, Massachusetts 02148
USA

British Library Cataloguing in Publication Data

A CIP catalogue record for this book is available from the British Library.

Library of Congress Cataloging-in-Publication Data

Theology and sexuality : classic and contemporary readings / edited by Eugene F. Rogers, Jr.
    p. cm. — (Blackwell readings in modern theology)
Includes bibliographical references and index.
ISBN 0–631–21276–0 (alk. paper) — ISBN 0–631–21277–9 (pbk. : alk. paper)
1. Sex—Religious aspects—Christianity. I. Rogers, Eugene F. II. Series.

BT708 .T45 2002
233′.5—dc21

2001037565

Typeset in 10½ on 12 pt Ehrhardt
by Ace Filmsetting Ltd, Frome, Somerset
Printed in Great Britain by MPG Books Ltd, Bodmin, Cornwall

This book is printed on acid-free paper.

for
Susan Dodson Rogers
1931–1999

Contents

Contents ───

Contents ——————————————————————————————

Contributors

Marilyn McCord Adams is Horace Tracy Pitkin Professor of Historical Theology in Religious Studies, Philosophy, and Divinity at Yale University.

James Alison is a Catholic priest, theologian, and author.

St. Thomas Aquinas (1225–74) was a Dominican theologian.

St. Augustine (354–430) was Bishop of Hippo.

Karl Barth (1886–1968) was a Swiss Calvinist theologian.

John Boswell (1947–94) was A. Whitney Griswold Professor of History at Yale University.

Thomas Breidenthal is John Henry Hobart Professor of Moral Theology at the General Theological Seminary, New York.

Paul Evdokimov (1901–70) was a Russian Orthodox priest and theologian.

Susan A. Harvey is Associate Professor of Religious Studies at Brown University.

Stanley Hauerwas is Gilbert T. Rowe Professor of Theological Ethics at Duke Divinity School.

Charles Hawes is Chaplain of St. Mary's House, University of North Carolina at Greensboro.

Robert W. Jenson is Senior Scholar for Research at the Center for Theological Inquiry, Princeton.

St. John Chrysostom (ca. 347–407) was Patriarch of Constantinople.

St. John of the Cross (1542–91) was the founder of the Discalced Carmelites.

Luke Timothy Johnson is R. W. Woodruff Professor of New Testament at Candler Divinity School, Emory University.

Mark D. Jordan is Asa Griggs Candler Professor of Religion at Emory University.

David Matzko McCarthy is Assistant Professor of Theology at Mount St. Mary's College.

Sebastian Moore, OSB, is at Downside Abbey.

Thomas Nagel is Professor of Philosophy and Law, New York University.

Oliver O'Donovan is Regius Professor of Moral Theology at Oxford University.

Eugene F. Rogers, Jr., is Associate Professor of Religious Studies at the University of Virginia.

George P. Schner, SJ (1946–2000) was Associate Professor of Systematic Theology at Regis College, the University of Toronto.

Jeffrey Stout is Professor of Religion, Princeton University.

Andrew Sullivan is Senior Editor of *The New Republic*.

St. Symeon the New Theologian (942–1022) was Abbot of Saint Mamas.

Rowan D. Williams was formerly Lady Margaret Professor of Divinity at Oxford University, and is now Archbishop of Wales.

Acknowledgments

I wish to thank Blackwell Publishers, especially Alex Wright, who commissioned this anthology, and L. Gregory Jones and James J. Buckley, in whose series it appears.

I wish to thank the National Humanities Center for support during a leave year 1998–9 when I began this project. At the Humanities Center I am especially grateful to Robert Connor, the Director; Kent Mullikin, the Deputy Director; Karen Carroll, the wonderful Coordinator of Editorial Services; and the splendid librarians, Alan Tuttle, Jean Houston, and Eliza Robertson, who not only found all sorts of out-of-the-way materials, but found them fast and often even xeroxed them – tremendous help for an anthologizer.

I wish to thank the University of Virginia for additional support during 1998–9, for Summer Research Grants in several years, as well as for a University Seminar Research Grant that allowed me to teach this material twice. Thanks also to Library Express On-Grounds, which delivers books, xeroxes, and electronic files to my office or computer, especially Lew Purifoy and Winston Barham.

And I wish to thank the students of those seminars; my research assistant, Trent Pomplun; and my indexer, Willis Jenkins.

Finally, I wish to thank Derek Krueger for moral support.

For errors I have only myself to thank.

The publishers gratefully acknowledge the following for permission to reproduce copyright material.

"Embodiment in Time and Eternity: A Syriac Perspective," by Susan Harvey, from *St. Vladimir's Seminary Quarterly* 43 (1993): 106–30. Used by permission of St. Vladimir's Theological Quarterly, 575 Scarsdale Road, Crestwood, NY 10707.

"The Appeal to Experience," by G. P. Schner, from *Journal of Theological Studies* 53 (1992): 40–59 (1992). Reprinted by permission of Oxford University Press Journals.

Extracts from *The Book of Common Prayer* (1979), Episcopal Church, USA.

"Betrothal Service" and "Order of Second Marriage" from *Service Book of the Holy Orthodox-Catholic and Apostolic Church*, 6th ed., trans. Isabel Hapgood, pp. 291–3 and 302–5. Reprinted by permission of Antiochan Orthodox Christian Archdiocese of North America, New Jersey.

Extract from the "Office of Same-Sex Union," Grottaferrata Gamma B II, in John Boswell, *Same-Sex Unions in Premodern Europe*, Villard Books, 1994, pp. 294–8.

"Tomorrow Shall Be My Dancing Day" (II), English Traditional, Sandys 1833.

Augustine, "The Good of Marriage," partially translated in *Marriage in the Early Church*, ed. and trans. David G. Hunter, *Sources of Early Christian Thought*, pp. 102–21. Reprinted by permission of Augsburg Fortress Publishers, Minneapolis.

"Homily on Marriage," partially translated as *Sermon on Marriage* in *On Marriage and Family Life*, trans. Catherine P. Roth and David Anderson (Crestwood, NY: St. Vladimir's Seminary Press, 1997), pp. 81–8. Used by permission of St. Vladimir's Press, 575 Scarsdale Road, Crestwood, NY 10707.

"Against the Opponents of the Monastic Life," by John Chrysostom, in *A Comparison of Treatises by John Chrysostom*, trans. David G. Hunter, Studies in the Bible and Early Christianity, 13, published by Edwin Mellen Press, 1988, pp. 162–3. Reprinted by permission of Edwin Mellen Press.

"Hymns of Divine Love 15," St. Symeon the New Theologian, *Hymns of Divine Love*, trans. George A. Maloney, pp. 51–8, 2nd ed. March 1999, published by Dimension Books Inc. Reprinted with permission.

St. John of the Cross, "The Spiritual Canticle: Songs Between the Soul and the Bridegroom," in John Frederick Nims trans., *The Poems of St. John of the Cross*, a bilingual edition, 3rd ed., published by University of Chicago Press, 1979, pp. 3–17, odd-numbered pages only. Reprinted by permission of University of Chicago Press.

"An den Etnologen Rolf Italiaander, Hamburg," from *Offene Briefe 1945–1986*, by Karl Barth, ed. Diether Koch, in Jürgen Fangmeier and Hinrich Stoevesadt, eds., *Karl Barth Gesammtausgabe V Briefe*, pp. 542–3 © 1984. Reprinted by permission of Theologischer Verlag, Zurich.

Extract from *The Epistle to the Romans* by K. Barth, trans. from the 6th ed. by E. C. Hoskyns, 1933. Reprinted by permission of the publishers, Oxford University Press.

Thomas Nagel, "Sexual Perversion," in *Mortal Questions*, published by Cambridge University Press New York, 1979, pp. 39–52. Reprinted by permission of Cambridge University Press New York.

Jeffrey Stout, "Moral Abominations," from *Ethics after Babel: The Languages of Morals and their Discontents*, by Jeffrey Stout. Copyright © 1988 by Jeffrey Stout. Published by Beacon Press. Reprinted by permission of Beacon Press, Boston.

Sebastian Moore, "The Crisis of an Ethic Without Desire," in *Jesus the Liberator of Desire*, published by Crossroad, 1989, pp. 89–107. Reprinted by kind permission of the author.

John Paul II, selections from *The Original Unity of Man and Woman: Catechesis of the Book of Genesis*, published by St. Paul Editions, *L'Osservatore Romano*. Reprinted by permission of *L'Osservatore Romano*.

Paul Evdokimov, selections from "Introduction" and "Marriage and the Monastic State," in *The Sacrament of Love: The Nuptial Mystery in the Light of the Orthodox Tradition*, trans. Anthony P. Gythiel and Victoria Steadman, published by St. Vladimir's Seminary Press in 1985, pp. 15–19, 21–2, 41–5, 65–71, and 81–3. Used by permission of St. Vladimir's Press, 575 Scarsdale Road, Crestwood, NY 10707.

"Faithfulness" by Robert W. Jenson, from *Dialog* 14 (1975): 38–41. Reprinted by permission of Blackwell Publishers Limited.

"The Relationship of Bodies: A Nuptial Hermeneutics of Same-sex Unions" by David Matzko McCarthy in *Theology and Sexuality* 8 (1998): 96–112. Reprinted by permission of Sheffield Academic Press.

"Sanctification, Homosexuality, and God's Triune Life" by Eugene F. Rogers from *Sexual Orientation and Human Rights in American Religious Discourse*, eds. Martha Nussbaum and Saul Olyan. Copyright © 1998 Oxford University Press Inc. Used by permission of Oxford University Press, Inc.

Extracts from the "Letter to the Bishops of the Catholic Church on the Pastoral Care of Homosexual Persons." Reproduced by permission of Libreria Editrice Vaticana, 2001.

Mark Jordan, "The Pope Converts: Imagination, Bureaucracy, Silence," ch. 1 in *The Silence of Sodom: Homosexuality in the Catholic Church*, published by

University of Chicago Press, 2000, pp. 1–17. Reprinted by permission of University of Chicago Press.

"Alone Again, Naturally: The Catholic Church and the Homosexual," by Andrew Sullivan, from *The New Republic*, Nov. 26, 1994, pp. 47, 50, 52, 54, 55. Reprinted by permission of *The New Republic* © 1994 The New Republic Inc.

Excerpt from "Faith Healing" from *Collected Poems* by Phillip Larkin. Copyright © 1988, 1989 by the Estate of Phillip Larkin. Reprinted by permission of Farrar, Strauss & Giroux, LLC. This excerpt also reproduced by courtesy of Faber and Faber Ltd.

Stanley Hauerwas, "Gay Friendship: A Thought Experiment in Catholic Moral Theology," in *Sanctify Them in the Truth: Holiness Exemplified*, published by T. & T. Clark, 1998, pp. 105–21. Reprinted by permission of the publishers.

Rowan D. Williams, "The Bodies Grace," 10th Michael Harding Memorial Address – Institute for the Study of Christianity and Sexuality, 1989, reprinted in *Our Selves, Our Souls and Bodies: Sexuality and the Household of God*, ed. C. Hefling, Cowley Press, 1996. Reprinted by permission of Lesbian & Gay Christians.

"Trinitarian Friendship: Same-Gender Models of Godly Love in Richard of St. Victor and Aelred of Rievaulx" by Marilyn McCord Adams, Horace Tracy Pitkin Professor of Historical Theology in Religious Studies, Philosophy, and Divinity, Yale University.

Copyright 1986 by Charles Hefling. All rights reserved. Reprinted from *Our Selves, Our Souls and Bodies* edited by Charles Hefling, from the essay *Sanctifying Nearness* by Thomas Breidenthal, published by Cowley Publications, 28 Temple Place, Boston, MA 02111. Www.cowley.org (1 800 225 1534)

Introduction in *Uncommon Calling: A Gay Man's Struggle to Serve the Church* by Chris Galser, published by Westminster John Knox Press. Copyright © 1988 Chris Galser. Used by permission of Westminster John Knox Press.

Charles Hawes (chaplain of St. Mary's House, University of North Carolina at Greensboro), sermon at Richey/Smith wedding, Black Mountain Presbyterian Church, May 28, 1994. Used with permission.

"Disputed Questions: Debate and Discernment, Scripture and the Spirit" by Luke Timothy Johnson, in *Commonweal*, Jan. 28, 1994. Copyright (c) 1994 Commonweal Foundation, reprinted by permission. For subscriptions call toll-free 1-888-495-6755.

"Theology amidst the Stones and Dust" by James Alison, from *Faith Beyond*

Resentment: Fragments Catholic and Gay. Reprinted by permission of Darton Longman & Todd Ltd. and Crossroad Publishing Co., New York.

The publishers apologize for any errors or omissions in the above list and would be grateful to be notified of any corrections that should be incorporated in the next edition or reprint of this book.

Introduction

What is the body for? What does marriage mean? What is the purpose of Christianity? What does God want with sex, anyway?

A remarkable convergence is emerging with short, catechetical answers to questions like these from among Protestant, Catholic, and Eastern Orthodox writers. The convergence is remarkable both because it comes from so many corners, and because it arises from an area in which the arguments have usually been particularly long and dreary: theology and sexuality.

Theology and sexuality studies have often talked past each other or gone unheard in a shouting match. Charges of question-begging abound. That is particularly the case these days on the issue of homosexuality and Christianity. Thus liberals find that natural-law approaches beg the question of what's natural. Or they find that divine-command approaches beg the question of how God created us. Similarly, conservatives find that psychological approaches find no foothold in Scripture or tradition, or that constructivist approaches may remain theologically inert.

Numerous anthologies have appeared. They tend to support one side or the other. In rarer cases they announce debates. Both the one-sided and the debating anthologies tend to present hardened positions. More rarely still they claim to get "beyond the impasse." The current anthology originally approached that form. It was divided into biblical, liturgical, and classical resources, from which several modern positions derived: those who would prohibit homosexual activity, those who would permit it under marriage-like circumstances, and what I called an emerging consensus. That organization of the recent material, however, simply re-presented the format of debate.

The interesting thing about the dispute, however, was not at all the predictable debates, but how it had caused Christians generally, and not just those concerned with sexuality debates and culture wars, to recover marriage metaphors for the relation of God and God's people, and how it had begun to answer the question of what marriage might be for in the church, apart from what Evdokimov calls functionalisms of control of lust or procreation of children. I have found students often at a loss to say what marriage might be for. They tend not to believe that it is practically necessary any more to legitimate sexual intercourse or children, and they cannot imagine more for it to mean. It is the point of this volume to recover that "more," which is the ascetic more, the pearl of great price that the body might have more to mean. The late twentieth-century texts, conservative and liberal, all treat sexuality and marriage as ways in which God can produce human beings who become, over time, aware of grace and communities of virtue. The interesting thing was the recovery of rationales for our creation with bodies, the purpose of Christianity, of sexuality, of marriage, now without regard for the debates that had caused their recovery, and even without regard for one's position in those debates. One can agree with all of the positions below, whether one comes to them approving of same-sex marriage or not. For that reason, the essays now appear under theological rubrics, rather than under rubrics pro and con. The point is that both conservatives and liberals have much to learn from those recovering the tradition – which is to say, from each other – about the point of bodies, sexualities, marriages, and Christianity itself. Thus authors in this volume have proved able to answer the opening questions in ways like these:

The body exists to perceive and manifest the glory of God. It is in the body that God comes to meet and save and elevate human beings.[1]

Marriage is a means by which a couple donate their bodies to be signs to the community of the faithful of God's reconciliation.[2] Marriage displays the promise-keeping that God practices in the trinitarian communion and toward Israel.[3]

Christianity has as its rationale the task of teaching us that God loves us as God loves God, that we may perceive ourselves, therefore, as occasions of joy.[4]

Sexuality is a sign that we cannot escape of our vulnerability to the neighbor[5] and to God who "penetrates the creature . . . completely naked before Him," or, if you prefer a feminine metaphor, to Wisdom, who "envelopes all things."[6] It is a means God can use to "catch us up into" God's own life,[7] not least because it "ropes us into" commitments and disciplines from which also we cannot easily escape.[8] Sexuality is primarily, therefore, for sanctification, not for satisfaction – or for the consummation that sanctification brings.

None of this means any kind of sex-mysticism or Christian tantra. A friend of mine wrote that Christian couples are worried enough that their sex life is not measuring up to society's standards; "the last thing we need is *spiritually significant* sex, God help us!" Rather, what are significant are the commitments and disciplines, the practices of community and sanctification, that God and the church catch sexually linked couples up into. The goal here is the goal in all parts of human life – the fostering of faith, hope, and charity.

That goes especially when the raising of children comes into view. The great contribution of early Christianity to the raising of children had to do with its view of itself. Jesus himself was a humanly fatherless child, adopted by Joseph. Baptism was a rite of adoption. Through it Gentiles became children of the God of Israel. Monastic communities and others did a good deed unto Christ as they did it unto the least of their children when they adopted children abandoned in their midst. In raising natural children they enacted an analogate to the raising up of spiritual children to God in baptism. In this theology, as David McCarthy mentions, child-rearing becomes essentially the task of the faithful community, even if delegated to natural parents. From Chrysostom in the fourth century to Zizioulas in the twentieth, many authors have regarded compulsory procreation as undermining Christians' belief in the resurrection. Because the resurrection, rather than natural childbirth, secures the future for Christians, adoption becomes the type of child-rearing (the theologically correct way of understanding it), because it shows how childbirth and parenting, like baptism and godparenting, are not natural entitlements but reciprocal occasions for thanksgiving.

Multiple criteria have motivated the inclusion of readings in this collection. Earlier texts provide liturgical and classical theological resources cited or taken for granted in the contemporary essays, that students often will not read, teachers sometimes will not have, and scholars occasionally will not be aware of, unless they appear in the same volume.

The selections also share an attitude toward the appeal to "experience," a prominent feature of modern theology. Liberals appeal to gay and lesbian, divorced and remarried folks' "experience" to get a hearing from conservatives. Conservatives in turn castigate the "experience" as having vitiated the standing of the ones reporting it. What grants authority with one group undermines it in another. The arguments prove more fruitful when couched in other terms. Because of this indirection, the book might almost be called "After the Body." In the essays that follow, experience is always mediated through reason, tradition, sense of the faithful, the work of the Spirit – because only as mediated is experience communal and communicable.

As I was putting together this anthology, I was also planning another book, to be called *After the Spirit* (under contract for Westview). Its topic is in part the continual lip-service and equally continual lack of substance accorded the Holy Spirit in modern Christian thought. Committed to talk of the Spirit by its tradition, modern Christian thought has increasingly little to say about it. Spirit talk in the twentieth century is ever more invoked, and ever more substance-free. The Spirit, who in classical Christian discourse "makes all things new," had, in modern Christian discourse, become boring.

It did occur to me that I was writing books at two ends of a spectrum, body and spirit. But it was not until I had an urge to get organized that I realized what was happening. It was hard to divide the "spirit" books from the "body" books. I was duplicating articles to file them in two places at once. I was reaching for a center from two ends.

What if the Spirit had grown boring because it no longer had anything to do with the body? And what if bodily experience led to mutual dismissal because too individualist, because my subjects no longer dared argue in terms of a common Spirit?

In the first four centuries of the Christian era, talk of the Holy Spirit was almost always strictly tied to talk of holy places, holy people, and holy things. It did not float free of bodily existence as it does in modern Christian thought. Indeed, it was embodied. One locus was baptism, in which the Spirit descended upon a person. Another was the Eucharist, where, according to the Syriac tradition, it dwelt as a fire in consecrated bread and wine. A third was unction, in which "oil is the dear friend of the Holy Spirit,"[9] as Ephrem the Syrian wrote. It breathed on the water at creation; it moved in Mary's womb; it animated the churches; it appealed to the senses as light, fire, incense, wine, and song. The Spirit was not merely transcendent; it was immanent in bodily things.

Christian worship constructs the body liturgically. So, for example, the notorious asceticisms of Symeon the Stylite – one of a number of such saints who spent years standing atop a pillar – turn out to be keyed to the mass and the calendar. Symeon's own ecclesiastical superiors, worrying lest his self-denial would lead to death, persuaded him to put them at the service of others. So he was induced to preach from his pillar, the people processing in and out as if at mass – and restricting his homilies to reasonable length. He was encouraged to save his greatest austerities for penitential seasons: he must eat more in ordinary time so as to eat less during Lent. One hagiographer even suggested that in standing on pillar-top he made of his body a living sacrifice rising like incense up to God. His body becomes a communicative sign, a liturgical formation – or as the traditional language would put it, imbued with the Spirit. (See Susan Harvey, "The Sense of a Stylite."[10]) The same kind of liturgical construction of the body is going on when modern Christian groups decide who may marry, who may offer themselves as communicative signs to the community.

Thus the anthology opens with two essays that may seem off-topic – but they provide crucial context. Susan Harvey's "Embodiment in Time and Eternity: A Syriac Perspective" argues that the liturgy, as the place in which the body comes most explicitly to perceive and manifest God's glory, rather than sexuality, is the site from which to understand Christianity's construction of the body. George Schner's "Appeal to Experience" examines the rhetorical and argumentative roles covered by that word. It appears in times of trouble, much as Wittgenstein thought the word "meaning" did, and may at other times disappear.

The rest of the essays are sometimes self-explanatory, and sometimes not. In any case I will introduce them better in one or more paragraphs that precede them directly.

Notes

1 Susan Harvey, "Embodiment in Time and Eternity: A Syriac Perspective," in this volume.
2 David McCarthy Matzko, "The Relationship of Bodies: A Nuptial Hermeneutics of Same-Sex Unions," *Theology and Sexuality* 8 (1998):96–112.
3 Robert W. Jenson, "Faithfulness," in this volume.
4 Rowan Williams, "The Body's Grace," in this volume.
5 Thomas Breidenthal, "Sanctifying Nearness," in this volume.
6 John Paul II, in this volume, quoting Heb. 4:13 (where we are *panta gymna* before God), and Wis. 7:24.
7 Williams, "The Body's Grace."
8 Jenson, "Faithfulness," Williams, "The Body's Grace," Breidenthal, "Sanctifying Nearness," and Rogers, "Sanctification," in this volume.
9 Ephrem the Syrian, *Hymn on Virginity*, no. 7, in Sebastian P. Brock, trans., *The Harp of the Spirit: Eighteen Poems of St. Ephrem*, Studies Supplementary to *Sobornost* (Society of St. Alban and St. Sergius, 1983), p. 48.
10 Susan Harvey, "'The Sense of a Stylite,' Perspective on Symeon the Elder," *Vigiliae Christianae* 42 (1988): 376–94.

PART

How and How Not to Think Theologically about the Body

Embodiment in Time and Eternity: A Syriac Perspective

Susan A. Harvey

This article provides a context for the entire anthology, in that it challenges the common assumption that Christianity's concern with the body is reducible to Christianity's concern with sexuality. Rather, the body is the place in which alone Christians perceive and reflect the glory of God. Thus Christianity constructs the body liturgically, that is, as a place of prayer and praise.

For some years now, scholarship has been heavily preoccupied with discussion of the "the body."[1] What constitutes our body, what it means to be embodied, and what the body contributes to our human or individual identities are topics that receive frequent and lengthy discussion in every kind of scholarly forum. Needless to say, religionists and theologians have been active participants in this area of interest.[2] For those who study ancient Christianity, discussion has been dominated by a focus on sexuality, with emphasis on asceticism as a devotional practice of sexual renunciation or control of the body as a sexual body.[3] While ancient Christians were surely concerned about these issues, such overriding emphases may owe more to our contemporary social debates than to the primary interests of those who pursued the Christian life in its formative centuries. For if they, too, worried about the body as an essential component of human identity, they also developed a Christian devotional life strikingly dependent on the direct engagement of bodily experience as its context.

In a basic sense, the ancients shared our questions. Why do we have a body? Having one, what are we to do with it? How are we to understand the purpose of embodied existence in the human relationship with God? Early Syriac Christianity maintained consensus on these matters: we have a body because

God created us with one. Moreover, God created the body to be a means of knowing God and of being in God's presence. Syriac writers further present the body with this epistemological goal as the point of continuity between the present world and the hereafter. In their eyes, the body held an ontologically locative significance across time and eternity. An essential and inextricable component of *who* we are, both here and in the world to come, it was also seen to be *where* we are, both now and in eternity. Bodily experience and bodily expression become primary epistemological tools in both realms of existence, as we seek relation to God; the knowledge they convey is a knowledge that cannot be gained in any other way. Therein lies the purpose of the body: it provides the context for how and what we can and will know of God, now and in the life to come.

Before considering these matters, however, some orientation to early Syriac Christianity may be helpful.

Another History

Syriac is a dialect of Aramaic, itself a dialect of Hebrew. Syriac arose in the region of Edessa (Urfa, in modern southeastern Turkey) in the first century AD and became the primary Christian language throughout the Middle East and beyond. To this day, the Syriac-speaking churches pride themselves on using "the language of Our Lord," "the language Jesus spoke." Syriac Christianity was long neglected by western scholars, for whom Christian discourse has been dominated by Greek and Latin traditions. In recent years, by contrast, historians have increasingly acknowledged that the Greek and Latin church Fathers do not present the whole story of Christianity's emergence; nor, indeed, do the confines of the Roman Empire adequately allow us to map "the mission and expansion of Christianity" during its early centuries.[4] As scholars have considered afresh the ancient patterns, Syriac Christianity has been an area of particular interest because of its distinctive modes of devotional piety, its rich and profound theological writings, and its presence sometimes within, sometimes far beyond the eastern Roman frontier.

Still, misrepresentations have been plentiful. Among modern scholars of ancient Christianity, the Syrian Orient is notorious as a hotbed of dualism:[5] gnosticism, Marcionism, and Manichaeism flourished widely in this region (Manichaeism was born there, after all). Nicene orthodoxy did not dominate until the fifth century; Ephrem complained bitterly that the Nicene "party" of his day (mid-fourth century) was a minority group called "Palutians" after the late second century bishop Palut, while the more numerous Marcionites (among others) claimed the name "Christian."[6] Modern scholarship has also tended to see a direct continuity between these early, widespread dualistic movements and the particularly harsh ascetic forms that characterized Syrian monasticism during late antiquity, perhaps best known in the exotic figure of Simeon the Stylite, the fifth century holy man who lived 40 years in the Syrian wilderness atop a 60-foot pillar, standing midway between heaven and earth, a living icon of prayer ascending.[7]

However, the simplistic terms "dualistic" or "extreme" do little to illumine Syrian tradition, especially with regard to embodiment. Indeed, one of the most striking characteristics of ancient Syriac Christianity in all its forms is its intense physicality. Across a broad spectrum of beliefs, for good and for ill, the body provided a central focus of concern for religion in this region, and the primary instrument of religious expression. This is not discordant with the developments of Greco-Latin traditions. Nonetheless, in the Syrian Orient we find it often demonstrated in more vivid terms, and not only in the popularity of religious movements like gnosticism or Manichaeism, or an ascetic tradition infamous for its sometimes extravagant self-mortifications. Throughout the spirituality of the Syrian Orient – in its liturgical forms, its monasticism, its devotional piety, its exquisite hymnography, even its startling use of gendered God language – one finds a heightened awareness of sensory experience, of physical expression, of bodily knowing, of embodiment as the medium in which and by which the encounter between human and divine takes place.

In the present discussion I draw upon Syriac writers from the second through sixth centuries, with primary attention to Ephrem Syrus (304–373 AD), whose ancient title "the Harp of the Holy Spirit" bespeaks his status in Syriac tradition as a theologian of unparalleled brilliance and a writer of astonishing beauty. Early Syriac theology was most often presented in poetic form. Hymnography and metrical homilies comprise our major sources rather than the philosophical treatises such as Greek and Latin writers often produced, although such prose treatises do come to predominate in the later patristic period as Syriac theological discourse became increasingly hellenized. Following the dictates of their form, Syriac poetical works employ religious language in terms that differ significantly from the language of philosophical discourse. Consequently, early Syriac theology is rendered in richly textured images that utilize metaphor to explore and convey meaning rather than to define it. Early Syriac writers are self-conscious in their role as poet-theologians, and are wary of the dangers in any intellectual effort to explain, define, or delimit God through the use of rational language.[8]

Ephrem admonished that all religious language is metaphorical because no language is adequate to convey God; rather, it is a sign of God's loving compassion for us that the incarnation took place not only into the body, but into language as well. Just as God put on the "garment of flesh," so, too, did God put on the "garment of names," entering into human language as into the body so that we might approach and in our limited way know about God.[9] In the course of their metaphorical explorations, early Syriac theologians engaged bodily experience as a deliberate strategy in the task of understanding God.[10]

Embodiment: A Way of Living

Early Syriac Christianity displayed a profoundly physical sensibility. Physical experience was seen to reveal both the good and the bad of life in its total cosmic reality, and physical action was seen to be the appropriate response to that reality. A clear eye and a limpid heart[11] were necessary to discern the Truth contained in experience and activity. But at the core of early Syriac Christianity lies an unequivocal understanding of the "oneness" of the human person, a oneness of body and soul, in which the physical and the spiritual are essential to one another in relation to God, for neither has meaning without the other. As Ephrem marveled, "The soul is Your bride, the body Your bridal chamber."[12] Even in its expectation of the eternal life that awaits when this world will pass away, Syriac writers present an eschatological vision of concretely physical nature, experienced in bodily terms.

From earliest Syriac tradition, the body is the location of Christianity. It is so in the first place as part of God's creation, a creation lovingly conceived and fashioned by God as God's own, marked indelibly by its Maker, and hence revelatory. In harmony with the written revelation of scripture, the created world of nature proclaims this God, God's self, and God's presence. Ephrem explains:

> In every place, if you look, [God's] symbol is there,
> and when you read, you will find His types.
> For by Him were created all creatures,
> and He engraved His symbols upon His possessions.
> When He created the world,
> He gazed at it and adorned it with His images.
> Streams of His symbols opened, flowed and poured forth
> His symbols on His members.[13]

The whole of creation is marked as God's work, yet the human person is the summit of that work as God's own image: "According to the greatness of His beauty He made me."[14] Earliest Syriac tradition speaks of humanity's creation as an act of love surpassing our understanding but profoundly known by us. The creation of our bodies was the creation of our very selves, and the enormity of this realization evoked stark bodily imagery in the effort to glimpse the impulse that compelled God's effort. The second-century *Odes of Solomon* portray God's voice describing this human creation:

> I fashioned their members,
> and my own breasts I prepared for them,
> That they might drink my holy milk and live by it.
> I am pleased by them,
> And am not ashamed by them.
> For my workmanship are they,
> and the strength of my thoughts.
> . . .
> I willed and fashioned mind and heart,
> And they are my own.[15]

Here as elsewhere in early Syriac literature, God's own self can be imaged in bodily terms, not as a literal representation but to convey a truth that defies the confines of rational language and to express knowledge of God through the play of metaphor. Ephrem marveled at the thought of Mary nursing the infant Christ through a similar use of gendered imagery for God's activity, setting in parallel the first creation in which we were given life, and our new creation into eternal life at the final resurrection:

> He [Christ] was lofty but He sucked Mary's milk,
> and from His blessings all creation sucks.
> He is the Living Breast of living breath;
> by His life the dead were suckled, and they revived.
> Without the breath of air no one can live;
> without the power of the Son no one can rise.
> Upon the living breath of the One Who vivifies all
> depend the living beings above and below.
> As indeed He sucked Mary's milk,
> He has given suck – life to the universe.
> As again He dwelt in His mother's womb,
> in His womb dwells all creation.[16]

In God's creation the human person is fashioned complete, body and soul, just as the whole of God performs the fashioning. The *Odes of Solomon* describe a relationship between believer and God in which the believer is wholly given to God: "I will call out to Him with all my heart / I will praise and exalt Him with all my limbs."[17] In these Odes, the right relationship between Creator and created must, in turn, demonstrate the same oneness of being as that between body and soul: "As the wind moves through the harp / and the strings speak, / So the Spirit of the Lord speaks through my members / and I speak through His love."[18] Worship requires the whole person, body and soul, even as it enacts the intimate love that binds the believer to God:

My heart bursts forth the praise of the Lord,
And my lips bring forth praise to Him.
And my tongue becomes sweet with His anthems,
and my limbs are anointed with His psalms.
And my face rejoices in His exaltation,
and my spirit rejoices in His love,
And my being shines in Him.[19]

The oneness of the believer is God's intention. The separation, or disharmony, of body and soul that we know as mortality is consequently how we experience and know our fallen condition. Ephrem addresses God from the midst of this tragic division:

You looked upon the body, as it mourned,
and on the soul in its grief,
for You had joined them together in love,
but they had parted and separated in pain.
. . .
Body and soul go to court to see
which caused the other to sin;
but the wrong belongs to both,
for free will belongs to both.[20]

Thus the body is at fault, but is not in itself the cause of our fallen condition. Rather, its state reveals (or expresses) our soul or the inward disposition of the heart. Although separated in the fall, body and soul remain an entity for Syriac writers in which the distinctions between the two matter far less than the single person both comprise. In the *Odes of Solomon*, the believer who is not wholly devoted to God is utterly given to the corrupt and corrupting falsehood of the Evil One.[21] A late fourth–century cycle of hymns on baptism provides a vivid image of the failure of even sacramental action if the interior and exterior conditions of the human person are not mutually expressive of true faith: the sacramental anointing at baptism – the physical act of consecration – can only be effective if the "odor of the heart" exuded by the one anointed accords with the holy fragrance of the chrism.[22]

To be sure, the body remains central because of Christianity's insistence that the salvation process is worked by Christ's physical incarnation and physical resurrection. In Syriac the same term is used to mean both "salvation" and "life" (*hayye*). We know our fallen condition through the corruptibility and mortality of the body; we will know salvation through its incorruptibility and immortality as revealed in original creation. The most prevalent image for salvation in early Syriac literature is that of healing. Christ is the Treasury of Healing[23] and the Medicine of Life, a title also commonly employed for the eucharist. Again, Christ is the Good or Wise Physician.[24] Syriac legend attributes the conversion of Edessa to Christ's healing of King Abgar the Great and his nobles, through the apostle Addai (identified with Thaddeus, one of the 70 sent out in Luke 10:1).[25] In the *Odes of Solomon*, the Odist describes his worship or contemplation of God as a dynamic state in which he is created anew in the presence of God, with new limbs "for my very self, / And there was no pain in them, / nor affliction, nor suffering."[26]

For early Syriac writers, then, Christianity was located in the body because the body, in the most literal sense, was what God had fashioned in the beginning and where God had chosen to find us in our fallenness. This was why God acted through the incarnation. Ephrem declares, "Glory to You who clothed Yourself with the body of mortal Adam, and made it a fountain of life for all mortals!"[27] This, too, explains the ritual process of the liturgy, as one enacted in and with the body. Ephrem evokes the liturgy as that which teaches us not only how to experience with our bodies, but further, what to experience.

> His body was newly mixed with our bodies,
> and His pure blood has been poured out into our veins,
> And His voice into our ears, and His brightness into our eyes.
> All of Him has been mixed with all of us by His compassion.[28]

Our bodies have received His body, our blood His blood; our ears have heard the Word through scripture readings; our eyes, through the eyes of the apostles, beheld divine glory in the Theophany.[29] Christ fills us, our bodies, our senses.

The healing of the sacraments restores our oneness of being and our appropriate sensory experience. Yet there is more to be done. In the body of Christ, the cosmic war between good and evil was fought in earnest. Our bodies are the battleground in which the struggle between God and Satan, good and evil, life and death continues. The fallen order in which we live, Death's dominion, is one we know because of bodily suffering at the level of the individual (who suffers sickness, hunger, weariness, despair) and at the level of society (which suffers poverty, injustice, tyranny, and war). Just as Christ defeated Satan in and by his body, so, too, must the victory be rendered in the whole body of Christ: the body of the believer, the body of the church. Thus, what one does with the body, how one lives in the body, what one knows with the body are all matters vital to the process of salvation – a process in which God's ultimate triumph will grant us eternal life. The oneness of the believer, body and soul, keeps the body at the center of the process throughout its long duration.

Here is the point from which to assess the pervasive presence of ascetic practice early Syriac Christianity. At the far end of the spectrum (Marcionites, Manichaeans, encratites), asceticism represented renunciation of a body and a world produced by an evil power. By contrast, at the heart of "mainstream" Syriac tradition the ascetic mode of life renounced not the physical world, but a world gone awry. Celibacy or chastity in marriage; simplicity of food, clothing, and possessions; care for the poor, sick, and suffering – such were the requisite features of the Christian mode of life from Christianity's inception. In earliest Syriac literature, the body of the true believer is a body rendered chaste, healed and holy in marriage to its Heavenly Bridegroom by living a Christian life. In turn, the condition of the believer's body must be mirrored in the community as a whole body. Caring for others, and especially for the suffering, not only fulfilled the command to love one another, but also forged into existence a community whose life as a healed and consecrated community literally reflected Paradise regained – the image by which Edessa recalled the experience of its conversion to Christianity.[30] Even when a distinct monastic movement was set in motion during the fourth century, Syriac monasticism was characterized by its location in or near to villages and cities, and by its active ministry to the larger community, especially the poor and the suffering. Monasticism continued to represent a dedicated life of service within the body of the church, not a turning away or withdrawal from the world.[31] Simeon the Stylite was as noted for the extraordinary extent of his works of service as he was for his mortifications: from the pillar he devoted hours each day to preaching, counseling, healing, exorcising, and mediating disputes (personal, civic, and ecclesiastical) among the hordes of pilgrims who flocked to his pillar in endless streams. His body imaged the defeat of Satan's wiles through his conquest of hunger, sickness, and despair in himself by means of his ascetic practices. As a result, in his presence the sick were healed, the hungry were fed, the weary received their rest. Where Simeon's body was, there, too, the whole body knew its healing.

The body is the place in which salvation happens and the instrument by which it is done. The body is more than the physicality of our existence; it provides the activity, or external expression, by which the salvific process takes place. Bodily acts express the believer's interior condition even as they display the living image of the body, individual and collective, redeemed. Thus in his treatise *On Prayer*, Aphrahat can admonish that care for the weary, the sick and the poor is also the activity of prayer.[32] Ephrem describes an eschatological vision in which virgins who perform no ministry will be shut out of Paradise, while married women who have done good works for the needy will be let in.[33] More pointedly, Ephrem's call for the life of faith is one in which the believer will manifest the image of God by literally enacting God's saving, healing activity:

> Let charity be portrayed in your eyes
> and in your ears the sound of truth.
> Imprint your tongue with the word of life

and upon your hands [imprint] all alms.
Stamp your footsteps with visiting the sick,
and let the image of your Lord be portrayed in your heart.
Tablets are honored because of the image of Kings.
How much [more will] one [be honored] who portrayed his
  Lord in all his senses.[34]

The sometimes extreme idiosyncrasies of Syrian ascetic practice have their purpose from just this iconic understanding of the body. If one considers the literary imagery by which it is conveyed, and not merely the physical actions described, Syrian asceticism shines forth as physical metaphor. The stylite on the pillar was incense on an altar, the embodiment of prayer rising heavenward (as Ps. 141:2); he was Ezekiel in his flaming chariot; he was the new Moses atop the new Mount Sinai, dispensing the New Law; he was a living crucifix.[35] The ascetic who lived naked in the wilderness, grazing on wild food and living among wild beasts, held two dichotomized images in tension: the penance of Adam expelled from Paradise, fulfilled as by Nebuchadnezzar, struck with divine madness and wandering in the wild, grazing like an animal, his hair like eagles' feathers, his nails like claws (Dar. 118. 4:28–33); and the life of Adam and Eve in Paradise before the fall, who lived naked without shame, who ate the food of the earth without toil, who lived in harmony among the animals (Gen. 2). In an anonymous hymn describing these "grazers," the ascetic's body is imaged as the ecclesial body in microcosm, the body serving as sanctuary, the mind as altar, tears as the incense on that altar.[36]

What in the earliest Syriac tradition can best be characterized as the experience of "realized eschatology" (seen in the descriptions of the worship experience in the *Odes of Solomon*, for example), over time becomes the more profound consciousness that although we live in historical time, our religious life allows us to participate in the sacred time which is God's eternal reality. The iconic activity of the body is symbolic in our time and place, while participating in an existence where past, present, and future are brought together in the single outworking of God's salvation drama. The body thereby offers continuity even now, into the life we will only fully know in the world to come. Such, for example, is the sense regarding worship as described in the fifth-century *Book of Steps*:

by starting from these visible things [church, altar, and baptism], and provided our bodies become temples and our hearts altars, we might find ourselves in their heavenly counterparts which cannot be seen by the eyes of the flesh, migrating there and entering in while we are still in this visible church with its priesthood and its ministry acting as fair examples for all those who imitate there the vigils, fasting and endurance of our Lord and of those who have preached him.[37]

In the oneness of the human person that Syriac writers portray, the only real separation of body and soul is at death. Although a tragic severance, death is but a temporary suspension of their union: in the resurrected life they will again be joined. To live now and here as one person, body and soul, is to declare what we will be then and there. This is realized eschatology, yes, but also a process understood to bring into actuality that saved condition we seek. As Ephrem presents it, now we inhabit two times, chronological and sacred; but we await a life when we will know only one.[38]

Embodiment: A Way of Knowing

What was the separation of body and soul at death, that Syriac writers should hold embodiment as our essential condition even in eternity?

After many years in ascetic practice atop his pillar, Simeon the Stylite (d. 459) suffered a life-threatening outbreak of gangrene in his foot. In most accounts of the episode, Simeon suffered grievously for months until at last he was healed by a miracle. Jacob of Serug, in a homily written some decades later, tells the story rather differently: Simeon refused to succumb to this affliction sent by Satan, and finally amputated the diseased foot. Simeon then bid a poignant farewell to his severed limb, which had labored so valiantly in God's service:

> Why are you shaken and grieved since your hope is kept (quoting from Ps 42:5)? For again onto that tree from which you have been cut off you will be grafted. Go, wait for me until I come and do not grieve. For without you I will not rise up on the last day. Whether to the bridal chamber or to Gehenna I will walk on you. And whether to heaven or to the abyss, our way is one. We will be one when we are resurrected just as we have been, for death or life, for judgement or fire, or for the kingdom . . .[39]

More than a vehicle of suffering, the body was also the loyal companion, the steadfast comrade in the cosmic battle between good and evil. Physical torment, whether caused by ascetic mortification or by illness, was understood to be an affliction from Satan, a test such as Job endured or Christ during the forty days in the wilderness. Devotion to God required extreme endurance because to be *with God* was to be *at battle against Satan*. The believer's body was the battleground, as Christ's had been. And just as his body was the place in which Christ defeated hunger, thirst, weariness, and death, so, too, must the believer also defeat Satan by refusing Satan victory in these assaults on the weaknesses of the mortal body. While scholars have interpreted Syrian asceticism as manifesting hatted of the body, the texts often display the opposite view (as

Ephrem: "We love our bodies, which are akin to us, of the same origin: / for our roots are dust"[40]). Hence the sorrow that afflicts where the dead repose, as the soul yearns for its faithful partner.

Ephrem spoke of the souls of the dead camped at the gates of Paradise, awaiting their reunion with their bodies so that they might enter therein, together to praise their Savior.[41] For Jacob of Serug, the period of separation was rather more harrowing. He vividly describes the souls of the dead huddled around the eucharistic offering at the memorial masses offered on their behalf. There they drink the "fragrance of life" (*riha d-hayye*) emanating from the holy oblation, for sustenance until the eschaton when they will be rejoined to their bodies for eternity.[42]

Syriac writers shared the Pauline vision that in the final resurrection "we shall all be changed" (1 Cor. 15:51); the resurrected body will not be this same body we now inhabit.[43] Yet nowhere does the physicality of Syriac tradition resound more clearly than in its vision of our existence in eternity, where the oneness of the believer, body and soul, will find its true life and indeed its true meaning.[44] For the body changed in the eschaton will remain the body in which and through which we know God – and in the eschaton, knowing God will be the sum total of our life. Freed of the earthly uses and weaknesses of the body, we will find the continuity from our mortal life to our immortal life through the body's continuation as our instrument of knowledge. Indeed, the body will continue its existential role: it will be the location in which we receive God's revelation. It will continue its expressive role: it will enact and manifest our relationship with our Creator. And, it will at last fulfill its epistemological role: if, in this life, the body provides us limited knowledge of God, there, in the world to come, the body will be unlimited in what it can convey of the divine. In a very real sense, all that we have considered thus far as expressions of what embodiment means in early Syriac tradition rests on the conviction that whatever the changes in our resurrected body, it is the continuity of our bodily existence in time and eternity that matters.

Syriac tradition finds its most distinctive articulation of this understanding in Ephrem's writings, especially in his *Hymns on Paradise*.[45] The relation between sense perception and religious epistemology is a major concern for Ephrem, for whom, as noted earlier, all of creation is marked with the imprint of its Maker.[46] Ephrem insists that sense perception and bodily experience are necessary for our knowledge of and encounter with God in eternity no less than in the present dispensation.

In Ephrem's view, soul and body require each other for existence even in the world to come. Without the body, the soul would not be able to perceive or be conscious of Paradise (the root here is *rgsh*, to feel, perceive, be conscious or aware of). Ephrem discusses this in *Hymns on Paradise* 8, from which I quote at length:

> . . . I considered
> how the soul cannot
>   have perception of Paradise
> without its mate, the body,
>   its instrument and lyre.
>   . . .
>
> That the soul cannot see
>   without the body's frame,
> the body itself persuades,
>   since if the body becomes blind
> the soul is blind in it
>   groping about with it;
> see how each looks
>   and attests to the other,
> how the body has need of the soul
>   in order to live,
> and the soul too requires the body
>   in order to see and to hear.
>
>   . . .
> Though the soul exists
>   of itself and for itself,
> yet without its companion
>   it lacks true existence;
>   . . .
> If the soul, while in the body,
>   resembles an embryo
> and is unable to know
>   either itself or its companion,
> how much more feeble will it then be
>   once it has left the body,
> no longer possessing on its own
>   the senses
> which are able to serve
>   as tools for its use.
> For it is through the senses of its companion
>   that it shine forth and becomes evident.[47]

Ephrem then notes that God did not place Adam in Paradise until he was fully made, body and soul: "The soul could not enter there [into Paradise] / of itself and for itself." Together body and soul entered Paradise, together they left after the Fall, together they will enter again in the resurrection.[48] Ephrem is positing two important points here. First, knowledge has a sensory, noncognitive base. Gaining access to knowledge requires the body's active receptivity to what lies outside it. Sensory experience is not the whole content of what is to be known, but without its contribution nothing can be fully encountered or comprehended. Second, the soul itself has no real existence without the body to render it present and active. Ephrem bypasses the problem of a mind/body split, and leaves aside the problematic of rationality as a basis for knowledge. Instead, he posits sense perception as an essential method of knowing, particularly crucial to that which defies the limitations of human understanding – God.

There is a recognition here that we know first by encounter, by bodily experience, before we can process understanding. This epistemological function of the body is what makes the body crucial to human existence. It is for this purpose, it seems, that God created the body in the first place. God's consistent activity in relation to humanity, whether in creation or in redemption, has been the revelation of God's being. As we have noted, Ephrem declares that all that God has wrought is stamped with God's mark. For Ephrem this is true in this world and in Paradise: "In Eden and in the inhabited earth are parables of our Lord. / Who is able to gather the likeness of the symbols of Him, / all of Whom is portrayed in all? / In scripture He is written, in nature He is engraved."[49] The *raison d'être* for Paradise, then, no less than for this world, is to manifest God's revelation.

What is the nature of Paradise that we should need our bodies to perceive it? Why should we need to experience it in bodily terms? Ephrem's *Hymns on Paradise* are a *tour-de-force* for the senses, reminiscent of the *Song of Songs* in their lush sensuality. Paradise here is a place of breathtaking, sumptuous beauty: shimmering in resplendent light, billowing with myriad exquisite scents, its colors gleaming, its tastes and sounds a marvel. Flowers, fountains, perfumes, blossoms, trees laden with fruits abound "in endless variety." The body, healed and glorified in its resurrected state, is robed now in "garments of glory" that replace its former "garments of shame." In this condition the body, no longer hindered, receives utterly the sensory onslaught that Paradise pours forth on every side. "Being unburdened, / the senses stand in awe and delight / before the divine Majesty."[50] In Paradise one's entire being will be permeated by the encounter with the divine. Living there will be the absolute experience of God's presence.

Cognitivity, or rational thought, positions a person apart from the object of consideration. What Ephrem describes is an encounter between subject and object in which the person will be saturated at every level of awareness and being by the object sought, to the point where the subjective encounter is swallowed up by the immensity of presence in the midst of what is divine. Significantly, however, the human self is not lost in this event, nor obliterated by the power of God's Being. Rather, here is a relationship between creature and Creator of completion, of full realization of self within Self. The resurrected life is that condition in which nothing separates us from God. Bathed in divinity from without, we will radiate divinity from within, aglow from our inmost heart to our outermost limbs. Those who enter Paradise will be astonished at what they become:

> People behold themselves
> in glory
> and wonder at themselves,
> discovering where they are.
> The nature of their bodies,
> once troubled and troublesome,
> is now tranquil and quiet,
> resplendent
> from without in beauty,
> and from within with purity,
> the body in evident ways,
> the soul in hidden ways.[51]

Ephrem describes Paradise as a "total encounter." Yet he admonishes that his description is itself a didactic metaphor: ultimately, the instrument of the body, or the medium of sense perception, provides a pale analogy for what will be.

> Do not let your intellect
> be disturbed by mere names,
> for Paradise has simply clothed itself
> in terms that are akin to you;
> it is not because it is impoverished
> that it has put on your imagery;
> rather, your nature is far too weak
> to be able
> to attain to its greatness,
> and its beauties are much diminished
> by being depicted in the pale colors
> with which you are familiar.[52]

For Ephrem, the incarnation is not only an action of redemption, it is also an action of revelation in terms of exactly this epistemological quality of bodily experience. "That unreachable power came down and put on limbs that could be touched so that the needy could approach Him and, embracing His humanity, become aware of His divinity."[53] In our fallen condition, the revelation of nature and indeed of scripture proved insufficient for returning us to God. Christ incarnate brought a directness of encounter that we could not experience in any other way, ironically so since it was Christ's incarnate body that seemed to deny his divinity: "[Scribes and Pharisees] spoke ill of our Lord because of His body and thought that He was not God. They threw Him down, yet it was because of His body – the body they experienced as passing among them – that they recognized that He is God."[54] Ephrem depicts Death as shocked when the risen Christ returned to Sheol for His body, paradoxically that which separates us from God and that by which God would join us again to Godself: "Death was amazed at You in Sheol, / that You sought Your garment and found [it]. / O Wise One Who lost what was found / in order to find the lost!"[55]

God's activity is revelation; the means by which we ourselves know that revelation is the sensory experience of the body in which we encounter it. In the incarnation God poured Godself into the body, the instrument of our knowing. In sacrament, Christ enters into each of our bodies, so that nothing separates our bodies from His. "Ears even heard Him, eyes saw Him, / hands even touched Him, the mouth ate Him. / Limbs and senses gave thanks to / the One Who came and revived all that is corporeal."[56]

Ephrem insists that sense perception is the foundational experience of the human–divine encounter, while he repeatedly admonishes that the senses are insufficient for the task.[57] Inadequate at best, the senses are a feeble medium through which to receive knowledge of God. Nonetheless, in Ephrem's view it is precisely their inadequacy that renders them crucial. When open to God, the senses receive God's revelation at every turn; they take it in, they convey it, they mediate, they actively encounter and transmit. What they do *not* do is intentionally, willfully, or consciously manipulate what they receive; they do not function as does the rational mind. For Ephrem, rationality is the process of "investigation." The autonomous effort of the mind to investigate God is where humanity falls astray, since God cannot be fathomed by the human intellect. Investigation is, in Ephrem's formulation, the source of all error, all heresy, precisely because it depends on the radical separation of subject from object. It takes place when the mind attempts to be the source of its own knowledge. Investigation is, so to speak, the seeking of *disembodied* knowledge: therein it fails.

For all its weaknesses, the body remains our constant epistemological source in relation to God. When its experiences are received by us in our whole selves – when body and mind function as the unity they were created to be – then the hubristic dangers of intellectual autonomy are averted. We cannot know God by separating ourselves from God. We can only know God by allowing God's revelation to permeate the whole of our being.

> Our Lord has become our living bread,
> and we shall delight in our new cup.
> Come, let us eat it without investigation,
> and without scrutiny let us drink His cup.
> Who disdains blessings and fruits

and sits down to investigate their nature?
A human being needs to live. Come let us live and not die
in the depth of investigation.[58]

Ancient Christianity defined God as ineffable and inconceivable. It thereby heightened the significance of sense perception specifically as a noncognitive process of knowing. From such a view, the body becomes the instrument by which God is known in relation to the believer and the believer in relation to God. In existential terms the body is where we experience God; it is where we receive divine initiative. Further, the body expresses our response to what we receive: it provides the activity by which we articulate our relationship to the divine. Above all, the body fulfills an epistemological role: it is the medium through which we first encounter the divine and it offers a knowledge of God through that encounter that cannot be gained in any other way. In early Syriac tradition, embodiment is the condition that defines our existence in time, as it will also define it in eternity. For these writers, the existential, expressive, and epistemological qualities of life in the body are seamlessly interwoven, right across the divide between this world and the eschaton. This is why Ephrem can say that the works we do now will be the healing we experience there, in Paradise:

> Whoever has washed the feet of the saints
>   will himself be cleansed in that dew;
> to the hand that had stretched out
>   to give to the poor
> will the fruits of the trees
>   themselves stretch out;
> the very footsteps of him
>   who visited the sick in their affliction
> do the flowers make haste
>   to crown with blooms,
> jostling to see
>   which can be first to kiss his steps.[59]

Here, for these writers, is our healing and our hope: salvation is a life we will live. And because we know this now in our limited, temporary, mortal body, we will know it there in a fullness that defies our rational understanding but brings to completion the nature of our embodiment. We will be at home, and we will know it.

Notes

1 An earlier version of this paper was presented to the American Theological Society, Princeton Theological Seminary, April, 1997. I am grateful to the Society for fruitful discussion, and also to Dr. Flora Keshgegian. This paper is dedicated to my father, Professor James B. Ashbrook, in the presence of whose long dying it was originally conceived and with whose passing it has finally been completed.

2 For an excellent entry into some primary points of debate, see now Sarah Coakley, ed., *Religion and the Body* (Cambridge: Cambridge University Press, 1997).

3 Again, the bibliography is massive. Arguably the most influential work has been Peter Brown, *The Body and Society: Men, Women and Sexual Renunciation in Early Christianity* (New York: Columbia University Press, 1988), a study itself much influenced by Michel Foucault, *The Use of Pleasure* (History of Sexuality, vol. 2), trans. Robert Hurley (New York: Pantheon Books, 1985), and *idem, The Care of the Self* (History of Sexuality, vol. 3), trans. Robert Hurley (New York: Vintage Books, 1986). See also Aline Rouselle, *Porneia: On Desire: The Body in Antiquity*, trans. Felicia Pheasant (New York: Blackwell, 1988); and Vincent Wimbush and Richard Valantasis, eds., *Asceticism* (New York: Oxford University Press, 1995).

4 I deliberately refer to the classic work of Adolph von Harnack, *The Mission and Expansion of Christianity in the First Three Centuries*, trans. J. Moffatt (New York: Harper, 1962). For a survey of the story beyond Roman borders, see now Samuel H. Moffett, *A History of Christianity in Asia*: vol. 1: *Beginnings to 1500* (San Francisco: Harper Collins, 1992).

5 The characterization owes much to the pervasive influence of Walter Bauer, *Rechtgläubigkeit und Ketzerei im ältesten Christentum*, which first appeared in 1934; revised with supplements by Georg Strecker in 1964; first English translation, *Orthodoxy and Heresy in Earliest Christianity*, eds. R. A. Kraft and G. Krodel (Philadelphia: Fortress Press, 1971). Chapter 1 is devoted to Edessa. A similar view, though argued from a different perspective, has been vigorously put forward by H. J. W. Drijvers, *East of Antioch: Studies in Early Syriac Christianity* (London: Variorum, 1984) and *idem, History and Religion in Late Antique Syria* (Brookfield, VT: Ashgate Publishing, 1994).

6 Ephrem, *H Contra Haer.* 22.5–6. Ephrem's polemical battles are especially clear in this cycle of hymns, ed. and trans. E. Beck, *Des heiligen Ephraem des Syrers Hymnen contra Haereses*. Corpus Scriptorum Christianorum Orientalium [hereafter CSCO] 169–70/Scr.Syr. 76–7 (Louvain, 1957); and C. W. Mitchell, *S. Ephraim's Prose Refutations of Mani, Marcion, and Bardaisan* (London and Oxford, 1912, 1921) 2 vols. To be fair, Nicene orthodoxy was not the predominant theological stance anywhere in the Roman Empire much before the fifth century. Consider the doctrinal battles fought by the Cappadocian Fathers contemporaneously with those of Ephrem, and in the decades following.

7 See the well-known but deeply flawed study by Arthur Vööbus, *History of Asceticism in the Syrian Orient*, CSCO 184/Sub. 14, 197/Sub. 17 (Louvain 1958), and CSCO 500/Sub. 81 (Louvain, 1988).

8 E.g., Robert Murray, *Symbols of Church and Kingdom: A Study in Early Syriac Tradition* (Cambridge: Cambridge University Press, 1975); Sebastian P. Brock, *The Luminous Eye: The Spiritual World Vision of St. Ephrem the Syrian* (Kalamazoo: Cistercian, 1992);

Tanios Bou Mansour, *La pensée symbolique de Saint Ephrem le Syrien* (Kaslik, Lebanon 1988).

9 Ephrem, *H Fid* 31, ed. and trans. E. Beck, *Des heiligen Ephraem des Syrers Hymnen de Fide*. CSCO 154–5/Scr. Syr. 73–4 (Louvain, 1955). Cf. Brock, *Luminous Eye*, pp. 43–8: and see also Bou Mansour, *La pensée symbolique*, 160–87 on Ephrem's understanding of the divine names.

10 For most of the twentieth century, the view prevailed that Syriac Christianity prior to the late fourth century represented a purely Semitic Christianity, untainted by Hellenic thought or culture, which therefore was either insignificant or extremely important (depending on one's view) as representing an entirely autonomous form of earliest Christianity. In recent years, our understanding of the complex multilingual, multicultural society that comprised the eastern Mediterranean world in antiquity has improved tremendously. We have come to appreciate that Hellenic, Semitic, and west Asian traditions were deeply intermingled in this region, and that the resulting cultural matrix was far more cosmopolitan and sophisticated than we had previously recognized.

11 Brilliantly conveyed in Brock, *The Luminous Eye*.

12 *H Fid* 14.5.

13 *H Virg* 20.12; here translated by Kathleen McVey, *Ephrem the Syrian: Hymns* (New York: Paulist Press, 1989) 348–9. Ephrem elsewhere speaks of God or Christ playing three harps – the Old and New Testaments, and nature – in a perfect harmony of revelation. E.g., H Virg 29.1,30.1; ed. and trans. E. Beck, *Des heiligen Ephraem des Syrers Hymnen de Virginitate*, CSCO 223–4/Scr.Syr. 94–5 (Louvain, 1962).

14 *Odes Sol.* 15.7b; ed. and trans. James H. Charlesworth. *The Odes of Solomon*, 2nd edn. (Missoula, MT, 1977; repr. Chico, CA: Scholars Press, 1982). Translations from the *Odes* are my own throughout.

15 *Odes Sol.* 8:14–18. For the gendered God language of the *Odes of Solomon*, cf. S. A. Harvey, "Feminine Imagery for the Divine. The Holy Spirit, the Odes of Solomon, and Early Syriac Tradition," *St. Vladimir's Theological Quarterly* 37 (1993): 111–39.

16 *H Nat* 4: 149–54; here trans. McVey, *Ephrem*, 100. Text ed. and trans. E. Beck, *Des heiligen Ephraem des Syrers Hymnen de Nativitate (Epiphania)*. CSCO 186–7/Ser. Syr. 82–3 (Louvain, 1959).

17 *Odes Sol.* 26:4.

18 *Odes Sol.* 6:1–2.

19 *Odes Sol.* 40:2–4.

20 *H Nis* 69.3.5; here trans. Sebastian P. Brock, *The Harp of the Spirit: Eighteen Poems of Saint Ephrem*, 2nd edn. (London: Fellowship of St. Alban and St. Sergius, 1983), 77. Text ed. and trans. E. Beck, *Des heiligen Ephraem des Syrers Carmina Nisibena*, CSCO 218–19/Scr. Syr. 92–3 (Louvain, 1961).

21 E.g. *Odes Sol.* 33, 38.

22 *H Epiph.* 3; for the text, see above n. 14. Although attributed to Ephrem, the cycle is clearly by his disciples.

23 Ephrem, *Hom. on Our Lord*, 18.2; ed. and trans. E. Beck, *Des heiligen Ephrem des Syrers Sermo de Domino Nostro*, CSCO 270–1/Scr. Syr. 116–17 (Louvain, 1966).

24 Cf. Brock, *The Luminous Eye*, 40, 99–114.

25 As preserved in the *Doctrina Addai*, ed. G. Phillips (1876) and trans. George Howard, *The Teaching of Addai* (Missoula, MT: Scholars Press, 1981).

26 *Odes Sol.* 21:4.

27 *Hom on Our Lord*, 9.1: here trans. Joseph P. Amar and Edward G. Mathews, Jr., *St. Ephrem the Syrian: Selected Prose Works*, Fathers of the Church 91 (Washington, DC; Catholic University of America Press, 1994), 284.

28 *H Virg.* 37.2; trans. McVey, *Ephrem*, 425.

29 The Syriac term here translated "brightness" is *denha*, "shining forth," "manifestation," "epiphany," "theophany."

30 In the *Doctrina Addai*, Howard, at p. 100. The same imagery is used to characterize what happened to Edessa during the episcopate of its great bishop Rabbula (in office 411/12–435/6AD). Cf. the *Vita S. Rabbulae*, ed. Paul Bedjan, *Acta Martyrum et Sanctorum* 4 (Paris/Leipzig: Otto Harrassowitz, 1894; repr. Hildesheim: Georg Olms, 1968) 396–450.

31 It is absolutely crucial to understand the origins of Syrian monasticism within the service of the church. See now the superb study by Sidney H. Griffith, "Asceticism in the Church of Syria: The Hermeneutics of Early Syrian Monasticism," in *Asceticism*, ed. Vincent Wimbush and Richard Valantasis (New York: Oxford University Press, 1995), 220–45; and *idem*, "Ephraem, the Deacon of Edessa, and the Church of the Empire," in *Diakonia: Studies in Honor of Robert T. Meyer*, ed. T. Halton and J. P. Williman (Washington, DC: Catholic University of America Press, 1986), 22–52. See S. A. Harvey, *Asceticism and Society in Crisis: John of Ephesus and the 'Lives of the Eastern Saints'* (Berkeley: University of California Press, 1990) and Andrew Palmer, *Monk and Mason on the Tigris Frontier: The Early History of Tur 'Abdin* (Cambridge: University of Cambridge Press, 1990), for discussions of the continuing Syriac tradition.

32 Aphrahat, *Demonstration* 4.14; ed. J. Parisot, *Patrologia Syriaca* 1 (1894) cols. 37–82. There is an English translation in Sebastian P. Brock, *The Syriac Fathers on Prayer and the Spiritual Life* (Kalamazoo: Cistercian Publications, 1987), 1–28.

33 Ephrem, *Letter to Publius*, 15. The text is edited with translation by Sebastian P. Brock in *Le Muséon* 89 (1976): 261–305. There is also a translation in Mathews and Amar, *St. Ephrem the Syrian: Selected Prose Works*, 335–55.

34 *H Virg* 2.15; trans. McVey, *Ephrem*, 270.

35 Most vividly seen in the Syriac *Vita S. Simeonis Stylitae*, ed. P. Bedjan, *Acta Martyrum et Sanctorum* 4 (Paris 1894): 507–644; the imagery is even more powerful in the Greek vita of Simeon the Younger, ed. and trans. P. Van den Ven, *La vie ancienne de S. Syméon Stylite le jeune* (521–92), Subsidia Hagiographica 32 (Bruxelles, 1962–70), 2 vols. See the discussion in S. A. Harvey, "The Sense of a Stylite: Perspective on Simeon the Elder," *Vigiliae Christianae* 42 (1988): 376–94.

36 The anonymous hymn, wrongly attributed to Ephrem, "On Hermits and Desert Dwellers," ed. and trans. E. Beck, *Des heiligen Ephraem des Syrers Sermones* IV, CSCO 334–5/Scr. Syr. 148–9 (Louvain, 1973); and trans. J. P. Amar, in *Ascetic Behavior in Greco-Roman Antiquity: A Sourcebook*, ed. Vincent Wimbush (Minneapolis: Fortress Press, 1990), 66–80. I am indebted to Gary Anderson for sharing with me his work on Nebuchadnezzar and Syriac penitential tradition.

37 *Book of Steps*, Discourse 12.2; here trans. Brock, *Syriac Fathers on Prayer*, p. 46. Text ed. M. Kmosko, *Patrologia Syriaca* 3 (1926).

38 Cf. Brock, *The Luminous Eye*, 29–30.

39 Jacob of Serug, "Homily on Simeon the Stylite," ed. Bedjan, *Acta Martyrum et Sanctorum* 4, 650–65; here trans. S. A. Harvey, in Wimbush, *Asceticism in Greco-Roman Antiquity*, 15–28, at p. 22.

40 *H Nis.* 50.3; trans. Brock, *Harp of the Holy Spirit*, p. 56.

41 *H Par* 8.10. Ed. and trans. E. Beck, *Des heiligen Ephraem des Syrers Hymnen de Paradiso und Contra Julianum*, CSCO 174–5/Scr. Syr. 78–9 (Louvain, 1957).

42 Jacob of Serug, *Homily* 22, ed. P. Bedjan, *Homiliae Selectae Mar Jacobi Sarugensis* (Paris/ Leipzig: Otto Harrasowitz, 1905) at I: 546. Cf. Michael Guinan, *The Eschatology of James of Serug* (Ann Arbor: University Microfilms, 1972). On the phrase, "fragrance of life" in Syriac tradition, see S. A. Harvey, "St. Ephrem on the Scent of Salvation," *Journal of Theological Studies* n.s. 49 (1998): 109–28.

43 E.g., Aphrahat, *Demonstrations* 6.14, 18: 8: 22. Ephrem, *H Par* 5:8–10. See the fine study by Caroline Walker Bynum, *The Resurrection of the Body in Western Christianity, 200–1336* (New York: Columbia University Press, 1995), including her interesting discussion of Aphrahat and Ephrem, at pp. 71–8.

44 Cf J. Daniélou, "Terre et Paradis chez les Pères de l'Église," *Eranos Jahrbuch* 22 (1953): 433–72, where the Ephrem's *Hymns on Paradise* are his case study for the physicality of the afterlife. For a striking example of patristic diversity on this matter, however, compare the totality of sensory experience evoked in Ephrem's *Hymns on Paradise*, with Augustine of Hippo, *City of God*, 22.30. In Augustine's presentation, the bodily dimension of the resurrected life is dominated by the experience of perfect sight, to the virtual exclusion of the other senses.

45 I will use the translation by Sebastian P. Brock, *St. Ephrem the Syrian: Hymns on Paradise* (Crestwood, NY: St. Vladimir's Seminary Press, 1990). This book includes an excellent introduction and commentary on these hymns.

46 See the discussion in Harvey, "St. Ephrem on the Scent of Salvation."

47 *H Par* 8.2b, 4, 5b, 6. Trans. Brock, *Hymns on Paradise*, 132–3.

48 *H Par* 8.9.

49 *H Virg* 8.2–3; trans. McVey, *Ephrem*, 298.

50 *H Par* 9.6, 17; Brock, *Hymns on Paradise*, 138, 142.

51 *H Par.* 7.12; trans. Brock, *Hymns on Paradise*, 123.

52 *H Par* 11.6; trans. Brock, *Hymns on Paradise*, 156.

53 *Hom on Our Lord*, 10.2; trans. Mathews and Amar, *Ephrem: Prose*, p. 286.

54 *Hom on Our Lord*, 21.5; trans. Amar, *Ephrem: Prose*, p. 297.

55 *H Virg* 30. 12; trans. McVey, *Ephrem*, 397.

56 *H Nat* 4.144–5; trans. McVey, *Ephrem*, 100.

57 E.g., *H Nat* 3.16, 21; *H Nat* 25.14–15; *H Par* 9.27; *H Par* 11.6–8.

58 *H Virg* 16.5; McVey, *Ephrem*, 330.

59 *H Par* 7.17; trans. Brock, *Hymns on Paradise*, 125.

2

The Appeal to Experience

George P. Schner, SJ

This article argues that bare experience, experience "as such," enters theological discourse as a peculiarly modern category. Appeal to individual experience creates a discontinuity between recent and earlier theology. Experience has always played a role in theology, but not as individual or incorrigible. Aquinas did not begin his response to disputed questions with the remark, "In my experience, . . ." Individual experience was not, that is, authority-granting. Thus Schner elaborates and anticipates a thesis of this collection that experience gains its authority under other theological rubrics that shape and discipline it: reason, tradition, scripture, the sense of the faithful, the form of the liturgy, the work of the Spirit.

Somewhere in this century the term "experience" begins to appear with regularity in the titles of articles and books in Christian theology and makes its way into proposals for methodological and doctrinal developments. Similarly, in the common parlance of the Christian faithful, and especially of students of theology, a similar appeal to "my experience," or the experience of a particular group, has become theological common sense. When one asks about what sort of appeal it is, whether it is philosophically coherent, and whether it is appropriate to the task of Christian theology, such questions are often greeted with surprise. What could be more obvious than the appeal to experience, its inevitability, or even its momentous appropriateness at this point in the history of Christianity and its theology?

All theology, it would be agreed, should be "experiential" in a manner analogous to the way in which it ought all to be "scriptural," "philosophical," and "logical," and in a way in which it cannot all be Roman Catholic, or

Anglican, or perspectival in a great variety of ways. In claiming that one's theology is "experiential," however, one has not yet said very much. What is the form of appeal to experience? How is the use of experience in the theological argument related to the content of the experience? How is the appeal to experience related to other elements of theological construction?

This essay offers a sketch of this appeal to experience in three parts: the first section will ask about the rhetorical use of the appeal, and its function as an appeal to authority; a second section will propose four basic characteristics of experience as a general philosophic category, and consider the oddity of two common usages; the final section will propose a continuum of possible uses of the appeal to experience within theological arguments.

In the course of the remarks in each section there will be few direct references to recent authors since my purpose here is not to analyze particular usages but to provide a conceptual map. My conclusions result as much from listening to students as from analyzing theological texts. Those familiar with David H. Kelsey's *The Uses of Scripture in Recent Theology*[1] might notice a resemblance of this essay to the sort of exercise he engaged in concerning the appeal to Scripture in Christian theology. Just as his typology is illuminating beyond the specific authors he discusses, so my proposal is intended to be broad and heuristic. As the sentence "Scripture is authoritative for Christian theology" is the invocation of a self-involving rule that commits the speaker to *function* in a particular way, so the appeal to experience is a similar invocation. But not every appeal to experience is an appeal to the same construal of experience, nor does it function in the same role in the argument structure. This essay is an initial exploration of these differences, not with attention to the exact placement of experience in any particular argument, but with attention to types of possible use.

Rhetorical Appeal to Experience

By comparison to many philosophical analyses of experience, it seems easy yet illuminating to explore first the rhetorical use of phrases such as "in my experience . . ." or "personally speaking . . ." In a minimalist fashion, they are used as a linguistic cipher before the speaker states an opinion or inserts something confirming or new, differing or even contradictory, into a conversation. The appeal to oneself might carry the weight of an assurance of authenticity, the promise of self-manifestation, or an assertion of the right to speak. It is meant to give force or credibility to a particular stage in an argument. Moreover, it often implicitly questions the authenticity, force, or credibility of one's conversation partners and their opinions, though with the appearance of not actually doing so. The cipher invokes a supposed common ground, experience, within which differing opinions will be placed, and may, perhaps, be reconciled. It adds no content to what follows, but does more than the obvious, which would be to remind the listener that the opinions being expressed belong to the speaker. It is important to note that in the rhetorical appeal to experience, the noun "experience" does not *refer* to anything, neither an object nor a "state" of the subject. The same result might be achieved by changing the tone of voice, or by a gesture or change of posture. The nuance of meaning must be determined from the context, and such usage is never "exact" since its function as rhetorical depends upon many inexact factors.

Prefacing what is about to be said as "mine," an emphasis I will call "perspectival," seems to imply that it is not merely that of a group, or of people in general, but rather is uniquely my own; or, the need to call attention to the opinion as mine might be precisely as a member of a specific group which stands in opposition to another group, or any other group at all. It can also be an extremely brief way in which to remind the listener or reader that the sentence to follow is the result of serious, perhaps prolonged, consideration by the individual or the group. It is somewhat like the preface "I believe that . . ." or more emphatically "I'd stake my life (reputation) on it" or "I would be untrue to myself if I were not to say that . . ." or "as a concerned member of such-and-such a group, I must point out that . . ." The rhetorical appeal is thus in no sense trivial, though it may range from emphasis without content to well-considered urgency precisely because of who the subject of the experiencing is and what has been experienced.

Two general observations can be made to locate this use of experience and differentiate it from other rhetorical uses. First, the usual historical reference is to the Enlightenment origins of this appeal and its dependence upon such notions as: (1) a Cartesian, Hobbesian, or Kantian self; (2) the autonomy of reason in face of the heteronomous vehicles of authority which were seen to be in opposition to free inquiry; and (3) the rationalist and empiricist programme of deriving all judgments from individual observation or, as it comes to be called, experience. The presupposition of a self-regulating human rationality dependent upon interior and exterior senses common to us all, which can detect errors in knowledge through a sort of self-policing exercise, is not the discovery of the Enlightenment, of course. It was well known to the ancients and the medievals, but took a quite particular turn in the seventeenth century. The construal of experience as individual, oppositional, and in some sense self-authenticating is essential to the origin and maintenance of a notion that all opinions have a "right" to be heard. Thus, though an opinion is different from that of one's interlocutor, it has a right to be heard, perhaps even a priority over other opinions.

Second, the by now familiar trio of Nietzsche, Marx, and Freud are then invoked as principal expositors of a suspiciousness about this "autonomous" and "pure" reason, such that though opinions are indeed to be heard they are to be suspected of carrying more freight than appears to be the case. An unqualified appeal to experience is thus seen as naive unless the social, psychological, and philosophical determinants of experience are exposed. Any such appeal must include a retrieval of the inevitable presence of interpretation and tradition in even the simplest of appeals to "my" experience. A further moment of this analysis and critique is prefigured in Hegel and carried out in two quite different philosophical investigations by Heidegger and Wittgenstein, for example. They dismantle the metaphor of the subject as "inside" and the world as "outside," leave the modern preoccupation with the subject, and rejoin the premodern philosophical study of the forms of mediation, of language, symbols, and culture in general, as the proper topic for the investigation of just what experience is and is not. In a manner parallel to the critique of the subject's states of consciousness by psychoanalysis for example, criticism of the moment of mediation – of language use, social structures, the embodiment of power, and so forth – must also be carried out.

A contemporary rhetorical use of phrases referring to "my experience" must, therefore, acknowledge this critique and go beyond the maintenance of enlightened subjectivity. The appeal as a form of "locating" what is to be said adverts to the knowledge, implicit or explicit, of the existence of "worlds of discourse" which are variously overlapping or incommensurate. The individual might be thought of as proposing what is about to be said in a tentative way, acknowledging that it consists of only one possible articulation, and possibly one that the conversation partners may find only partially intelligible or even wholly obscure, beyond the obvious sense of the words being uttered. Such a usage seems to be the moment of second naivete, in which the confident utterance of self-assertion, chastened by a hermeneutic of personal and cultural suspicion, gives way to a second articulation of meaning which of necessity is prefaced by a relativizing "in my experience," meaning "in my experience as one perspective among many . . ." One might actually withhold one's opinion, for purposes of education or politeness, in some circumstances because of precisely this sort of self-awareness.

Whether modern or postmodern, it is the oddity of making the appeal at all that I wish to take note of. Where else would an opinion come from except from "my experience," whether it is a result of direct learning or appropriation on the word of another? Much like the phrase "personal experience," one might ask: what other kind is there? Have you ever expressed your "impersonal experience" when giving an opinion? The use of the rhetorical cipher derives from the need to give some sort of emphasis to what follows it, to cause a particular kind of attention to be paid to both the speaker and the opinion. At least two sorts of emphasis appear to be intended.

As to the first sort of emphasis, whether it is naive, self-suspicious, or self-effacing, the appeal to experience is a variation on the appeal to authority, a rhetorical style and a feature of argumentation which has a venerable role in Christian theology.[2] As with any appeal to authority, so too the appeal to experience is a *counterappeal*, whether acknowledged as such or not. It is essentially a claim for the dominance of one opinion over another, for the right of the opinion to be heard and possibly to be determinative of thought, speech, or action, not on the basis of the content of the opinion or the logic used to construct the argument, but because of the genesis and possession of the opinion by a particular person or group. If the opinion were thought to stand on its own account, the rhetorical appeal to experience would be unnecessary. However, to employ the rhetorical appeal need not be taken as a clue to the weakness of the opinion it prefaces. The nature of its strength or value, that is, the warrant for its authority, is another kind of emphasis given by the appeal to experience.

Second, then, the cipher "in my experience . . ." can be taken as making the claim that what is about to be said is not ideological, but is the articulation of the actual form of life of an individual or a group. The claim is that what is about to be said is not merely an abstract concept or theory, a mere repetition of past opinions, but is the articulation of the actual operative principles or convictions of the individual or group. As such it can be in the mode of an appeal which calls into question the interlocutor's opinion or the received opinion, and asserts by contrast the truth (or at least what the speaker claims should prevail); moreover, it is presumed there is a right, if not a necessity, that it be heard and considered, more because of its function as actual operative content than for any other reason. The activity of "making myself heard" through articulation of "my experience" may be analyzed psychologically, socially, and philosophically in terms of identity formation or conflicts of power which require self-assertion, regardless of the content of the opinion. Questions are raised when the emphasis on a "right to be heard" is taken to mean that the position has authority *on the basis* of its being the articulation of actual operations.

The two forms of emphasis should not be confused. A careful distinction is needed between "experience" as a term to name the authentic articulation of how I happen to function as a human person, and the appeal to that opinion qua "experience" as the warrant for its acceptance as a norm or model (not to be confused with truth, licitness, or value), in a word, as a warrant for the "authority" of my opinion over a particular form of life, even over a particular community.[3] There is a moment of passage between these two uses which depends upon judgments of reality and value. To assert my opinion as part of the dialectic of an argument is one thing, to presume the assertion is the conclusion of the argument is another. The rhetorical ciphers are also evidence of the sense of being misunderstood which is expressed in similar phrases, such as "now look here . . ." or "now listen to me . . ." It articulates the sense that one's having been heard is a form of not being heard. One's opinion has a right

27

to be heard, or more precisely to be heard and understood, on the grounds of its own principles of construction. It carries a sophisticated, even if intuitive, awareness that opinions in their differing are the articulation of differing principles, and that more is at stake than simple self-assertion. However, the appeal to experience can inaugurate a foreclosure on the necessary dialectic of opinions rather than initiate it. When the appeal is actually a demand for "my experience" to be dominant, to overcome and displace the other opinions of the conversation, then the appeal to experience degenerates to an appeal to authority in the pejorative sense, resulting in an antinomy of opinions at best, an unmoving opposition at worst.

The rhetorical appeal to experience is thus both a maintenance of the Enlightenment desire to set aside the tutelage of any group or text so as to exercise reason in full freedom of inquiry, and also an instance of the displacement of authority from the dominant community to the individual or to particularized groups within the community. As the history of philosophical, psychological, and social criticism subsequent to the Enlightenment confirms, this form of an appeal to experience must itself be subjected to critique and is never literally a disinterested appeal. That is not to say it is purposefully ignorant let alone ill willed. Rather, it points out that an appeal to experience as the authorization of the status of a given opinion is dependent upon a theory of rationality, of human nature, of the relation of the individual to society and history, and of language and all other forms of mediation. The rhetorical appeal to experience, once examined, leads us to a nest of philosophic problems.

Thus, if the rhetorical appeal to experience is to be useful, particularly in Christian theology, it will benefit from two kinds of philosophical analysis, one which will consider the chief characteristics of experience and another which will consider its role in arguments. The latter will investigate the appeal to experience as the moment in an argument which invites analysis and appreciation of the inherently dialectical character of the occurrence. The appeal to experience is a negative moment which alerts us, not to the obvious, i.e. the fact that the speaker is speaking, but to the unexpressed, i.e. the fact that the speaker is absent, is not represented by the other conversation partner's self-articulation. The occurrence of the rhetorical appeal, while it indeed calls attention to the content of what follows, seems to raise issues rather than settle them, and a foremost issue is why the appeal itself is needed at the moment of its occurrence in the argument.

As to the former analysis, it must be remembered that as a rhetorical cipher the phrase "in my experience . . ." offers no content and need not be construed as a description of states of the self. Rather, it serves as a preparatory remark before the statement of content, giving an indirect clue to a state of affairs in the community of believers, the realm of public discourse, or in the academy. What is masked in the rhetorical appeal is the fact that, like any such appeal to authority, one is simultaneously appealing to a tradition and its multiple origins and connections. The appeal to "my experience" is of particular interest, then, because its linguistic form appears to be the opposite of what it actually is, an appeal to a particular tradition of experience and authority, and its being anchored in a particular self likewise belies its dependence on others and its intent to be determinative of others.

I turn first to a statement of some general characteristics of experience as a philosophical category, and then to a proposal about a range of uses for the notion within a theological argument.

Experience as a Philosophic Category

A thorough philosophical investigation of the notion "experience" and its use in arguments would require a lengthy digression into the history of the rise to prominence of this notion in the seventeenth and eighteenth centuries, though it obviously had been present previously in Western philosophy in some guise or other. The philosophers and psychologists of the last three centuries have developed many schemata within which to define "experience" as a particular moment and relate it to the other activities essential to the full range of human knowledge. Rather than repeat the usual history of that succession of theories, I will articulate four general rules governing the notion "experience" which emerge despite differing epistemologies and psychologies.

Experience is a construct

Whether one examines the most rudimentary occurrence of experience as interior or exterior awareness, in relatively isolated instances or in large collections of "my life experience," one discovers a construction, dependent upon a variety of operations and elements; it is composed of what is past, projective of the future, elusively in the present; it is shaped by a complex of physiological, psychological, and linguistic activities; and, as a result, it is multilayered in its potential for sense, reference, and meaning. By the time some moment of the interrelation of self and other is actually adverted to reflectively and appealed to as "experience," it has undergone a process of construction which a phenomenology can deconstruct only by stopping the flow of consciousness so as to dissect the living. Experience is therefore investigated through some form of mediation, whether through memory or imagination, through thought by means of conceptualization or judgment, through language by means of articulation, or through symbolic representation of some kind.

Thus certain phrases become problematic: experience as the given, experience as immediate, experience as incorrigible, experience as consisting of

◈ 29

discrete moments. At the very point at which I am able actually to appeal to experience, I have achieved a level of awareness in which I implicitly know that I am appealing to something which I have constructed, which is therefore revisable, and subject to a request for justification of some kind. Thus experience is neither given, nor unmediated, nor incorrigible, nor atomistic: it is constructed.

Experience is intentional

An appeal to experience always includes, implicitly or explicitly, a prepositional phrase following it, beginning with "of" or "about" or "with" or a similar connective, which will convey the intentional (in the sense of the "tending towards") character of experience. Hegel discusses it in terms of the interpenetration and mutual dependence of self and other, and Heidegger unfolds the great variety of relations to things and to others which human "being-in-the-world" implies, exploring the movement into the "there" of the "being-there." Wittgenstein's intensive analysis of various language uses not only criticizes the positivist limitation of language to empirical reference, but also encourages an expansion of our understanding of intentionality in its plurality of forms. The forms of appeal which are problematic in relation to this general rule of intentionality are those which presume that experience is self-contained or private. Such construals of experience remain enthralled by the invention of that particular kind of subjectivity called "modern"; they tend to forget the social, mediated, and linguistic character of consciousness.

Thus certain usages become problematic when they employ the term "experience" in place of "feeling" or "intuition" in the sense of an unthematic or vague state of consciousness. Such a substitution can be accompanied by a claim to the uniqueness of such "experience," to its superiority as unarticulated, or perhaps to its immunity to requirements for authentication or justification as to its use in an argument. Most sophisticated theories of knowledge make careful distinctions between these two moments of knowing, and assign them relative merit and use based upon the teleology of the whole range of ways of knowing.

Experience is derivative

This is a corollary of the constructed and intentional character of experience. When I preface a remark with the phrase "in my experience," I am in part saying "according to what I have received." Rudimentarily, I am appealing to what has shaped my consciousness from both beyond myself and through the structuring operations of consciousness itself, those which are natural and those which are learned. I am also saying "as I have been taught," not referring simply to formal schooling or education, but to family customs, and to my socialization in a variety of groups. I indirectly admit to membership in those groups which have formed my person, given me my language, shaped attitudes and capacities for feeling, and habituated me with notions, concepts, rules, and attitudes.

Thus a phrase like "personal experience" is problematic when it is used to claim uniqueness or irreducibility, or exemption from critique. There is a sense in which no experience is strictly "mine." In fact, were I not to live in a common and agreed upon world of experiencing, communication and interaction would be impossible. As Hegel puts it in the *Phenomenology*, self-consciousness comes about through the discovery of the "we," and the full development into Spirit depends upon language and culture. As Heidegger puts it, we live most consistently in the "they," in modes of alienation, and authenticity is only a modified form in which everydayness is taken up. Or, as Wittgenstein puts it, meaning is found through the investigation of use, and language use has its foothold in a form of living.

Experience is dialectical

This also is a corollary of the constructed and intentional character of experience. We employ the term "dialectical" here, but we could just as accurately characterize experience at this point as dynamic, self-altering, self-displacing, or inventive. As inherently unstable, experience is never perfectly balanced between "self" and "other," never simply "of the present" but always coming from the past and projecting the future, never simply "mine" but also "theirs," and never merely "a position" or "an opinion" but also "a counterposition" and "an opposing opinion." Most philosophers and psychologists have proposed some form of teleology for human consciousness, either one which is imposed upon it or one it has by nature. Thus each moment is a nest of relations "on the move," a configuration or gestalt which adds its necessary but not sufficient conditions to the ever-complexifying self-and-other awareness. We easily consider consciousness to be developmental, historical, and relative to circumstances, somewhat in contradiction of phrases like "in my experience" or "personally speaking." So "in my experience" *may* connote: "I refuse to move." Thus certain phrases become problematic, such as "you can't possibly understand my experience" or "no one will ever persuade me that . . ." When experience is collapsed into the subject itself *simpliciter*, the appeal has obviated itself.

These four characteristics – constructed, intentional, derivative, and dialectical – are applicable to the common sense uses of the word "experience" which one finds in a dictionary definition: "experience" as the conscious apprehension of inner or outer reality through senses and mind; as active participation in specific events and the knowledge gained by such participation;

as the undergoing of life and the accumulation of knowledge thereby; as experimentation, testing, or trial.[4] Philosophers and psychologists interested in epistemology or cognitional structure produce theories which map out the multiple activities between the unconscious and the mystical, giving the word "experience" a technical role as referring to a specific human operation in a series of operations. Since these activities occur as a whole, anticipating one another or being built upon one another, experience can be said to participate in those characteristics which belong to the whole. In the case of its use in theological works, experience is often used as a nontechnical comprehensive term covering the whole range of cognitional and emotional operations without being too precise or limiting. In other cases, the term is used in a predetermined, technical sense.

The four general rules concerning experience lead me to question two phrases which are common in theological arguments and range between common sense and technical uses. First, the phrase "common human experience" is sometimes used to imply a foundation of human operations common to all human beings, either as to content or structure. Such a rarified abstraction would be asymptotically approaching emptiness in its efforts to be as common as possible, or would function more as a prescription as to how we ought to speak about human beings from other cultures or religions *as if* they were ourselves. That there are family resemblances among human beings, analogous descriptions of human activities, can hardly be denied. That there is literally a "common experience" would presume either a single subjective substrate, which is contradictory, or a singularity of history, culture, and language, which is counterfactual. The best sense one can make of such a phrase as "common human experience" is to treat it as a cipher for "experience." Human beings experience; in that they are all alike. Beyond that, irreducible diversity enters in as the constructive, intentional, derivative, and dialectical character of experience is grasped in the concrete. Another use of the phrase could be as part of a prescriptive theory of the transcendental conditions of all human experience, a notion which may indeed be needed by some theologians to make their arguments work, but one which is more ideal and prescriptive than empirical and descriptive.

A second phrase to be reconsidered is "religious experience." It can be used to imply that there are specific sorts of human operation which are "religious" or that there are specific foci of the intentionality that can be called "religious." If the phrase means the experience of the various elements which make up the actual functioning of a specific religion, then such experience is only different from other experience in having particular modes of construction, intention, derivation, and dialectic. The phrase can then be seen to be as ordinary as "teaching experience," "dish-washing experience," "fund-raising experience." The word "experience" is used to signify acquaintance with, expertise in, certain states of affairs and human interaction with them commonly called religion (and more properly named with a specific adjective, Christian, Jewish, Hindu, etc). If it is taken to mean human operation with a particular quality, namely "religiousness," then the phrase "religious experience" would be like the phrases "frightening experience," "comforting experience," or "confusing experience." In both of these cases, as acquaintance with a state of affairs or as a quality of experience, the phrase "religious experience" is subjected to investigation by many sciences and disciplines, and is often reduced to other more elemental forms of experience. Isolating its nonreducible character would presumably depend upon discovering, beyond the obvious use of generally accepted religious terms, its peculiar interpretive, revelatory, regenerative, numinous, or even mystical characteristics.[5]

As early as the sixteenth century but particularly since the nineteenth century, the growing need to preserve a domain for religious belief in face of its ineffectualness occasioned the development of a theory about historic religions and human nature, in which the phrase "religious experience" has come to mean a peculiar kind of human operation which, in the various developments of the theory, exhibits a unique form of construction, intention, derivation, and dialectic. Thus, what was denied as possible for the human mind by Kant and made a constituent of all consciousness by Hegel, was made foundational yet inaccessible by Schleiermacher. The moment of religiousness is prior to experience yet inseparable from it. As Rahner will describe it a century later, it is the unthematic transcendental condition which is inseparable from categorical experience and known through a careful process of philosophical reflection. In determining what religiosity is, Rahner adopts Kant's demand for critical justification of it, Hegel's placement of it within an optimistic teleological anthropology, and Schleiermacher's preconceptual status for it. Thus there is actually no religious experience, per se, to point to, but only a religious dimension of all experience. What we are after seems better served by the phrase "the religious dimension of all experience."

Adjectival or adverbial additions to "experience" can be indicative of deeply rooted cultural imperatives and forms of functioning that human beings might be said to be struggling with. They do not necessarily "refer" to anything as such, but do alert us to a state of affairs within which a regaining of certain ways of speaking, thinking, and functioning are essential for the health of humanity, or specifically for the health of the Church. I suggest this is the case with the phrases "religious experience" and "common human experience," which are in themselves troublesome expressions. While they may appear to do valuable service in certain theological contexts, they can also be symptomatic of the situation which Michael Buckley's analysis of the origins of modern atheism discloses.[6]

Appeal to Experience in Theology

Beyond the rhetorical use of an appeal to experience, and keeping in mind the four general rules I have suggested about the notion itself, I would propose a continuum of broad possibilities for the meaning and use of the notion "experience" when it constitutes a major element in the work of a theologian. The range of possibilities, of course, admits of a succession of slight variations and I will only highlight certain significant moments of change from one type to another. The two ends of the continuum, which might well join one another from opposite directions, are an objectification of experience in a theological anthropology at one end, and a radical loss of the self in the transcendent Other, beyond articulation and identity, at the other end. While these extremes seem easy to locate, the nodes which mark transition between are not necessarily so obvious. I will attempt to describe three other types of appeal and what they entail. Essential to each stage or moment will be noting the role which the transcendent and the community (or tradition) play in the construal of experience.

The appeal transcendental

When experience enters a theological argument in the form of an appeal to an anthropology, it functions as an extreme of the objectification of experience. In effect, experience is a term for philosophy, or some such theory about the common elements or structures of actual human life, often of cognition and volition taken as the essential operations which constitute human activity. The appeal is not to any actual descriptions of experience, but to the "conditions of possibility" of all experience, of the structuring elements which make experience human. For theological arguments it is crucial whether this appeal presumes there is a transcendent dimension to all experience or not. On the one hand, if it presumes such an horizon, then the argument can proceed apologetically, requiring the interlocutor to admit self-contradiction if she does not admit of the intelligibility of a given doctrine of an historical religion's self-description. The doctrine, derived from the transcendental conditions of all experience, could only be denied if the transcendental conditions are denied. This would involve the contradiction of denying what one is using for the denial. On the other hand, if the appeal transcendental excludes the possibility of a transcendent dimension to all experience, then the appeal would proceed in the argument to "explain away" anything distinctively religious or theological that cannot be adequately explained by other sciences or disciplines. In both cases, through the appeal to experience before experience (that is, to the transcendental conditions of all experience known only through a special process of reflective thinking), the argument can proceed to the necessity of particular doctrinal content, either by a logical unfolding or reduction.

As to the community, the appeal transcendental with a transcendent dimension potentially appeals to all possible human beings, living or otherwise. "Experience" and the "community" coincide, so that appeal to experience is appeal to the community and in effect its tradition, i.e. its inherent structures. If there is no transcendent dimension by necessity, then the appeal to the community is to provide negative instances, as it were. What everyone has is an experience of the absence of God. In either case there is no need for an appeal to a specific community or to specific forms of experience. One might conclude that an appeal transcendental which does not include a transcendent dimension inherent in its community (i.e. in human nature) ultimately obviates strictly theological argument.

The appeal hermeneutical

What I am calling the appeal hermeneutical is an appeal to experience marked by modes of suspicion. If the appeal transcendental consists in asserting a universal and self-establishing conception of the conditions of human life, then the appeal hermeneutical questions the very possibility of such an assertion by making explicit in the appeal the perspectival, limited, and even alienating characteristics of experience. Every appeal has a companion caution expressed with it, which questions what is appealed to, articulated in description, assertion, or some other linguistic form. Unlike the appeal transcendental which is foundational, the appeal hermeneutic emphasizes the dialectical character and function of any appeal. Unlike the appeal transcendental whose inner principles would not require movement on the continuum, the appeal hermeneutical admits of two obvious moves. Experience so invoked could be expected to resolve itself either into the appeal transcendental by way of correction of the presumed normative structure identical with human nature, or into the appeal constructive. What is invited is, so to speak, an unpacking of the story provided in the account of experience so as to discover its ideological features, with the possibility that the experience is corrigible by adoption of "the normative" conceived as either universal or particularistic. For an argument to remain in the appeal hermeneutical would seem to me to invite a form of skepticism to prevail in one's theoretical constructions. Every possible position would be subjected to scrutiny, based upon altering construals of reality in "experience" and accompanied by a persistent hesitation ever to settle upon any construal as normative. In such a usage no evidence ever suffices to authorize any experience as normative, and the appearance of movement in an argument, from construal to construal without rest, must, I think, give away to some other form of appeal.

The transcendent and communal dimensions of experience share in the unstable and skeptical character of this appeal. If the transcendent is an ingredient at all, it is likely to be inaccessible or at least subject to the same scrutiny as any other element or dimension of experience. It would admit of a variety of embodiments, none of them normative, as the procedure of suspicion requires. As for the community, it is multiple in its manifestations but limited in its viability. As the procedures of suspicion are carried out, adherence to any particular community or tradition is made increasingly difficult, and would ultimately produce a situation in which the appeal to experience would be a form of refined, philosophical skepticism contrasted to "common life" or the possibilities of change through the acceptance of a normative narrative.

The appeal constructive

In the appeal constructive, experience is invoked as the moment of transformation, being a construal of experience as possessing neither the inevitability of a transcendental condition of human nature, nor simply a relativity consequent upon its being representative of a community of persons, things, ideas, language, habits and similar formative historical and social influences. As such it enters into a theological argument without imposing a universal structure independent of the particularities of the religion's community and its beliefs, or without depriving itself of normativity through a presupposed relativity of all experience as mere convention or incommensurate subjectivities. The appeal constructive is a dual appeal to possibility and necessity. It is possible through experience to change one's life, and to accomplish change it is necessary for experience to interact with already operative determinants. What is appealed to as experience must be capable of bearing necessity in itself, and yet be a "possibility," neither simply structurally inevitable nor radically disparate from the context into which it is brought. Experience is, then, not unqualifiedly the "source" of theological construction, nor is it incapable of being normative as in the appeal hermeneutical. It can be known and articulated, as the appeal immediate or mystical will not readily admit, and it does not collapse into a theory of human nature in order to establish its normativity.

I would envision the appeal to proceed, not necessarily explicitly each time it is invoked, but implicitly involving the following stages or moments. Experience as a form of encounter is recognized for its characteristics as constructed, intentional, derivative, and dialectical. As such it enters an argument not as foundational but as interruptive. It enters as a moment of discontinuity into a larger, already established context. It is interruptive since, if it were simply continuous with what is already operative, it would not need to be adverted to precisely as "experience." It might well be considered *disruptive*, and as such takes its place in an argument (or in life) as a challenge to be learnt from or refused. Thus, the insertion invites consideration, discussion, revision, change. As the element of experience becomes incorporated into the argument (and ultimately into the form of life the argument might be proposing or redescribing), it becomes subsumed so that it need no longer be appealed to precisely as "experience." It has become, so to speak, part of the structuring environment which will be the context for the next incursion of "experience" which will invite consideration. Experience passes into habit, an appeal to what challenges passes into an appeal to the tradition.

In this form of appeal, in Christianity, the role of the transcendent is congruent with the interruptive, critical, and determining role that experience plays in theological construction, mirroring its role in Christian life. As such, the transcendent enters into the established and performs the tasks of experience in a transcendent way, interrupting, questioning, and norming in an absolute way. If intervention by the transcendent is denied as a possibility (which seems to me self-contradictory in this sort of appeal to experience), then the whole point of attentiveness to experience is undercut. In this form of appeal, it is not human nature in general, the needs of a particular part of humanity, but the agency of the transcendent which is "experience."

As to the role of the community and of tradition, it has a dual face. On the one side it functions as the medium within which the transcendent can appear, and on the other side it remains opaque, if not resistent, to this revelatory agency. If one emphasizes the *content* of new and startling experience which requires special attention, one mitigates the "startling" character in favor of an interpretation which inserts it into the established tradition and community, at worst in a reductive fashion. If one emphasizes the *interruptive character* of experience, one moderates the organic and continuous nature of experience in favor of radical change, at worst in a schismatic or schizoid fashion. Christianity, it seems to me, profits from an appeal constructive which maintains a balance between these two forms of communal presence and tradition.

The appeal confessional

The appeal confessional agrees with the appeal constructive in its use of experience as normative, taking on a contemporary urgency when it addresses the difficulties which the appeal hermeneutic causes by engendering a kind of relativism or skepticism. This appeal could be an outright appeal to authority, with or without a mention of "experience." It might consist in simply "telling the story," recounting the experience, in the hope that the mere hearing of it will inaugurate the moment of transformation and reconstruction. The appeal to experience is an appeal to "the way things are" or at least "the way things should be." In the life of the Church, the liturgical use of the Bible, for example, might be thought of as an appeal confessional, and some forms of preaching consist of the simple rendering of an account of experience.

As such, this appeal might be called "naive," though we should distinguish between a favorable and a pejorative usage. It is naive on account of its convictions, not necessarily unaware of criticism, but setting it aside, perhaps avoiding it, even possibly repudiating some forms of it which endanger the integrity of the experience. This appeal can be called naive with a pejorative intent, if one has the conviction that no human experience can have ultimate significance, perhaps as the appeal hermeneutical, when absolutized, would require. Just as the appeals constructive, hermeneutical, and transcendental seem apt for some situations yet not for others, so the appeal confessional can be appropriate or counterproductive. Particularly when it would foreclose upon forms of suspicion, the appeal turns authoritarian and is often given the epithet "fideistic" or "fundamentalist." If it moves to become an appeal immediate or mystical, of course, in changing ground it gains credibility. One might even consider the appeal confessional to follow upon some sort of appeal mystical, as the highly dissonant experience of the transcendent is mediated through a metaphor or narrative.

As to the transcendent and the community, the appeal confessional maintains a close connection between these two and the experience itself, presuming the transcendent to be mediated to the community by the experience itself, and the community to be established, as it were, by the experience. This obviously lends considerable weight to the appeal to experience, but unlike the appeal transcendental which does a similar thing in generalities, the appeal confessional "speaks" for the community and the transcendent in particularities. Denial of the transcendent altogether would seem unlikely in the appeal confessional, since it would degenerate into a kind of hypocrisy to have an almost apodictic (absolute) assertion of experience without a firm assertion of the transcendent (as absolute) which the experience conveys. Such seems to have been the unsuccessful attempt of those kinds of "death of God" theology which wished to marry denial of a transcendent God with personal piety devoted to Jesus in all His particularity. Similarly, the community and tradition are vital to this form of appeal, since they are its principal audience and source; the presumption is that a particular account of experience can be normative for the community as a whole and that the recounting of the experience is not oppressive for the group but preservative.

This appeal, like the appeal hermeneutical, could deflect theology from its constructive work by rendering it into mere translation or rephrasing of the account of experience, as given in the Bible for example, just as the hermeneutical appeal become skeptical would discourage the normativity of any text, of any experience.

The appeal immediate or mystical

In this form of appeal to experience, the ultimate collapse of the subject into that which is experienced causes the appeal to be paradoxically an indescribable one, yet one which requires articulation if it is to be used for the good of the community in various forms of theological construction. Radical self-transcendence into that which is beyond the self does not admit of mediation, though one might move back into a former mode of appeal and attempt a description of the state of self and its object, with the help of the imagination. Or, one might provide a symbolic, especially artistic, representation of the experience with or without words, with the caution that the actual experience was the occasion or instrumental cause of the expression, but remains unmediated. Experience ceases to be experience, in the sense of what is constructed, intentional, derivative, and dialectical. There is a similarity to the appeal transcendental, inasmuch as what is appealed to is the experience before experience. If the radically subjective is rendered objective as transcendental structures, so here the radically subjective is left as it is. Concerning the two important relations to the transcendent and to the community, this mode of experience posits a coincidence of the human with the transcendent, and that can be either an empty nothingness or a divine fullness. It may be presented as momentary and utterly gratuitous or as a universal, foundational structure of human life itself, or of a given religion. While in some forms of the experience itself the community is finally utterly absent, in the moment of being alone with the Alone, there are obviously other forms of mysticism which occur in the midst of the everyday and through attention to very determinate manifestations of the transcendent. Just as there are nuances within each of the previous moments on the continuum of options, so here also there are variations of the degree to which the individual is withdrawn from all limitations of the human, and hence of community or tradition in any sense.

In one sense there is no manner in which to "test" such experiences because of their uniqueness to the subject, and so they carry an apodictic weight in an argument. Even so, there is a complex tradition within each historic religion precisely about the testing of such experiences, according to the norms of the particular religion, particularly its notions of both the community and the transcendent. Thus two significant difficulties arise when such an appeal mystical is made without grounding within a given religion's community of faith. If it is an appeal to a generic form of absorption into the transcendent, then it admits of any and all particularities indifferently and loses its usefulness precisely as an appeal to experience. Similarly, as an appeal originating outside of any particular religious tradition and community, it would, because of its rootlessness, lack real effectiveness as critical and potentially transformative.

Thus another form of the appeal mystical is the appeal immediate, the simple assertion or expression of opinions by sheer force of the subject, with the claim that because the appeal is made it is to be taken as authoritative or true or requiring respect. The one who makes the appeal mystical has utter confidence in the experience beyond experience, of what is "because it is so," whereas the one who makes the appeal immediate has utter confidence because "I say so." Both appear to be without community, since in the former case the subject collapses into the transcendent beyond all awareness, and in the latter case the transcendent, and all else, collapses into the subject producing what is technically called solipsism. Perhaps at its best, the appeal immediate is the appeal rhetorical in its polyvalent forms.

Conclusion

These remarks are the result of observing the notion of experience at work in a variety of texts, pedagogical situations, and moments of church life. My continuum admittedly hovers between being a description of and a proposal for constructive theology, since it proposes a dialectic of positions beyond merely identifying them. Before concluding I will offer a brief indication of the evidence for my analysis, with one important caution. As is the case in Kelsey's work on the use of Scripture, showing the presence of a particular usage in an author is not to suggest that that form of appeal to experience is the only one the author uses or the situation requires. Deciding when to use which form of appeal is a further issue. A simple mention of authors is inadequate, but for heuristic purposes let me suggest that the moments of the continuum can be located in the following typical forms. The appeal transcendental can be found in various types of transcendental Thomism, though an author such as Rahner need not be construed as employing an unqualified appeal as Kant did, but rather an ad hoc transcendental proposal. Perspectival theologians employ various sorts of the hermeneutical, and much of the modern philosophy of religion uses the skeptical form of this appeal. Hume's *Dialogues Concerning Natural Religion* are an excellent example of this. Barth's discussion of the place of experience in theology in the *Church Dogmatics* 1.1, or in his work on Anselm, offers one instance of a theoretical exposition of the appeal constructive, and some contemporary narrative theology attempts to employ that form of appeal. Various forms of homiletic and devotional literature use the appeal confessional, and certain forms of evangelism and its popular literature give instance of the appeal naive. The appeal mystical has a very influential exposition by Schleiermacher in his *Speeches,* and is found with varying effect in texts ranging from classical mystical texts to New Age writings. Inasmuch as the appeals mystical and transcendental join one another in closing the circle of possibilities, it would not be incorrect to observe passages in Rahner, for example, where the two intersect.

In conclusion I would suggest that the appeal to experience seems to be an instance of itself: it is itself evidence of a particular kind of experience and of a particular context for theological work within church life and culture at large. As such it is a Janus figure, poised between worlds of discourse and construction. As its doors open to offer those employing it a reconsideration of previous agenda and principles, it returns the contemporary theologian to many past problems and issues which have intricate and well-established histories. As the doors open upon the future, then the ladder by which they have reached the position can be thrown away, as Wittgenstein suggested in another context, so that the work of Christian theology can go forward. There is the potential for a certain bewitchment by "experience" as an element of theological construction which, like Scripture and philosophy, can become disproportionately preoccupying and autocratic. It is equally important to note that the theologian who neglects the appeal to experience does so at great peril. My attempt here at an analysis and clarification has functioned equally as a critique of inadequate and inconsistent uses of experience in Christian theology and as an appreciation of its vital function. The fabric of theological work and of church life profits from a harmonious blend of the three elements of philosophy, Scripture, and experience. A change in relation among these three signals a change in ecclesiastical, cultural, and institutional climates.

Notes

1 Philadelphia: Fortress, 1974.
2 It could be fascinating to read the *sed contra* of the *quaestio*, as used by Aquinas for example, as prefaced by the phrase "however, in my experience . . ."
3 I am aware that I am presupposing that "truth" has or is an "authority," in contradistinction to other possible determinates such as power, numerical majority, historical precedent, temporal age, and so on.
4 This list is a synthesis of the lists of definitions found in *The Oxford English Dictionary* (1937) and *The American Heritage Dictionary* (1976).
5 Cf., for example, Caroline Franks Davis, *The Evidential Force of Religious Experience* (Oxford: Clarendon, 1989) ch. 2; Nicholas Lash, *Easter in Ordinary* (Notre Dame: University of Notre Dame Press, 1990).
6 Michael J. Buckley, *At the Origins of Modern Atheism* (New Haven: Yale University Press, 1987).

PART

Liturgical Resources

3

The Celebration and Blessing
of a Marriage

from *The Book of Common Prayer*

This wedding service descends from the one by Thomas Cranmer, often considered the greatest liturgical writer in English. Note the nuptial hermeneutics, or statement of what marriage means or represents: "It signifies to us the mystery of the union between Christ and his Church." Note too that there are two sets of vows, the "declaration of consent," answered with "I will," and the marriage vows proper, answered with "I do."* The second set is marked with the exchange of rings and the joining of hands. In the West, the couple are together the ministers of the sacraments.

[* For more about this feature, see the work of Adrian Thatcher. For a shorter version, see Adrian Thatcher, "Beginning Marriage: Two Traditions," in Michael A. Hayes, Wendy Porter, and David Tombs, eds., Religion and Sexuality, *Studies in Theology and Sexuality, 2 and Roehampton Institute London Papers, 4 (Sheffield: Sheffield Academic Press, 1998), pp. 415–26. For a longer account, see Adrian Thatcher,* Marriage After Modernity: Christian Marriage in Postmodern Times *(Sheffield: Sheffield Academic Press, 1999), esp. ch. 4.]*

At the time appointed, the persons to be married, with their witnesses, assemble in the church or some other appropriate place.

During their entrance, a hymn, psalm, or anthem may be sung, or instrumental music may be played.

Then the Celebrant, facing the people and the persons to be married, with the woman to the right and the man to the left, addresses the congregation and says

Dearly beloved: We have come together in the presence of God to witness and bless the joining together of this man and this woman in Holy Matrimony. The bond and covenant of marriage was established by God in creation, and our Lord Jesus Christ adorned this manner of life by his presence and first miracle at a wedding in Cana of Galilee. It signifies to us the mystery of the union between Christ and his Church, and Holy Scripture commends it to be honored among all people.

The union of husband and wife in heart, body, and mind is intended by God for their mutual joy; for the help and comfort given one another in prosperity and adversity; and, when it is God's will, for the procreation of children and their nurture in the knowledge and love of the Lord. Therefore marriage is not to be entered into unadvisedly or lightly, but reverently, deliberately, and in accordance with the purposes for which it was instituted by God.

Into this holy union *N.N.* and *N.N.* now come to be joined. If any of you can show just cause why they may not lawfully be married, speak now; or else for ever hold your peace.

Then the Celebrant says to the persons to be married

I require and charge you both, here in the presence of God, that if either of you know any reason why you may not be united in marriage lawfully, and in accordance with God's Word, you do now confess it.

The Declaration of Consent

The Celebrant says to the woman

N., will you have this man to be your husband; to live together in the covenant of marriage? Will you love him, comfort him, honor and keep him, in sickness and in health; and, forsaking all others, be faithful to him as long as you both shall live?

The Woman answers

I will.

The Celebrant says to the man

N., will you have this woman to be your wife; to live together in the covenant of marriage? Will you love her, comfort her, honor and keep her, in sickness and in health; and, forsaking all others, be faithful to her as long as you both shall live?

The Man answers

I will.

The Celebrant then addresses the congregation, saying

Will all of you witnessing these promises do all in your power to uphold these two persons in their marriage?

People We will.

If there is to be a presentation or a giving in marriage, it takes place at this time.

A hymn, psalm, or anthem may follow.

The Ministry of the Word

The Celebrant then says to the people

The Lord be with you.
People And also with you.

Let us pray.

O gracious and everliving God, you have created us male and female in your image: Look mercifully upon this man and this woman who come to you seeking your blessing, and assist them with your grace, that with true fidelity and steadfast love they may honor and keep the promises and vows they make; through Jesus Christ our Savior, who lives and reigns with you in the unity of the Holy Spirit, one God, for ever and ever.
Amen.

Then one or more of the following passages from Holy Scripture is read. If there is to be a Communion, a passage from the Gospel always concludes the Readings.

Genesis 1:26–28 (Male and female he created them)
Genesis 2:4–9, 15–24 (A man cleaves to his wife and they become one flesh)
Song of Solomon 2:10–13; 8:6–7 (Many waters cannot quench love)
Tobit 8:5b–8 (*New English Bible*) (That she and I may grow old together)

1 Corinthians 13:1–13 (Love is patient and kind)
Ephesians 3:14–19 (The Father from whom every family is named)
Ephesians 5:1–2, 21–33 (Walk in love, as Christ loved us)
Colossians 3:12–17 (Love which binds everything together in harmony)
1 John 4:7–16 (Let us love one another for love is of God)

Between the Readings, a Psalm, hymn, or anthem may be sung or said. Appropriate Psalms are 67, 127, and 128.

When a passage from the Gospel is to be read, all stand, and the Deacon or Minister appointed says

The Holy Gospel of our Lord Jesus Christ according to——.
People Glory to you, Lord Christ.

Matthew 5:1–10 (The Beatitudes)
Matthew 5:13–16 (You are the light . . . Let your light so shine)
Matthew 7:21, 24–29 (Like a wise man who built his house upon the rock)
Mark 10:6–9, 13–16 (They are no longer two but one)
John 15:9–12 (Love one another as I have loved you)

After the Gospel, the Reader says

The Gospel of the Lord.
People Praise to you, Lord Christ.

A homily or other response to the Readings may follow.

The Marriage

The Man, facing the woman and taking her right hand in his, says

In the Name of God, I, *N.*, take you, *N.*, to be my wife, to have and to hold from this day forward, for better for worse, for richer for poorer, in sickness and in health, to love and to cherish, until we are parted by death. This is my solemn vow.

Then they loose their hands, and the Woman, still facing the man, takes his right hand in hers, and says

In the Name of God, I, *N.*, take you, *N.*, to be my husband, to have and to hold from this day forward, for better for worse, for richer for poorer, in sickness and in health, to love and to cherish, until we are parted by death. This is my solemn vow.

They loose their hands.

The Priest may ask God's blessing on a ring or rings as follows

Bless, O Lord, *this ring* to be *a sign* of the vows by which this man and this woman have bound themselves to each other; through Jesus Christ our Lord. *Amen.*

The giver places the ring on the ring-finger of the other's hand and says

N., I give you this ring as a symbol of my vow, and with all that I am, and all that I have, I honor you, in the Name of the Father, and of the Son, and of the Holy Spirit (*or* in the Name of God).

Then the Celebrant joins the right hands of husband and wife and says

Now that N. and N. have given themselves to each other by solemn vows, with the joining of hands and the giving and receiving of *a ring*, I pronounce that they are husband and wife, in the Name of the Father, and of the Son, and of the Holy Spirit.

Those whom God has joined together let no one put asunder.

People   Amen.

The prayers

All standing, the Celebrant says

Let us pray together in the words our Savior taught us.

People and Celebrant

Our Father, who art in heaven,
   hallowed be thy Name,
   thy kingdom come,
   thy will be done,
     on earth as it is in heaven.
Give us this day our daily bread.
And forgive us our trespasses,
   as we forgive those
     who trespass against us.
And lead us not into temptation,
   but delivér us from evil.
For thine is the kingdom,
   and the power, and the glory,
   for ever and ever. Amen.

Our Father in heaven,
   hallowed be your Name,
   your kingdom come,
   your will be done,
     on earth as in heaven.
Give us today our daily bread.
Forgive us our sins
   as we forgive those
     who sin against us.
Save us from the time of trial,
   and deliver us from evil.
For the kingdom, the power,
   and the glory are yours,
   now and for ever. Amen.

If Communion is to follow, the Lord's Prayer may be omitted here.

The Deacon or other person appointed reads the following prayers, to which the People respond, saying, Amen.

If there is not to be a Communion, one or more of the prayers may be omitted.

Let us pray.

Eternal God, creator and preserver of all life, author of salvation, and giver of all grace: Look with favor upon the world you have made, and for which your Son gave his life, and especially upon this man and this woman whom you make one flesh in Holy Matrimony. *Amen.*

Give them wisdom and devotion in the ordering of their common life, that each may be to the other a strength in need, a counselor in perplexity, a comfort in sorrow, and a companion in joy. *Amen.*

Grant that their wills may be so knit together in your will, and their spirits in your Spirit, that they may grow in love and peace with you and one another all the days of their life. *Amen.*

Give them grace, when they hurt each other, to recognize and acknowledge their fault, and to seek each other's forgiveness and yours. *Amen.*

Make their life together a sign of Christ's love to this sinful and broken world, that unity may overcome estrangement, forgiveness heal guilt, and joy conquer despair. *Amen.*

Bestow on them, if it is your will, the gift and heritage of children, and the grace to bring them up to know you, to love you, and to serve you. *Amen.*

Give them such fulfillment of their mutual affection that they may reach out in love and concern for others. *Amen.*

Grant that all married persons who have witnessed these vows may find their lives strengthened and their loyalties confirmed. *Amen.*

Grant that the bonds of our common humanity, by which all your children are united one to another, and the living to the dead, may be so transformed by your grace, that your will may be done on earth as it is in heaven; where, O Father, with your Son and the Holy Spirit, you live and reign in perfect unity, now and for ever. *Amen.*

The Blessing of the Marriage

The people remain standing. The husband and wife kneel, and the Priest says one of the following prayers

Most gracious God, we give you thanks for your tender love in sending Jesus Christ to come among us, to be born of a human mother, and to make the way of the cross to be the way of life. We thank you, also, for consecrating the union of man and woman in his Name. By the power of your Holy Spirit, pour out the abundance of your blessing upon this man and this woman. Defend them from every enemy. Lead them into all peace. Let their love for each other be a seal upon their hearts, a mantle about their shoulders, and a crown upon their foreheads. Bless them in their work and in their companionship; in their sleeping and in their waking; in their joys and in their sorrows; in their life and in their death. Finally, in your mercy, bring them to that table where your saints feast for ever in your heavenly home; through Jesus Christ our Lord, who with you and the Holy Spirit lives and reigns, one God, for ever and ever. *Amen.*

or this

O God, you have so consecrated the covenant of marriage that in it is represented the spiritual unity between Christ and his Church: Send therefore your blessing upon these your servants, that they may so love, honor, and cherish each other in faithfulness and patience, in wisdom and true godliness, that their home may be a haven of blessing and peace; through Jesus Christ our Lord, who lives and reigns with you and the Holy Spirit, one God, now and for ever. *Amen.*

The husband and wife still kneeling, the Priest adds this blessing

God the Father, God the Son, God the Holy Spirit, bless, preserve, and keep you; the Lord mercifully with his favor look upon you, and fill you with all spiritual benediction and grace; that you may faithfully live together in this life, and in the age to come have life everlasting. *Amen.*

The peace

The Celebrant may say to the people

The peace of the Lord be always with you.
People　　And also with you.

The newly married couple then greet each other, after which greetings may be exchanged throughout the congregation.

When Communion is not to follow, the wedding party leaves the church. A hymn, psalm, or anthem may be sung, or instrumental music may be played.

At the Eucharist

The liturgy continues with the Offertory, at which the newly married couple may present the offerings of bread and wine.

Preface of Marriage

At the Communion, it is appropriate that the newly married couple receive Communion first, after the ministers.

In place of the usual postcommunion prayer, the following is said

O God, the giver of all that is true and lovely and gracious: We give you thanks for binding us together in these holy mysteries of the Body and Blood of your Son Jesus Christ. Grant that by your Holy Spirit, *N.* and *N.*, now joined in Holy Matrimony, may become one in heart and soul, live in fidelity and peace, and obtain those eternal joys prepared for all who love you; for the sake of Jesus Christ our Lord. *Amen.*

As the wedding party leaves the church, a hymn, psalm, or anthem may be sung; or instrumental music may be played.

4

The Betrothal Service

from the *Service Book of the Holy Orthodox-Catholic Apostolic Church*

In Eastern Orthodox churches, a service of betrothal may occur when a couple get publicly engaged, marked by an exchange of rings. The wedding service proper is marked not by the exchange of rings but by an imposition of crowns, the crowns of marriage. Acknowledging the ascetic, sanctifying discipline of marriage remarked upon by many of the authors in this volume, Orthodox theologians interpret the crowns (positively!) as crowns of martyrdom. Usually the service of betrothal occurs as the first half of a wedding ceremony, so that like the Western rite the wedding consists in a double commitment. Unlike the Western rite, in the East it is the priest, representing God, who makes the marriage, rather than the parties thereto. In the time of Tertullian, the wedding rite took place during the Eucharist; then the couple fed each other the bread and wine of the Eucharist, so that the eucharistic body of Christ (bread and wine) entered the newly one flesh as the one flesh newly entered the eucharistic body of Christ (the community of the faithful). Now the wedding ends as the couple offer each other the "common cup" of blessed wine, indicating that they will share the bitterness and sweetness of life.* The following prayer, marking the exchange of rings, is remarkable for its use of typology, that is, for its integration of the couple into a whole catena of biblical predecessors also marked by rings.

[* See Paul Evdokimov, The Sacrament of Love: The Nuptial Mystery in the Light of the Orthodox Tradition, *trans. Anthony P. Gythiel and Victoria Steadman (Crestwood, NY: St. Vladimir's Seminary Press, 1985), pp. 157–8. For a more complete account of the history of the rite, see John Meyendorff,* Marriage: An Orthodox Perspective, *2nd ed. (Crestwood, NY: St. Vladimir's Seminary Press, 1975), pp. 18–34; and Alvian N. Smirensky, "The Evolution of the Present*

Rite of Marriage and Parallel Canonical Developments," St Vladimir's Seminary
Quarterly 8 (1964): 38–47.]

The Betrothal Service

After the Divine Liturgy, the Priest being in the Temple, those who desire to be joined
together take their stand before the Holy Door. The two rings lie on the right-
hand side of the Holy Altar. The Priest maketh, thrice, the sign of the cross over
the heads of the bridal pair; and giveth them lighted tapers. And the Deacon saith:
Bless, Master.

Priest. Blessed is our God always, now, and ever, and unto ages of ages.
Choir. Amen.

Deacon. In peace let us pray to the Lord.
Choir. Lord, have mercy.

For the peace of the whole world: *and the rest, ending:* That he will aid them: . . .

For the servant of God, N., and for the handmaid of God, N., who
now plight each other their troth, and for their salvation: ℞

That there may be granted unto them children for the continuation
of their race, and all their petitions which are unto salvation: ℞

That he will send down upon them perfect and peaceful love, and
succour: ℞

That he will preserve them in oneness of mind, and in steadfastness
of faith: ℞

That he will bless them with a blameless life: ℞

That the Lord our God will grant unto them an honourable
marriage, and a bed undefiled: ℞

That he will deliver us from all tribulation, wrath, and necessity: ℞

let us pray to the Lord. Choir. Lord, have mercy.

Succour us, save us, have mercy upon us, and keep us, O God, by thy grace.
Choir. Lord, have mercy.

Calling to remembrance our most holy, all-undefiled, most blessed and
glorious Lady, the Birth-giver of God and ever-virgin Mary, with all the Saints,
let us commend ourselves, and each other, and all our life unto Christ our God.
Choir. To thee, O Lord.

Priest. For unto thee are due all glory, honour and worship, to the Father,
and to the Son, and to the Holy Spirit, now, and ever, and unto ages of ages.
Choir. Amen.

Priest. O eternal God, who hast brought into unity those who were sundered,
and hast ordained for them an indissoluble bond of love; who didst bless Isaac
and Rebecca, and didst make them heirs of thy promise: Bless also these thy
servants, N. and N., guiding them unto every good work. For thou art a
merciful God, who lovest mankind, and unto thee do we ascribe glory, to the

Father, and to the Son, and to the Holy Spirit, now, and ever, and unto ages of ages.

Choir. Amen.

Priest. Peace be with you all.

Choir. And with thy spirit.

Deacon. Bow your heads unto the Lord.

Choir. To thee, O Lord.

Priest. O Lord our God, who hast espoused the Church as a pure Virgin from among the Gentiles: Bless this Betrothal, and unite and maintain these thy servants in peace and oneness of mind.

For unto thee are due all glory, honour and worship, to the Father, and to the Son, and to the Holy Spirit, now, and ever, and unto ages of ages.

Choir. Amen.

Then taking the rings, the Priest blesseth the bridal pair therewith, making the sign of the cross with the ring of the Bride over the Bridegroom, and with that of the Bridegroom over the Bride, saying to the Man:

The servant of God, N., is betrothed to the handmaid of God, N.: In the Name of the Father, and of the Son, and of the Holy Spirit. Amen.

And to the Woman:

The handmaid of God, N., is betrothed to the servant of God, N.: In the Name of the Father, and of the Son, and of the Holy Spirit. Amen.

And when he hath spoken thus to each one thrice, he placeth the rings on their right hands. Then the bridal pair exchange the rings, and the Priest saith the following Prayer:

Let us pray to the Lord. —— *Choir.* Lord, have mercy.

O Lord our God, who didst accompany the servant of the patriarch, Abraham into Mesopotamia, when he was sent to espouse a wife for his lord Isaac; and who, by means of the drawing of water, didst reveal unto him that he should betroth Rebecca: Do thou, the same Lord, bless also the betrothal of these thy servants, N. and N., and confirm the word which they have spoken. Establish them in the holy union which is from thee. For thou, in the beginning, didst make them male and female, and by thee is the woman joined unto the man as a helpmeet, and for the procreation of the human race. Wherefore, O Lord our God, who hast sent forth thy truth upon thine inheritance, and thy covenant unto thy servants our fathers, even thine elect, from generation to generation: Look thou upon thy servant, N., and upon thy handmaid, N., and establish and make stable their betrothal in faith, and in oneness of mind, in truth and in love. For thou, O Lord, hast declared that a pledge should be given and confirmed in all things. By a ring was power given unto Joseph in Egypt; by a ring was Daniel glorified in the land of Babylon; by a ring was the uprightness of Tamar revealed; by a ring did our heavenly Father show forth his bounty upon his Son; for he saith: Put a ring on his hand, and bring hither the fatted calf, and kill it, and eat, and make merry. By thine own right hand, O Lord, didst thou arm

Moses in the Red Sea; by the word of thy truth were the heavens established, and the foundations of the earth were made firm; and the right hands of thy servants shall be blessed also by thy mighty word, and by thine upraised arm. Wherefore, O Lord, do thou now bless this putting-on of rings with thy heavenly benediction: and let thine Angel go before them all the days of their life.

For thou art he who blesseth and sanctifieth all things, and unto thee do we ascribe glory, to the Father, and to the Son, and to the Holy Spirit, now, and ever, and unto ages of ages.

Choir. Amen.

5

Order of Second Marriage

from the *Service Book of the Holy Orthdox-Catholic Apostolic Church*

The Eastern Orthodox tradition allows remarriage in rare cases as a concession to human frailty. It is to this frailty that the central prayer of the rite refers. As Gregory of Nazianzus said, "A first marriage is in full conformity with the law [of the Church]; a second marriage is tolerated by indulgence." (He goes on to say, "A fourth marriage [not permitted at all] makes one resemble a pig."*) Perhaps idiosyncratically, Paul Evdokimov summarizes reasons for annulment given at the Synod of Moscow in 1918 as all forms of death: "the death of the very matter of the sacrament (love) through adultery, religious death through apostasy, civil death through condemnation, and physical death through absence."** The prayer beginning "O thou who knowest the frailty of human nature" is at once severe and witty – in the sense of knowing. The originators of that prayer also know human nature.

[* PG 36:292C, translated in Evdokimov, pp. 185–6.   ** Evdokimov, p. 184.]

The Priest beginneth:
Blessed is our God always, now and ever, and unto ages of ages.
Choir. Amen.
O heavenly King . . .
O Holy God, Holy Mighty, Holy Immortal One, have mercy upon us. (*Thrice.*)
Glory to the Father, and to the Son, and to the Holy Spirit, now, and ever, and unto ages of ages. Amen.
O all-holy Trinity, have mercy upon us. O Lord, wash away our sins. O Master, pardon our transgressions. O Holy One, visit and heal our infirmities, for thy Name's sake.

Lord, have mercy. (*Thrice.*) Glory ... now, and ever, ...

Our Father, who art in heaven, Hallowed be thy Name. Thy kingdom come. Thy will be done on earth, As it is in heaven. Give us this day our daily bread. And forgive us our trespasses, As we forgive those who trespass against us. And lead us not into temptation; But deliver us from the Evil One:

Priest. For thine is the kingdom, and the power, and the glory, of the Father, and of the Son, and of the Holy Spirit, now, and ever, and unto ages of ages.

Choir. Amen. —— *Choir.* Lord, have mercy. (*Twelve Times.*)

The Hymn for the Day.

Deacon. In peace let us pray to the Lord. —— *Choir.* Lord, have mercy.

For the peace of the whole world: *and the rest, ending:* That he will aid them ...

For the servants of God, N. and N., and for the protection which is from God; and for their life together: let us pray to the Lord.

Choir. Lord, have mercy.

That they may dwell together uprightly and in oneness of mind: let us pray to the Lord.

Choir. Lord, have mercy.

Succour us, save us, have mercy upon us, and keep us, O God, by thy grace.

Choir. Lord, have mercy.

Calling to remembrance our most holy, all-undefiled, most blessed and glorious Lady, the Birth-giver of God and ever-virgin Mary, with all the Saints, let us commend ourselves, and each other, and all our life unto Christ our God.

Choir. To thee, O Lord.

Priest. For unto thee are due all glory, honour and worship, to the Father, and to the Son, and to the Holy Spirit, now, and ever, and unto ages of ages. —— *Choir.* Amen. —— *Deacon.* Let us pray to the Lord.

Choir. Lord, have mercy.

The Priest saith this Prayer:

O eternal God, who hast brought into unity those who were sundered; and hast ordained for them an indissoluble bond of love; who didst bless Isaac and Rebecca, and didst make them heirs of thy promise: Bless also these thy servants, N. and N., directing them unto every good work.

For thou art a merciful God, who lovest mankind, and unto thee do we ascribe glory, to the Father, and to the Son, and to the Holy Spirit, now, and ever, and unto ages of ages.

Choir. Amen. —— *Priest.* Peace be with you all. —— *Choir.* And with thy spirit. —— *Deacon.* Bow your heads unto the Lord. —— *Choir.* To thee, O Lord.

The Priest prayeth:

O Lord our God, who hast espoused the Church as a pure Virgin from among the Gentiles: Bless this Betrothal, and unite and maintain these thy servants in peace and oneness of mind.

For unto thee are due all honour, glory and worship, to the Father, and to the Son, and to the Holy Spirit, now, and ever, and unto ages of ages.

Choir. Amen.

Then the Priest, taking the rings, giveth one first to the Man, and to the Woman another, and saith to the Man:

The servant of God, N., is betrothed to the handmaid of God, N.: In the Name of the Father, and of the Son, and of the Holy Spirit. Amen.

And in like manner to the Woman:

The handmaid of God, N., is betrothed to the servant of God, N.: In the Name of the Father, and of the Son, and of the Holy Spirit. Amen.

Then he maketh with the rings the sign of the cross over their heads, and pulleth the rings on the fingers of their right hands. The Sponsor of the bridal pair exchangeth them. Then the Deacon:

Let us pray to the Lord.

Choir. Lord, have mercy.

Priest. O Master, Lord our God, who showest pity upon all men, and whose providence is over all thy works; who knowest the secrets of man, and understandest all men: Purge away our sins, and forgive the transgressions of thy servants, calling them to repentance, granting them remission of their iniquities, purification from their sins, and pardon of their errors, whether voluntary or involuntary. O thou who knowest the frailty of man's nature, in that thou art his Maker and Creator; who didst pardon Rahab the harlot, and accept the contrition of the Publican: remember not the sins of our ignorance from our youth up. For if thou wilt consider iniquity, O Lord, Lord, who shall stand before thee? Or what flesh shall be justified in thy sight? For thou only art righteous, sinless, holy, plenteous in mercy, of great compassion, and repentest thee of the evils of men. Do thou, O Master, who hast brought together in wedlock thy servants, N. and N., unite them to one another in love: vouchsafe unto them the contrition of the Publican, the tears of the Harlot, the confession of the Thief; that, repenting with their whole heart, and doing thy commandments in peace and oneness of mind, they may be deemed worthy also of thy heavenly kingdom.

For thou art he who ordereth all things, and unto thee do we ascribe glory, to the Father, and to the Son, and to the Holy Spirit, now, and ever, and unto ages of ages.

Choir. Amen.

Priest. Peace be with you all.

Choir. And with thy spirit.

Priest. Bow your heads unto the Lord.

Choir. To thee, O Lord.

The Priest saith this Prayer:

O Lord Jesus Christ, the Word of God, who wast lifted up on the precious and life-giving cross, and didst thereby destroy the handwriting against us, and deliver us from the dominion of the Devil: Cleanse thou the iniquities of thy servants; because they, being unable to bear the heat and burden of the day and the hot desires of the flesh, are now entering into the bond of a second marriage, as thou didst render lawful by thy chosen vessel, the Apostle Paul, saying, for the sake of us humble sinners, It is better to marry in the Lord than to burn. Wherefore, inasmuch as thou art good and lovest mankind, do thou show mercy and forgive. Cleanse, put away, pardon our transgressions; for thou art he who didst take our infirmities on thy shoulders; for there is none sinless, or without uncleanness for so much as a single day of his life, save only Thou, who without sin didst endure the flesh, and bestowest on us passionlessness eternal.

For thou art God, the God of the contrite in heart, and unto thee do we ascribe glory, to the Father, and to the Son, and to the Holy Spirit, now, and ever, and unto ages of ages.

People. Amen.

Deacon. Let us pray to the Lord.

Choir. Lord, have mercy.

Then the Priest saith the Prayer:

O holy God, who didst create man out of the dust, . . .

And the rest, as in the First Rite of Marriage.

Office of Same-sex Union (eleventh century)

from *Same-Sex Unions in Premodern Europe*

This is a ceremony for adelphopoiesis, *literally the making of brothers. John Boswell argues that the brother imagery does not necessarily exclude a sexual relationship, so that the "same-sex union" is like a gay marriage. He mentions that Abraham refers to his wife Sarah as his sister, and that Montaigne, observing such ceremonies, describes them as marriages "male to male."* The ceremonies share some features in common with Eastern Orthodox marriages. The most crucial of those features is the lifting of crowns at the end of the ceremony, which implies the imposition of those crowns. In Eastern Orthodox marriages, the central event is the crowning of the couple with crowns of martyrdom, since marriage is a form of ascesis, and in Greek the wedding ceremony is known as the crowning (as opposed to the betrothal, marked by the exchange of rings).*

Critics of Boswell's argument make much of two facts about this text. One is that it mentions only the lifting and not the previous imposition of the crowns. Does the oddity suggest a conflation of manuscripts? The second is that the crucial lifting appears after a line in the text. What does the line mean? Boswell argues in a footnote that it separates parts of a unitary liturgy. He notes that the second part is not complete by itself, and has no other beginning than the beginning of the adelphopoiesis. Critics reply, on the other hand, that the line must separate the full ceremony of adelphopoiesis from something else, not a marriage rite complete in itself, but part of one simply misplaced.**

Three questions remain unanswered, and given the current state of the evidence, unanswerable:

1) If the two halves of Grottaferata B are the conflation of adelphopoiesis with the end of a wedding, why did some redactor put them together in this way? Did he not know what he was doing? (If not, why not?) Or did someone think they belonged together? If someone thought they belonged together, did enough other people think they belonged together too, in that they got performed that way? How often? With what feeling of rightness or unrightness?

2) Whether or not the ceremonies of adelphopoiesis might end with a lifting of previously imposed crowns, they have other features of marriages. How then were they lived out? If the meaning of a rite depends on its use, the question becomes, what did different couples use it to do? *Heterosexual marriages are used to do many different things, some at the same time: to cement family alliances, to transfer wealth, to produce children, to celebrate romance, to obtain citizenship rights, to build up the community of the faithful, to legitimize sexual intercourse, to model the relationship of God and the church, to empower commitment, and so on. Since the public display of bloody first-night sheets has passed out of custom, no part of the ceremony graphically affirms "and they have sex." Similarly, we should expect that adelphopoiesis also served many purposes – and not expect that it would explicitly announce, "and they have sex." Did some instances of adelphopoiesis represent romantic attachments between men who lived and slept together? What proportion took this form? Was such a use of the ceremony considered its purpose, or a common use, or a disapproved use, by the community at large? If the high theology disapproves, while the liturgical practice celebrates, which governs,* lex orandi *(law of prayer, or what people do in church),* or lex credendi *(law of belief, or official doctrine)? The general rule is* "lex orandi, lex credendi," *which means that what people do in church generates and governs official doctrine, which becomes a critical reflection of it.*

3) To what use will these ceremonies now *be put? If modern same-sex couples appear before ministers and priests and persuade them to say the ancient ceremonies over them, what will those ceremonies* come to mean?

Orthodox theologians descended from Russian romanticism provide erotic but nonsexual interpretations of adelphopoiesis. *See Pavel Florensky,* The Pillar and Ground of the Truth *(Princeton: Princeton University Press, 1997), pp. 284–330. Serge Boulgakof calls adelphopoiesis "a spiritual pairing of syzygy" given by the Spirit for building up the church; see* Le Paraclet *(Paris: Aubier, 1944), pp. 307–9.*

[* John Boswell, Same-Sex Unions in Premodern Europe *(New York: Villard Books, 1994), pp. 264–5, esp. n. 16.* ** Brent D. Shaw, Review of Same-Sex Unions in Premodern Europe, *in* The New Republic 211 *(July 18–25, 1994), pp. 33ff.; and Ralph Hexter and Brent D. Shaw, 'Same-Sex Unions in Premodern Europe: An Exchange," in* The New Republic 211 *(Oct. 3, 1994), pp. 39–41.]*

i.

The priest shall place the holy Gospel on the Gospel stand and they that are to be joined together place their <right> hands on it, holding lighted candles in their left hands. Then shall the priest cense them and say the following:

ii.

In peace we beseech Thee, O Lord.

For heavenly peace, we beseech Thee, O Lord.

For the peace of the entire world, we beseech Thee, O Lord.

For this holy place, we beseech Thee, O Lord.

That these thy servants, N. and N., be sanctified with thy spiritual benediction, we beseech Thee, O Lord.

That their love abide without offense or scandal all the days of their lives, we beseech Thee, O Lord.

That they be granted all things needed for salvation and godly enjoyment of life everlasting, we beseech Thee, O Lord.

That the Lord God grant unto them unashamed faithfulness, <and> sincere love, we beseech Thee, O Lord.

That we be saved, we beseech Thee, O Lord.

Have mercy on us, O God.

"Lord, have mercy" shall be said three times.

iii.

The priest <shall say>:

Forasmuch as Thou, O Lord and Ruler, art merciful and loving, who didst establish humankind after thine image and likeness, who didst deem it meet that thy holy apostles Philip and Bartholomew be united, bound one unto the other not by nature but by faith and the spirit. As Thou didst find thy holy martyrs Serge and Bacchus worthy to be united together, bless also these thy servants, N. and N., joined together not by the bond of nature but by faith and in the mode of the spirit, granting unto them peace and love and oneness of mind. Cleanse from their hearts every stain and impurity, and vouchsafe unto them to love one other without hatred and without scandal all the days of their lives, with the aid of the Mother of God and all thy saints, forasmuch as all glory is thine.

iv.

Another Prayer for Same-sex Union

O Lord Our God, who didst grant unto us all those things necessary for salvation and didst bid us to love one another and to forgive each other our failings, bless and consecrate, kind Lord and lover of good, these thy servants who love each other with a love of the spirit and have come into this thy holy church to be blessed and consecrated. Grant unto them unashamed fidelity [and] sincere love, and as Thou didst vouchsafe unto thy holy disciples and apostles thy peace and love, bestow <them> also on these, O Christ our God, affording to them all those things needed for salvation and life eternal. For Thou art the light [and] the truth and thine is the glory.

v.

Then shall they kiss the holy Gospel and the priest and one another, and conclude:[1]

Ecclesiastical Canon of Marriage of the Patriarch Methodius

O Lord our God, the designer of love and author of peace and disposer of thine own providence, who didst make two into one and hast given us one to another, who hast [seen fit?] to bless all things pure and timeless, send Thou now down from heaven thy right hand full of grace and lovingkindness over these thy servants who have come before Thee and given their right hands as a lawful token of union and the bond of marriage. Sanctify and fill them with thy mercies. And wrapping the pair in every grace and in divine and spiritual radiance, gladden them in the expectation of thy mercies. Perfect their union by bestowing upon them peace and love and harmony, and deem them worthy of the imposition and consecration of the crowns, through the prayers of her that conceived Thee in power and truth, and those of all thy saints, now and forever.

vi.

And after this prayer the priest shall lift the crowns and dismiss them.

Notes

Some 35 notes have been omitted. Interested readers should consult consult the original cited in the Acknowledgements. – *Editor.*

1 A line is drawn between the preceding prayer and the following one, but such lines in manuscripts do not reliably indicate the beginning of a new office. It is not really possible that this prayer should constitute part of an office different from what precedes. This would be the grossest scribal error imaginable: the entire prayer would have to have been copied into the manuscript by mistake, and then not crossed out or corrected. Even so, it would be difficult to believe that it was not inserted here *for a reason.* It is surely the more difficult and less likely argument that the scribe copied this prayer into the text from an *unrelated* ceremony. The apparent confusion of priestly dismissal *followed* by a prayer is closely paralleled in many other liturgical collections. In the *Euchologion* of Porphyre Uspenski εὐχὴ ἀντιφώνου δ' της απολύσεως occurs on fol. 57v and 59r, as part of a series in each case, and in each case is followed by other prayers. In Sinai 957 there is a dismissal *before the Communion prayer* in the heterosexual marriage ceremony (καὶ μετὰ τὸ 'Αμὴυ μεταδιδοὺς αὐτοῖς ζωοποιοῦ κοινωνίας ἀπολύει): *then* there is the εὐχὴ τοῦ ποτηρίου (Dmitrievskij, p. 5). In the Barberini Greek 336 εὐχὴ ἤγουυ

ἀπόλυοις occurs at least *four times* without indicating the end of a ceremony. In Istanbul 615 (757) (Dmitrievskij XCVI, pp. 743–4), the final rubric says ``the partners kiss each other and [the priest] gives them Communion and they depart. If they wish to have a liturgy after the reading of the Gospel, the office [of same-sex union] takes place, and those joined together are commemorated again at the blessing, and then there is the dismissal." This is very similar to this office in providing two possible endings. Brightman, in his Greek index, s.v. ἀπόλυσις (p. 595), defines the term as "the conclusion of an office and the formula with which it is concluded." Moreover, the major part of the *beginning* of the liturgy of St. John Chrysostom is called the ἀπολυτίκιον ("conclusion"). The ODB [*Oxford Dictionary of Byzantium*] also observes of "dismissal" (1:639) that it is "a formula pronounced at the end of a liturgical service or sometimes of one of its parts" Cf. Athos Panteleimon 149 [15], in which the rubrics prescribe καὶ γίνεται ἀπόλυσις καὶ ἀσπάζονται τὸ ἅγιον εὐαγγέλιον καὶ ἀλλήλους καὶ ἀπέρχονται, and Athos Panteleimon 780 (No. 13 in this appendix, No. 6 in the next), which is otherwise *almost identical*: the ending is καὶ ἀσπάζονται τὸ ἅγιον εὐαγγέλιον καὶ ἀλλήλους καὶ ἀπόλυσις. In the first, ἀπόλυσις is mentioned, then final acts are prescribed. In the second, derived from it, the final acts are followed by ἀπόλυσις. There is the clear possibility that in either case ἀπόλυσις stands for the final acts themselves, separately mentioned, or is a final blessing not actually given in the text. In any event, these examples show that something important could follow ἀπόλυσις. Other examples of ἀπολύσις occurring *within* (rather than at the end of) a ceremony, all from Dmitrievskij: XXIII (Sinai 966, thirteenth century), p. 214; LIX (Athos Vatoped. 322 [934], BC 1468), p. 422; LXI (Athos Athanas. 88, fifteenth century), p. 442; LXV (Athos Pantocrator 149, fifteenth century), p. 488; LXXI (Athos Panteleimon 364, fifteenth century), p. 569; LXXIV (Sinal 984, fifteenth century), p. 595; LXXXIII (Patmos Ilitari 690, fifteenth century), p. 651; XCIX (Athos Athanasios 21 [91], CE 1536), p. 760.

Tomorrow Shall Be My Dancing Day

from *The Shorter New Oxford Book of Carols*

This old carol uses the image of Christ as bridegroom of the church to unfold the whole story of salvation history. It conceives of salvation as finally sharing in the life of the Trinity, or "participation in the divine nature," as II Peter 1:4 has it. The trinitarian sharing of space, or perichoresis, *is traditionally thought of as a kind of dancing around, here "the general dance" of a wedding feast into which Christ pulls humanity. Note the anti-semitism of vv. 6 and 8.*

English traditional
(Sandys, 1833, arr. editors)

of___ my play, To call my true___ love to___ the dance.
man's_ na - ture, To call my true___ love to___ the dance. *Sing*
sil - ly poor ass, To call my true___ love to___ my dance.

O my___ love, O___ my love, my love, my
*Sing*___ O my love,___

love, *This have I done___ for my___ true love.*

4   Then afterwards baptized I was;
     The Holy Ghost on me did glance,
    My Father's voice heard from above
     To call my true love to my dance.

5   Into the desert I was led,
     Where I fasted without substance;
    The devil bade me make stones my bread,
     To have me break my true love's dance.

6   The Jews on me they made great suit,
     And with me made great variance,
    Because they loved darkness rather than light,
     To call my true love to my dance.

7   For thirty pence Judas me sold,
     His covetousness for to advance:
    'Mark whom I kiss, the same do hold!'
     The same is he shall lead the dance.

8   Before Pilate the Jews me brought,
     Where Barabbas had deliverance;
    They scourged me and set me at nought,
     Judged me to die to lead the dance.

9   Then on the cross hangèd I was,
     Where a spear my heart did glance;
    There issued forth both water and blood,
     To call my true love to my dance.

10   Then down to hell I took my way
      For my true love's deliverance,
    And rose again on the third day,
      Up to my true love and the dance.

11   Then up to heaven I did ascend,
      Where now I dwell in sure substance
    On the right hand of God, that man
      May come unto the general dance.

PART

Classical Resources

from The Good of Marriage

St. Augustine (354–430), Bishop of Hippo

*This famous passage sets the terms for what counts as marriage in the West. In an earlier passage, Augustine commends companionship (*societas*), but in summary Augustine lists three criteria,* fides, proles, *and* sacramentum, *or fidelity, offspring, and sacrament, for the paradigm case. Interesting questions arise when one or more of the criteria are lacking. What of adultery? Childlessness? Common-law marriages? When do those conditions defeat a marriage, and when can they be forgiven or overlooked? Have conditions for marriage changed over time?*

(I.1) Every human being is part of the human race, and human nature is a social reality and possesses a great and natural good, the power of friendship. For this reason God wished to create all human beings from one, so that they would be held together in human society, not only by the similarity of race, but also by the bond of blood relationship. Therefore, the first natural union of human society is the husband and wife. God did not create even these as separate individuals and join them together as if they were alien to each other, but he created the one from the other. The power of the union was also signified in the side from which she was taken and formed, for they are joined to each other's side, when they walk together and together look where they are walking. The result is the bonding of society in children, who are the one honorable fruit, not of the union of male and female, but of sexual intercourse. For there could have been some kind of real and amiable union between the sexes even without sexual intercourse, a union in which the one rules and the other obeys.

(II.2) There is no need at this time for us to examine and set forth a definite opinion on the question of how the offspring of the first humans could have come into being, whom God had blessed, saying: *Increase and multiply, and fill the earth* [Gen. 1:28], if they had not sinned. For it was by their sin that their bodies deserved the condition of death, and there could be no intercourse except of mortal bodies. Many different views have been expressed on this subject, and if we were to examine which of them is most congruent with the truth of the divine Scriptures, there is matter for an extended discussion.

One possibility is that, if they had not sinned, they would have had children in some other way without any act of intercourse, by a gift of the almighty Creator, who was able to create the first human beings without parents, who was able to form the flesh of Christ in a virgin's womb, and – to speak now even to unbelievers – who was able to give offspring to bees without intercourse.

Another possibility is that much of that passage should be interpreted in a mystical and figurative way. For example, *Fill the earth and master it* [Gen. 1:28] could refer to a fullness and perfection of life and power, so that the increase and multiplication that is expressed in the text, *Increase and multiply*, would mean a development of the intellect and an abundance of virtue, just as it is said in the psalm: *You have increased my soul in virtue* [Ps. 138:3]. In this case the human race would not have received a succession of offspring, if sin had not caused there to be a succession unto death.

Yet another possibility is that the bodies of the first human beings were originally created as animal, not spiritual, so that later by the merit of obedience they would have become spiritual in order to achieve immortality. This would have happened not after death, since death entered the world through the envy of the devil [cf. Wis. 2:24] and became the punishment for sin, but through that transformation which the apostle describes when he says: *Then those of us who are still alive and left will be caught up with them in the clouds to meet Christ in the air* [1 Thess. 4:17]. In this interpretation the bodies of the first married couple would have been created mortal in their initial formation, but would not have died, if they had not sinned, just as God had threatened. It is just as if God might threaten a wound, since the body is vulnerable to wounding, although the wounding would not happen unless his commands were violated.

So, then, generations of bodies such as these could have come into being through sexual intercourse. They would have developed up to a certain point, but would not have advanced to old age; or they would have grown to old age, but would not have died, until the earth was filled by the multiplication that was promised in the blessing. If God allowed the clothes of the Israelites to retain their proper state without decay for forty years [cf. Deut. 29:5], how much more would he have rendered to the bodies of those who obey his commands a kind of happy equilibrium of a fixed state, until they were changed into something better, not by human death, in which the soul deserts the body, but by a blessed transformation from mortality to immortality, from an animal to a spiritual quality.

(III) It would take too long to investigate and to discuss which of these opinions is true, or whether the text is susceptible of one or more other interpretations.

(3) This is what we now say: according to that state of birth and death, which we experience and in which we were created, the union of male and female is something good. The divine Scripture commends this alliance to such an extent that a woman who is divorced by her husband is not allowed to marry another, while her husband is still alive; and a man who is divorced by his wife may not take another, unless the wife who has left him has died. It is right, therefore, to inquire why the good of marriage is a good, which even the Lord confirmed in the gospel, not only because he prohibited divorce, except in cases of fornication [cf. Matt. 19:9], but also because when he was invited to the wedding, he attended [cf. John 2:1–11].

I do not believe that marriage is a good solely because of the procreation of children: there is also the natural association (*societas*) between the sexes. Otherwise, we would no longer speak of a marriage between elderly people, especially if they had lost or had never produced children. But now in a good marriage, even if it has lasted for many years and even if the youthful ardor between the male and female has faded, the order of charity between husband and wife still thrives. The earlier they begin to refrain from sexual intercourse, by mutual consent, the better they will be. This is not because they will eventually be unable to do what they wish, but because it is praiseworthy not to wish to do what they are able to do.

If, therefore, they keep faithful to the honor and the conjugal duties that each sex owes the other, even if both of their bodies grow weak and almost corpselike, yet the chastity of spirits joined in a proper marriage will endure; the more it is tested, the more genuine it will be; the more it is calmed, the more secure it will be. There is an additional good in marriage, namely the fact that carnal or youthful incontinence, even the most wicked, is directed toward the honorable task of procreating children. As a result, conjugal intercourse makes something good out of the evil of lust (*libido*), since the concupiscence of the flesh, which parental affection moderates, is then suppressed and in a certain way burns more modestly. For a sort of dignity prevails over the fire of pleasure, when in the act of uniting as husband and wife the couple regard themselves as father and mother.

(IV.4) To this we would add that in the very act of paying the conjugal debt, even if they demand it somewhat intemperately and incontinently, the spouses still owe to each other mutual fidelity (*fides*). The apostle attributed to this fidelity so much authority that he called it a "power," saying: *A wife does not have power over her body, but her husband does; likewise, a husband has no power over his body, but his wife does* [1 Cor. 7:4]. The violation of this fidelity is called adultery, when one has intercourse with another man or woman contrary to the marriage agreement, either at the instigation of one's own lust or out of consent to another's lust. In this way fidelity, which is a great good of the spirit even in the insignificant affairs of the body, is broken. Therefore, it is certain that fidelity ought to be preferred even to the health of the body, by which life itself is sustained. A little straw may be almost nothing compared to a great amount of gold; yet, when fidelity is genuinely preserved in a matter of straw as if in one of gold, it is no less valuable because it is preserved in a thing that is less valuable.

When fidelity is used to commit sin, of course, we wonder whether it should still be called fidelity. But whatever it is, if one acts contrary to it, one becomes worse, unless one is abandoning it in order to return to a true and legitimate fidelity, that is, in order to make amends for a sin by correcting the wickedness of the will. Take, for example, someone who is unable to rob a man by himself and so finds an accomplice and agrees with him that they will commit the crime together and then share the loot; but after the crime is committed, he takes it all himself. The accomplice, of course, will be sad and will complain that fidelity to him was not kept. But in his very complaint he ought to realize that he should have kept his fidelity to human society by leading a good life and by not unjustly plundering another human being, if he recognizes how unjust it was that fidelity to him in the society of sin was not preserved.

Of course, the first robber, who is guilty of infidelity on two counts, should be judged the more guilty of the two. But if the first regretted the evil they had done and for this reason refused to share the loot with his accomplice, in order to return it to the man from whom it was stolen, not even the unfaithful accomplice would call him unfaithful. Thus, if a wife who has violated the fidelity of marriage keeps her fidelity to the adulterer, she is still evil; but if she is not faithful even to the adulterer, she is worse. Yet if she repents of her wickedness and returns to her marital chastity, there-by repudiating her adulterous agreements and purposes, I do not think that even the adulterer will regard her as violating fidelity.

(V.5) It is often asked whether this situation should be called a marriage: when a man and a woman, neither of whom is married to another, have intercourse with each other, not in order to have children, but out of incontinence solely to have sex, and yet faithfully pledge not to do this with anyone else. Perhaps it would not be absurd to call this a marriage, if they made this agreement to last until the death of one of them, and if, although they have not come together for the sake of procreation, they at least do not avoid it, either by not wishing to have children or by acting in an evil way to prevent children from being born. But if one or both of these conditions are absent, I do not see how we could call this a marriage.

For if a man is living with a woman only until he finds someone else who is worthy either of his position or of his wealth, whom he can marry as an equal, in his heart he is an adulterer, not with the woman whom he would like to find, but with the woman with whom he is living but not in a marital union. The same applies to the woman, if she is aware of this and is still willing to have unchaste intercourse with a man, with whom she does not have a commitment as a wife. But if she preserves her fidelity to him as to a spouse after he has taken a wife, and if she refuses to marry and decides to remain completely continent, I would not find it easy to call her an adulteress. Yet who would not call it a sin, knowing that she had intercourse with a man who was not her husband?

But if all the woman wanted from the sexual relations was to have children, and if she unwillingly bore whatever else was involved beyond the desire for procreation, surely this woman ranks higher than many matrons. Some of them, even if they are not guilty of adultery, force their husbands, who often desire to be continent, to pay the debt of the flesh. They make intemperate use of their right, not out of a desire for offspring, but solely out of the passion of concupiscence. Nonetheless, in the marriages of such women there is this good, namely that they are married. For this is why they were married, so that concupiscence itself might be directed toward a legitimate bond and thereby cease to flow in a disordered and disgraceful way. Concupiscence has in itself a weakness of the flesh that cannot be restrained, but in marriage it has an association of fidelity that cannot be dissolved. On its own, concupiscence leads to immoderate intercourse, but in marriage it finds a means of chaste procreation. Even if it is shameful to use a husband in a lustful way, nevertheless it is honorable to choose to have sex only with a husband and to bear children only with a husband.

(VI) Likewise, there are men who are so incontinent that they do not spare their wives even during pregnancy. But whatever immodest, shameful, and sordid acts are committed by married persons with each other, these are the result of human vice, not the fault of marriage itself.

(6) Furthermore, even when people make an excessive demand for the payment of the carnal debt – which the apostle did not give to them as a command but granted as a concession [cf. 1 Cor. 7:6] – so that they engage in intercourse even without the purpose of procreation; even if immoral conduct leads them to this sort of intercourse, nevertheless marriage protects them from adultery and fornication. It is not that this sort of behavior is permitted because of marriage; rather, it is forgiven because of marriage. Therefore, not only do married people owe each other the fidelity of sexual intercourse for the sake of procreation, which is the first association of the human race in this mortal life, but they also owe each other a sort of mutual service for the sustaining of each other's weakness, so that they may avoid illicit intercourse. As a result, even if one of them would prefer to adopt perpetual continence, it is not permitted without the consent of the partner. For in this matter *a wife does not*

have power over her body, but her husband does; likewise, a husband has no power over his body, but his wife does [1 Cor. 7:4].

Therefore, they should not deny one another that which the husband seeks from matrimony and that which the wife seeks from her husband, even if this proceeds not from a desire to have children but only from weakness and incontinence. This is to prevent them from falling into damnable seductions at the temptation of Satan because of the incontinence of one or both of them. Conjugal intercourse for the sake of procreation carries no fault; intercourse for the sake of satisfying lust, provided that it takes place with a spouse, carries a forgivable fault (*venialis culpa*) because of marital fidelity; but adultery or fornication carries a mortal fault. Therefore, abstention from all intercourse is better even than marital intercourse that takes place for the sake of procreation.

(VII) But while continence has greater merit, it is no sin to pay the conjugal debt; and although to demand it beyond the need for procreation is a forgivable fault, certainly fornication and adultery are crimes that must be punished. Therefore, the charity of marriage must be careful that, in seeking greater honor for itself, it does not create a situation in which a spouse incurs damnation. For *whoever divorces his wife, except in the case of fornication, makes her commit adultery* [Matt. 5:32]. Once the nuptial agreement has been made, it is a kind of sacrament to such an extent that it is not made void even by separation, since as long as the husband who left her still lives, she commits adultery if she marries someone else, and the husband who left her is the cause of this evil.

(7) Since it is permissible to divorce an adulterous wife, I wonder whether it is also permissible to marry again after the divorce. In this case Sacred Scripture creates a difficult problem, since the apostle cites a precept of the Lord saying that a woman ought not to leave her husband, but that if she leaves him, she should remain unmarried or be reconciled to her husband [cf. 1 Cor. 7:10–11]. She definitely should not withdraw and remain unmarried, except in the case of an adulterous husband, because by withdrawing from a husband who is not adulterous she may cause him to commit adultery. But, perhaps, she can be justly reconciled to her husband, either by tolerating him, if she is unable to restrain herself, or after he has been corrected. But I do not see how a man can be permitted to marry another woman when he leaves an adulterous wife, if a woman is not permitted to marry again when she leaves an adulterous husband.

If this is the case, the unifying bond of marriage is so strong that, although it is created for the purpose of procreation, it may not be dissolved for the purpose of procreation. A man may be able to divorce a barren wife and marry someone who can bear his children, but in our times and according to Roman law, a man is not permitted to take a second wife, as long as he still has one wife who is alive. Certainly, when an adulterous wife or husband has been abandoned, it would be possible for many human beings to be born, if the woman or the man chose to marry again. But if this is not permitted, as the divine law seems to prescribe, who could fail to acknowledge the demands that the great strength of the conjugal bond makes for itself?

I do not think that it could be so powerful if there were not attached to it a kind of sacramental significance (*sacramentum*) of something greater than could arise from our feeble mortality, something that remains unshaken in order to punish those who abandon or wish to dissolve this bond. For even when there is a divorce, the nuptial alliance is not abolished, and the persons involved remain spouses, even when they are separated. Furthermore, they commit adultery if they have intercourse with anyone else after the divorce, and this applies both to the man and to the woman. This is not the case for the woman, however, except *in the city of our God, on his holy mountain* [Ps. 48:1].

(VIII) But who does not know that the laws of the non-Christians are different? Among them when a divorce has been issued, both the woman and the man are free to marry whomever they wish, without any liability to human punishment. This custom is similar to something that Moses apparently permitted regarding a written notice of divorce because of the Israelites' hardness of heart [cf. Deut. 24:1; Matt. 19:8]. In this case there appears to be more of a rebuke than an approval given to divorce.

(8) *Let marriage be held in honor by all and the marriage bed be undefiled* [Heb. 13:4]. We do not say that marriage is a good merely in comparison with fornication; in that case there would be two evils, one of which is worse. In that sense even fornication would be a good because adultery is worse – since to violate another person's marriage is worse than to have sex with a prostitute; and adultery would be a good because incest is worse – since it is worse to have intercourse with your mother than with another man's wife; and on it would go until you reach things which, as the apostle said, *it is disgraceful even to mention* [Eph. 5:12]. On this rendering all things would be good in comparison with something worse. But who has any doubts that this is false?

Marriage and fornication, therefore, are not two evils, one of which is worse, but marriage and continence are two goods, one of which is better. Similarly, bodily health and sickness are not two evils, one of which is worse, but health and immortality are two goods, one of which is better. Likewise, knowledge and vanity are not two evils, of which vanity is the worse, but knowledge and love are two goods, of which love is the better. For *knowledge will be destroyed*, the apostle says, and yet it is a necessity in the present life; but *love will never fail* [1 Cor. 13:8]. In the same way, the procreation of mortal bodies, which is the purpose of marriage, will be destroyed; but freedom from all sexual relations is a participation in the angelic life (*angelica meditatio*) here and now, and it will remain so forever.

Just as the feasting of the just is better than the fasting of the sacrilegious, so the marriages of the faithful are to be ranked higher than the virginity of the impious. But this does not mean that feasting is preferable to fasting, only that justice is preferable to sacrilege; similarly, marriage is not preferable to virginity, but faith is preferable to impiety. For the just will feast when it is necessary in order to give to their bodies what is right and proper, as good masters do to their servants, but the sacrilegious fast in order to serve demons. The faithful marry in order to have chaste intercourse with their spouses; but the impious adopt virginity in order to commit fornication against the true God.

Therefore, just as Martha did something good when she ministered to the saints, but her sister Mary did something better when she sat at the Lord's feet and listened to his words [cf. Luke 10:38–42], so likewise we praise the good of Susanna in her conjugal chastity, and yet we rank more highly the good of the widow Anna, and much more highly the good of the virgin Mary. It was a good thing that they did, when they supplied Christ and his disciples with the necessities out of their own resources; but those who abandoned all their resources in order to follow the same Lord more readily did an even better thing. Yet, in both of these goods, whether that of Martha and Mary or that of the disciples, the better thing could not be done without bypassing or abandoning the lesser good.

It must be understood, therefore, that marriage is not to be regarded as an evil simply because abstention from it is necessary in order to achieve the chastity of a widow or the integrity of a virgin. It is not the case that what Martha did was an evil simply because her sister had to abstain from it in order to do the better thing. Nor is it an evil to invite a just man or a prophet into one's house simply because the person who wishes to follow Christ perfectly is required to abandon his house in order to do the better thing.

(IX.9) Surely, it must be acknowledged that God gave us some goods to be sought for their own sake, such as wisdom, good health, and friendship, and other goods that are necessary for the sake of something else, such as learning, food, drink, sleep, marriage, and sexual intercourse. Some of these goods are necessary for wisdom, such as learning; some are necessary for good health, such as food and drink and sleep; and some are necessary for friendship, such as marriage and sexual intercourse, for these lead to the propagation of the human race, in which a friendly association is a great good.

Thus the person who does not use these goods, which are necessary because of something else, for the purpose for which they were intended, sometimes sins in a forgivable way, sometimes in a damnable way. But the person who uses them for the purpose for which they were given does well. Therefore, the person who abstains from using things that are unnecessary does better. In the same way, when we have need of these things, we do well to want them; but we do better not to want them than to want them, since we possess them in a better way when we do not possess them as necessities.

For this reason, it is good to marry, since it is good to produce children, to be the mother of a family. But it is better not to marry, since it is better, even in regard to human society itself, not to have any need of marriage. For the state of the human race is such that not only do some make use of marriage because they are unable to be continent, but also many others indulge in illicit intercourse. Since the good Creator sees to it that good comes of their evils, numerous offspring are born and an abundant succession is produced, out of which holy friendships may be sought.

This leads me to conclude that in the earliest times of the human race the saints were required to make use of the good of marriage, not as something to be sought for its own sake, but as a good necessary for something else, namely the propagation of the people of God, through which the Prince and Savior of all peoples was both prophesied and born. But in the present, since there is abundant opportunity for spiritual kinsmen to enter into holy and genuine associations everywhere and among all nations, even those people who wish to marry solely for the sake of procreation are urged to practice the better good of continence.

(X.10) But I know what they will murmur: "What if all people wish to abstain completely from sexual intercourse? How would the human race survive?" If only all people had this desire, as long as it proceeds from *a pure heart and a good conscience and a sincere faith* [1 Tim. 1:5]! The City of God would be filled up much more quickly, and the end of time would be hastened. What else does the apostle seem to encourage when he says; *I would like everyone to be as I am* [1 Cor. 7:7]? Or, in another place: *What I mean, my friends, is that the time is short. From now on even those who have wives should live as if they had none; those who mourn, as if they were not mourning; those who rejoice, as if they were not rejoicing; those who buy, as if they were not buying; and those who use this world, as if they were not using it. For the form of this world is passing away. I want you to be without care.* Then he adds: *The man without a wife is concerned about the Lord's affairs, how to please the Lord. But the married man is concerned about the affairs of the world, how to please his wife, and he is divided. And the unmarried woman and virgin, she is concerned about the Lord's affairs, that she may be holy in body and spirit. But the married woman is concerned about the affairs of the world, how to please her husband* [1 Cor. 7:29–34]. For this reason, it seems to me that in the present time only those who do not restrain themselves should marry, in accord with that saying of the same apostle: *But if they cannot control themselves, they should marry, for it is better to marry than to burn* [1 Cor. 7:9].

(11) Not even in this case, however, is marriage a sin. For if marriage were preferable only by comparison with fornication, it would be a lesser sin than fornication, but still it would be a sin. But, as it is now, what shall we say in response to the very clear message that the apostle declares: *He may do whatever he wishes; he does not sin; let him marry* [1 Cor. 7:36]? And: *If you have taken a wife, you have not sinned; and if a virgin marries, she does not sin* [1 Cor. 7:28]?

This is now clear evidence that it is wrong to have any doubts about the sinlessness of marriage.

Therefore, it was not marriage that the apostle granted *as a concession* – for would it not be quite absurd to say that a concession is granted to those who did not sin? Rather, he granted *as a concession* that sexual union which takes place because of incontinence, not solely for the sake of procreation and sometimes not even for the sake of procreation at all. Marriage does not force this sort of intercourse to occur, but it does obtain for it a pardon, as long as it is not so excessive that it impedes the times that ought to be set aside for prayer, and as long as it does not lead to that use which is contrary to nature.

The apostle was unable to remain silent about this when he spoke about the extreme depravities that impure and wicked people practice. The intercourse that is necessary for the sake of procreation is without fault, and only this belongs properly to marriage. Intercourse that goes beyond the need of procreation follows the dictates of lust (*libido*), not of reason. Nevertheless, to render this to a spouse (though not to demand it), so that the spouse may avoid the damnable sin of fornication, is a duty of the married person. But if both partners are subject to such a desire (*concupiscentia*), they are doing something that clearly does not belong to marriage.

Nevertheless, if in their union they love what is honorable more than what is dishonorable (that is, if they love what belongs to marriage more than they love what does not belong to marriage), this is granted to them *as a concession* by the authority of the apostle. Their marriage does not encourage this fault; rather, it intercedes for it, if they do not turn away from the mercy of God, either by failing to abstain on certain days in order to be free for prayer (since abstinence, like fasting, lends support to one's prayers) or by exchanging a natural use for one that is contrary to nature, for this is more damnable in a spouse.

(XI.12) For when the natural use [of sexual relations] extends beyond the marriage pact (that is, beyond what is necessary for procreation), this is pardonable in a wife but damnable in a prostitute. Conversely, the use of sex beyond nature, which is abominable in a prostitute, becomes even more abominable in a wife. The ordinance of the Creator and the order of creation have such great force that an excessive use of something that is granted to be used is much more acceptable than even a single or rare excess in the use of something that has not been granted. That is why a spouse's immoderation must be tolerated when it is a question of licit sexual relations, so that lust will not erupt into illicit relations. This is also the reason why it is much less sinful to make constant demands of one's wife than to make even the rarest use of fornication.

But if a man wishes to use that part of his wife's body that has not been granted for this purpose, the wife is more shameful if she allows this to happen to herself than to another woman. The glory of marriage, therefore, is the chastity (*castitas*) of procreation and fidelity (*fides*) in rendering the duty of the flesh. This is the work of marriage, and this is what the apostle defends from all blame when he says: *If you have taken a wife, you have not sinned; and if a virgin marries, she does not sin* [1 Cor. 7:28]. And: *He may do whatever he wishes; he does not sin; let him marry* [1 Cor. 7:36]. Married persons are granted *as a concession* the right to demand from each other in a somewhat immoderate or excessive manner the payment of the conjugal debt, for the reasons that he gave above.

(13) Therefore, when the apostle says that *the unmarried woman thinks about the things of the Lord, that she may be holy in body and spirit* [1 Cor. 7:34], we should not take this to mean that the chaste Christian spouse is not holy in body. Indeed, this word was addressed to all the faithful: *Do you not know that your bodies are a temple of the Holy Spirit who is in you, whom you have received from God?* [1 Cor. 6:19]. Therefore, even the bodies of married people are holy when they keep faithful to each other and to the Lord. Even a spouse who is a nonbeliever is no obstacle to the holiness of either spouse; on the contrary, the apostle himself bears witness that the holiness of a wife benefits an unbelieving husband and the holiness of a husband benefits an unbelieving wife: *For the unbelieving husband is sanctified in his wife, and the unbelieving wife is sanctified in her husband* [1 Cor. 7:14].

Furthermore, in the previous passage Paul spoke of the greater holiness of the unmarried woman compared with that of the married woman, and indicated that a greater reward belonged to the unmarried because her good was greater than the other good, since the unmarried woman thinks only about how to please the Lord. This does not mean, however, that the Christian woman who preserves her conjugal purity does not think about how to please the Lord, but only that she thinks about this less, because she also thinks about the things of the world, how to please her husband. For Paul's intention was to let them know what marriage would require of them, namely that they would have to think about the things of the world, how to please their husbands.

• • •

(XIV.17) It is clear that a couple who have entered into an illicit union [i.e., concubinage] can still contract a valid marriage, if they subsequently make an honorable agreement.

(XV) But once they have entered into a marriage in the City of our God, where even from the very first intercourse of two human beings marriage derives a kind of sacramental quality (*quoddam sacramentum*), the marriage cannot be dissolved in any way, except by the death of one of the spouses. For the bond of marriage remains, even if children, for the sake of which the marriage was entered into, do not result because of a clear case of sterility.

Therefore, it is not permissible for married persons who know that they will not have children to separate from each other and have intercourse with others, even for the sake of having children. If they do so, they commit adultery with those with whom they have intercourse because they remain married persons.

Among the ancient fathers, of course, it was permissible to take another woman, with the permission of one's wife, and to produce children that were shared in common, the husband providing the seed and the intercourse, the wife providing the right and authorization. Whether this is also permitted in our own day I would not be so rash as to say. For today there is not the same need of procreation that there was in the past. In those days it was even permissible for husbands who could have children to take other wives in order to produce more numerous progeny, which is something that is certainly not allowed today.

The mysterious difference in times brings with it such a great opportunity for doing or not doing a thing properly that today a man who does not marry even one wife does the better thing, unless he cannot remain continent. But in the past they took many wives blamelessly, even those who would have been able easily to remain continent, if piety had not demanded something else at the time. For just as that wise and just man, who desired for a long time to be dissolved and to be with Christ [cf. Phil. 1:23], who took the greatest delight not in his desire to live but in his duty to serve, ate food in order to remain in the flesh (something that was necessary for the sake of other people), so also did the holy men in ancient times have intercourse with women, making use of the right of marriage not out of desire but out of duty.

(XVI.18) For sexual intercourse is to the health of the human race what food is to the health of a human being, and neither exists without some carnal pleasure (*delectatio carnalis*). When this pleasure is moderated and directed toward its natural use by the restraint of temperance, it cannot be lust (*libido*). What illicit food is to the sustaining of life, however, that fornication or adulterous intercourse is to the desire for offspring. And what illicit food is in the indulgence of the stomach and the palate, that illicit intercourse is in the lust that does not seek children. And an immoderate desire for licit food is to some people what to spouses is the pardonable use of intercourse. Therefore, just as it is better to die of hunger than to eat food that has been sacrificed to idols, so it is better to die without children than to seek to have children by illicit intercourse.

But from whatever source human beings may come, as long as they do not pursue the vices of their parents and as long as they worship God properly, they will be honorable and safe. For human seed is God's creation, no matter what sort of person it comes from, and it will be evil for the person who uses it in an evil way, although in itself it will never be evil. Just as the good children of adulterers cannot be used to defend adultery, so the wicked children born to married people cannot be used to disparage marriage.

In the same manner, just as the fathers in New Testament times took food because of their duty to care for others and just as they ate it while enjoying the natural pleasure of the flesh – although their pleasure was in no way comparable to the pleasure experienced by those who ate of sacrificial offerings or by those who consumed licit foods in an immoderate way – so, likewise, the fathers in Old Testament times had sexual intercourse because of their duty to care for others. The natural pleasure that they enjoyed did not give way to any sort of irrational or forbidden lust, nor should it be compared either to the wickedness of fornication or to the intemperance of married persons. Indeed, it was the same vein of charity, which once led them to produce children in a fleshly way, which now leads us to propagate in a spiritual way for the sake of our mother, Jerusalem. Only the difference of times caused the fathers to do different works. Just as it was necessary that the noncarnal prophets copulate in a carnal manner, so it was necessary that the noncarnal apostles eat in a carnal manner.

(XVII.19) Therefore, the married women of our own day, of whom it is said: *If they cannot control themselves, they should marry* [1 Cor. 7:9], ought not to be compared even to the holy women who married in ancient times. Marriage itself, of course, in all nations exists for the same purpose, the procreation of children. No matter how these children turn out in the end, marriage was instituted in order that they might be born in an ordered and honorable way. Now people who are unable to control themselves have taken a step up in honor, as it were, by marrying; but those who without a doubt would have controlled themselves, had the conditions allowed this, have taken a step down in piety, so to speak, by marrying. Because of this, even though the marriages of both types of people are equally good, in respect to the marriage itself, since they both exist for the sake of procreation, nevertheless the married people of our day are not to be compared to the married people of ancient times.

Married people today have something that is granted to them *as a concession* because of the honorable state of marriage, although this concession does not pertain to the essence of marriage itself; I am referring to the use of intercourse beyond the need of procreation, something that was not conceded to the ancients. Even if some married people today desire and seek in marriage only that for which marriage was instituted, even these spouses cannot be compared to the people of ancient times. For in people today the very desire for children is carnal, whereas in the ancients it was spiritual because it was in harmony with the sacred mystery (*sacramentum*) of the times. In fact, in our day no one who is perfect in piety seeks to have children except in a spiritual way, whereas in the past to have children in a carnal way was itself an act of piety, since the propagation of that people was a proclamation of future events and participated in the dispensation of prophecy.

(20) That is why a man was allowed to have several wives, while a woman

was not allowed to have several husbands, not even for the sake of offspring, if perhaps she was able to bear children when her husband was not able to beget them. For according to the mysterious law of nature, things that serve as ruling principles love singularity. In fact, it is fitting that subordinate things should be subject not only as individuals to individual rulers, but also (if the natural and social conditions allow it) as a group to a single ruler. That is why one servant does not have several masters, whereas several servants do have one master.

In the same manner, nowhere do we read that any of the holy women served two or more living husbands. But we do read that one husband had several wives, when the social customs of that people permitted it and when the character of the times required it, since this does not contradict the nature of marriage itself. For several women can become pregnant by one man, but one woman cannot become pregnant by several men – this is the power of the ruling principle – just as it is right that many souls should be subject to one God. For this reason the only true God of souls is one: although one soul is able to commit fornication through many false gods, it cannot be made fruitful by them.

(XVIII.21) Since there will be one City constructed out of the many souls who have one soul and one heart in God – this perfect state of unity will be achieved only after our pilgrimage in this life, when the thoughts of all will be revealed and all hostility will cease – the sacramental bond (*sacramentum*) of marriage in our day has been restricted to one man and one woman, with the result that it is forbidden to ordain a man as a minister in the church, unless he is the husband of [only] one wife [cf. 1 Tim. 3:2; Titus 1:6]. Those who have rejected the ordination of a man, who as a catechumen or a pagan had taken another wife, understood this most perceptively. What is involved is not the matter of sin, but rather the nature of the sacramental bond. For in baptism all sins are forgiven. But when the apostle said: *If you have taken a wife, you have not sinned. And if a virgin marries, she does not sin*, and: *He may do whatever he wishes, he does not sin; let him marry* [1 Cor. 7:28, 36], he declared clearly enough that marriage is no sin.

It is analogous to the case of a woman who has been corrupted while still a catechumen. Just as she cannot be consecrated among the virgins of God after her baptism on account of the holiness of the sacrament, so likewise it does not seem unfair that a man who has had more than one wife should have lost, as it were, the standard (*norma*) appropriate to the sacrament, even if he has committed no sin. This standard is not necessary for the merit of a good life, but it is required for the sign-value (*signaculum*) of ecclesiastical ordination.

For the very same reason, just as the several wives of the ancient fathers signified our churches that would come into being from the many nations and would be subject to the one man Christ, so our high priest, a man of one wife, signifies the unity that derives from the many nations and is subject to the one man Christ. This unity will be perfected in the future, when *he will reveal what is hidden in darkness and will make manifest the hidden motives of the heart, so that each will receive his praise from God* [1 Cor. 4:5]. In the present, however, there are disagreements, both manifest and hidden, even among those who, if charity is preserved, are to be one and in One. In the future these disagreements will be no more.

Therefore, just as in the past the sacrament of multiple marriages signified the multitude that would be subject to God in all the lands of the Gentiles, so in our time the sacrament of single marriages signifies the unity of all of us who will one day be subject to God in the heavenly City. Thus, just as servants do not serve two or more masters, so in the past it was forbidden (and is now forbidden and will always be forbidden) for a woman to marry another man while her husband is still alive. For it is always wrong to apostasize from the one God and to enter into the adulterous and superstitious worship of another god. Not even for the sake of more numerous offspring did our holy fathers do what the Roman Cato is said to have done, namely to have handed over his wife, while he was still alive, to fill the house of another man with children. Indeed, in the marriages of our women the holiness of the sacrament is more important than the fruitfulness of the womb.

(22) Therefore, even those who marry solely for the purpose of procreation, for which purpose marriage was instituted, are not to be compared to the ancient fathers, for they sought to have children in a manner quite different from those who live today. Take, for example, the devout and intrepid Abraham, who was ordered to sacrifice his son, whom he had received only after great desperation. Abraham, who had lifted his hand at God's command, would not have spared his only son, had not God himself prevented him and made him lower his hand [cf. Gen. 22:1–14].

• • •

(XXIV.32) The good of marriage, therefore, among all nations and peoples lies in the purpose of procreation and in the faithful preservation (*fides*) of chastity. But for the people of God the good of marriage lies also in the holiness of the sacramental bond (*sacramentum*). Because of this holiness, it is wrong for a woman to marry another man, even if she leaves with a bill of divorce, as long as her husband is alive, even if she does this for the sake of having children. Even if the first marriage took place solely for the sake of procreation and even if that for the sake of which the marriage was made did not happen, the marriage bond is not dissolved until the spouse dies.

In a similar way, if a cleric is ordained in order to form a congregation and if the congregation does not come into being, nonetheless the sacramental sign of ordination remains in those who have been ordained. If a cleric is removed from office because of some fault, he will not lose the sacramental sign of the Lord that was imposed once and for all, although it remains as a mark of judgment.

The apostle, therefore, testifies that marriage was made for the purpose of procreation. *I want the younger widows to marry*, he said [1 Tim. 5:14]. Then, as if someone had asked him, "But why?" he immediately added: *to bear children, to become the mothers of the households*. This passage also pertains to the faithful preservation of chastity: *A wife does not have power over her body, but her husband does; likewise, a husband has no power over his body, but his wife does* [1 Cor 7:4]. This passage also speaks of the holiness of the sacrament: *A wife should not separate from her husband; but if she does separate, she must remain unmarried or else be reconciled to her husband, and a man may not divorce his wife* [1 Cor. 7:10–11]. All these are the goods on account of which marriage is a good: offspring, fidelity, sacrament.

Surely, it is better and holier in the present time not to seek after offspring in the flesh and thereby to keep oneself perpetually free, as it were, from all this activity and to be subject in a spiritual way to the one man Christ, but only if people use this freedom in order to think *about the things of the Lord, how to be pleasing to God* [1 Cor. 7:32]. In other words, continence must constantly be on guard so that it does not fall short in respect to obedience. In their deeds the holy fathers of ancient times practiced the virtue of obedience as the root and mother, so to speak, of all their actions, whereas they possessed continence in the disposition of their souls. Indeed, through their obedience they even would have abstained from intercourse altogether, had they been ordered to, since they were righteous and holy people who were always prepared for every good work. For it would have been much easier for them to follow God's command or exhortation and to have abstained from sex, when they were able to sacrifice out of obedience the very offspring, whose propagation they were ensuring by their sexual intercourse.

from Homily I on Marriage

St. John Chrysostom

Note how Chrysostom calls for the establishment of new marriage customs "if they are not evil." Chastity, which in marriage is faithfulness, is more important than children: "We have as witnesses all those who are married but childless." Chrysostom treats the presence or absence of children in the light of the resurrection, which alone guarantees the future of the human race. Spiritual children (baptized Christians) are better than physical ones.

In pagan books, if anything good happens to be said, most writers hardly utter one healthful word out of many. In the holy Scriptures it is quite the reverse. There you never hear any evil word, but everything filled with salvation and great wisdom. Such are the words which have been read to us today. What are they? "Concerning the matters about which you wrote," Paul says, "it is well for a man not to touch a woman. But because of the temptation to immorality, each man should have his own wife and each woman her own husband."[1] Paul legislates concerning marriage without being ashamed or blushing, and with good reason. His Master honored a marriage, and so far from being ashamed of it, adorned the occasion with His presence and His gift. Indeed, He brought a greater wedding gift than any other, when He changed the nature of water into wine. How then could His servant blush to legislate concerning marriage?

Marriage is not an evil thing. It is adultery that is evil, it is fornication that is evil. Marriage is a remedy to eliminate fornication. Let us not, therefore, dishonor marriage by the pomp of the devil. Instead, let those who take wives now do as they did at Cana in Galilee. Let them have Christ in their midst. "How can they do this?" someone asks. By inviting the clergy. "He who receives you," the Lord says, "receives Me."[2] So drive away the devil. Throw out the lewd songs, the corrupt melodies, the disorderly dances, the shameful words, the diabolical display, the uproar, the unrestrained laughter, and the rest of the impropriety. Bring in instead the holy servants of Christ, and through them Christ will certainly be present along with His mother and His brothers. For He says, "Whoever does the will of My Father is My brother and sister and mother."[3]

I know that some people think I am burdensome and difficult, giving advice like this and uprooting ancient custom. But I do not care at all about their objections. I do not seek your favor but your benefit. I do not ask for the applause of praise, but the profit of wisdom. Let no one tell me that this is the custom. Where sin is boldly committed, forget about custom. If evil things are done, even if the custom is ancient, abolish them. If they are not evil, even if they are not customary, introduce them and establish them. Actually it was not an ancient custom to celebrate weddings in a disgraceful way, but some kind of innovation. Consider how Isaac married Rebecca, how Jacob married Rachel. Scripture tells us of these weddings, and how these brides entered the households of their bridegrooms. Nothing is said about such customs. They gave banquets and dinners more lavish than usual, and invited their relatives to the weddings. Flutes, pipes, cymbals, drunken cavorting, and all the rest of our impropriety were avoided. Nowadays on the day of a wedding people dance and sing hymns to Aphrodite, songs full of adultery, corruption of marriages, illicit loves, unlawful unions, and many other impious and shameful themes. They accompany the bride in public with unseemly drunkenness and shameful speeches. How can you expect chastity of her, tell me, if you accustom her to such shamelessness from the first day, if you present in her sight such actions and words as even the more serious slaves should not hear? For such a long time her father has striven along with her mother to protect the virgin, to keep her from speaking or hearing any of these words. He has arranged for private chambers, women's apartments, guards, doors, and locks. He has allowed her to go out only in the evening, to be seen only by members of the family. Have you overthrown all these precautions in one day, teaching her shamelessness by that disgraceful retinue, and introducing corrupt thoughts into the soul of the bride? Do not the subsequent evils begin here? Is not this the beginning of childlessness and widowhood and untimely orphanhood?

When you invoke demons by your songs, when you fulfill their desires by your shameful speeches, when you bring mimes and effeminate actors and the whole theater into your house, when you fill your house with harlots and arrange for the whole chorus of demons to make merry there, what good can you expect, tell me? Why do you even invite the clergy, if you are planning to celebrate these rites on the next day? Do you wish to demonstrate a beneficial munificence? Invite the choirs of the poor. Are you ashamed at this idea? Do you blush? What could be more unreasonable than this? When you drag the devil into your house, you do not think that you are doing anything shameful, but when you plan to bring Christ in, you blush? Just as Christ is present when the poor enter, so when effeminates and mimes dance there, the devil is carousing in their midst. From this extravagance there is no benefit, but rather great harm. From the other expenditure you might quickly receive a great reward.

No one in the city has done this, you say? Why don't you hurry to be the founder of this good custom, so that posterity may attribute it to you? If anyone envies or imitates this custom, your descendants will be able to say to inquirers that you first introduced this practice. In the competitions of the unbelievers, at symposia, many people sing the praises of those who have improved these unedifying rites. All the more in the spiritual rite everyone will give praise and thanks to the one who first introduces this wonderful innovation. This will bring both honor and benefit to him. When this is tended by others, it will bring the reward of its fruits to you who first planted it. This will make you quickly a father, this will help your children prosper, this will aid the bridegroom to grow old together with his bride. Just as God continually threatens the sinners, saying, "Your children shall be orphans and your wives widows,"[4] so also He promises to those who are always obedient a pleasant old age together with every good gift.

We can also hear Paul saying this, that a multitude of sins often causes untimely deaths. "That is why," he says, "many of you are weak and ill, and some have died."[5] From the story of the girl in Joppa we can learn that the poor who have been fed do not allow anything like this to happen. If any misfortune occurs, they bring a quick restoration. When she was lying dead, the poor whom she had fed stood around weeping. They raised her up and restored her to life.[6] So much more beneficial is the prayer of the widows and the poor than any amount of laughter and dancing. The latter gives pleasure for one day; the former brings lasting benefit. Think how good it is for a bride to enter the house of her bridegroom with such blessings on her head. Are not these more noble than any crowns? Are not they more useful than any wealth? Whereas the present customs represent the greatest madness and insanity.

Marriage was not instituted for wantonness or fornication, but for chastity. Listen to what Paul says: "Because of the temptation to immorality, each man should have his own wife and each woman her own husband."[7] These are the two purposes for which marriage was instituted: to make us chaste, and to make us parents. Of these two, the reason of chastity takes precedence. When desire began, then marriage also began. It sets a limit to desire by teaching us to keep to one wife. Marriage does not always lead to child-bearing, although there is the word of God which says, "Be fruitful and multiply, and fill the earth."[8] We have as witnesses all those who are married but childless. So the purpose of chastity takes precedence, especially now, when the whole world is filled with our kind. At the beginning, the procreation of children was desirable, so that each person might leave a memorial of his life. Since there was not yet any hope of resurrection, but death held sway, and those who died thought that they would perish after this life, God gave the comfort of children, so as to leave living images of the departed and to preserve our species. For those who were about to die and for their relatives, the greatest consolation was their offspring. To understand that this was the chief reason for desiring children, listen to the complaint of Job's wife. "See," she says, "your memory has perished from the earth, your sons and your daughters."[9] Likewise Saul says to David, "Swear to me that you will not destroy my seed, and my name along with me."[10] But now that resurrection is at our gates, and we do not speak of death, but advance toward another life better than the present, the desire for posterity is superfluous. If you desire children, you can get much better children now, a nobler childbirth and better help in your old age, if you give birth by spiritual labor.

So there remains only one reason for marriage, to avoid fornication, and the remedy is offered for this purpose. If you are going to practice fornication after marriage, you have approached marriage uselessly and in vain; or rather not merely in vain, but to your harm. It is not as serious for an unmarried man to practice fornication as to do the same after marriage. For then the same act is no longer fornication but adultery. Even if this statement seems strange, it is true. I realize that many people think it is adultery only when one corrupts a married woman. But I say that if a married man treats wickedly and wantonly an unmarried woman, even a prostitute or a servant girl, this act is adultery. The charge of adultery is determined not only by the status of the person wronged but also by that of the wrongdoer.

Do not tell me about the laws of the unbelievers, which drag the woman caught in adultery into court and exact a penalty, but do not demand a penalty from the married men who have corrupted servant girls. I will read to you the law of God, which is equally severe with the woman and the man, and which calls the deed adultery. When Paul says, "Let each woman have her own husband," he adds, "Let the husband show his wife the good will which is due."[11] What does he mean when he says this? Is it to preserve her access to her money? Is it to keep her dowry intact? Is it to provide her with expensive clothes, or an extravagant table, or a conspicuous display when she goes out? Is it to have her attended by many servants? What do you say? What kind of good will do you seek? All of these things show good will, do they not? I do not mean any of these, Paul says, but chastity and holiness. The husband's body is no longer the husband's, but the wife's. Therefore he must keep her property intact, without diminishing it or damaging it. We say that that servant has good will who takes charge of his master's property and does not damage any of it. Since therefore the husband's body is the wife's property, the husband must show good will in regard to the property entrusted to him. When Paul says, "Let him show the good will which is due," he adds, "the wife does not rule over her own body, but the husband does; likewise the husband does not rule over his own body, but the wife does."[12] So when you see a prostitute setting snares, plotting against you, desiring your body, say to her, "This body is not mine. It belongs to my wife. I do not dare to mistreat it nor to lend it to another woman." The wife should do the same. Here there is complete equality.

I grant that in other matters Paul gives the husband superior authority, when he says, "Let each one of you love his wife as himself, and let the wife see that she respects her husband."[13] He also says, "The husband is the head of the wife," and, "The wife ought to be subject to her husband."[14] In the Old Testament it is written, "Your desire shall be for your husband, and he shall rule over you."[15] How then in this passage has Paul introduced an equal exchange of service and mastery? In saying, "The wife does not rule over her own body, but the husband does; likewise the husband does not rule over his own body, but the wife does,"[16] he introduces a great measure of equality. Just as the husband is master of her body, so the wife is mistress of his body. Why does Paul introduce so much equality? Although in other matters there needs to be a superior authority, here where chastity and holiness are at stake, the husband has no greater privilege than the wife. He is punished equally with her if he breaks the laws of marriage, and with good reason. Your wife did not come to you, leaving her father and mother and her whole house-hold, so that you could dishonor her, so that you could take a cheap servant girl in her place. It was not in order to start a thousand battles that you took a companion, a partner for your life, a free woman of equal honor with yourself. Would it not be foolish to receive her dowry, treat it with all good will, and diminish nothing of it, but to corrupt and ruin that which is more valuable than the whole dowry, namely chastity and holiness, as well as your own body which is her possession? If you diminish her dowry, you give cause for a lawsuit to your father-in-law. If you diminish chastity, you will pay the penalty to God who instituted marriage and protects the wife. To know that this is true, hear what Paul says about adulterers: "Whoever disregards this, disregards not man but God, who gives His Holy Spirit to you."[17] Do you see how definitely his words prove that it is adultery to corrupt not only a married woman but even a prostitute, if the man is married? Just as we say that a married woman is made an adulteress whether she sins with a servant or any other man, so we should say that a married man commits adultery if he sins with a servant girl or any loose woman. Therefore do not neglect your own salvation. Do not offer your soul to the devil by this kind of sin. By such sins many families are broken, many battles are started. Such sins empty out love and undermine good will. Just as a virtuous man can never neglect or scorn his wife, so a wanton and licentious man can never love his wife, no matter how beautiful she is. Virtue gives birth to love, and love brings innumerable blessings.

(St John continues to exhort the husband to fidelity.)

Notes

1 1 Cor. 7:1–2.
2 Mt. 10:40.
3 Mt. 12:50.
4 Ex. 22:24.
5 1 Cor. 11:30.
6 Acts 9:36–41.
7 1 Cor. 7:2.
8 Gen. 1:28.
9 Cf. Job 18:17.
10 1 Kings 24:22 (1 Sam 24:21).
11 1 Cor. 7:2–3 var.
12 1 Cor. 7:3–4.
13 Eph. 5:33.
14 Eph. 5:23, 24.
15 Gen. 3:16.
16 1 Cor. 7:4.
17 1 Thess. 4:8.

from Against the Opponents of the Monastic Life

St. John Chrysostom

In this passage Chrysostom seeks to defend the childlessness of the monastics, and in the process makes further comments about the necessity of children in marriage – or lack thereof. Indeed, he makes marriage and monasticism two forms of the same discipline, the discipline or asceticism that leads to holiness.

If other people acted like this, it would not be so terrible. But when it is the parents, who have enjoyed a full worldly life, who have learned from experience that earthly pleasures are cold, when it is they who are so mad that they lead others to these pleasures, when they are too old to indulge themselves, when it is they who should have proclaimed themselves miserable because of their prior experiences, but who instead throw others onto the same road, when they themselves are already close to death, judgment, and punishments, what excuse will be left to them, what pardon, what pity? They will pay the penalty not only for their own sins, but also for the wicked deeds of their children, whether or not they succeed in upsetting them.

16. But perhaps you long to see your children's children? How is this, when you are not yet parents yourselves? For the act of begetting does not a parent make. And this is agreed upon by those parents who, when they see their sons reach the height of wickedness, reject and disown them as if they were not their own, and neither nature, nor birth, nor any such bond can restrain them. Therefore, those who are far inferior to their children with respect to philosophy should no longer be considered parents; only when they also have given birth to them in this way should they desire grandchildren; only then will they be able to see them. For the monks also have children; they are born *not*

of flesh and blood nor of the will of man, but they have been begotten *of God* [John 1:13]. Such children as these have no need to torment their parents over money, or marriage, or any such thing; on the contrary, they allow them to be free of all care and provide them with a greater pleasure than their natural parents enjoy. They are not born and raised for the same purposes as natural children, but for a much greater and more splendid destiny. Thus they delight their parents even more.

Besides these considerations, I also will add one more: it is not unreasonable that those who disbelieve in the resurrection should grieve about having descendants, since this is the only consolation left to them. But we, who think that death is a sleep, who have been taught to despise all things in this life, what pardon would we merit if we mourned about such matters and desired to see children and to leave them behind in this place, from which we are hastening to depart and in which we groan when we are present? This is what we would say to those who are more spiritual. But if there are some who are lovers of the body, who are quite attached to the present life, I would say this to them: first, it is not certain that a marriage will produce children at all; second, if children do come, there will be even greater discouragement. For the happiness which children bring us is far outweighed by the grief which comes from the daily care, anxiety, and fear which they cause.

"And to whom," you say, "will we leave our fields, houses, servants, and gold?" For I also hear you lamenting about these things. The child who previously was to inherit these goods will now be a much safer guardian and master of the property than before. Previously many things threatened to ruin his property: moths, the length of time, robbers, sycophants, jealous persons, the uncertainty of the future, the unstable character of human affairs, and ultimately death would have robbed your son of both his money and these possessions. But now he has stored his wealth beyond all this; he has found a safe place where none of the obstacles we have mentioned can intrude. This place is heaven, which is free of all treachery, more fertile than any land, a place where those who have deposited their wealth are allowed to reap the fruit of this deposit. Since this is the case, there is no need for you to make these complaints; but if your child wanted to live in the world, then you should lament and complain: "To whom shall we leave our fields, our gold and the rest of our goods?" Now our dominion over these goods is so extensive that not even after death will we lose control over them, but we will enjoy their fruit most when we have gone to the next life.

But if you wish to see someone who is master of his goods even in this life, you also could see this happen more to the monk than to the person in the world. Who, tell me, is the more lordly: the one who spends and gives with great fearlessness, or the one who does not dare to touch anything on account of his parsimony, but who hoards these goods and keeps away from his own property as if it were another's? The one who spends rashly and without purpose, or the one who does this only when necessary? The one who sows on earth, or the one who plants his seeds in heaven? The one who is not allowed to give all his goods to whomever he wishes, or the one who is free of all who demand such high taxes? The farmer and the businessman are set upon from all sides by many who compel them to pay tribute, each one demanding part of their property. But you would never see anyone threatening him who desires to give to the needy; thus, even in this life he is more lordly.

Hymns of Divine Love, 15

St. Symeon the New Theologian (942–1022), Abbot of Saint Mamas

In Eastern Orthodoxy, three and only three thinkers have received the epithet "the Theologian." Theories abound about why these three and no others deserve the name. One theory is this. A theologian is one who first identifies God in an irreversible way. John the Theologian, the evangelist, deserves the name because he first identifies God as Jesus in the prologue to John's Gospel. Gregory the Theologian, Gregory Nazianzen, deserves the name because he first identifies God as the Holy Spirit in his Theological Orations. Symeon the New Theologian deserves the name, according to this theory, because he most emphatically identifies God as in human beings as a result of the indwelling of the Holy Spirit, indeed of the entire Trinity – so that anyone who denies it commits blasphemy against the Holy Spirit.* This identification seems to make Symeon another theologian of the Holy Spirit, and it does. But the surprise to us moderns is that it also, and by the same reasoning, makes Symeon a theologian of the Spirit's dwelling, the human body. One who delights in provoking his opponents, Symeon aims to shock the reader with the consequences of identifying Christ with the human body in its entirety.

[* Symeon the New Theologian, The Discourses, *XV–XVI, XXXII, trans. C. J. deCatanzaro (New York: Paulist Press, 1980), pp. 193–204, 335–8.]*

How, in the sight of the glory of God, the author was directed by the activity of the most Holy Spirit; and that the divinity is interior and exterior to all, much more, at once seizable and unseizable for those who are worthy of it; and that we are the "House of David" that, becoming many members, Christ our God is and remains the only, the same and indivisible.

When You reveal Yourself, Master of the Universe,
and show the glory of Your face with more clearness,
I begin to tremble all over, to see You,
as far as is possible, to the lowliness of my nature,
I am filled with fear and, full of fright, I say:
"All that belongs to You, my God, is above my comprehension,
for I am impure, absolutely unworthy
to see You, You, the pure and holy Master
whom the angels venerate and serve trembling
and whose face disturbs the whole creation."
– But when I would speak thus and cover my eyes,
I mean, when I turn my mind towards earth, incapable
of looking at You or of contemplating You, unbearable vision,
then deprived of Your beauty, my God, I lament,
without being able to bear to be separated from You,
unique Friend of man – and while I weep and complain,
You surround me completely with Your light,
oh, amazement! and, upset, I weep more copiously,
admiring Your mercy towards me, the Prodigal.
Then I see all the shamefulness of my body,
and the unworthiness of my wretched soul,
and when I realize it, I exclaim beyond myself:
"To be sure who am I, O God, Creator of the universe
and to be sure what good have I done in all my life,
which one of Your commandments have I ever practised,
for You to glorify me, with such glory, in spite of my baseness?
and how is it, how does it happen that You have deigned
to surround me thus with Your light, night and day,
in spite of my wretchedness?
O my King, I have ever pined away with thirst in Your pursuit,
I have never grieved, suffered, for your commandments,
I have never endured trials and blows, like all
Your saints have endured them, forever,
so as to save me, O Christ, by counting me among them!
No, you will not save me, a slothful person, devoid of works,
as strong as Your love for man may be, this man whom You have made.
I hear Paul saying that faith without works is dead, and I
shiver over the punishments
which certainly await me down there, for my long negligence.
How then, as a faithful one, will I dare to be counted,
Master, in the ranks of those who have worked,
I who have never observed a single one of Your commandments?
But I know, You can do everything, You do all according to
Your will, and, Master, You give as much to the last as You
give to the first, indeed to the last, O marvel, before the first!"
While I speak thus, Creator of the world, You

who at first shone above me and then one day hid Yourself,
and who, afterwards, enveloped me completely with Your rays,
I suddenly contemplate You completely present in me,
You at first having appeared suddenly above, then hidden
behind a cloud, deprived of its rays like the sun.
Yes, as this star shows itself to whomever contemplates it,
and then, especially, all see it completely so to say,
similarly, You also show Yourself hidden within me,
yes seen, You, the inaccessible one, to the eyes of my intellect,
How? You know it –, gradually increasing,
redoubling with light, redoubling with brilliancy;
and another time, You show Yourself to me absolutely inaccessible.
That is why I magnify Your incomprehensibility
and, proclaiming your kindness, I cry to you:
"Glory to the one who has so glorified our essence,
glory, O my Savior, to Your incommensurable condescension,
glory to Your mercy, glory to Your power,
glory to You! because, remaining immutable and without change,
You are completely immovable and always completely in movement,
completely outside creation and completely in every creature,
You fill everything completely, You who are completely
outside everything, above everything, O Master, above all
beginning, above all essence, above the nature of nature,
above all ages, above all light, O Savior,
above intellectual Essences – for they too are Your work
or rather the work of Your mind.
Indeed, You are none of these creatures, but superior to
all creatures, for You are the cause of all creatures, in
so far as You are Creator of all
and that is why You are apart from them all,
very lofty, for our mind, above all creatures,
invisible, inaccessible, unseizable, intangible,
escaping all comprehension, You remain without change,
You are simplicity itself and yet You are all diversity –
and our mind is totally incapable of fathoming
the diversity of Your glory and the splendor of Your beauty.
You then, who are nothing of all that is, for You are above
everything, You who are outside everything, for You are
the God of everything, invisible, inaccessible, unseizable,
intangible, yes, You became a man, You came into the world
and showed Yourself to all, accessible, in the body that
You assumed.
But to believers, You made Yourself known in the glory of
Your divinity, You became seizable for them, You who are
totally unseizable, and completely visible, You the
invisible one to all; only the believers have seen Your

glory, O divine Divinity, and they alone contemplated it,
while all the unfaithful remained blind, they who saw You,
You, the light of the world.
So the faithful, now as then, see You ceaselessly and
possess You, You, the Creator of all things,
You live and You dwell with them in the darkness of this life,
like a non-setting sun, like a lamp which cannot be extinguished,
which darkness will never be able to seize
but which does not stop enlightening those who see You.
But, I repeat, since You are outside all things,
those whom You illumine also, You make them come out from
the visible and, just as You, while remaining above with
Your Father, You are equally, without separation, completely
present with us and at the same time being in the world
You are not separated from the world, for You are in
everything, but above everything –
in the same way we, your servants, in the midst of sensible
things are plunged in visible things, You make us come out
of them and draw us completely with You, resplendent with
Your light, and You make us mortals, immortals:
remaining what we are, by Your grace we become
sons, like You, and gods, seeing God.
In these conditions, who would not run towards You,
man's only Friend?
who would not follow You, who, urged by love, would not say:
"Behold, having left everything we are going to follow You,
You, the Master, filled with compassion, gentleness, mercy,
who always await our return to You,
who do not want the death of those who have offended You,
who now realize in us the dreadful marvels
that we hear formerly happened in the House of David,
to our astonishment!" Which ones? There they are;
We are the House of David, for we belong to Your race,
since You Yourself, Creator of the universe, became His
own Son, and we have become Your sons by grace.
By the flesh You belong to our race, by divinity we belong
to Yours, since, by assuming our flesh, You gave us your
Divine Spirit, and, all together, we have become the unique
House of David through what belongs to You only, by our
community of race with You.
Therefore, You are Lord of David in the Spirit,
but, all of us, we are children of David, we, Your divine seed!
And when we assemble, we become one single family,
that is to say, that we are all of the same race, we
are all Your brothers.
How not tremble in the presence of this marvel, or who

could without shivering no matter how little, conceive
this idea, welcome this revelation:
You are with us, now and forever,
You make Your home in each one and You live in everyone
and for all of us You become our home and we live in You,
each one of us entirely, O Savior, with You entirely,
with each one of us, You are along with him alone
and above us all, You are also, alone and all entire.
So You are, then, in us, about to do all these awesome marvels;
what marvels? – Among many, listen to these few:
for even if all we have already said surpasses all amazement,
nevertheless, listen, now, to still more formidable marvels!
We become members of Christ – and Christ becomes our members,
Christ becomes my hand, Christ, my miserable foot;
and I, unhappy one, am Christ's hand, Christ's foot!
I move my hand, and my hand is the whole Christ
since, do not forget it, God is indivisible in His divinity –;
I move my foot, and behold it shines like That – one!
Do not accuse me of blasphemy, but welcome these things
and adore Christ who makes you such,
since if you so wish you will become a member of Christ,
and similarly all our members individually
will become members of Christ and Christ our members,
and all which is dishonorable in us He will make honorable
by adorning it with His divine beauty and His divine glory,
since living with God at the same time, we shall become gods,
no longer seeing the shamefullness of our body at all,
but made completely like Christ in our whole body,
each member of our body will be the whole Christ;
because, becoming many members, He remains unique and
indivisible, and each part is He, the whole Christ.
Now, well you recognized Christ in my finger,
and in this organ . . . – did you not shudder, or blush?
But God was not ashamed to become like you
and you, you are ashamed to be like Him?
No, I am not ashamed to be like Him,
but, when you said, like a shameful member,
I feared that you were uttering a blasphemy.
Well, you were wrong to fear, for there is nothing shameful,
but they are the hidden members of Christ, because one
covers them, and for that reason they are more worthy of
honor than the others, as hidden members, invisible to all,
of the One who is hidden, of the One who sows the seed in
divine union, divine seed, made, amazingly, according to
the image of God, born of the divinity itself, completely –
for He is completely God –, the One who unites Himself

with us, O frightful mystery!
It is truly a marriage which takes place, ineffable and divine:
God unites Himself with each one – yes, I repeat it,
it is my delight – and each becomes one with the Master.
If therefore, in your body, you have put on the total Christ,
you will understand without blushing all that I am saying;
but if you have done nothing about it, or if of the
immaculate garment, I am speaking of Christ,
you have only put on a small piece to your soul,
plain piece on old material, it covers but one spot
and you are ashamed of all the remainder of your members,
or rather it is your whole body which is soiled.
Indeed how would you not blush, clad with soiled garments?
When I utter these formidable words about holy members,
and, with an enlightened mind that I consider all their glory,
filled with joy, without thinking of anything sensual,
you consider your own flesh, all soiled
and in spirit you run over your infamous actions
where your mind ever crawls like a worm;
that is why you project your shame on Christ and on me
saying: "Do you not blush at these shameful words,
and above all to disparage Christ to shameful members?"
But I say in my turn: "See Christ in the womb of His mother;
picture to yourself the interior of this womb and He
escaping from it, and whence my God had to pass to come out of it!
You will find there much more than what I have spoken about
and He accepted all that for our glory,
so that no one would blush to imitate Him
nor to say nor to suffer Himself what He suffered.
He became totally man, He, truly, totally God,
He the Unique One, without division, perfect man without
any doubt, and the same One is completely God, in the
totality of His members.
So there was, even now in these latter days,
Symeon the saint, the pious one, the Studite.
He did not blush before the members of anyone,
neither to see other men naked, nor to show himself naked,
for he possessed Christ completely, and he was completely
Christ, and all his own members and everybody else's members,
all and each one were always like Christ in his eyes;
he remained motionless, unhurt and impassive;
he was all Christ himself and as Christ he considered
all the baptized, clothed with the whole Christ.
While you, if you are naked and your flesh touches flesh,
there you are in heat like a donkey or a horse,
how do you dare then to speak against the saint himself,

and blaspheme Christ, the One who united Himself with us
and has given impassiveness to His holy servants?
For He becomes a spouse – do you hear? – each day,
and all the souls with whom the Creator unites Himself
become spouses and they, in turn, with Him, O wholly
spiritual marriage, divine embrace with which He embraces them!
Without dishonoring them in any way, away with the thought!
but even if He takes them already dishonored, by uniting Himself
with them, He at once restores their integrity, and what was
formerly soiled by corruption, in their eyes,
is no longer but sanctity, incorruption, perfectly healed.
They glorify the Merciful One, they are in love with the
most beautiful One. They are entirely united to His total love;
or rather, by receiving as we have already said, His holy
seed, within themselves, they completely possess God who
has taken the form of man.
Well, Fathers, isn't all that the truth?
Didn't we correctly speak of these divine realities?

Doesn't what I said truly correspond with the Scriptures?
But if you are clothed with the shamefulness of your flesh
if you have not bared your mind, nor stripped your soul,
if you have not succeeded in seeing the light,
buried as you are in darkness, what could I really do for you,
how should I show you the formidable mysteries?
Alas, how should I introduce you into the House of David?
For it is inaccessible for cowards like me,
it is entirely invisible to blind persons like me,
infinitely distinct for unbelievers and lazy persons
and very far from all the wicked, from all the friends
of the world, as for the conceited, without comparison,
it is distinct from them much more than the heights of the
heavens, than the depths of the abyss.
And who could, or how, ascend completely to heaven
or descend underground to explore the abysses?
While seeking a pearl, as minute
as a mustard seed, how could one find it?
Assemble, children, come, women,
hasten, fathers, before the end comes,
and, with me, all weep and lament,
since after having received God in Baptism as infants,
or rather, having become sons of God as little children,
soon, sinners, we have been expelled
from the House of David and that happened to us
without our realizing it! Let us hasten by penance
since it is by it that all the expelled return

and that there is no other way, do not be mistaken by it,
to enter into the interior
nor to see the mysteries which were accomplished there
and are still accomplished there now and till the end of
time in Christ, my God, to whom is due all glory,
all honor and all adoration, now and forever. Amen.

from Commentary on Romans 1:18–29

St. Thomas Aquinas

In sexual ethics, Thomas Aquinas is usually known for his natural law theory, which occupies only a few pages, and for his theory of the virtues, which runs for hundreds. Here the genre is biblical commentary, in which both natural-law and virtue-theory arguments appear fleetingly as part of a larger whole. Indeed, since "the mode of this science is narrative," they appear as part of a story. Thomas follows Paul to tell a story, discernible in the light of the gospel, in which both Gentiles and Jews need liberation from sin. Ignorance about the truth of God does not arise on its own, but follows from injustice, so that human beings involved in injustice cannot expect to have a correct discernment of right and wrong. Indeed, under conditions of injustice, natural law becomes a self-consuming artifact; it ceases to function to lead human beings to the good. Shocking to those who hold a high view of natural law, Thomas elsewhere does not shy away from the assertion that "The law of nature had already been destroyed" ("Lex natura . . . destructa erat," De duobus praeceptis charitatis, prologue*). One might nowadays take it to imply that those involved in the injustice of discrimination against gay and lesbian people will not find themselves in a position to know the truth about their relationships. But that is not the conclusion that Thomas draws.*

For rhetorical purposes, Paul stereotypes Gentile sin in a particular way (in order to turn the tables on the stereotyper at Romans 2:1, "you who judge are without excuse"). Thomas has adopted Pauline and rabbinic accounts according to which Gentiles fell into idolatry when the law was given to Israel at Sinai. (This is a distinct fall from the one in Eden.) Because of Gentile idolatry, God afflicted Gentiles (non-Jews) with an appropriate punishment, which was a further sin, on the form of idolatry, by which they would die out. Thomas called it the vice against nature. Note

104 ◆

how "nature" language and "virtue–vice" language, now relatively separate approaches in religious ethics, have not yet come apart. Note too how "nature" language causes Thomas to slide from Gentiles as non-Jews to Gentiles as generic human beings. Contemporary ethicists who wish to follow Thomas on sexual ethics will presumably not wish to follow him here: No one now holds that God afflicted Gentiles as a group with homosexuality; no one now holds that God did this as a result of a separate, historical fall of Gentiles at the time of Sinai. No one now holds that Gentile homosexuality occurs in connection with idolatry of the literal, graven-image-worshiping sort, or in necessary connection with other sins, indeed "all vice." And no one now holds that God did this in order that the group would die out.*

[* For more see Eugene F. Rogers, Jr., "The Narrative of Natural Law in Aquinas's Commentary on Romans 1," Theological Studies *59 (1998), pp. 254–76, and "Aquinas on Natural Law and the Virtues in Biblical Context: Homosexuality as a Test Case,"* Journal of Religious Ethics *27 (1999), pp. 29–56.]*

The true cognition of God, insofar as it is in itself, leads the human being to the good. But it is bound, as if held in captivity, by the affect of injustice, by which, as Ps.11(12):1 has it, "truths are diminished by the children of human beings." . . .

Those having cognition of God no longer used it for good. For they recognized God in two ways. In one way, as the super-eminent of all, and so they owed God the glory and honor that is owed to the most excellent things. They are therefore called inexcusable . . . either because they did not pay God the due cult, or because they imposed an end to God's power and knowledge, subtracting somewhat from God's power and knowledge . . .

Second, they recognized God as the cause of all good things. Therefore thanksgiving was owing to God in all things, which however they were not intending; but rather they were ascribing their good things to their own ingenuity and virtue . . . .

Next [Paul] asserts the subsequent ignorance, saying "and [their heart] was darkened"; that is, because it was darkened, "their heart" was made "foolish," that is, deprived of the light of wisdom by which the human being recognizes God truly."

[Paul] says therefore first . . . that since [the Gentiles] changed the truth of God into a lie, "God gave them up," not, indeed, impelling them to evil, but deserting them "in ignominious passions," that is, in sins against nature . . . .

Now it is to be considered that something can be against the nature of the human being in two ways. In one way, against the nature of the constitutive distinction of the human being, which is "rational"; and in that way any sin is said to be against the nature of the human being, insofar as it is against right reason . . . .

In another way, something is said to be against the nature of the human being by reason of the genus, which is "animal." Now it is manifest that, according to the intention of nature, the intercourse of the sexes in animals is ordered to the act of generation, whence all manners of intercourse, from which generation cannot follow, are against the nature of the human being insofar as the human being is animal . . . .

And therefore it is to be noted that the Apostle asserts the penalty for idolatry reasonably enough as the vice against nature, which is the gravest among the carnal sins, since it seems to have begun at the same time as idolatry, namely in the time of Abraham, when idolatry is believed to have begun. For that reason and at that time it is first read of as having been punished among the Sodomites, in Genesis 19. Just as idolatry was increasing, such vices grew . . . .

[Paul] expands upon their guilt in two ways. First intensively, when he says "full (of all vice)." For the one seems to be full of iniquity whose affect is totally disposed toward sinning. . . . Second, extensively, since namely they did not sin only in one thing but in all things . . .

Consequently [Paul] enumerates specific sins . . .

from The Spiritual Canticle: Songs Between the Soul and the Bridegroom

St. John of the Cross

Rowan Williams notes that "To be formed in our humanity by the loving delight of another is an experience whose contours we can identify most clearly and hopefully if we have also learned, or are learning, about being the object of the causeless, loving delight of God's love for God through incorporation into the community of God's Spirit and the taking on of the identity of God's Child. It is because of our need to keep that perspective clear before us that the community needs some who are called beyond or aside from the ordinary patterns of sexual relation to put their identities directly into the hands of God in the single life. This is not an alternative to the body's grace. . . . [The] extraordinary experiment [of Christian celibacy] does seem to be 'justified in its children' " in, among other ways, "the great freedom of the celibate mystic in deploying the rhetoric of erotic love in speaking of God." St. John of the Cross provides a sample of this rhetoric, taking it from the Song of Songs.

In this passage, note the freedom of gender, even gender-bending, of the traditional rhetoric. John is very free – indeed the genre requires him – to adopt the gender of the woman, who desires to be penetrated by God's love. Whether or not the modern reader experiences those passages as homoerotic, their grammatical basis is that John is speaking in the person of the soul, and the soul is feminine in Spanish. More than that, the tradition constructs the human being as essentially, ontologically, or ecclesially feminine, passive to God's male, and identified with Mary or the Bride of Christ (that is, the Church). So the same human being may take up and rhetorically and liturgically perform several gendered roles – male as priest and *female as believer – without any of the modern anxieties about gender identity. (To complicate matters, the bridegroom, Jesus himself – and after him, the abbot of a monastery – may also be constructed as feminine, and suckle believers with the milk of his breasts – in sources as diverse as Clement of Alexandria, medieval Cistercians, and the mystic Julian of Norwich.)**

[* Caroline Walker Bynum, "Jesus as Mother and Abbot as Mother: Some Themes in Twelfth-century Cistercian Writing," in Jesus as Mother: Studies in the Spirituality of the High Middle Ages *(Berkeley: University of California Press, 1982), pp. 110–69.]*

> Where have you hidden away,   The bride
> lover, and left me grieving, care on care?
>   Hurt me and wouldn't stay
>   but off like a deer from there?
> I hurried forth imploring the empty air.
>
>   You shepherds, you that rove
> over the range where mountains touch the sky,
>   if you should meet my love
>   – my one love – tell him why
> I'm faint, and in a fever, and may die.
>
>   I'll wander high and low
> after the one I worship; never fear
>   the wild things where I go;
>   not gather flowers; get clear
> of all the mighty and over the frontier.
>
>   O fields and woods between,   A question to the creatures
> foliage planted by a lover's hand,
>   O bluegrass, evergreen,
>   with marigolds japanned,
> tell me, has he been lately in your land?
>
>   Lavishing left and right   Their reply
> a world of wonders he went streaming by
>   the woodland, quick as light.
>   And where it touched, his eye
> left a new glory on the earth and sky.

Left me new suffering too!
Once and for all be really mine, and cure it!
　　Yourself! No making do
　　with couriers – who'd endure it?
I want your living voice, and these obscure it.

　　All that come and go
tell of a thousand wonders, to your credit;
　　new rumors – each a blow!
　　Like death I dread it.
Something – the telltale tongue, a-stumble, said it.

　　How manage breath on breath
so long, my soul, not living where life is?
　　Brought low and close to death
　　by those arrows of his?
Love was the bow. I know. I've witnesses.

　　And wounds to show. You'd cleave
clean to the heart, and never think of healing?
　　Steal it, and when you leave
　　leave it? What sort of dealing,
to steal and never keep, and yet keep stealing?

　　O shorten the long days
of burning thirst – no other love allays them.
　　Let my eyes see your face,
　　treasure to daze them.
Except for love, it's labor lost to raise them.

　　If only, crystal well,
clear in your silver mirror could arise
　　suddenly by some spell
　　the long-awaited eyes
sketched in my heart of hearts, but cloudy-wise.

　　Love, cover those bright eyes!
I'm lifted! off on air!
　　　　　Come settle, dove.
　　The deer – look yonder – lies
　　hurt on the hill above,
drawn by your wing he loves the coolness of.

My love: the mountains' height,
forest ravines – their far-away recesses,
    torrents' sonorous weight,
    isles no explorer guesses,
the affectionate air, all whisper and caresses;

    night sunk in a profound
hush, with the stir of dawn about the skies,
    music without a sound,
    a solitude of cries,
a supper of light hearts and lovelit eyes.

    Our bed, a couch of roses,
guarded by lions sunning with their young;
    our room which peace encloses,
    her purple curtains swung;
our wall, with a thousand gold escutcheons hung.

    Seeing your sandal-mark
girls whirl to the four winds; their faces shine
    stung by a sudden spark,
    flushed with the glorious wine.
Their breath a very heaven – the air's divine!

    Shown deeper than before
in cellars of my love I drank; from there
    went wandering on the moor;
    knew nothing, felt no care;
the sheep I tended once are who knows where?

    There he made gently free;
had honey of revelation to confide.
    There I gave all of me;
    hid nothing, had no pride;
there I promised to become his bride.

    Forever at his door
I gave my heart and soul. My fortune too.
    I've no flock any more,
    no other work in view.
My occupation: love. It's all I do.

The bride

If I'm not seen again
in the old places, on the village ground,
    say of me: lost to men.
    Say I'm adventure-bound
for love's sake. Lost on purpose to be found.

    In the cool morning hours
we'll go about for blossoms, sweet to wear;
    match emeralds and weave flowers
    sprung in love's summer air;
I'll give for their entwining the very hair

    curling upon my shoulder.
You loved to see it lifted on the air.
    You loved it, fond beholder
    caught fascinated there;
caught fast by an eye that wounds you unaware.

    Your eyes in mine aglow
printed their living image in my own.
    No wonder, marveling so,
    you loved me, thought me grown
worthier to return the fervor shown.

    But thought me, cheek and brow,
a shade too Moorish, and were slow to praise.
    Only look this way now
    as once before: your gaze
leaves me with lovelier features where it plays.

    Now that the bloom uncloses
catch us the little foxes by the vine,
    as we knit cones of roses
    clever as those of pine.
No trespassing about this hill of mine.

    Keep north, you winds of death.
Come, southern wind, for lovers. Come and stir
    the garden with your breath.
    Shake fragrance on the air.
My love will feed among the lilies there.

She enters, the bride! closes
the charming garden that all dreams foretold her;
    in comfort she reposes
    close to my shoulder.
Arms of the lover that she loves enfold her.

    Under the apple tree,
hands joined, we spoke a promise, broke the spell.
    I took you tenderly,
    hurt virgin, made you well
where all the scandal on your mother fell.

    Wings flickering here and there,
lion and gamboling antler, shy gazelle,
    peak, precipice, and shore,
    flame, air, and flooding well,
night-watchman terror, with no good to tell,

    by many a pleasant lyre
and song of sirens I command you, so:
    down with that angry choir!
    All sweet and low
and let the bride sleep deeper. Off you go!

    Girls of Jerusalem,
now that the breath of roses more and more
    swirls over leaf and stem,
    keep further than before.
Be strangers. And no darkening our door.

    Stay hidden close with me,
darling. Look to the mountain; turn your face.
    Finger at lips. But see
    what pretty mates embrace
the passer of fabulous islands in her chase.

    The little pearl-white dove
with frond of olive to the Ark returns.
    Wedded, the bird of love
    no longer yearns,
settled above still water, among ferns.

Hers were the lonely days;
in loneliest of solitudes her nest.
    Her guide on lonesome ways
    her love – ah, loneliest,
that arrow from the desert in his breast.

    A celebration, love!   The bride
Let's see us in *your* beauty! Jubilees
    on the hill and heights above!
    Cool waters playing! Please,
on with me deep and deeper in the trees!

    And on to our eyrie then,
in grots of the rock, high, high! Old rumor placed it
    far beyond wit of men.
    Ah but we've traced it,
and wine of the red pomegranate – there we'll taste it!

    There finally you'll show
the very thing my soul was yearning for;
    and the same moment, O
    my dearest life, restore
something you gave the other day: once more

    the breathing of the air,
the nightingale in her affectionate vein,
    woods and the pleasure there
    in night's unruffled reign –
these, and the flames embracing without pain.

    With none around to see.
Aminadab the demon fled offended.
    Above, the cavalry,
    their long siege ended,
sighted the shining waters and descended.

Freedom for Community

Karl Barth

Barth delegated to his assistant Eberhard Busch the task of answering a letter, which Busch drafted under Barth's direction on 21 June 1968. The letter (under the title "Freedom for Community") was sent with over 80 other answering letters in a special edition in October 1968 to the Commission for Reform of the Penal Code in the German Federal Parliament, all federal representatives, and other interested parties in the Federal Republic of Germany. The text of the special edition appeared together with Italiaander's open letter in 1969 as the second part of a collection published by him called Neither Sickness nor Crime.

Dear Mr. Italiaander:

Professor Karl Barth has taken your letter of June 10th under consideration and is glad that you have thought to let his voice too be heard in your planned collection about the problem of homosexuals and their social station and recognition.

In fact he has once already expressed himself on this problem (*Kirchliche Dogmatik* III/4, 1951, p. 184f.)[1] – granted, in a sense which does not allow that section to seem appropriate and fitting for your collection. In order that you do not falsely evaluate or unduly stress his predominantly negative assessment of homosexual relationships there, be it briefly noted:

1) that the merely *incidental* comment made there is only to be understood and evaluated against the background of the whole *context* of that section: a context, in which K. Barth expounds the human being as creature and the command of God given in human creatureliness under one aspect of many, namely under that of "*freedom* for community." Whereby for him the primal

form of all co-human community is the (not only "nuptial," but the whole natural) counterparts of man and woman.

2) In this context homosexuality appears to him according to its *essence* as a form of *unfree* community – that is, as a conduct in which the human being closes off and retracts his freedom for community. But you may be sure that this opinion of his on this point as such implied and implies for him in principle no excuse for "defamation," let alone for (an indeed irrational) juridical "penalizing" of homosexuals (in any case as far as they do not "seduce" or "harass" others). These are not the ones he regards as really bad, but far more the emotional Phariseeism that marches in or speaks against them, whether in degrading (often inequitably applied) sections of the legal code, or in condemnatory whispers. By no means!

3) Prof. Barth is today not completely satisfied any more with his former, incidental comments and would certainly formulate them today somewhat differently – with respect to what has changed or been newly recognized since they were written down. One might also think that, *precisely* against the background of the context that God's command also wants to be perceived and followed as "freedom in community," he could, in conversation with doctors and psychologists, come to a new judgment and exposition of the phenomenon.

Naturally you would gladly hear that from him. But since he must allow all kinds of restrictions befall him as an over-82-year-old man, he does not now have the requisite time left for it. That time he thinks he ought to deploy, with the powers remaining to him, to the work on the themes and tasks that seem to him still more important. Please have a friendly understanding for that!

Sincere greetings on his behalf.
Eberhard Busch

Notes

1 English translation: Karl Barth, *Church Dogmatics*, 4 vols. in 13 part-volumes; here, vol. III, part-vol. 4 (Edinburgh: T. & T. Clark, 1961), pp. 165–6.

from The Epistle to the Romans

Karl Barth

In this famous manifesto from the beginning of the twentieth century, Karl Barth sharply distinguishes what God is doing from what the bourgeois church is doing. In the process, he identifies the idolatry of Romans 1 not with homosexuality but with excessive concern for what we would now call heterosexuality, procreation, and family.

v. 22. Professing themselves to be wise, they became fools.
The picture of a world without paradox and without eternity, of knowing without the background of not-knowing, of a religion without the unknown God, of a view of life without the memory of the 'No' by which we are encountered, has much to be said in its favour. It evokes confidence, for it is simple and straight-forward and uncramped; it provides considerable security and has few ragged edges; it corresponds, generally speaking, with what is required by the practical experiences of life; its standards and general principles are conveniently vague and flexible; and it possesses, moreover, a liberal prospect of vast future possibilities. Once the possibility that things can be *clearly seen* (i. 20) is abandoned, men are able against this background to profess that they are wise. The Night, too, has its wisdom. But, nevertheless, the vanity of the mind and the darkness of the heart still remain facts to be reckoned with. The brilliance of this unbroken wisdom cannot be maintained in the actual course of events, for they have passed inevitably under the wrath of God. That God is not known as God is due, not merely to some error of thought or to some gap in experience, but to a fundamentally wrong attitude to life. Vanity of mind and blindness of heart inevitably bring into being corrupt conduct. The

more the unbroken man marches along his road secure of himself, the more surely does he make a fool of himself, the more certainly do that morality and that manner of life which are built up upon a forgetting of the abyss, upon a forgetting of men's true home, turn out to be a lie. It is indeed not difficult to show that this is so.

vv. 23, 24. And changed the glory of the incorruptible God for an image made like to corruptible man, and to birds, and fourfooted beasts, and creeping things. Wherefore God gave them up in the lusts of their hearts unto uncleanness, that their bodies should be dishonoured among themselves.

They changed the glory of the incorruptible – for an image of the corruptible. That is to say, the understanding of what is characteristic of God was lost. They had lost their knowledge of the crevasse, the polar zone, the desert barrier, which must be crossed if men are really to advance from corruption to incorruption. The distance between God and man had no longer its essential, sharp, acid, and disintegrating ultimate significance. The difference between the incorruption, the pre-eminence and originality of God, and the corruption, the boundedness and relativity of men had been confused. Once the eye, which can perceive this distinction, has been blinded, there arises in the midst, between here and there, between us and the 'Wholly Other', a mist or concoction of religion in which, by a whole series of skilful assimilations and mixings more or less strongly flavoured with sexuality, sometimes the behaviour of men or of animals is exalted to be an experience of God, sometimes the Being and Existence of God is 'enjoyed' as a human or animal experience. In all this mist the prime factor is provided by the illusion that it is possible for men to hold communication with God or, at least, to enter into a covenant relationship with Him without miracle – vertical from above, without the dissolution of all concrete things, and apart from THE truth which lies beyond birth and death. But, on whatever level it occurs, if the experience of religion is more than a void, or claims to contain or to possess or to 'enjoy' God, it is a shameless and abortive anticipation of that which can proceed from the unknown God alone. In all this busy concern with concrete things there is always a revolt against God. For in it we assist at the birth of the 'No-God', at the making of idols. Enveloped in mist, we forget not merely that all that passes to corruption is a parable, but also that it is ONLY a parable. The glory of the incorruptible God has been confused with the image (Ps. cvi. 20) of corruptible things. Some one of the relationships of men to the objects of their fear or of their desire, to some means of their subsistence, to some product of their own thought or action, to some impressive occurrence in nature or in history, is taken to be in itself significant and of supreme importance, as though even this selected relationship were not broken by the witness it bears to the unknown Creator whose glory cannot be confused with the known glory of an image, however pure and delicate. From such supposed direct communion with God – genuine only when it is not genuine, when it is not romanticized into an 'experience', when it is at once dissolved and claims to be merely an open space, a sign-post, an occasion, and an opportunity – there emerge precisely all those intermediary, collateral, lawless divinities and powers and authorities and principalities (viii. 38) that obscure and discolour the light of the true God. In the realm of romantic direct communion – in India, for example – these divinities are thrown up in the most extravagant numbers. Wherever the qualitative distinction between men and the final Omega is overlooked or misunderstood, that fetishism is bound to appear in which God is experienced in **birds and fourfooted things,** and, finally, or rather primarily, in the **likeness of corruptible man** – Personality, the Child, the Woman – and in the half-spiritual, half-material creations, exhibitions, and representations of His creative ability – Family, Nation, State, Church, Fatherland. And so the 'No-God' is set up, idols are erected, and God, who dwells beyond all this and that, is 'given up'.

Wherefore God gave them up. The confusion avenges itself and becomes its own punishment. The forgetting of the true God is already itself the breaking loose of His wrath against those who forget Him (i. 18). The enterprise of setting up the 'No-God' is avenged by its success. Deified nature and deified spirits of men are, in truth, very gods; like Jupiter and Mars, Isis and Osiris, Cybele and Attis, they come to be the very breath of our life. Our conduct becomes governed precisely by what we desire. By a strict inevitability we reach the goal we have set before us. The images and likeness, whose meaning we have failed to perceive, become themselves purpose and content and end. And now men have really become slaves and puppets of things, of 'Nature' and of 'Civilization', whose dissolution and establishing by God they have overlooked. And now there is no higher power to protect them from what they have set on high. And, moreover, the uncleanness of their relation to God submerges their lives also in uncleanness. When God has been deprived of His glory, men are also deprived of theirs. Desecrated within in their souls, they are desecrated also without in their bodies, for men are one. The concreteness of the creatureliness of their lives becomes now dishonour; and lust – sexuality both in the narrower and in the wider sense of the word – becomes, as the primary motive-power of their whole desire and striving, altogether questionable and open to suspicion. The whole ignominy of the course of the world they must now bear and bemoan and curse as ignominy; and further, in their separation from God they must continue to give it ever new birth. They have wished to experience the known god of this world: well I they have experienced him.

vv. 25–7. They exchanged the truth of God for a lie, and worshipped and served the creature rather than the Creator, who is blessed for ever. Amen. For

*this cause God gave them up unto vile passions: for their women changed the
natural relation of the sexes into that which is against nature: and likewise also
the men, leaving the natural use of the woman, burned in their lust one toward
another, men with men working unseemliness, and receiving in their own body
that recompense of their error which was due.*

They exchanged the truth for a life. Complete rebellion from God soon
takes to itself more pronounced forms. It would not be unexpected were direct
experience of God to have occasioned some occasional and rather humorous
changes, some superficial errors, some dissolution of the Truth of God into a
number of worldly-wise maxims. But thought this is, no doubt, possible, it is
not long before the Truth is quite seriously exchanged for a lie. The tiny mist
between God and man, by which the far distance is obscured, soon becomes
a veritable sea of clouds. Some half-conscious resentment at the unknown God
very soon becomes fully conscious. The dazzled eye is soon damaged.
Principalities and powers, formerly but seldom exalted to the throne, are soon
established there, encircled with a halo of *everlasting power and divinity* (i. 20).
The Creator, the eternal Archetype, meanwhile grows ever more and more
'abstract', 'theoretical', insignificant, and unloved. The completely concrete
'No-God' has won his victory, even though there may, perhaps, remain some
bleak survival of the Unknown behind what is thought to be genuinely
significant and magnificent, some occasional reference to a final secret in the
midst of so much busy service of him whom we name 'God'. The only reality,
the unknown, living God, appears nebulous, problematical, and unreal, whereas
the world, separated from Him, and men, necessity, and reality. The world is
worshipped and served – if it be necessary, quite apart from its Creator. In
their general view of the world scientists and historians are in far closer
agreement with philosophers and theologians than is normally recognized. It
is not merely that the world exists side by side with God: it has taken His place,
and has itself become God, and demands 'the same devotion which the old-
fashioned believer offered to His God' (Dr. F. Strauss). Contradictions within
the deified world – Nature and Civilization, Materialism and Idealism,
Capitalism and Socialism, Secularism and Ecclesiasticism, Imperialism and
Democracy – are not so serious as they give themselves out to be. Such
contradictions are contradictions within the world, and there is for them no
paradox, no negation, no eternity.

For this cause God gave them up. Unbroken naturalness is not pure.
Nor are matters improved when 'naturalness' is penetrated by piety. In
'naturalness' there is always secreted that which is non-natural, and, indeed,
that which actually contradicts nature. This contradictory factor awaits the hour
when it will break forth. When, by allowing nature to run its course freely and
uncontradicted, God and the world have become confused with one another,
there comes into prominence a further confusion: what cannot be avoided or

escaped from becomes confused with some necessity of nature, and this is in very truth a demonic caricature of the necessity of God. These two confusions stand altogether on one line, they belong together and cohere together. What is at first merely open to suspicion moves inexorably on to what is positively absurd. Everything then becomes Libido: life becomes totally erotic. When the frontier between God and man, the last inexorable barrier and obstacle, is not closed, the barrier between what is normal and what is perverse is opened.

vv. 28–31.

A final and even sharper pointing of the whole situation is not only conceivable but actually takes place. In the perversity of this relation to God there still, however, remains a relic of clarity of sight, a last, warning recollection of the secret of God that withstands the arrogance of religion. A reflection of this secret lies even in the deified forces of the world, even in the deified universe itself. From time to time this bare relic of the Unknown reasserts itself in the presentiment of awe. But even this can cease. The damaged eye may become blind. Defective knowledge can become ignorance of God; it may become AGNOSIA (I Cor. xv. 34). **Even as they refused to have God in their knowledge** – That is to say, they became no longer capable of serious awe and amazement. They become unable to reckon with anything except feelings and experiences and events. They think only in terms of more or less spiritual sophistry, without light from above or from behind. – **God gave them up to a reprobate mind, to do those things which are not fitting; being filled with all unrighteousness, wickedness, covetousness, maliciousness; full of envy, murder, strife, deceit, malignity; whisperers, backbiters, haters of God, insolent, haughty, boastful, inventors of evil things, disobedient to parents, without understanding, covenant-breakers, without natural affection, unmerciful.** Here is the final vacuity and disintegration. Chaos has found itself, and anything may happen. The atoms whirl, the struggle for existence rages. Even reason itself becomes irrational. Ideas of duty and of fellowship become wholly unstable. The world is full of personal caprice and social unrighteousness – this is not a picture merely of Rome under the Caesars! The true nature of our unbroken existence is here unrolled before us. Our ungodliness and unrighteousness stand under the wrath of God. His judgement now becomes judgement and nothing more; and we experience the impossibility of men as the real and final impossibility of God.

v. 32.

It ought not to be difficult for us to perceive this sequence, but – **Knowing the ordinance of God, that they which practise such things are worthy of death, not only do the same, but also consent with them that practise them.** This is the wisdom of the Night issuing in folly (i. 22): folly, because it holds firmly to a two-dimensional plane, a plane persistently contradicted by actual occurrence. The wisdom of the Night knows whither the unbroken road is leading. It understands quite clearly the meaning of its direction and of its goal. It knows the Cause; it sees the Operation; but it dare not give the command to halt. The road of those who forget their Creator is accompanied always by a strange complaint against the frailty of human existence, and by indictments against human sinfulness. But in spite of all this, with their eyes fixed upon the earth, they affirm the edifice which is erected on it, concentrate their desire upon it, approve it, hope for its continued existence, and, regardless of every protest, constitute themselves its guardians. But why is it so difficult to remember what has been forgotten, though it is quite clear that the operation of this forgetfulness and the end of our wandering in the Night is – Death?

PART

Contemporary Philosophical Resources

Sexual Perversion

Thomas Nagel

In this famous article, the philosopher Thomas Nagel works out a phenomenology of sexual desire. That is, he tries to see how sexual desire might mean in itself, apart from functional accounts of the preservation of the species or the control of lust. What kind of perception of the other and of oneself is sexual desire, and how does it transform us? How does desire work, how does it grow, how does it bounce back and forth, how does it become mutual and reciprocal? And from such an analysis, can we form any account of how it might fail to work, or work badly, that is, be perverted, not morally, but phenomenologically, be malformed as transformative perception? Students unfamiliar with analytic philosophy have sometimes misread this article in three ways. (1) The title, "Sexual Perversion," is provocative. The primary purpose is not to talk about perversion, but to figure out what sexual desire is like when it works. Some students have leapt to the conclusion that Nagel is a theological conservative because the word "perversion" appears. That would be silly. (2) How sexual desire "works" is, to be sure, a value judgment; but it is not in the first instance a moral judgment. The genre of the article is not moral theology, but philosophical phenomenology. Nagel forms judgments first of all about what sort of perception sexual desire is. (3) That Nagel seeks to understand and explain the judgments of others on these matters does not necessarily mean that he shares those judgments; he seeks to strengthen his own account by showing that it can improve on the accounts of others.

There is something to be learned about sex from the fact that we possess a concept of sexual perversion. I wish to examine the idea, defending it against the charge of unintelligibility and trying to say exactly what about human sexuality qualifies it to admit of perversions. Let me begin with some general conditions that the concept must meet if it is to be viable at all. These can be accepted without assuming any particular analysis.

First, if there are any sexual perversions, they will have to be sexual desires or practices that are in some sense unnatural, though the explanation of this natural/unnatural distinction is of course the main problem. Second, certain practices will be perversions if anything is, such as shoe fetishism, bestiality, and sadism; other practices, such as unadorned sexual intercourse, will not be; about still others there is controversy. Third, if there are perversions, they will be unnatural sexual *inclinations* rather than just unnatural practices adopted not from inclination but for other reasons. Thus contraception, even if it is thought to be a deliberate perversion of the sexual and reproductive functions, cannot be significantly described as a *sexual* perversion. A sexual perversion must reveal itself in conduct that expresses an unnatural *sexual* preference. And although there might be a form of fetishism focused on the employment of contraceptive devices, that is not the usual explanation for their use.

The connection between sex and reproduction has no bearing on sexual perversion. The latter is a concept of psychological, not physiological, interest, and it is a concept that we do not apply to the lower animals, let alone to plants, all of which have reproductive functions that can go astray in various ways. (Think of seedless oranges.) Insofar as we are prepared to regard higher animals as perverted, it is because of their psychological, not their anatomical, similarity to humans. Furthermore, we do not regard as a perversion every deviation from the reproductive function of sex in humans: sterility, miscarriage, contraception, abortion.

Nor can the concept of sexual perversion be defined in terms of social disapprobation or custom. Consider all the societies that have frowned upon adultery and fornication. These have not been regarded as unnatural practices, but have been thought objectionable in other ways. What is regarded as unnatural admittedly varies from culture to culture, but the classification is not a pure expression of disapproval or distaste. In fact it is often regarded as a *ground* for disapproval, and that suggests that the classification has independent content.

I shall offer a psychological account of sexual perversion that depends on a theory of sexual desire and human sexual interactions. To approach this solution I shall first consider a contrary position that would justify skepticism about the existence of any sexual perversions at all, and perhaps even about the significance of the term. The skeptical argument runs as follows:

'Sexual desire is simply one of the appetites, like hunger and thirst. As such it may have various objects, some more common than others perhaps, but none in any sense "natural". An appetite is identified as sexual by means of the organs and erogenous zones in which its satisfaction can be to some extent localized, and the special sensory pleasures which form the core of that satisfaction. This enables us to recognize widely divergent goals, activities, and desires as sexual, since it is conceivable in principle that anything should produce sexual pleasure and that a nondeliberate, sexually charged desire for it should arise (as a result of conditioning, if nothing else). We may fail to empathize with some of these desires, and some of them, like sadism, may be objectionable on extraneous grounds, but once we have observed that they meet the criteria for being sexual, there is nothing more to be said on *that* score. Either they are sexual or they are not: sexuality does not admit of imperfection, or perversion, or any other such qualification – it is not that sort of affection.'

This is probably the received radical position. It suggests that the cost of defending a psychological account may be to deny that sexual desire is an appetite. But insofar as that line of defense is plausible, it should make us suspicious of the simple picture of appetites on which the skepticism depends. Perhaps the standard appetites, like hunger, cannot be classed as pure appetites in that sense either, at least in their human versions.

Can we imagine anything that would qualify as a gastronomical perversion? Hunger and eating, like sex, serve a biological function and also play a significant role in our inner lives. Note that there is little temptation to describe as perverted an appetite for substances that are not nourishing: we should probably not consider someone's appetites *perverted* if he liked to eat paper, sand, wood, or cotton. Those are merely rather odd and very unhealthy tastes: they lack the psychological complexity that we expect of perversions. (Coprophilia, being already a sexual perversion, may be disregarded.) If on the other hand someone liked to eat cookbooks, or magazines with pictures of food in them, and preferred these to ordinary food – or if when hungry he sought satisfaction by fondling a napkin or ashtray from his favorite restaurant – then the concept of perversion might seem appropriate (it would be natural to call it gastronomical fetishism). It would be natural to describe as gastronomically perverted someone who could eat only by having food forced down his throat through a funnel, or only if the meal were a living animal. What helps is the peculiarity of the desire itself, rather than the inappropriateness of its object to the biological function that the desire serves. Even an appetite can have perversions if in addition to its biological function it has a significant psychological structure.

In the case of hunger, psychological complexity is provided by the activities that give it expression. Hunger is not merely a disturbing sensation that can be quelled by eating; it is an attitude toward edible portions of the external world, a desire to treat them in rather special ways. The method of ingestion: chewing, savoring, swallowing, appreciating the texture and smell, all are important components of the relation, as is the passivity and controllability of the food (the only animals we eat live are helpless mollusks). Our relation to food depends also on our size: we do not live upon it or burrow into it like aphids or worms. Some of these features are more central than others, but an adequate phenomenology of eating would have to treat it as a relation to the external world and a way of appropriating bits of that world, with characteristic affection. Displacements or serious restrictions of the desire to eat could then be described as perversions, if they undermined that direct relation between man and food which is the natural expression of hunger. This explains why it is easy to imagine gastronomical fetishism, voyeurism, exhibitionism, or even gastronomical sadism and Masochism. Some of these perversions are fairly common.

If we can imagine perversions of an appetite like hunger, it should be possible to make sense of the concept of sexual perversion. I do not wish to imply that sexual desire is an appetite – only that being an appetite is no bar to admitting of perversions. Like hunger, sexual desire has as its characteristic object a certain relation with something in the external world; only in this case it is usually a person rather than an omelet, and the relation is considerably more complicated. This added complication allows scope for correspondingly complicated perversions.

The fact that sexual desire is a feeling about other persons may encourage a pious view of its psychological content – that it is properly the expression of some other attitude, like love, and that when it occurs by itself it is incomplete or subhuman. (The extreme Platonic version of such a view is that sexual practices are all vain attempts to express something they cannot in principle achieve: this makes them all perversions, in a sense.) But sexual desire is complicated enough without having to be linked to anything else as a condition for phenomenological analysis. Sex may serve various functions – economic, social, altruistic – but it also has its own content as a relation between persons.

The object of sexual attraction is a particular individual, who transcends the properties that make him attractive. When different persons are attracted to a single person for different reasons – eyes, hair, figure, laugh, intelligence – we nevertheless feel that the object of their desire is the same. There is even an inclination to feel that this is so if the lovers have different sexual aims, if they include both men and women, for example. Different specific attractive characteristics seem to provide enabling conditions for the operation of a single basic feeling, and the different aims all provide expressions of it. We approach the sexual attitude toward the person through the features that we find attractive, but these features are not the objects of that attitude.

This is very different from the case of an omelet. Various people may desire it for different reasons, one for its fluffiness, another for its mushrooms, another for its unique combination of aroma and visual aspect; yet we do not enshrine the transcendental omelet as the true common object of their affections. Instead we might say that several desires have accidentally converged on the same object: any omelet with the crucial characterstics would do as well. It is not similarly true that any person with the same flesh distribution and way of smoking can be substituted as object for a particular sexual desire that has been elicited by those characteristics. It may be that they recur, but it will be a new sexual attraction with a new particular object, not merely a transfer of the old desire to someone else. (This is true even in cases where the new object is unconsciously identified with a former one.)

The importance of this point will emerge when we see how complex a psychological interchange constitutes the natural development of sexual attraction. This would be incomprehensible if its object were not a particular person, but rather a person of a certain *kind*. Attraction is only the beginning, and fulfillment does not consist merely of behaviour and contact expressing this attraction, but involves much more.

The best discussion of these matters that I have seen appears in part III of Sartre's *Being and Nothingness*.[1] Sartre's treatment of sexual desire and of love, hate, sadism, masochism, and further attitudes toward others, depends on a general theory of consciousness and the body which we can neither expound nor assume here. He does not discuss perversion, and this is partly because he regards sexual desire as one form of the perpetual attempt of an embodied consciousness to come to terms with the existence of others, an attempt that is as doomed to fail in this form as it is in any of the others, which include sadism and masochism (if not certain of the more impersonal deviations) as well as several nonsexual attitudes. According to Sartre, all attempts to incorporate the other into my world as another subject, i.e. to apprehend him at once as an object for me and as a subject for whom I am an object, are unstable and doomed to collapse into one or other of the two aspects. Either I reduce him entirely to an object, in which case his subjectivity escapes the possession or appropriation I can extend to that object; or I become merely an object for him, in which case I am no longer in a position to appropriate his subjectivity. Moreover, neither of these aspects is stable; each is continually in danger of giving way to the other. This has the consequence that there can be no such thing as a *successful* sexual relation, since the deep aim of sexual desire cannot in principle be accomplished. It seems likely, therefore, that the view will not permit a basic distinction between successful or complete and unsuccessful or incomplete sex, and therefore cannot admit the concept of perversion.

I do not adopt this aspect of the theory, nor many of its metaphysical underpinnings. What interests me is Sartre's picture of the attempt. He says that the type of possession that is the object of sexual desire is carried out by 'a double reciprocal incarnation' and that this is accomplished, typically in the form of a caress, in the following way: 'I make myself flesh in order to impel the Other to realize *for herself* and *for me* her own flesh, and my caresses cause my flesh to be born for me in so far as it is for the Other *flesh causing her to be born as flesh*' (*Being and Nothingness*, p. 391; Sartre's italics). The incarnation in question is described variously as a clogging or troubling of consciousness, which is inundated by the flesh in which it is embodied.

The view I am going to suggest, I hope in less obscure language, is related to this one, but it differs from Sartre's in allowing sexuality to achieve its goal on occasion and thus in providing the concept of perversion with a foothold.

Sexual desire involves a kind of perception, but not merely a single perception of its object, for in the paradigm case of mutual desire there is a complex system of superimposed mutual perceptions – not only perceptions of the sexual object, but perceptions of oneself. Moreover, sexual awareness of another involves considerable self-awareness to begin with – more than is involved in ordinary sensory perception. The experience is felt as an assault on oneself by the view (or touch, or whatever) of the sexual object.

Let us consider a case in which the elements can be separated. For clarity we will restrict ourselves initially to the somewhat artificial case of desire at a distance. Suppose a man and a woman, whom we may call Romeo and Juliet, are at opposite ends of a cocktail lounge, with many mirrors on the walls which permit unobserved observation, and even mutual unobserved observation. Each of them is sipping a martini and studying other people in the mirrors. At some point Romeo notices Juliet. He is moved, somehow, by the softness of her hair and the diffidence with which she sips her martini, and this arouses him sexually. Let us say that *X senses Y* whenever *X* regards *Y* with sexual desire. (*Y* need not be a person, and *X*'s apprehension of *Y* can be visual, tactile, olfactory, etc., or purely imaginary; in the present example we shall concentrate on vision.) So Romeo senses Juliet, rather than merely noticing her. At this stage he is aroused by an unaroused object, so he is more in the sexual grip of his body than she of hers.

Let us suppose, however, that Juliet now senses Romeo in another mirror on the opposite wall, though neither of them yet knows that he is seen by the other (the mirror angles provide three-quarter views). Romeo then begins to notice in Juliet the subtle signs of sexual arousal, heavy-lidded stare, dilating pupils, faint flush, etc. This of course intensifies her bodily presence, and he not only notices but senses this as well. His arousal is nevertheless still solitary. But now, cleverly calculating the line of her stare without actually looking her in the eyes, he realizes that it is directed at him through the mirror on the opposite wall. That is, he notices, and moreover senses, Juliet sensing him. This is definitely a new development, for it gives him a sense of embodiment not only through his own reactions but through the eyes and reactions of another. Moreover, it is separable from the initial sensing of Juliet; for sexual arousal might begin with a person's sensing that he is sensed and being assailed by the perception of the other person's desire rather than merely by the perception of the person.

But there is a further step. Let us suppose that Juliet, who is a little slower than Romeo, now senses that he senses her. This puts Romeo in a position to notice, and be aroused by, her arousal at being sensed by him. He senses that she senses that he senses her. This is still another level of arousal, for he becomes conscious of his sexuality through his awareness of its effect on her and of her awareness that this effect is due to him. Once she takes the same step and senses that he senses her sensing him, it becomes difficult to state, let alone imagine, further iterations, though they may be logically distinct. If both are alone, they will presumably turn to look at each other directly, and the proceedings will continue on another plane. Physical contact and intercouse are natural extensions of this complicated visual exchange, and mutual touch can involve all the complexities of awareness present in the visual case, but with a far greater range of subtlety and acuteness.

Ordinarily, of course, things happen in a less orderly fashion – sometimes in a great rush – but I believe that some version of this overlapping system of distinct sexual perceptions and interactions is the basic framework of any full-fledged sexual relation and that relations involving only part of the complex are significantly incomplete. The account is only schematic, as it must be to achieve generality. Every real sexual act will be psychologically far more specific and detailed, in ways that depend not only on the physical techniques employed and on anatomical details, but also on countless features of the participants' conceptions of themselves and of each other, which become embodied in the act. (It is familiar enough fact, for example, that people often take their social roles and the social roles of their partners to bed with them.)

The general schema is important, however, and the proliferation of levels of mutual awareness it involves is an example of a type of complexity that typifies human interactions. Consider aggression, for example. If I am angry with someone, I want to make him feel it, either to produce self-reproach by getting him to see himself through the eyes of my anger, and to dislike what he sees – or else to produce reciprocal anger or fear, by getting him to perceive my anger as a threat or attack. What I want will depend on the details of my anger, but in either case it will involve a desire that the object of that anger be aroused. This accomplishment constitutes the fulfillment of my emotion, through domination of the object's feelings.

Another example of such reflexive mutual recognition is to be found in the phenomenon of meaning, which appears to involve an intention to produce a belief or other effect in another by bringing about his recognition of one's intention to produce that effect. (That result is due to H. P. Grice,[2] whose position I shall not attempt to reproduce in detail.) Sex has a related structure: it involves a desire that one's partner be aroused by the recognition of one's desire that he or she be aroused.

It is not easy to define the basic types of awareness and arousal of which these complexes are composed, and that remains a lacuna in this discussion. In a sense, the object of awareness is the same in one's own case as it is in one's sexual awareness of another, although the two awareness will not be the same, the difference being as great as that between feeling angry and experiencing the anger of another. All stages of sexual perception are varieties of identification of a person with his body. What is perceived is one's own or another's *subjection* to or *immersion* in his body, a phenomenon which has been recognized with loathing by St Paul and St Augustine, both of whom regarded 'the law of sin which is in my members' as a grave threat to the dominion of the holy will.[3] In sexual desire and its expression the blending of involuntary response with deliberate control is extremely important. For Augustine, the revolution launched against him by his body is symbolized by erection and the other involuntary physical components of arousal. Sartre too stresses the fact that the penis is not a prehensile organ. But mere involuntariness characterizes other bodily processes as well. In sexual desire the involuntary responses are combined with submission to spontaneous impulses: not only one's pulse and secretions but one's actions are taken over by the body; ideally, deliberate control is needed only to guide the expression of those impulses. This is to some extent also true of an appetite like hunger, but the takeover there is more localized, less pervasive, less extreme. One's whole body does not become saturated with hunger as it can with desire. But the most characteristic feature of a specifically sexual immersion in the body is its ability to fit into the complex of mutual perceptions that we have described. Hunger leads to spontaneous interactions with food; sexual desire leads to spontaneous interactions with other persons, whose bodies are asserting their sovereignty in the same way, producing involuntary reactions and spontaneous impulses in *them*. These reactions are perceived, and the perception of them is perceived, and that perception is in turn perceived; at each step the domination of the person by his body is reinforced, and the sexual partner becomes more possessible by physical contact, penetration, and envelopment.

Desire is therefore not merely the perception of a pre-existing embodiment of the other, but ideally a contribution to his further embodiment which in turn enhances the original subject's sense of himself. This explains why it is important that the partner be aroused, and not merely aroused, but aroused by the awareness of one's desire. It also explains the sense in which desire has unity and possession as its object: physical possession must eventuate in creation of the sexual object in the image of one's desire, and not merely in the object's recognition of that desire, or in his or her own private arousal.

Even if this is a correct model of the adult sexual capacity, it is not plausible to describe as perverted every deviation from it. For example, if the partners in heterosexual intercourse indulge in private heterosexual fantasies, thus avoiding recognition of the real partner, that would, on this model, constitute a defective sexual relation. It is not, however, generally regarded as a perversion. Such examples suggest that a simple dichotomy between perverted and unperverted sex is too crude to organize the phenomena adequately.

Still, various familiar deviations constitute truncated or incomplete versions of the complete configuration, and may be regarded as perversions of the central impulse. If sexual desire is prevented from taking its full interpersonal form, it is likely to find a different one. The concept of perversion implies that a normal sexual development has been turned aside by distorting influences. I have little to say about this causal condition. But if perversions are in some sense unnatural, they must result from interference with the development of a capacity that is there potentially.

It is difficult to apply this condition, because environmental factors play a role in determining the precise form of anyone's sexual impulse. Early experiences in particular seem to determine the choice of a sexual object. To describe some causal influences as distorting and others as merely formative is to imply that certain general aspects of human sexuality realize a definite potential whereas many of the details in which people differ realize an indeterminate potential, so that they cannot be called more or less natural. What is included in the definite potential is therefore very important, although the distinction between definite and indeterminate potential is obscure. Obviously a creature incapable of developing the levels of interpersonal sexual awareness I have described could not be deviant in virtue of the failure to do so. (Though even a chicken might be called perverted in an extended sense if it had been conditioned to develop a fetishistic attachment to a telephone.) But if humans will tend to develop some version of reciprocal interpersonal sexual awareness unless prevented, then cases of blockage can be called unnatural or perverted.

Some familiar deviations can be described in this way. Narcissistic practices and intercourse with animals, infants, and inanimate objects seem to be stuck at some primitive version of the first stage of sexual feeling. If the object is not alive, the experience is reduced entirely to an awareness of one's own sexual embodiment. Small children and animals permit awareness of the embodiment of the other, but present obstacles to reciprocity, to the recognition by the sexual object of the subject's desire as the source of his (the object's) sexual self-awareness. Voyeurism and exhibitionism are also incomplete relations. The exhibitionist wishes to display his desire without needing to be desired in return; he may even fear the sexual attentions of others. A voyeur, on the other hand, need not require any recognition by his object at all: certainly not a recognition of the voyeur's arousal.

On the other hand, if we apply our model to the various forms that may be taken by two-party heterosexual intercourse, none of them seem clearly to qualify as perversions. Hardly anyone can be found these days to inveigh against oral–genital contact, and the merits of buggery are urged by such respectable figures as D. H. Lawrence and Norman Mailer. In general, it would appear that any bodily contact between a man and a woman that gives them sexual pleasure is a possible vehicle for the system of multi-level interpersonal awareness that I have claimed is the basic psychological content of sexual interaction. Thus a liberal platitude about sex is upheld.

The really difficult cases are sadism, masochism, and homosexuality. The first two are widely regarded as perversions and the last is controversial. In all three cases the issue depends partly on causal factors: do these dispositions result only when normal development has been prevented? Even the form in which this question has been posed is circular, because of the word 'normal'. We appear to need an independent criterion for a distorting influence, and we do not have one.

It may be possible to class sadism and masochism as perversions because they fall short of interpersonal reciprocity. Sadism concentrates on the evocation of passive self-awareness in others, but the sadist's engagement is itself active and requires a retention of deliberate control which may impede awareness of himself as a bodily subject of passion in the required sense. De Sade claimed that the object of sexual desire was to evoke involuntary responses from one's partner, especially audible ones. The infliction of pain is no doubt the most efficient way to accomplish this, but it requires a certain abrogation of one's own exposed spontaneity. A masochist on the other hand imposes the same disability on his partner as the sadist imposes on himself. The masochist cannot find a satisfactory embodiment as the object of another's sexual desire, but only as the object of his control. He is passive not in relation to his partner's passion but in relation to his nonpassive agency. In addition, the subjection to one's body characteristic of pain and physical restraint is of a very different kind from that of sexual excitement: pain causes people to contract rather than dissolve. These descriptions may not be generally accurate. But to the extent that they are, sadism and masochism would be disorders of the second stage of awareness – the awareness of oneself as an object of desire.

Homosexuality cannot similarly be classed as a perversion on phenomenological grounds. Nothing rules out the full range of interpersonal perceptions between persons of the same sex. The issue then depends on whether homosexuality is produced by distorting influences that block or displace a natural tendency to heterosexual development. And the influences must be more distorting than those which lead to a taste for large breasts or fair hair or dark eyes. These also are contingencies of sexual preference in which people differ, without being perverted.

The question is whether heterosexuality is the natural expression of male and female sexual dispositions that have not been distorted. It is an unclear question, and I do not know how to approach it. There is much support for an aggressive–passive distinction between male and female sexuality. In our culture the male's arousal tends to initiate the perceptual exchange, he usually makes the sexual approach, largely controls the course of the act, and of course penetrates whereas the woman receives. When two men or two women engage in intercourse they cannot both adhere to these sexual roles. But a good deal of deviation from them occurs in heterosexual intercourse. Women can be sexually aggressive and men passive, and temporary reversals of role are not uncommon in heterosexual exchanges of reasonable length. For these reasons it seems to be doubtful that homosexuality must be a perversion, though like heterosexuality it has perverted forms.

Let me close with some remarks about the relation of perversion to good, bad, and morality. The concept of perversion can hardly fail to be evaluative in some sense, for it appears to involve the notion of an ideal or at least adequate sexuality which the perverions in some way fail to achieve. So, if the concept is viable, the judgment that a person or practice or desire is perverted will constitute a sexual evaluation, implying that better sex, or a better specimen of sex, is possible. This in itself is a very weak claim, since the evaluation might be in a dimension that is of little interest to us. (Though, if my account is correct, that will not be true.)

Whether it is a moral evaluation, however, is another question entirely – one whose answer would require more understanding of both morality and perversion than can be deployed here. Moral evaluation of acts and of persons is a rather special and very complicated matter, and by no means all our evaluations of persons and their activities are moral evaluations. We make judgments about people's beauty or health or intelligence which are evaluative without being moral. Assessments of their sexuality may be similar in that respect.

Furthermore, moral issues aside, it is not clear that unperverted sex is necessarily *preferable* to the perversions. It may be that sex which receives the highest marks for perfection *as sex* is less enjoyable than certain perversions; and if enjoyment is considered very important, that might outweigh considerations of sexual perfection in determining rational preference.

That raises the question of the relation between the evaluative content of judgments of perversion and the rather common *general* distinction between good and bad sex. The latter distinction is usually confined to sexual acts, and it would seem, within limits, to cut across the other: even someone who believed, for example, that homosexuality was a perversion could admit a distinction between better and worse homosexual sex, and might even allow that good homosexual sex could be better *sex* than not very good unperverted sex. If this is correct, it supports the position that, if judgments of perversion are viable at all, they represent only one aspect of the possible evaluation of sex, even *qua* sex. Moreover it is not the only important aspect: sexual deficiencies that evidently do not constitute perversions can be the object of great concern.

Finally, even if perverted sex is to that extent not so good as it might be, bad sex is generally better than none at all. This should not be controversial: it seems to hold for other important matters, like food, music, literature, and society. In the end, one must choose from among the available alternatives, whether their availability depends on the environment or on one's own constitution. And the alternatives have to be fairly grim before it becomes rational to opt for nothing.

Notes

1 *L'Etre et le Néant* (Paris: Gallimard, 1943), trans. Hazel E. Barnes (New York: Philosophical Library, 1956).
2 'Meaning.' *Philosophical Review* LXVI, no. 3 (July, 1957): 377–88.
3 See Romans 7:23; and the *Confessions*, bk. VIII, pt V.

Moral Abominations

Jeffrey Stout

As in the preceding essay, the title intends to provoke interest, while the exposition exposes the title category to question. Religious ethicist Jeffrey Stout draws on the work of anthropologist Mary Douglas to see how people respond to phenomena that cross their conceptual boundaries, that is, seem not to fit with the way in which they divide up the world in their heads. In such accounts, the word "anomaly" appears as a technical term. Like Nagel's use of the word "perversion," it expresses no moral disapproval. It simply identifies the statistically less prevalent or the conceptually unaccounted for. Whether what one finds less prevalent or what one's categories leave unaccounted for is of significance for how one ought to behave is another and a complex question, the answers to which vary from case to case, depending on whether the categories are good ones or not.

Suppose the action I am imagining is a harmless and highly pleasurable expression of loving respect between consenting adults bound to each other by public commitments of fidelity. Could such an action be an abomination on a par with cannibalism, bestiality, and intercourse with corpses? Evidently not, for in granting that the action brings about harmless pleasure, derives from the mutual commitment and informed consent of competent adults, and expresses loving respect, we seem to have excluded all possible grounds for a conclusion so extremely negative. Utility measures up well; no rights have been violated; both parties have been treated as ends in themselves. How could such an action be abominable? But add that the action in question is sodomy and that the adults in question are both males, and we see at once that many people would indeed view this action as an abomination.

How can this be so? The idea that such an action might be symptomatic of psychological traits we would not want to commend is perfectly intelligible, even to those liberals who would finally disagree. Yet to find such an action abominable seems like mere superstition or taboo – an attitude that cannot be explained by the presence of good reasons. Small wonder, then, that debates over homosexuality often degenerate quickly into ad hominem attacks. Each side considers the other either too irrational or too depraved to profit from reasoned argument.

Perhaps we can profit, however, from giving the notion of moral abomination more thought. We stand to learn something not only about the impasse just mentioned but also about ourselves. For most of us have experienced intense revulsion at the thought, the sight, or the artistic representation of some action Jerry Falwell would classify as an abomination. Many were the liberals who, sometime during the late 1960s, succumbed to nausea at the cinema after witnessing simulations of acts against which they had no principled objection. Where sacrilege and sodomy fail to offend, necrophilia, bestiality, and cannibalism often succeed. It behooves us to understand these reactions of ours and their possible relevance to ethical theory. We still, on occasion, use the language of abomination to express these reactions. Whatever distance we may feel from certain traditional judgments of abomination, talk of the abominable persists.

Yet recent ethical theory is virtually silent on the topic. Modern moral philosophers rarely invoke, much less systematically elucidate, the notion of abomination. When they do use the term to decry the deeds they most abhor, it seems to supply little more than rhetorical flourish. If a moral abomination is simply an especially serious violation of human rights, a particularly striking sign of disrespect for those who should never be treated as means only, or an act with unusually sweeping bad consequences, then such concepts as rights, respect, and utility, not the notion of abomination itself, will demand attention. I have already noted, however, that outside philosophy the notion of abomination sometimes plays a much more prominent role – one not always easily explained by means of the more familiar concepts of ethical theory. It belongs to a language that moral philosophers, *qua* moral philosophers, do not speak. The notion does, of course, appear prominently in the practical discourse of other cultures, including those that immediately precede our own in the history of the West. The concept is central to some strands of the biblical traditions, for example, and (as we shall see) ethical theorists working in close proximity to those traditions once felt bound to account for the specific judgments of abomination present in the biblical materials.

These thoughts raise interesting questions. Is it possible to make sense of the abominable at all? Is the notion finally unintelligible, or at best a vestige of primitive thought essentially unrelated to the realm of morality properly conceived? What explains the silence on the abominable in contemporary ethical theory? I propose to elucidate the notion of an abomination as I understand it, drawing on a theory that is by now old hat in anthropology although rarely discussed by ethical theorists. I have nothing new to add to the theory, but I do hope to show how it can be used to determine the kinds of social and cognitive contexts in which the language of abomination tends to take hold and also the kinds of contexts in which certain specific judgments of abomination are likely to be rendered. I shall then reflect briefly on the relevance of the theory to moral reflection in our context. My purpose will not be to revive the language of abomination but rather to come to grips with it philosophically. Let me begin, then, with a relatively unthreatening example of the repulsive from personal experience. This example possesses no moral interest of its own, but it will direct us toward salient features of cases that might.

I

Cabbits are said to be produced by crossbreeding. Take any cat and any rabbit meeting certain conditions of appropriateness and fecundity, subject them to the standard procedures, and (barring mishap) you will soon have a cabbit. Or so I heard one evening while watching television and read the next morning in a local tabloid. It was probably a single cabbit making the rounds. The hind parts were those of a rabbit, the head unmistakably feline. It may have been nothing more than a Manx cat with a rabbit's tail attached, but both the television producer and the newspaper editor knew that this combination would hold an audience. The televised version proved more effective because it conveyed the anomaly in more dimensions. It also afforded an opportunity to observe the responses of other observers. This cabbit was no mere object of quiet curiosity. The audience was clearly fascinated, at once attracted and repelled.

You may find all this unconvincing if the thought of a cabbit does not disconcert you. I doubt that the thought of a cabbit, by itself, would have bothered me. I have no objection in principle to cabbits. Yet the sight of a living cabbit did affect me. I found it revolting. Even the sight of a cabbit, of course, would not thus affect everyone. The question is how to explain the variation.

My daughter has never seen a cabbit. Yet I am certain she would not have found a cabbit revolting had she seen one just after her second birthday. In those days she regularly confused cats with rabbits. She had not yet learned to treat them as distinct kinds of thing, having only begun to master the requisite vocabulary. A person who lacks the concepts of cat and rabbit would not be fascinated by the anomalous combination: no distinction, no anomaly. So it is not the cabbit-in-itself or the cabbit as immediately given to the senses that offends. The offense one takes depends upon the concepts one brings to the scene.

It seems reasonable to suppose that my daughter and I then stood at opposite ends of the spectrum of attitudes toward cabbits. Unable to recognize the anomaly, those at her end of the spectrum would not be offended by cabbits. Those at my end, equipped with sharp distinctions between cats and rabbits, would be much more likely to be offended. I speculate that my daughter has moved closer to my end of the spectrum during the years since her second birthday. Sharpen someone's concepts, and they will be more likely to find the corresponding anomalies repulsive.

Repulsive perhaps, but not abominable. We need to look elsewhere for full-fledged abominations. Horror movies are full of them, as are ancient myths, folk tales, and side shows at circuses. Monsters and freaks make ideal abominations. There seems to be a recipe for constructing them – a procedure akin to crossbreeding. An abomination must be anomalous. Like the cabbit, it must combine characteristics uniquely identified with separate kinds of thing, or at least fail to fall unambiguously into any recognized class. But the recipe for abominations should include another injunction: if possible, load the anomaly with social significance. A combination of characteristics that straddles the line between *us* and *them* will be highly effective. Darwin's culture (or at least some classes within it) guarded the line between human and nonhuman. In such a culture the man-beast may well be an abomination. The elephant-man is famous; the cabbit is not. Where the line between masculine and feminine roles becomes accentuated and forms the basis of the division of labor or the rules of inheritance, we may see bearded women and hermaphrodites turning up in freak shows.

An abomination, then, is anomalous or ambiguous with respect to some system of concepts. And the repugnance it causes depends on such factors as the presence, sharpness, and social significance of conceptual distinctions. For a detailed defense and elaboration of these marks of the abominable, readers should consult the work of Mary Douglas, whose sociological reflections on the relevant ethnography inspired the approach I am taking here.[1] There is no need in this context to pursue the details of Douglas's theories or their application to specific anthropological cases. My present purposes require only a very thin conception of how the categories of someone's cosmology and social structure might render intelligible their attitudes toward abominations. I need just enough theory to stimulate reflection on how judgments of abomination might be related to what I have said in other essays about such matters as moral truth, justification, and the spectrum of relativity. We have thus far concentrated on monsters and freaks. The next task is to extend the account to abominable acts, where moral relevance may start to figure in. We should then be in a better position to address questions at the level of ethical theory.

Before going any further, however, I should enter one caveat. I have not claimed that *all* objects, events, or acts that seem anomalous or ambiguous relative to the categories of someone's cosmology and social structure will be treated by that person as abominable. Douglas and others have shown, to the contrary, that an entire range of phenomena demand explication in such terms. Leviticus proscribes eating the flesh of the pig and the hare, which fail to fit neatly into biblical cosmology. But the Lele revere the pangolin, which is similarly ambiguous relative to their concepts of natural kinds. Many sorts of defilement and even humor, according to Douglas, follow closely related patterns. Wayne Proudfoot has offered a similar explanation of mystical experience.[2]

So anomalous and ambiguous objects, events, and acts are often emotionally charged, but whether they make our eyes glaze over in rapture, our sides ache with laughter, or our stomachs turn with disgust requires further explanation. And while Douglas has much of interest to say about how these phenomena can be correlated with types of social significance, this too must be only partially developed here. All we need for my purposes is the vague notion that an anomalous or ambiguous act is more likely to seem abominable where it seems to pose, or becomes symbolic of, a threat to the established cosmological or social order. One form of humor owes its excitement to flirtation with the line between joking and obscenity or abomination. When we sense that playful inversion of the norms, which gives us the delight of momentary release from them, has given way to direct assault, we know that a comic has crossed the line.[3] Likewise, we might well revere an anomalous creature, as the Lele revere the pangolin, if its way of crossing conceptual boundaries becomes symbolic of some beneficial kind of boundary-crossing in our social life.[4] A great deal hangs, therefore, on whether the anomaly in question is viewed as a mediator between realms or as a transgressor across boundaries that guard cosmic and social order.

I shall henceforth confine the term *abomination* to transgressors (or transgressions) of this kind, ignoring any other types of abomination there might be. In a looser sense of the term, anything loathsome would count as an abomination. My (still rather loose) definition of the term is designed to abbreviate a theory in which reactions to such creatures as monsters and freaks and to such actions as cannibalism, bestiality, and homosexual sodomy are grouped together and explained along the same lines. The basic idea is this: in contexts where the anomalous or ambiguous character of an object, event, or act seems to threaten disruption of the natural-social order, rather than promising to knit that order together, the object, event, or act will be abominated. In such contexts, one should expect to find talk of abominations. To see what this idea comes to, let us now consider attitudes toward cannibalism, bestiality, and sodomy in turn.

II

A man enters a seaside restaurant, orders albatross, and is served. After a single taste of the bird, he removes a gun from his pocket, presses its barrel to his forehead, and pulls the trigger. Why? I first heard this question put while playing parlor games as a teenager. The riddler poses the problem. The audience, using only these scraps of evidence and whatever can be gleaned from the riddler's answers to yes–no questions, tries to piece together a plausible narrative making sense of the circumstances of the suicide.

Here is the solution. Three men were adrift at sea in a lifeboat. One died. The survivors had killed an albatross for food, but knew that at most one of them could stay alive until the rescue party arrived if they ate nothing but the albatross. The only other available food was the flesh of their dead comrade. Neither had ever eaten albatross before, let alone human flesh, and the thought of cannibalism appalled them. Hoping to avoid overwhelming guilt, they devised a method of culinary disguise. One would eat the albatross; the other, human flesh. But neither would know which he was eating. The disguise worked, at least for the time. By keeping them ignorant, it held their consciences at bay. After the rescue, however, our protagonist found a way to satisfy his curiosity. He went to the restaurant because he knew that a taste of albatross would tell him what he had eaten on the lifeboat. If the taste was unfamiliar, he must have been eating human flesh at sea. Otherwise, his conscience would be clear. As it turned out, the taste was unfamiliar, and he shot himself dead.

Notice that this puzzle would make sense only in a culture that treated cannibalism as utterly repulsive. If the audience cannot recognize the protagonist's discovery as a plausible reason for his suicide, the puzzle falls flat. The reason need not be compelling, yet it must be plausible. But what did our hero have to feel guilty about? He had not taken his comrade's life. He had, indeed, saved a life (his own) by taking his comrade's flesh for food. So the balance of utility was favorable. It is certainly not clear that he had violated anyone's rights. The puzzle remains plausible even if we stipulate that the dying comrade expressed the hope that the others would eat his remains rather than starve at sea. Why? Because our hero's sense of guilt is akin to defilement. His concern is not simply for his comrade but also for himself. His action has stained him. He is repulsed at the thought of himself. The abominable act has made him abominable.

My hypothesis is that cannibalism offends us for the same reason that the thought of becoming a werewolf does: it threatens our unambiguous status as human beings. A creature that usually resembles humans in all respects but, when the moon is full, becomes more wolflike than human has slipped into an ambiguous position between heretofore delimited classes. The same thing happens, in our culture, to cannibals. Being unambiguously human entails, for us, a kind of dietary restraint. Some objects in the environment count as food, others do not. Ingestion of the wrong objects threatens one's status as human. Eating dirt or feces is degrading in the straightforward sense that it puts you in a different (lower) class. Eating human flesh strays outside the normative diet in another direction, but the effect is the same – to render the diner's status as a human insecure. Nonhuman carnivores make no bones about eating human flesh. To eat human flesh is to become like them, to straddle the line between us and them, to become anomalous.

None of this applies in the same way, of course, where the line between us and them – between members of the community and outsiders – is drawn in a different place. Some vegetarians embrace a community that extends well beyond the confines of our species. Jain monks have been known to go further, including even most vegetables as members of the community. Jains abominate most human meals. I would be surprised if they singled out cannibalism for special disapprobation. At the other extreme, there are tribal societies whose moral community excludes most of humanity. The line between us and them is drawn tightly around the tribe itself, and no broader conception of the species appears to be present. If such a tribe were to practice cannibalism (whether such tribes actually exist is highly disputed in the scholarly literature), it would not surprise me if their victims were always strangers while making meals of one's kin was fully abominated.

I am tempted to generalize by inverting Feuerbach's dictum that you are what you eat. As far as social identity goes, what you eat is what you are not. Most societies define themselves in part by proscribing the use of their members as food. Violation of this proscription threatens the boundary of the social order. Not every society, however, defines its boundary with a sharp line. A society that does not will, if I am right, show relatively little concern over cannibalism. Its attitude toward cannibals will be like a toddler's attitude toward cabbits. It takes sharp lines to bring anomalies into focus. Most societies impose sexual as well as dietary constraints upon their members, and restraint in the use of sexual organs is often at least as important as proper habits of ingestion in maintaining identity as a member of the group. Sexual intercourse with beasts, like eating human flesh, is beastly. It calls into question one's social identity.

I have argued that the social identity of the cannibal is the basic issue at stake when a social group abominates cannibalism. Respect for the dead might be seen as the real issue: cannibalism is simply a kind of desecration of corpses. While cannibalism may be that as well, I want to insist on the centrality of the cannibal's social status. The parallel to bestiality strengthens my case, for bestiality is structurally similar to cannibalism but also simpler. To whom does bestiality show disrespect? Surely not the beast. When the shepherd's lust takes his flock as its object, it is the shepherd, not the flock, that we fear for. What we fear, I suggest, is that the shepherd has become too beastly to maintain a firm grip on his social identity. His abominable act has made him an abomination. The violated sheep, on the other hand, is not an end-in-itself and therefore makes no claim on the shepherd's respect for persons. If our shepherd has shown disrespect for anyone, it must be himself. What makes the action abominable is its degrading character – its capacity, within some social settings, to make the agent himself seem (or be) less human.

Sodomy,[5] like bestiality, involves a use of sexual organs that can render one's social identity anomalous or ambiguous, but, unlike both bestiality and cannibalism, it does not concern the line between human and nonhuman or the boundary of the social structure. On this score, sodomy is more like the bearded woman and the hermaphrodite in its relation to the distinction between masculine and feminine roles. The line that becomes crucial here is one internal to the social structure, not the external boundary. Once again, I assume that the line must be both sharp and socially significant if trespassing across it is to generate a sense of abomination. Attitudes toward homosexuality can be expected to vary accordingly. The sharper the line between masculine and feminine roles and the greater the importance of that line in determining matters such as the division of labor and the rules of inheritance, the more likely it is that sodomy will be abominated.

So once again, as with cannibalism and bestiality, social identity is at stake, although the issue is access to stereotypically defined roles, not membership in the group. If your society defines masculine and feminine roles, as many do, partly in reference to socially legitimated uses of sexual organs, then sexual activity of the wrong kind can threaten your claim to play a certain role. You become, in effect, a social anomaly – ambiguous with respect to the partition of available roles. You become, that is, the social equivalent of a monster – an object of abomination.

John Boswell has recently contrasted attitudes toward homosexuality in two general types of social organization, which he calls urban and rural.[6] According to Boswell, urban societies, which "are characteristically organized in political units which transcend kinship ties" (p. 34), tend to show more tolerance of homosexuality than do rural societies, in which kinship structures are the primary or sole elements of social organization. But Boswell is bothered by exceptions to the rule. He grants that the growth of intolerance of homosexuality in Catholic Europe during the late middle ages seems to have nothing to do with his distinction between urban and rural societies. In fact, urbanization was increasing along with intolerance. He also grants that some rural societies – in particular, nomadic societies such as bedouins and American Indians – "are generally favorable to gay people." Boswell therefore concludes that his "generalizations must be viewed with extreme caution." He even laments that the "complexity of human existence must inevitably frustrate efforts at logical analysis . . ." (p. 36).

That may well be true, but the problem with Boswell's analysis is that his contrasting types give only a crude description of the relevant features of social structure. What matters, if I am right, is the line between masculine and feminine roles: how sharply it is drawn, how much and what kind of social significance it has, and how stereotypical definitions of these roles harness sexual activity to socially legitimated purposes. Clearly, Boswell's distinction between urban and rural societies is insufficiently subtle to handle the crucial variables. A society in which political units transcend kinship ties might still display the very features that, on my view, tend to make homosexuality seem abominable. And a society in which kinship ties remain primary might lack these features. To transcend kinship ties in some respects by introducing political structures of a certain kind is not necessarily to supplant a sharp distinction between masculine and feminine roles stereotypically defined or to make such a distinction socially insignificant. By the same token, to place the entire burden of social organization on the structure of the extended family is not necessarily to make everything depend on an exhaustive and mutually exclusive distinction between masculine and feminine roles or to establish stereotypical conceptions of these roles that will make homosexual activity seem anomalous.

Boswell points out, when listing counterexamples to his generalizations, that some rural societies "recognize homosexual marriages, as long as one partner agrees to play the role of wife" (p. 34 n. 63). Such societies, on my account, maintain the line between male and female roles, although without defining these roles specifically in reference to the possession of male and female sexual organs. Male roles are not restricted to men; female roles are not restricted to women. In such societies, homosexuals will have clearly defined roles to play, so they will probably not seem utterly anomalous. Nor is this the only way of providing homosexuals with clearly defined roles. Some rural societies keep the distinction between masculine and feminine roles in place while setting aside additional roles specifically restricted to homosexuals.[7] The distinction between standard masculine and feminine roles need not be exhaustive. In such a social setting, homosexuals are marginal but not anomalous. They constitute an independent kind with its own defining traits. They are not likely to be abominated.

So much, then, for cannibalism, bestiality, and sodomy. The account could easily be extended to cover other acts often thought to be abominable, such as incest (which might be called the familial equivalent of cannibalism) and the pointless or sadistic murder of innocents (acts so gruesome, like the recent carving of crosses in the body of a nun, or so massively destructive, like those which set the holocaust in motion, that we hesitate to call them human). I leave speculation on such matters to my readers, assuming that my approach is relatively clear. The next task is to draw out some implications of the foregoing discussion for ethical theory.

III

I shall begin by making a couple of remarks reminiscent of points made before by Rodney Needham.[8] The first is that, given what I said in chapter 3 [of *Ethics After Babel*, from which this chapter is excerpted] about the relativity of expressibility, we should not expect our terms for the various kind of prohibited acts we have been considering (such as *cannibalism, bestiality*, and *sodomy*) to have exact equivalents in every culture we wish to compare with our own. The significance of such a term, and of the proscriptions in which it appears, will depend on features of social and cognitive context that may well frustrate attempts at cross-cultural comparison. It is misleading to speak, say, of prohibitions of sodomy without making clear that these prohibitions do not necessarily comprise a definite class. Some cultures may lack the concept of sodomy altogether; others may possess only inexact equivalents of our term. Any responsible comparison must proceed cautiously and with all possible sensitivity to context. The same point would apply, as I hinted briefly in an earlier chapter, to a concept like slavery.

The second remark is related to the first. Part of the context in which prohibitions appear consists of permissions and prescriptions. As Needham says, it is "methodically defective" to consider only prohibitions.[9] Judgments of abomination are typically the reverse side of affirmative valuations and cannot be understood without keeping these in mind. This point bears on the relativity of justification. A table of abominations tends to appear pointless, and therefore especially lacking in justification, if it is considered apart from the positive value of a harmonious social and cosmic order.

Abominable acts sometimes overpower us with a sense of revulsion that does not lend itself readily to discursive elaboration. The reason should now be clear. We occasionally have trouble saying anything coherent about the abominable precisely because of its anomalous or ambiguous character. The more severe the anomaly or ambiguity at hand, the more paradoxical and mysterious our speech is apt to become. This helps explain not only the character of our revulsion, given the uneasiness that can be produced whenever coherent interpretation of experience is impossible,[10] but also the suspicion that the very notion of abomination is somehow beyond comprehension.

We need not conclude, however, that this notion is unintelligible. To treat the abominable as a cultural artifact and our sense of revulsion as a function of cognitive context is to make sense of them, to demystify, to render the repellent approachable. This does not mean, of course, that we cease to experience revulsion in the face of ambiguous or anomalous phenomena. I still find cannibalism repulsive, theory or no theory. But we are in a better position to ask dispassionately what status our sense of revulsion should have in moral deliberation.

Revulsion tends to be immediate in this sense: we do not normally arrive at revulsion as we arrive at the conclusion of an argument, by moving through a series of inferential steps. We may therefore be tempted to think of our responses to the abominable as a kind of prelinguistic given – an incorrigible datum to which any ethical theory must be held responsible. In fact we do, as noted in the previous two chapters, tend to demand that ethical theories account for our deepest moral feelings and hunches. Any theory that cannot explain what seem to be the paradigmatic cases of evil hardly deserves credence. Philosophers have often spoken of these deepest moral feelings and hunches as deliverances of the moral sense or as a species of intuitive cognition. Alternatively, the immediacy of the experience and its insusceptibility to discursive elaboration can be taken as grounds for suspicion. We may fear that sheer revulsion is too primitive to be trusted and too mute to be factored into deliberation. The experience of revulsion is to ethical theory as mystical experience is to philosophical theology. The same aspects of the experience that can make it seem foundational and revelatory can also make it seem nonsensical or superstitious, depending on one's philosophical leanings.

I happily grant that revulsion need not involve inference. It can, in that sense, be immediate. I also grant that we do (and should), in most cases at least, hold ethical theories accountable to our deepest feelings and hunches, including our sense of revulsion in the face of the abominable. But the other conclusions do not follow. We need not think of revulsion as prelinguistic or incorrigible, as a product of an unchanging moral sense, or as a species of intuitive cognition. Nor need we simply reject it out of hand as blind emotion that must remain forever unintelligible. Indeed, if my account is correct, these additional conclusions must be false, for they are incompatible with the context-dependence of responses to the abominable.

I said early on that it is not the prelinguistic cabbit that offends. Responses to cabbits are neither incorrigible intuitions nor blind emotions, however primitively noninferential they may seem. They depend, to the contrary, on a (usually unacknowledged) cognitive context. So too with responses to other abominations, including abominable acts. We can understand these responses if we set them in their context – the network of cosmological and social categories relative to which some phenomena are bound to seem anomalous or ambiguous. We see at once that the responses are hardly a matter of blind emotion. They are thoroughly informed by cognitive categories, the categories of a moral language infused with cosmological and sociological assumptions.

Nor are the responses incorrigible. Change the relevant network of categories enough, and you will alter the list of abominable acts while redirecting the corresponding sense of revulsion.

The intuitionist and the theorist of moral sense leave us at the mercy of our feelings and hunches. The answer is not, however, to ignore feelings and hunches altogether. Without them, ethical theory loses contact with the data of moral experience. But we need not merely accept feelings and hunches as given. The myth of the given is as naive and misleading in morals as it is in science. Even the most immediate perception is, in either arena, deeply implicated in cognitive context. To recognize this is to begin to achieve critical distance from the data we employ to test the theories we inherit and devise.

Most of us in the modern West share roughly the same sense of revulsion to cannibalism. Those of us who do not share this sense typically lack any motive for opposing the popular conclusion that cannibalism is morally abominable. In such an instance, we have little reason to theorize. Deeply felt and widely shared revulsion is reason enough for the conclusion. Theorizing would not strengthen the case. Cannibalism would become significant to theory only if theories devised for other purposes could not account for it. We might then be forced to decide whether the theories should be emended or the revulsion should be taken less seriously.

The issue is quite different with homosexuality, where some of us feel deep revulsion and others feel none at all. Rational disputation breaks down quickly in circumstances where the moral data against which one group tests its theories are not even recognized by another. What we need in such instances is the critical leverage an explanatory theory can provide. We want to know where the intuitions in question come from and how they may be assessed. It is here that my account should prove useful.

The debate over homosexuality need not end in appeals to conflicting intuitions. What requires defense, if I am right, is the battery of categories that gives rise to an intuition in the first place. If the issue is genuinely in dispute, it is not enough to appeal to one's own sense of revulsion (or lack thereof) and leave it at that. For the revulsion itself derives from antecedent commitment to categories that are themselves subject to dispute. The question is not whether homosexuality is intrinsically abominable but rather what, all things considered, we should do with the relevant categories of our cosmology and social structure. Addressing this question at all places us squarely within what Levi identifies as the "circular motion" of a moral tradition. If we wish to address it self-consciously, we shall need an account of the forces at work in the reconfiguration of our tradition's moral languages over time.

Traditional Christian natural law theory may be viewed (in part) as an attempt to explain and justify specific judgments of moral abomination by explicitly defending the corresponding features of cosmology and social structure. Contrary to the standard interpretation of Aquinas's ethics, he rarely used natural-law categories to justify specific moral judgments.[11] But when he turned to "unnatural vice," including bestiality and sodomy, natural-law categories become central to his argument. Unnatural vice, he said, is especially ugly because it conflicts with "the natural pattern of sexuality for the benefit of the species":

> Take any class of objects grouped together for comparison, and the worst of them all will be that which saps the basis on which all of them rest. The lines along which our minds work are those consonant with the nature of things; the fundamentals have been laid down for us by nature, we have to start with these, the presuppositions which our later development must respect. This is true of both theory and practice. A mistake in our thinking about the inborn principles of knowledge goes to the very bottom, and so does a practice opposed to the pattern set for us by nature.

Unnatural lust is the gravest kind of lust, then, because it "flouts nature by transgressing its basic principles of sexuality." Of the unnatural sins of lechery, "The greatest is that of bestiality, which does not observe the due species. . . . Afterwards comes sodomy, which does not observe the due sex."[12]

These are clearly the words of a man who recognized, and sought to explain, the connection between his table of abominations and a broader context of cosmological and social assumptions and categories. Whatever fault we find with the theory of natural law that Aquinas uses to frame his explanation – and I would be inclined to find much fault – it must be admitted that he is locating debate at the proper level. He does not merely appeal to an inarticulate sense of revulsion. He attempts to justify his revulsion in relation to his conception of the seams of the moral universe. If that conception can be sustained, the moral import of the revulsion would be established.

The social and cosmological categories of Aquinas's moral language have eroded greatly over the intervening centuries, and they were hardly unquestioned by his contemporaries. It would be hard for us to assume, as he did, that they are simply "laid down for us by nature" as "presuppositions which our later development must respect." My point, in any event, is not to defend Aquinas but rather to show that the notion of moral abomination does make sense when set within a context of assumptions and categories like his. If we wish to explain why the notion of abomination came to be neglected in ethical theory, the answer will surely lie, at least in part, in whatever makes our context different from his, in a story of the erosion, for example, of sharp lines between masculine and feminine roles.

Yet the erosion has not been complete – or, for that matter, uniform – and that is why the language of abomination is still with us and why it still repays philosophical scrutiny with morally relevant insight. If we dismiss it as entirely foreign, hoping to elevate ourselves above the "primitive" or "religious" thinkers of previous generations, we fail to come to terms with important features of our own moral experience. Most of us do abominate cannibalism, bestiality, and necrophilia. And even those of us who do not abominate homosexuality often interact with subcultures in which the language of unnatural vice and moral abomination survives as a primary means for appraising sexual activity. We had better try to understand them as well as ourselves.

Such subcultures, of course, are more prone to produce Jerry Falwells than academic ethical theorists. Ethical theorists of the kind I had in mind tend to hail, by the time they have become ethical theorists, from communities and subcultures in which the line between masculine and feminine roles has become blurred or is self-consciously viewed as provisional. Any such context is unlikely to prove hospitable to the attitudes Aquinas felt obliged to account for. So we should not find it surprising that the language in which modern moral philosophers frame their moral judgments differs from the languages in which Aquinas, the author of Leviticus, and Jerry Falwell have framed theirs.

We can understand their concepts, if we put our minds to it and learn enough about their use of words and their way of life. The notion of abomination is not so foreign that we lack the needed linguistic resources to translate their sentences. The relativity of expressibility is no barrier. We can also sensibly say that specific judgments of abomination we would not be inclined to make were justified under the circumstances in which Aquinas and the author of Leviticus found themselves. So the relativity of justification can help us avoid charging such people with irrationality by allowing us to understand the concepts and reasons at their disposal. What, then, about truth and falsity? Can we sensibly say of such people that their judgments about which acts or agents count as abominable were false? Can we meaningfully criticize people and actions in distant cultures or epochs as truly abominable, intending by this something more than the idea that we find them abominable or that they are revolting to us?

I do not see why not. At least some of the judgments of abomination we make seem to fall roughly where judgments about evil do on the spectrum of relativity.[13] When the Nazis made lampshades out of the skins of their human victims, that was truly abominable. I would be prepared to say the same thing about members of some more distant culture if they engaged in similar practices. In saying so, I would be doing more than simply reporting how things seem to me, although I would of course be presupposing that the line between human and nonhuman ought to have moral significance and that there are certain ways in which human beings (and their remains) shouldn't be treated. If members of a distant culture said that their (Nazi-like) treatment of their victims wasn't abominable, I could surely judge them wrong. I needn't simply call attention to differences in sensibility to explain why a practice they find morally indifferent is abominable "for us" and leave it at that, as if truth weren't at issue. And I wouldn't, unless judging them wrong had no point.

Supposing that the notion of the abominable is less central to our moral language than it used to be, we still need to determine why it should be virtually absent from, and not merely a marginal concept within, present-day moral philosophy. Why doesn't it receive at least some attention from theorists like Nielsen and Donagan? The answer, if I am on the right track, must have to do with the literary and argumentative means by which moral philosophers constitute their subject matter. But what made those means seem appropriate to so many philosophers throughout the modern period? To answer this question, we need to return to the issue of secularization raised in [an earlier chapter].

Rights, respect, and utility gained virtually exclusive priority in moral thought precisely when appeals to a wide range of assumptions and categories in the traditional ethos of our predecessor culture became more likely to generate conflict than agreement. Recoiling from Reformation polemics and the religious wars, modern ideologues and ethical theorists increasingly had good reason to favor a vocabulary whose sense did not depend on prior agreement about the nature of God and the structures of cosmos and society ordained by him. That the favored notions were abstracted from that same ethos should not surprise us. Neither should the fact that the resulting abstractions are ill-suited to interpret or explain much of the moral revulsion sustained by remnants of that ethos which still survive. But that these abstractions have powerfully influenced how many of us think and speak about morality can hardly be denied.

Early modern ethical theorists disagreed rather little about cannibalism, bestiality, and the like. But as religious discord grew, they found it necessary to devise a language in which highly contentious social and cosmological categories and assumptions would no longer be presupposed. Ethical theory, by sticking to this more austere language, drew a relatively tight circle around morality. That is, it gave itself a more narrowly delimited topic to be a theory of – a topic that looks more like the one Donagan tries to mark off than the one Aristotle discussed in his *Ethics* or Aquinas discussed in his *Summa*. With much of the old context no longer simply taken for granted, a notion like that of the morally abominable, which derives its intelligibility from features of a context in which certain lines are both sharp and socially significant, was bound to become less central. The sense that the abominable has something to do with morality came to seem paradoxical. The abominable and the moral now fell in distinct cultural spheres. Ethical theorists have consequently felt less and less comfortable about rendering judgments of abomination – especially, perhaps, in the area of sexual conduct, where the increasingly contested line between masculine and feminine roles assumes importance.

Kant, here as elsewhere, is the great transitional figure, the author who did more than anyone else to differentiate morality from other cultural domains. Like most of his immediate predecessors and contemporaries, he still experienced intense revulsion at the thought of bestiality and homosexuality, but the radical contraction of the moral sphere to which his own moral philosophy gave expression left him without the means to defend this revulsion convincingly or to explain it. A latter-day Kantian like Donagan, while granting that Kant had "put into words the horror of irregular sexual activity that appears to underlie both Jewish and Christian condemnations of it," concludes that his arguments "verge upon hysteria." Donagan finds Aquinas's arguments "more dispassionate," but "no more persuasive."[14]

My conjecture is that Aquinas, Kant, and Donagan represent, respectively, three crucial stages of the history of the abominable in ethical theory: an initial stage in which the abominable not only makes sense but occupies a central position in ethical theory; a transitional stage in which ethical theorists still largely share their gardeners' sense of revulsion at standard examples of the abominable but no longer find themselves able to defend this response except with raised voices; and a third stage in which much of the revulsion has come to seem alien and groundless, a datum even ethical theorists sympathetic to Jewish and Christian tradition are more concerned to explain away than to explain. To test this conjecture comprehensively would require a breadth of sociological and historical knowledge I lack. And it is surely possible that the ideas I have been borrowing from anthropology will have more trouble withstanding the scrutiny of comparative ethicists than I suppose. But if my hunches about the abominable are borne out by further inquiry, we will have clear confirmation of the need to make ethics more sensitive to its own history, the value of prying open the aperture through which we have been looking at that history, and the importance of tracing the fate and influence of religious assumptions and categories if we are to understand that history well.

Notes

1 Mary Douglas, *Purity and Danger* (London: Routledge & Kegan Paul, 1966); *Natural Symbols* (New York: Vintage Books, 1973), esp. ch. 3; and *Implicit Meanings* (London: Routledge & Kegan Paul, 1975).
2 Wayne Proudfoot, *Religious Experience* (Berkeley and Los Angeles: University of California Press, 1985).
3 See Douglas, *Implicit Meanings*, ch. 7.
4 Ibid., ch. 17.
5 For a discussion of the ambiguity of the term *sodomy*, see John Boswell, *Christianity, Social Tolerance, and Homosexuality* (Chicago: University of Chicago Press, 1980), p. 93

n. 2. I shall use the term to refer only to homosexual anal intercourse.

6 Ibid., pp. 31–6, 91, 119–21, 169–70, 208–9, 270.

7 See Boswell's reference (p. 34 n. 63) to the institution of the *berdache* among American Indians.

8 Rodney Needham, *Remarks and Inventions* (London: Tavistock, 1974), pp. 61–71. I owe this reference to Alasdair MacIntyre.

9 Ibid., p. 68.

10 See Proudfoot's development of this theme in *Religious Experience, passim.*

11 My interpretation of Aquinas is influenced by many conversations with my colleague, Victor Preller.

12 St. Thomas Aquinas, *Summa Theologica*, trans. Blackfriars (New York: McGraw Hill, 1968), 2a2ae. 154, 11.

13 I claim only that some such judgments fall there. Others might fall elsewhere on the spectrum. Some, for example, might presuppose what Harman calls inner judgments, thereby partaking in their relativity to an agent's reasons. Moreover, the issue might be complicated in other ways, for example by what Wong calls environmental relativity.

14 Alan Donagan, *The Theory of Morality* (Chicago: University of Chicago Press, Phoenix edn., 1979), p. 105.

PART

Nuptial Hermeneutics, Or What Marriage Means

The Crisis of an Ethic without Desire

Sebastian Moore, OSB

Sebastian Moore, a Benedictine monk, has one of the profoundest understandings of human sexuality, proving Rowan Williams's comment that the "extraordinary experiment" of Christian celibacy in community "does seem to be 'justified in its children,' " because, "paradoxical as it sounds, the celibate calling has, as one aspect of its role in the Christian community, the nourishing and enlarging of Christian sexuality."

In this essay, Moore argues two surprising theses. (1) In going to his death, Jesus is motivated by desire and not its denial. (2) Adam and Eve do not experience shame after the fall because their bodies are disobedient. Rather, their minds are disobedient, in that they want to be like God. Their bodies remain obedient in continuing to act in an appropriate, creaturely way. This obedience of their bodies makes Adam and Eve ashamed, because they do not want to be proved creatures, they want to be gods. Their bodies tell the truth, and give them the lie.

The crucifixion of Jesus with its pneumatic sequel is the final liberation of desire into the divine union that all desire is groping toward. But when we ask how these two realities, the saving cross of Jesus and human desire, have been connected historically, we get an amazing answer. First of all, we find in our history a systematic distrust and suppression of desire. Alice Miller's devastating account of this has already been referred to. From generation to generation, "what I feel I want" has been thrust from the child's mind by what Miller calls poisonous pedagogy. And philosophy since Descartes, for all its emancipatory intention, is virtually silent on desire. The amazing thing is that the cross of Jesus has been presented to us not as our liberation from this repressive mind, but as its endorsement! How has it come about?

Basically, there is the misunderstanding of suffering, the failure to distinguish between the suffering we bring on ourselves by our refusal to grow – by sin, in other words – and the suffering that growth itself entails. Of course they are intertwined, inextricably, but they are nonetheless distinct, and spiritual progress is discernibly the slow prevailing of transformative over ego-centered pain. Failure to observe this distinction makes "bearing the cross" mean bearing the suffering our sins deserve, and although this is called sharing in the suffering of Jesus which is *un*deserved, it is never made clear how our deserved suffering connects with his undeserved suffering. Nor can it be, for if the predominant idea of suffering is as something deserved by our sin as opposed to something inherent in our participation in a transcendence-oriented universe, what is the meaning of undeserved suffering? So suffering with Jesus means undergoing the suffering our sins deserve, with Jesus the sinless sufferer as our model. This hardly makes sense, but the words of the penitent thief suggest themselves here: "We are getting our just deserts, but what evil has he done?" If he who did no wrong accepts this suffering, *how much more* should we sinners accept ours! There is a kind of logic to this, but it does not take us far.

And what does it mean, to suffer what we deserve? It means, to this commonsense way of thinking, to suffer *for following our desires*. Jesus, it is implied, suffers not for following his desires but to fulfill the will of God.

The truth is surely that Jesus does suffer for following his desires. That is what the cross is all about. His desire, totally liberated toward union with God, totally resonant with God's will, draws upon him the vengeance of an unliberated and fearful world. And he draws us to follow him on this *via crucis*, this way of liberated desire in an unliberated world.

Once we see it this way, the sufferers for undenied desire, in their prisons all over the world, the Gandhis, the Kings, the Mandelas, who speak for the desires of the oppressed millions, come out of the Limbo to which a decadent Christianity has consigned them: men and women who have dared to desire. (From what a distance we admire them in movies like *A World Apart!*)

So what we learn from the cross is, not to deny our desires, to push them down, but on the contrary to *attend* to them, to ask of them, What *do* I want? and hence to begin to learn the difference between the compulsive, unfree, addictive movements that go by the name of desire and give desire a bad name, and the élan vital in us of which these movements are the arrest, the dead-ending; the difference between the desire of the ego to stay where it is and simply to repeat past satisfactions, and the desire that can say, "I want to want more," and that alone leads to suffering with Christ. Martin Luther King, Jr., suffered with Christ the desire for his people's dignity in a world that denied it.

What we learn from the cross is the difference between liberation *from* desire (the latter equated with the insatiable self-promoting ego) and liberation *of* desire from the chains of my customary way of being myself. Two contrary views of asceticism present themselves here. The conventional view is that it means denying ourselves things we want. A more discerning and disconcerting view is that it means dropping things we no longer want, admitting to ourselves we no longer want them, and thus giving our journey, our story, a chance to move on – to which our Pauline "old self" puts up a far greater resistance than to more seemingly self-afflicting deprivations that often minister to the ego.

Of course it is difficult to see the cross this way, and seems to be stretching meanings. There's the figure on the cross, naked and abandoned. And there's Paul saying, "Those who belong to Christ have crucified the flesh with its appetites" and "If by the Spirit we have put to death the deeds of the flesh we shall live" and "The spirit lusts against the flesh, the flesh against the spirit." And there's *The Imitation of Christ*. In vain do the Scripture scholars tell us that by "the flesh" Paul means our insatiable egoism that must utterly die if we are to come out of the half-life that goes for life in normal society. We know what the flesh is. It is sex. And we know what the spirit means. It means prayer and so forth. Yet such an interpretation will not bear examination once we ask, Did God create sex and say "That's good!" or didn't he? The idea that one of God's principal prophets is telling us to choose one half of God's creation and reject the other half is ludicrous. But still it won't go away, that naked tortured figure.

And God forbid that it should go away! A therapy I am using with myself is to switch from Jesus for the time being, and think about Nelson Mandela and those twenty-five unrecoverable youthful years spent behind bars. I ask myself, Does he put me to shame for my enjoyment of life "while he's in there"? Yes, but this is a cover story. Really, he puts me to shame for risking so little. Risk is the refusal to forget desire.

A comment suggests itself, in this connection, on *A Course in Miracles*. This charismatic, and extraordinarily prolific, "word" from a contemporary mystic takes the form of Jesus speaking to us today. The main theme is that our emphasis on the cross has been a huge mistake, and Jesus apologizes for giving rise to it. And, apart from this text, how often we meet that phrase "emphasis on the cross," generally used to deplore this emphasis. Of course what we are running into here is precisely this ruinous identification of the crucifixion with the negation of desire, of creativity, of the élan vital, whereas it is precisely the liberation of these things into the eternal life that is the heart of the universe. And the identification of the cross with repression stems from the deeper error of thinking of suffering only from the standpoint of the ego, never from the standpoint of transformation. The moralistic cross is the cross without transformation, without grace, without resurrection.

It is because we do not understand desire but equate it with egoism, that we see the cross of Jesus as opposed to it. Real desire is what the cross empowers, bringing us to the death that its liberation entails. The death is the death of our present ego, whose perpetuation is the work of egoism posing as desire.

Real desire, what I really want and have always wanted, is to be more and more myself in the mystery in which I am. It is the relatedness that I am to everything and everyone in the mystery, trying to realize itself. Desire is love trying to happen. It is the love that permeates all the universe, trying to happen in me. It draws into its fulfilling meaning all the appetites of our physical being. It turns the need for shelter into the sacrament that is a house. It turns the need for food and drink into – well, Babette's Feast! And it turns sexual passion into – ah, there we have a problem. The sentence ends with "marriage," and this is true. But the biggest ethical gap in the Christian tradition is the failure to say anything much as to *how* that taking up of sexual passion into authentic desire, of which marriage is the institutionalizing, happens.

What is authentic sexual desire, celebrated by the Song of Songs and in the first chapters of Genesis? To begin with, it is odd that we have no easy, comfortable common word for it. "Sexual desire" is very stilted. On the other hand, there are plenty of colloquialisms for it, but they all belong to what Renee Haynes once brilliantly called the shadow language. But there is nothing in between, in the world of "*Buon appetito!*" "That's because this is sacred." Oh, give me a break! Anyway, we're stuck with "sexual desire."

No desire is so prone to self-deception, to the very subtlest ploys of our egoism, as is sexual desire. No desire, therefore, is in such need of being understood correctly. But for no desire is this need less met by our Christian tradition.

Sin, misinterpretation of our godness,
Raises the spirit high above the flesh,
Looks with contempt at its resulting oddness:
So shame is born, and seeks to make redress.

With shame as teacher, we confound confusion
Asking of what we have to be ashamed.
Thus we accept as leader an illusion
And look around for what ought to be blamed.

We find the flesh at fault, blaming the victim
Of our impatient grab at what is ours,
Godhead in flesh: and when he came, we sticked him:
Even after his triumph, our heart cowers.

Will nothing teach us we are freed from sin?
Still under shame, we think we have to win.

But we must make an observation here. It is quite unhistorical simply to blame the Christian tradition, for the latter merely reflects an erotic incoherence deeply embedded in the culture. Indeed the charge against the Christian tradition here is of its failure to do much more than reflect this incoherence, indeed its tendency to capitalize on it, to say, You are right to be confused, repressive, fearful. The situation is further confused today, in a culture that appears to be anything but confused, repressive, and fearful, but is none the less so. The church's attitude to sexuality mirrors the fear and, above all, the hopelessness, in the culture. We must not mistake the mirror for a beacon. The beacon is Jesus on his cross made revelatory and gracious in Resurrection. The church needs to model her thinking about sexuality on this "dangerous memory" and not on our unconscious negative beliefs about life.

There is a very long history behind this basing of Christian moral doctrine on the bias of the culture. In the fourth century, when Christianity found itself the religion of the empire, it was necessary to elaborate a systematic ethic, and the one at hand was Stoicism. This regarded pleasure as not lawful in itself, only when had in the pursuit of a worthy end. The end, in the case of sexual pleasure, was procreation. Thus – and this is the point – sexual enjoyment did not have its own value, only the permission it got from the real value, procreation. And thus, when sexual moral problems presented themselves, the mutual enjoyment of husband and wife was not among the values that had to be respected and made space for. This lacuna became dramatically evident when, at Vatican II, questions were addressed to the traditional ban on contraception. As we know, the rest is history, and with *Humanae Vitae* the traditional ban was upheld.

Now what the copious discussion that preceded and, even more, followed *Humanae Vitae* brought to light was the intellectual and spiritual poverty of the Catholic tradition on sexuality. A morality evolved by celibates, it showed the fact in failing to see the joy of sex as a crucial factor. So our doctrine on sexuality, at last revealing the bankruptcy of a doctrine based not on Jesus the liberator of desire but on a very narrow human philosophy, is crying out for its true basis, the mystery of Christ crucified and risen.

The present pope is the first pope to attempt this. A few years ago, he devoted his weekly audiences for a whole year to building up a theory of sexuality on the first three chapters of Genesis, read with the eyes of a philosopher and man of profound faith. These talks were edited, paraphrased, and usefully commented upon by Mary Durkin, in a book entitled *Feast of Love: Pope John Paul II on Human Intimacy* (Loyola University Press, 1986).

The fundamental idea behind these talks is that the first three chapters of Genesis, heard with faith, offer a perspective on sexuality that is far wider and deeper than that to which we are accustomed. Further, there is a theological reason why we are accustomed to the narrower view with all the conflicts and contradictions it engenders: the Fall.

What the Fall means, according to Pope John Paul, is that we are very poorly in touch with our sexuality as it truly is, as it images the creating Godhead. To get a glimpse of this true perspective, we have to consider what the story is telling us, first about the deep existential solitude of the human being, which calls us into "partnership with the Absolute," and which reveals the partnership of man and woman as a sharing in this aloneness and partnership with God. Adam's ecstatic cry on seeing the woman – "Behold, bone of my bone, flesh of my flesh!" – is a prelude to the Song of Songs. Of this sublime condition, of intimacy in God, sexual union is the expression. This is the reinstatement of sexual union in its full context, the mystery of our transcendence-oriented and Christ-illuminated humanity. The connecting of Adam's cry "Bone of my bone, flesh of my flesh!" with the lyrics of the Song of Songs is a beautiful poet's touch. We are certainly in a world different from the standard papal pronouncement on sex.

Now the pope stresses with what great difficulty this full meaning of sexuality is realized in our present, fallen condition. And this raises a question: How do we know when we *are* realizing this intimacy with God? In other words, what *is* this full sexual experience? Is there anything in *sex as we know it,* "fallen" though it is, that evidences the beauty of sexual union as a covenantal expression? Or is there only *the idea* of a divinely shaped union, *of* which our sexual experience is the always deficient expression?

I keep getting the feeling, reading these profound reflections, that their author does not believe that there *is* any clue to the sublime reality in sexual experience itself. In reflection on one's body in its maleness or femaleness, its essential incompleteness, yes; in the mysteriousness of the union of two in one flesh, yes. But in *sex,* as we enjoy and suffer it? Somehow, no. That never comes through. This is a phenomenology of sexuality, descriptive of its intentionality. But we are light years away from the world of D. H. Lawrence. I mean that there is no feeling for the area of experience for which Lawrence has found such memorable words. Of course I don't want the pope to write like Lawrence! It's just that when I think of Lawrence, and then read this text, I get the feeling that, though phenomenological and existential, it really is not talking about what Lawrence is talking about at all.

Wondering why this was so, and seeking clues in this dense text, I came upon something that I believe may be the clue. It occurs, not surprisingly, where the moment of the Fall is being explored. John Paul's interpretation of this moment is as follows. The result of disobedience to God is that the harmony, in the human being, between the "higher" and the "lower" nature is lost. It is in the treatment of this lost harmony that I find the clue I have been seeking.

A loss of harmony may – and must, if we are to avoid a fatal distortion – be considered both as a failure of the "lower" to obey the "higher" *and* as a failure of the "higher" to befriend the "lower." But it is only the failure of the "lower" to obey that is considered. For what happens in the pope's account is that they eat the fruit, that is, disobey God, and as a result experience the lustful rebellion of their lower nature, *as a result of which experience* they are filled with shame and cover their sexual organs.

The Genesis story, on the other hand, features the corresponding failure of the "higher" to befriend the "lower." In fact, it makes this failure the key to the whole thing: they eat the fruit, and "immediately their eyes were opened, and they saw that they were naked." Ironically, the would-be god whom the serpent has duped finds the evidences of his/her own animality embarrassing. The thematic connection between shame and the act of disobedience is made no less than three times in the narrative. Before the event, it is said that "they were naked together, and knew no shame." In the event itself, their eyes are opened to their nakedness. And later, in the evening, God says, "Who told you you were naked?" This hubris-inspired embarrassment at being sexual is the experience of the fallen condition. Certainly the "lower nature," thus outlawed, gets its own back by behaving like the outlaw it now is – and this is lust. In other words, it is shame that sets the stage for lust. In the pope's account, it is the other way round: lust generates shame. He insists that "man is ashamed of his body because of lust."

This idea has serious consequences. Shame emerges as an appropriate reaction to the disorder of lust, whereas in the biblical account shame is how sexuality looks to the human pretending to be God; it is the looking down on sexuality that is the immediate effect of claiming divinity as one's own. What disappears from the account of original sin when we follow the pope's order of "shame because of lust" is the notion of sin *consisting in contempt for the flesh.* What is lost to view is that a failure to honor sexual union as an experience is the hubris of original sin. Much of traditional Catholic thinking on sexuality falls into this trap. The "sex, ugh!" of the fallen Adam becomes the "sex, ugh!" of the church. This is that reflecting by the church of the culture's attitude to sex, of which I was speaking just now.

The notion of shame is very tricky. There are the things one ought to be ashamed of, such as cowardice, treachery, lust. And there are the things being ashamed of which indicates a disorder, such as poverty, a humble family background, sexuality. The shame in the Genesis story is clearly and emphatically of the latter sort, and it says so three times. It is precisely the story of how shame comes to be where it should not be. To hear it as talking about a situation where shame *should* be – that is, a lustful situation – is to exclude from consideration just what the story is so forcefully presenting: the inappropriateness, in the divine perspective, of shame to sexuality. What we see of sex, in the story of the Fall as presented by Pope John Paul, is sex as shameful, but not the way the story intends, but rather the way he intends, that is, as shameful because of lust. "Man is ashamed of his body because of lust" is repeated twice in the text. But what the story is saying is that man is ashamed of his body because *it* remains faithful to God in being what it is while man tries to be God. To confuse this latter shame with the shame we appropriately feel over lust, to confuse inappropriate shame with appropriate shame, is ruinous, and grounds the negative view of sexuality out of which the Christian tradition is at last trying to grow.

These profound meditations are seeking in the Genesis account a deeper and truer perspective on sex. Yet at the crucial point where the Fall is dramatized as involving a subtle disesteem of our sexual experience, the implication is missed. What the biblical text can say to us here is not "Sexual experience is not what God meant it to be" but something more like "Beware of downgrading sex in your quest for God. Beware of Neoplatonism. It is not quite Christian."

One of the most significant moments at Vatican II was when the imperative of attention to people's sexual experience as an indispensable unitive value in the human community was thrust upon the representatives of a 2,000-year-old celibate tradition – when, in other words, the above implication of the story of the Fall became operative in the council's collective mind. The context was the debate on birth control. Could the value enshrined in sexual union be made subservient to a very rigid and long-unquestioned understanding of natural law? Patriarch Maximos, an octogenarian, suggested that church authority suffered from a "bachelor psychosis." Cardinal Suenens warned the fathers that we might, if we persisted in the traditional attitude to contraception, have another Galileo case on our hands, which might be one too many. And Charles Davis, a *peritus* at the council, told the press that evening. "Today, my role as a theologian changed."

The plunge was not taken. The birth control question was taken out of the council's hands and given to a papal commission, whose virtually unanimous vote for change was ignored. Not one of the small minority against change upheld the traditional doctrine. Their only argument was, "If we change, no one will ever believe in the authority of the church again," a prophecy ironically fulfilled by what has followed the decision *not* to change. It has been demonstrated sociologically that a far greater exodus of people from the American church can be traced to the encyclical *Humanae Vitae* than to any other of the many possible factors of our changing time.

In sum, the reason the pope's biblical mirror to sexuality does not show sexual experience as we know it, fallen though we are, as valid and revelatory of God, is that where the biblical text shows our fallenness to consist precisely in the downgrading of sexuality, with which we are only too familiar, the pope does not follow the text. On the contrary, by inverting the text's order of shame and lust, he gets *from* the text a downgrading of sexual experience. He sees the downgrading of sexual experience as *justified* by the fact of the Fall, whereas this downgrading *is* the Fall in its immediate effect. In short, he reads the text as justifying the attitude which the text is telling us we must deplore.

This is really the crux of the matter. The split between the lower and the higher nature happens in losing touch with the mystery I am in. That is to say, it is an *attitudinal* split. It is what the world gets to feel like when I am no longer in the mystery. The story captures this "consequential attitude" beautifully: "and immediately their eyes were opened." This means that "what the world looks like" – sexuality alienated and untrustworthy, for instance – is an illusion consequent upon the deepest alienation. It is not a new normative state of affairs. Original sin is not a regime. It is not a new quasi nature superimposed on the original. It is something we have to *allow for*, and massively, in our assessment of social and political situations – indeed it can turn politics into something like a dramatized lie, as in current electioneering – but it is not something to be *consulted*. To treat it as a regime is to succumb to it.

The Council of Trent fought to maintain the goodness of nature despite the Fall, against the tragic Christianity of the reformers. It is perhaps the acid test of Catholicity, closely allied with the dearly held consonance of faith with reason. But it needs to be recovered today in the context of a much more subjective understanding of the human condition. Any notion of original sin suggesting that it is a new norm resists this necessary advance into ever-living and unchanging truth.

I am not saying we can undo the Fall. I am saying that we have to learn from it, and that we do not learn from it by promoting the very attitude of shame at sex that results from the Fall. A correct reading of the text will demote, not promote, this attitude. Of course sexual shame is part and parcel of our condition. But a theology that fails to see farther than this is not faithful to "the oracles of God."

And I am not saying that any casual sexual experience is revelatory of God. I am saying that where sexual experience *is* so revelatory, it is so in the delightful way it happens, and not in the deep speculations of philosophy. This is the crux, of course. Whenever the Vatican talks of sex, it never seems to have in mind what people experience as sex, what they experience sex as. The gulf is always there. It was very nearly bridged at that historic moment during Vatican II, to which I have referred.

It is perhaps because this interpretation of Genesis reinstates, reestablishes, this gulf between the sexual reality and sexual theologizing, that the present pope has felt able to reverse the trend that followed *Humanae Vitae*, namely, the benign attitude of some national hierarchies to contraception, which has been authority's way of admitting, at last, the laity's experience as crucial in this whole affair. The sharp difference between the tone of Pius XI's *Casti Connubii* (1930) and that of the national hierarchies following the birth-control encyclical has not been sufficiently marked – least of all by the hierarchies themselves! It must be recalled, now that the supreme authority seems to be recovering the confidence of *Casti Connubii*. To anyone who is wondering how this can be happening, I would commend a close study of this profound text.

Nevertheless, with this text of a reigning pope, an important step is taken toward the recognition of sexual desire as an ethical value. And amidst all the press hoopla let loose by his statement that husbands should not lust after their wives, no one noticed that, for the first time in church history surely, a reigning pontiff was admitting that rape could happen in marriage. But the step was not completed, and the effect of this, curiously, is to reinforce the position before the step was taken. In the larger context of a millennial position based on Stoicism, the step was a momentous one, and this may account for the retreat. Feeling the heat of the fire, the hand is sharply withdrawn.

So the step has still to be taken. Only when it is, only when sexual desire is understood, by that massively powerful force Catholic tradition, in the light of Christianity's and humanity's central mystery, will the church be empowered to critique the appalling sexual derailment of our time. And the role of the Petrine office, which is to bring together the huge creative forces in Christianity, needs to be exercised here. It may turn out that one advantage of modern secularism, a good blown by this otherwise ill wind, is to render no longer attractive the pursuit of ecclesiastical power, which is the main obstacle to the emergence of the massive spiritual power of the church centered in Rome, the only worldwide and world-old institution that is committed to changing the world.

Once the step is taken, discrimination occurs. Sexual desire is no longer seen in a primitive and undifferentiated way as a powerful force that has to be curbed, but as a value that needs to be fostered. For desire as personal and person-oriented is not something automatic. On the contrary, it requires patient labor involving the deep differences between man and woman. "The difference between [me and my husband]," said a woman to psychologist Lillian Rubin, "is that for me foreplay begins at breakfast." The axiom explored earlier in this book [*Jesus the Liberator of Desire*, 1989, from which this chapter is reproduced], that real desire desires its own increase and is spiritual ("pneumatic") and not easily discovered in oneself, applies above all to sexuality. The most dramatic, indeed comic, instance of cross-purposes between the Vatican and the married, is that the Vatican sees the problem as one of curbing desire, whereas the married know that the problem is to keep desire going, which means to keep it growing, which means deepening. As Andrew Greeley puts it, the Vatican warns against "unbridled passion." When will they realize that the problem with most marriages is bridled passion? We all desire to be desired by one we desire, but the fulfillment of this longing involves much dying to ego. It is nothing less than the transition from the way ego wants to be desired – the ego still pursuing its childhood agenda – to the realization of my desirableness as a person, as a creature, as a body, as a disclosure of God. It means coming to that desire which flows out of the fullness of my being in the mystery that grounds all that is.

Finally, a word about St. Augustine. It is customary to lay the blame for much of the church's negative view of sexuality on St. Augustine. We all know Rosemary Reuther's protest to the effect that fifteen centuries dominated by the problem of Augustine's penis is enough. Actually, the way Augustine relates lust to original sin looks very like the notion I am using in critiquing Pope John Paul's notion of lust, for he sees sexual lust as a *subset* of the much more fundamental *libido dominandi* ("the impulse to dominate"). In other words, it derives from that trying to be God that is the essence of the Fall. And there is not all that much difference between contempt for sexuality and the use of sexuality to further one's ego-project. Lust, then, is not sexual passion out of the control of the will, but sexual passion acting as a cover-story for the will to be God.

This is well illustrated in Iris Murdoch's recent novel *The Good Apprentice*. Harry Cuno has an affair going with Midge, the wife of Tom McCaskerville. The affair has lasted two years, and Harry is bringing enormous pressure on Midge to tell Tom, get a divorce, and start a "real" marriage with him. After Murdoch, in her inimitable way, has had events shake up the human kaleidescope, the pieces settle with Midge deciding that she really does love Tom and their 12-year-old Meredith, and she tells Harry. The latter responds with a series of letters in which the rhetoric of passion excels itself. He writes, "I cannot and will not accept what you say. Please be clear about this. I will not accept it and you do not mean it. This is, how strange, my first love letter to you," and much more in this vein. Finally Midge replies with a single line, "No. I am sorry. No." And then Harry realizes, quite simply, that he has lost. And then comes the vague thought that there will be others. The hounds of passion have been called off by the ego, which thus reveals that it has been calling the shots all along. His love turns out to have been an extremely sophisticated form of lust.

So I'm inclined to say, "Hands off Augustine!" (In general, we've got to get beyond this trendy theology, Elaine Pagels and all that.) He tasted God, and while this did not result, as with Rabbi Akiba, in his getting sex straight, it did teach him that getting sex wrong came from trying to *be* God; that lust means not getting sex straight, and does not just mean letting sex rip. He cannot be invoked as the perpetrator of the great anomaly, of a desire that joins man to woman and creates the human future, yet of whose *intrinsic* holiness no account is given, whose need to be joined with deep life-commitment is insisted upon while the relational nature of this desire which *leads* it to seek commitment is not clarified; the anomaly, in short, of a lyric about which the only language we have is the language of control, of a hedonistic God proclaimed by a forbidding church.

The task before us is not to subject sexual passion to the will, but to restore it to desire, whose origin and end is God, whose liberation is of God's grace made manifest in the life, teaching, crucifixion, and Resurrection of Jesus Christ.

The wonder of arousal
Has never ceased to be
A source of speculation
Whose place is he and she.

Long before man or woman
Were lettered, self-aware,
Passion arose between them
Of quality so rare:

Alone among the passions
This one was ecstasy:
Alone it made two persons
Dream of eternity.

These two characteristics,
Pleasure and permanence,
Stood out, and holy mystics
Joined them without offense.

Most have preferred to keep them
In line as best they could,
Which wasn't very well – still
We must try to be good.

The Church that pushed our thinking
In other regions far,
In this one was most timid,
Her preference to bar.

Why ecstasy seeks bonding
She did not ask, invoked
Rather her power God-given
To keep the couple yoked.

The anomaly stays with us,
Stays our becoming whole:
A high, God-given lyric
Whose language is control.

Unplumbed is the resentment
Of those who know the joy
And hear the Church propounding
As though it were a toy.

But the discovery of sexuality in the light of desire seeking liberation in Christ is part of a wider strategy of recovery and discovery. In the next chapter *[of Moore's book], we shall ask the more far-reaching questions, How may we liberate the mind from the traps in which our senescent Western culture is caught? What are the traps? How did we get into them? How do we get out of them?

from The Original Unity of Man and Woman: Catechesis on the Book of Genesis

Pope John Paul II

In a series of Wednesday talks at the Vatican, Pope John Paul II works out a profound "nuptial hermeneutics," or discourse of the signification of bodies in communion. Many of the authors in this volume work out the thesis that sexuality is first of all somehow for God; it is a reflection of the fact that before human beings desire one another, God loves and desires them. John Paul puts this in a particularly graphic way: "God, according to the words of Holy Scripture, penetrates the creature, who is completely 'naked' before Him: 'And before him no creature is hidden, but all are open (panta gymna *[naked] and laid bare to the eyes of him with whom we have to do' (Heb. 4:13)." Even more surprisingly, this "penetration," which can sound so male-centered, need not be, because as John Paul also notes, "This characteristic belongs in particular to Divine Wisdom," usually gendered feminine, and associated with the Second Person of the Trinity, quoting Wis. 7:24: "Wisdom . . . because of her pureness pervades and penetrates all things" – which might better be translated "pervades (*dieko*) and envelopes (*choreo*, spread, make room for, hold, contain) all things." Thus the human being is bound for the beatific vision of God, because God sees the human being as good, that is, with desire. It is for this reason that the human being is granted "a body that expresses the person," because it is bound for a nuptial community, whether the marriage to which the adjective "nuptial" refers is one between human beings or between the human being and God.*

Man's vision of God

5. The whole biblical narrative, and in particular the Yahwist text, shows that the body through its own visibility manifests man and, manifesting him, acts as intermediary, that is, enables man and woman, right from the beginning, "to communicate" with each other according to that *communio personarum* willed by the Creator precisely for them. Only this dimension, it seems, enables us to understand in the right way the meaning of original nakedness. In this connection, any "naturalistic" criterion is bound to fail, while, on the contrary, the "personalistic" criterion can be of great help. Genesis 2:25 certainly speaks of something extraordinary, which is outside the limits of the shame known through human experience and which at the same time decides the particular fullness of interpersonal communication, rooted at the very heart of that *communio*, which is thus revealed and developed. In this connection, the words "they were not ashamed" can mean (*in sensu obliquo*) only an original depth in affirming what is inherent in the person, what is "visibly" female and male, through which the "personal intimacy" of mutual communication in all its radical simplicity and purity is constituted. To this fullness of "exterior" perception, expressed by means of physical nakedness, there corresponds the "interior" fullness of man's vision in God, that is, according to the measure of the "image of God" (cf. Gn. 1:17). According to this measure, man "is" really naked ("they were naked": Gn. 2:25),[1] even before realizing it (cf. Gn. 3:7–10).

We shall still have to complete the analysis of this important text during the meditations that follow.

Creation as Fundamental and Original Gift

General audience of January 2, 1980.

1. Let us return to the analysis of the text of Genesis (2:25), started some weeks ago. ("And the man and his wife were both naked and were not ashamed." Gn. 2:25)

According to this passage, the man and the woman see themselves, as it were, through the mystery of creation; they see themselves in this way, before knowing "that they are naked." This seeing each other is not just a participation in "exterior" perception of the world, but has also an interior dimension of participation in the vision of the Creator Himself – that vision of which the Elohist text speaks several times: "God saw everything that he had made, and behold, it was very good" (Gn. 1:31).

Seeing each other

"Nakedness" signifies the original good of God's vision. It signifies all the simplicity and fullness of the vision through which the "pure" value of humanity as male and female, the persons means existing in a mutual "for," in a relationship of mutual gift. And this relationship is precisely the fulfillment of "man's" original solitude.

Effected by love

3. This fulfillment is, in its origin, beatifying. It is certainly implicit in man's original happiness, and constitutes precisely that happiness which belongs to the mystery of creation effected by love, which belongs to the very essence of creative giving. When man – "the male," awakening from the sleep of Genesis, sees man – "the female," drawn from him, he says: "This at last is bone of my bones and flesh of my flesh" (Gen. 2:23). These words express, in a way, the subjectively beatifying beginning of man's existence in the world. Since it took place at the "beginning," this confirms the process of individuation of man in the world, and springs, so to speak, from the very depths of his human solitude, which he lives as a person in the presence of all other creatures and all living beings *(animalia)*.

This "beginning" belongs, therefore, to an adequate anthropology and can always be verified on the basis of the latter. This purely anthropological verification brings us, at the same time, to the subject of the "person" and to the subject of the "body-sex." This simultaneousness is essential. If, in fact, we dealt with sex without the person, the whole adequacy of the anthropology, which we find in the Book of Genesis, would be destroyed. And for our theological study the essential light of the revelation of the body, which appears so fully in these first affirmations, would then be veiled.

Body expresses person

4. There is a deep connection between the mystery of creation, as a gift springing from love, and that beatifying "beginning" of the existence of man as male and female, in the whole truth of their body and their sex, which is the pure and simple truth of communion between persons. When the first man exclaims, at the sight of the woman: "This is bone of my bones, and flesh of my flesh" (Gn. 2:23), he merely affirms the human identity of both. Exclaiming in this way, he seems to say: here is *a body that expresses the "person"!*

Following a preceding passage of the Yahwist text, it can also be said that this "body" reveals the "living soul," such as man became when God Yahweh breathed life into him (cf. Gn. 2:7), as a result of which there began his solitude before all other living beings. Precisely by traversing the depth of that original solitude, man now emerges in the dimension of the mutual gift, the expression of which – and for that very reason the expression of his existence as a person – is the human body in all the original truth of its masculinity and femininity.

The body, which expresses femininity, manifests the reciprocity and communion of persons. It expresses it by means of the gift as the fundamental characteristic of personal existence. This is the body: a witness to creation as a fundamental gift, and so a witness to Love as the source from which this same giving springs. Masculinity – femininity – namely, sex – is the original sign of a creative donation and of an awareness on the part of man, male-female, of a gift lived so to speak in an original way. Such is the meaning with which sex enters the theology of the body.

Called "nuptial"

5. That beatifying "beginning" of man's being and existing, as male and female, is connected with the revelation and discovery of the meaning of the body, which can be called "nuptial." If we speak of revelation and at the same time of discovery, we do so in relation to the specificness of the Yahwist text, in which the theological thread is also anthropological, appearing, in fact, as a certain reality consciously lived by man.

We have already observed that the words which express the first joy of man's coming to existence as "male and female" (Gn. 2:23) are followed by the verse which establishes their conjugal unity (Gn. 2:24), and then by the one which testifies to the nakedness of both, without mutual shame (Gn. 2:25). Precisely this significant confrontation enables us to speak of the revelation and at the same time the discovery of the "nuptial" meaning of the body in the very mystery of creation.

This meaning (inasmuch as it is revealed and also conscious, "lived" by man) confirms completely that the creative giving, which springs from Love, has reached the original consciousness of man, becoming an experience of mutual giving, as can already be seen in the archaic text. That nakedness of both progenitors, free from shame, seems also to bear witness to that – perhaps even specifically.

Blessing of fertility

6. Genesis 2:24 speaks of the finality of man's masculinity and femininity, in the life of the spouses-parents. Uniting with each other so closely as to become "one flesh," they will subject, in a way, their humanity to the blessing of fertility, namely, "procreation," of which the first narrative speaks (Gn. 1:28). Man comes "into being" with consciousness of this finality of his own

masculinity-femininity, that is, of his own sexuality. At the same time, the words of Genesis 2:25: "they were both naked, and were not ashamed," seem to add to this fundamental truth of the meaning of the human body, of its masculinity and femininity, another no less essential and fundamental truth. Man, aware of the procreative capacity of his body and of his sexuality, is at the same time free from the "constraint" of his own body and sex.

That original nakedness, mutual and at the same time not weighed down by shame, expresses this interior freedom of man. Is this what freedom from the "sexual instinct" is? The concept of "instinct" already implies an interior constraint, similar to the instinct that stimulates fertility and procreation in the whole world of living beings (*animalia*). It seems, however, that both texts of the Book of Genesis, the first and the second narrative of the creation of man, connected sufficiently the perspective of procreation with the fundamental characteristic of human existence in the personal sense. Consequently the analogy of the human body and of sex in relation to the world of animals – which we can call analogy "of nature" – is also raised, in a way, in both narratives (though in a different way in each), to the level of "image of God," and to the level of the person and communion between persons.

It will be necessary to dedicate other further analyses to this essential problem. For the conscience of man – also for modern man – it is important to know that in those biblical texts which speak of the "beginning" of man, there is found the revelation of the "nuptial meaning of the body." But it is even more important to establish what this meaning expresses precisely.

The Man-Person becomes a Gift in the Freedom of Love

General audience of January 16, 1980.

1. Let us continue today with the analysis of the texts of the Book of Genesis, which we have undertaken according to Christ's line of teaching. Let us recall, in fact, that in the talk about marriage He referred to the "beginning."

The revelation, and at the same time the original discovery of the "nuptial" meaning of the body, consists in presenting man, male and female, in the whole reality and truth of his body and sex ("they were naked") and at the same time in full freedom from any constraint of the body and of sex. The nakedness of our progenitors, interiorly free from shame, seems to bear witness to this. It can be said that, created by Love, that is, endowed in their being with masculinity and femininity, they are both "naked" because they are free with the very freedom of the gift.

This freedom lies precisely at the basis of the nuptial meaning of the body.

The human body, with its sex, and its masculinity and femininity seen in the very mystery of creation, is not only a source of fruitfulness and procreation, as in the whole natural order, but includes right "from the beginning" the "nuptial" attribute, that is, the capacity of expressing love: that love precisely in which the man-person becomes a gift and – by means of this gift – fulfills the very meaning of his being and existence. Let us recall here the text of the last Council, where it is declared that man is the only creature in the visible world that God willed "for its own sake," adding that this man "can fully discover his true self only in a sincere giving of himself."[2]

2. The root of that original nakedness free from shame, of which Genesis 2:25 speaks, must be sought precisely in that complete truth about man. Man or woman, in the context of their beatifying "beginning," are free with the very freedom of the gift. In fact, to be able to remain in the relationship of the "sincere gift of themselves" and to become such a gift for each other through the whole of their humanity made of femininity and masculinity (also in relation to that perspective of which Genesis 2:24 speaks), they must be free precisely in this way.

We mean here freedom particularly as mastery of oneself (self-control). From this aspect, it is indispensable in order that man may be able to "give himself," in order that he may become a gift, in order that (referring to the words of the Council) he will be able to "fully discover his true self" in "a sincere giving of himself." Thus the words "they were naked and were not ashamed" can and must be understood as the revelation – and at the same time rediscovery – of freedom, which makes possible and qualifies the "nuptial" sense of the body.

3. Genesis 2:25 says even more, however. In fact, this passage indicates the possibility and the characteristic of this mutual "experience of the body." And it enables us furthermore to identify that nuptial meaning of the body *in actu*. When we read that "they were naked and were not ashamed," we indirectly touch almost the root of it and directly already the fruits. Free interiorly from the constraint of his (her) own body and sex, free with the freedom of the gift, man and woman could enjoy the whole truth, the whole self-evidence of man, just as God Yahweh had revealed these things to them in the mystery of creation.

This truth about man, which the conciliar text states precisely in the words quoted above, has two main emphases. The first affirms that man is the only creature in the world that the Creator willed "for its own sake"; the second consists in saying that this same man, willed by the Creator in this way right from "the beginning," can find himself only in the disinterested giving of himself. Now, this truth about man, which seems in particular to grasp the original condition connected with the very "beginning" of man in the mystery of creation, can be reread – on the basis of the conciliar text – in both directions. This rereading helps us to understand even more the nuptial meaning of the body, which seems inscribed in the original condition of man and woman (according to Genesis 2:23–5) and in particular in the meaning of their original nakedness.

If, as we have noted, at the root of their nakedness there is the interior freedom of the gift – the disinterested gift of oneself – precisely that gift enables them both, man and woman, *to find one another*, since the Creator willed each of them "for his (her) own sake" (cf. *Gaudium et spes*, 24). Thus man, in the first beatifying meeting, finds the woman, and she finds him. In this way he accepts her interiorly: he accepts her as she is willed "for her own sake" by the Creator, as she is constituted in the mystery of the image of God through her femininity; and, reciprocally, she accepts him in the same way, as he is willed "for his own sake" by the Creator, and constituted by him by means of his masculinity. The revelation and the discovery of the "nuptial" meaning of the body consists in this. The Yahwist narrative, and in particular Genesis 2:25, enables us to deduce that man, as male and female, enters the world precisely with this awareness of the meaning of his body, of his masculinity and femininity.

4. The human body, oriented interiorly by the "sincere gift" of the person, reveals not only its masculinity or femininity on the physical plane, but reveals also such a value and such a beauty as to go beyond the purely physical dimension of "sexuality."[3] In this manner awareness of the nuptial meaning of the body, connected with man's masculinity–femininity, is in a way completed. On the one hand, this meaning indicates a particular capacity of expressing love, in which man becomes a gift; on the other hand, there corresponds to it the capacity and deep availability for the "affirmation of the person," that is, literally, the capacity of living the fact that the other – the woman for the man and the man for the woman – is, by means of the body, someone willed by the Creator "for his (her) own sake," that is, unique and unrepeatable: some one chosen by eternal Love.

The "affirmation of the person" is nothing but acceptance of the gift, which, by means of reciprocity, creates the communion of persons. The latter is constructed from within, comprising also the whole "exteriority" of man, that is, everything that constitutes the pure and simple nakedness of the body in its masculinity and femininity. Then – as we read in Genesis 2:25 – man and woman were not ashamed. The biblical expression "were not ashamed" directly indicates "the experience" as a subjective dimension.

5. Precisely in this subjective dimension, as two human "egos" determined by their masculinity and femininity, both of them, man and woman, appear in

the mystery of their beatifying "beginning" (We are in the state of man's original innocence and at the same time, original happiness). This appearance is a short one, since it comprises only a few verses in the book of Genesis; however it is full of a surprising content, theological and anthropological at the same time. The revelation and discovery of the nuptial meaning of the body explain man's original happiness and, at the same time, open the perspective of his earthly history, in which he will never avoid this indispensable "theme" of his own existence.

The following verses of the Book of Genesis, according to the Yahwist text of chapter 3, show, actually, that this "historical" perspective will be constructed differently from the beatifying "beginning" (after original sin). It is all the more necessary, however, to penetrate deeply into the mysterious structure, theological and at the same time anthropological, of this "beginning." In fact, in the whole perspective of his own "history," man will not fail to confer a nuptial meaning on his own body. Even if this meaning undergoes and will undergo many distortions, it will always remain the deepest level, which demands to be revealed in all its simplicity and purity, and to be shown in its whole truth, as a sign of the "image of God." The way that goes from the mystery of creation to the "redemption of the body" (cf. Rom. 8) also passes here.

Remaining, at present, on the threshold of this historical perspective, we clearly realize, on the basis of Genesis 2:23–5, the connection that exists between the revelation and the discovery of the nuptial meaning of the body and man's original happiness. This "nuptial" meaning is also beatifying and, as such, manifests in a word the whole reality of that donation of which the first pages of the Book of Genesis speak to us. Reading them, we are convinced of the fact that the awareness of the meaning of the body that is derived from them – in particular of its "nuptial" meaning – is the fundamental element of human existence in the world.

This "nuptial" meaning of the human body can be understood only in the context of the person. The body has a "nuptial" meaning because the man-person, as the Council says, is a creature that God willed for its own sake, and that, at the same time, can fully discover its true self only in a sincere giving of itself.

If Christ revealed to man and woman, over and above the vocation to marriage, another vocation – namely, that of renouncing marriage, in view of the kingdom of heaven – He highlighted, with this vocation, the same truth about the human person. If a man or a woman are capable of making a gift of themselves for the kingdom of heaven, this proves in its turn (and perhaps even more) that there is the freedom of the gift in the human body. It means that this body possesses a full "nuptial" meaning.

Notes

1 God, according to the words of Holy Scripture, penetrates the creature, who is completely "naked" before Him: "And before him no creature is hidden, but all are open (*pánta gymná*) and laid bare to the eyes of him with whom we have to do" (Heb. 4:13). This characteristic belongs in particular to Divine Wisdom: "Wisdom . . . because of her pureness pervades and penetrates all things" (Wis. 7:24).

2 "Furthermore, the Lord Jesus, when praying to the Father 'that they may all be one . . . even as we are one' (Jn. 17:21–2), has opened up new horizons closed to human reason by implying that there is a certain parallel between the union existing among the divine persons and the union of the sons of God in truth and love. It follows, then, that if man is the only creature on earth that God has willed for its own sake, man can fully discover his true self only in a sincere giving of himself" (*Gaudium et spes*, no. 24).

The strictly theological analysis of the Book of Genesis, in particular Gn. 2:23–5, allows us to refer to this text. This constitutes another step between "adequate anthropology" and "theology of the body," which is closely bound up with the discovery of the essential characteristics of personal existence in man's "theological prehistory." Although this may meet with opposition on the part of the evolutionist mentality (even among theologians), it would be difficult, however, not to realize that the text of the Book of Genesis that we have analyzed, especially Gn. 2:23–5, proves not only the "original," but also the "exemplary" dimension of the existence of man, in particular of man "as male and female."

3 Biblical tradition reports a distant echo of the physical perfection of the first man. The prophet Ezekiel, implicitly comparing the King of Tyre with Adam in Eden, writes as follows:

> "You were the signet of perfection.
> full of wisdom,
> and perfect in beauty;
> you were in Eden, the garden of God . . ."
> (Ez. 28:12–13).

from The Sacrament of Love: The Nuptial Mystery in the Light of the Orthodox Tradition

Paul Evdokimov

This account of marriage is an exercise not in ethics but in what we might call "nuptial symbolics," that is, the elaboration of what marriage means, or what its conceptual ramifications are, throughout a complex system of symbols such as Christianity. Radical for its day, Evdokimov's account depends on an ontology of "the masculine" and "the feminine" that will now strike most as dated. To be put off by it now, however, would prevent one from learning more important things that Evdokimov has to teach. He ties a twofold critique to a positive account. The critique charges both Protestants and Catholics with reducing sex to a mere means, whether that means is to the control of lust or the procreation of children. But sex, according to Evdokimov, is only secondarily for control of lust or procreation of children. Primarily, sex is for God. This does not mean it is for pleasure as such. Sex tends to bind us to another human being in a way that we cannot easily escape. It leads us into a community, that of marriage, in which we can hope to be made better. If marriage works, it leads to sanctification. That is the sense in which sex is for God. It is, or can be, a means by which God draws human beings to Godself by sanctifying them. Marriage improves people by ascesis, by showing them how to give up less meaningful goods in favor of more meaningful ones. Ascesis is not properly self-denial, but the self-betterment for which we in the modern West also (perhaps vainly) hope when we undertake diets and go to the gym. Marriage and monasticism become two modes, according to Evdokimov, of a single vocation: both promote sanctification by placing human beings into a community in which love makes them better.

Introduction

"Have you not read that He who made them from the beginning made them male and female, and said, '. . . man shall . . . be joined to his wife, and the two shall become one flesh'?" To the disciples who said, "If such is the case of a man with his wife, it is not expedient to marry," the Lord replies, "He who is able to receive this, let him receive it" (Mt. 19:1–12).

This brief dialogue throws into striking relief the vertiginous distance between the divine order and human institutions. At precisely what moment "that which was in the beginning" turned toward "that which is now" is covered by the mists of time and the "twilight of the idols." We can only follow a series of critical junctures which are at the same time dreadful judgments.

Christianity has raised the nuptial union to the dignity of a sacrament. However, this revolutionary move strikes against a tendency deeply anchored in the general mentality, which considers marriage only from the external viewpoint of sociological usefulness, from the point of view of rights and duties. The mystery of love itself, its hidden dimension which is always unique and personal, remains in the shadow and does not even reach the domain of morals and human customs. A "mental humus," formed through thousands of years, strongly resists the evangelical "metanoia," the "change of heart."

Modern psychology uses the term *über Ich* or *superego* to designate the collective consciousness. The latter possesses enormous influence; by means of ancestral atavisms, it bears down with all its weight on each individual consciousness. The archetypes and complexes act with their mysterious charm. The *superego* keeps watch over the apparent balance of accepted ideas. It expertly thrusts aside all "metanoia" (i.e. change of mind, conversion), having become capable of awakening anguish and pained awareness in the presence of adulterated values. Every spirit that dares run counter to conformity, that wonders whether it belongs to those that "can accept this word" of the Lord, is at once suspect in its orthodoxy. Such is the hypnotic power of all "ancient belief." But the ancient as such is never a valid criterion. It can become petrified in us, who stand in the temporal dimension of what was "in the beginning," in the mind of God ever present and new, in the dimension that transcends time.

On the other hand, the "constraint of repetition" always tries to reproduce the same situations; it creates false myths such as, for example, the masculine myth of virility, of man the generator, the stud. Thus through thousands of years, this constraint has subordinated woman to man, the pair to the necessity of the species, and love to the service of procreation.

The onerous heritage of Antiquity finds an echo in the formation of asceticism. In Essence circles, with the monks of Qumran, the perfect are those who cultivate celibacy. This becomes characteristic of early Judeo-Christianity. The enthusiastic praise of celibacy by the Syrians, who are somewhat inflexible by nature, becomes a condemnation of marriage, as in Satornilus, Tatian, Marcion, The Gospel of the Egyptians, and later Julius Cassian. Christian thought exalts virginity positively, as a separate value, but does not always remain at this height, turning as it does to the negative aspect, the depreciation of marriage. In its extremist currents, the struggle against the flesh identifies the flesh with concupiscence, then with woman, and advocates the flight from all that is feminine. At times, one has the impression that the problem of salvation is for men alone, and that he who wants to save himself must, above all, save himself from women. There is an echo of Gnosticism in this, where "redemption" means "deliverance from sex" and where woman is reduced to the purely sexual and, from there, to the demonic. A certain type of ascetic even refuses to see his own mother because she is a woman and exhibits disquieting attention to the accursed sex even in the animal world. The Cathari push this encratite[1] asceticism to its limit and declare marriage a satanic abomination.

Surprisingly, it is with the hermits that the "woman question" becomes most current, reducing it to its "passionate" aspect and compromising it forever. Certain theologians deem it useless to propagate the human race; they reduce marriage to the one aim of avoiding incontinence. This is why a conjugal love that is too passionate borders on adultery. On what scale should one weigh passion? Can one gauge the effects of similar calculations on an awakening love, most often chaste, that is free of all eroticism? Only an abstract being can "invent" such restraints and thereby poison with his distrust the dew of a blossoming flower. Women who react to the wishes of a misunderstood asceticism are nowadays identified as "frigid women"; doctors understand the tragedies that this attitude creates in marital intimacy. It renders men impotent or drives them to extramarital substitutions. On the other hand there are those, unhappy because of loneliness, who even with prostitutes look for a simple feminine presence, an illusion of love. In these extreme cases eroticism, sexuality properly understood, is no longer at work . . .

When it is simplistic, the exaltation of virginity borders on paradox. It seems to say that Christianity is defined by celibacy and makes of marriage only a tolerated exception. In the mysterious and irrational element of his being, man sees himself disembodied from his mystery, entirely determined by the most elementary physiology and the most pragmatic sociology. One could say that here the Gospel has not brought any great changes. One readily understands what deep uneasiness can be implanted in a woman's soul, sensitive and attentive, by the many affirmations of the Church's theologians – purely gratuitous affirmations, even though they are the product of spiritual authorities who are otherwise beyond dispute.[2] So much was this so that between the summit of humanity, the Virgin Mary who is "beyond compare more glorious than the Seraphim" and whose praise rises like a single spire, and an incomplete and demonic feminine being, there does not exist, so it appears, a third option. An amazing alienation has established itself in history as a normal situation.

The legally and finalistic principle of Jewish thought penetrates from within and strongly permeates certain Christian thought; the latter sometimes risks "sitting on the seat of Moses" and developing a transposed Rabbinism.[3] On the other hand, Monophysitism,[4] an easy solution, gains the advantage many times and warps the theological consciousness. The theologians of the patristic era center their interest on questions of dogma; monks themselves, and mostly virgins, they had neither the necessary experience nor the time and interest for a philosophy of love. Very rich in ascetical treatises, this era skirts the transphysiological mystery of the sexes. The magnificent heroism of the ascetics unleashed a decisive battle within man himself and exorcised the demonic powers from him, but at a price that verges on the dehumanization of relationships between man and woman. It appears that certain theologians' opinions on married love are taken from zoology manuals; the couple is seen from the viewpoint of reproduction and child-raising. One also finds entire systems that connect "ordination" to "subordination" and "superordination" to determine whether man is the chief or the head. The question of love in itself and of its meaning still remains open today and reveals a deep malaise: Scholasticism favors procreation, but castrates love . . .

[. . .]

The early Christian writers were not able to disregard the prevailing mentality. They were reacting against moral decadence; but in agreement with the ancients, they considered woman, socially, as a minor and the servant (*ancilla*) of her husband, being obliged before all else to serve the husband as a master (*servire viro sicut domino*). Within this mentality, especially in the West, procreation took precedence over everything else, and man was first procreator and *pater familias*. For St Ambrose, procreation is the sole reason for marriage: *Feminis haec [prolis] sola est causa nubendi.*[5] Likewise, for St Augustine, of the threefold good of marriage – offspring (*proles*), fidelity (*fides*), sanctification (*sacramentum*)[6] – the one that predominates in the end is procreation, and he considers that precisely here woman brings her "help" to man. St Thomas says: The begetting of children is most essential in marriage (*Proles est essentialissimum in matrimonio*). Roman Catholic Canon Law (canon 1013) faithfully expresses the thesis that has become classic: The primary end of marriage is the procreation and education of offspring (*Matrimonii finis primarius est procreatio atque educatio prolis*). Everything else is subordinated to this primary aim.

The command "be fruitful and multiply," addressed alike to the animal world and to the human being as "male and female,"[7] has caused Western theologians completely to lose sight of the fundamental fact that the institutional word of marriage, addressed to man as man-woman above the animal plane, does not even mention procreation.[8]

[. . .]

The personalistic conception of marriage

Social life requires married people just as it requires farmers and soldiers. Its utilitarianism can even justify the polygamy of the Old Testament or of the Code of Hammurabi (paragraph 145) that legalized fertile concubines and ranked them equal to wives. Here the good of the species comes before that of the individuals. Society is only interested in the biological and sociological content of nuptial unions. It does not have to arrive at a conclusion about love, and when it speaks of love, it implies the family and not love.

Love flees these forms and even escapes from the religious, when the latter does not address itself adequately to the mystery of love. Such a "sentimental education" produces divisions, secularizes, and in the end separates from the Church. On the other hand, current teaching hardly encourages nuptial spiritualization in itself; socialized, it merely sets forth banalities on procreative love. Yet, the doctrine of the Scholastics is not the only one and can in no way pretend to be the Tradition. It is appropriate to recall the words of St Benedict in his Rule: "There are ways which to men seem right, but the ends thereof lead to the depths of hell" (Pr 16:25).[9]

The seeds deposited in the Bible flower only after many centuries. A completely new spirituality is asserting itself today, one that is searching for neither more nor less than a priestly vocation in conjugal love: *The Nuptial Priesthood*.

It is only by rising above the philosophy of the "common good" that one can grasp the singular worth of those who love each other. It is this hidden and intimate element that is consecrated in the sacrament, it is love that constitutes its matter and receives the gift of the Holy Spirit, the nuptial Pentecost. Society knows but the surface. Between the two lovers there is only God who is the third term; this is why the meaning of marriage is taken precisely in this dual and direct relation to God.

In ancient Greek mysteries and rituals, marriage was called the *telos*, "end," in the sense of conclusion, plenitude. Pseudo-Dionysius the Areopagite explains this: "The Athenians called marriage '*telos*,' because it crowns a man for life."[10] Likewise, in Plato, *Eros* is the longing for completion.

V. Soloviev, in *The Meaning of Love*, which is perhaps the most perceptive of his writings, reconnects love not to the species, but to the person. Procreation fragments the person, love makes him whole. Soloviev shows that in lower organisms, there is at once great reproductive power and a complete absence of sexual attraction, from the very fact that the sexes are not differentiated. With more advanced organisms, the sexual attraction increases as the reproductive force diminishes, until, at the summit, with man, the strongest sexual love becomes visible, even in the case of a total absence of reproduction. And thus, if at the two extremes of animal life we find, on the one hand, reproduction without sexual love, and, on the other, sexual love without reproduction, it is apparent that these two phenomena are not indissolubly linked, that each one has its own significance and that reproduction does not emerge as the essential aim of the sexual life in its higher forms. In man the sexual differentiation finds its meaning independent of the species, of society, and of the common good. Indeed, between sexuality and procreation there is a direct physical link; it conditions the sexual attraction that is most often instinctive, impersonal, and common to to the entire animal kingdom. This power of the species over the individual reduces the persons to a simple, specific function, compatible with innumerable substitutions. On this level, sexual life visibly bears the mark of man's Fall. Both the preservation of the species and selfish sexual pleasure reduce the partner to a mere tool and destroy his dignity. Love alone bestows a spiritual meaning upon marriage, and justifies it by elevating it to perceive the countenance of the beloved in God, to the level of the one and only icon.

The Church, by instituting monasticism, unerringly professes the absolute value of the individual above the social, and affirms it once again by consecrating the unique being of the lovers, by placing this ordination at the heart of the sacrament of marriage. Married love proceeds from spiritual interiority and gazes toward the inside. Its visible aspect is but an outer manifestation. Its invisible aspect is open only to faith, because faith is precisely the perception of things not seen. "It is in the vision of the beloved that love grows," Theodoret says;[11] "the one who loves has another self," St John Chrysostom states.[12]

Without multiplying quotations, one can detect an entire tradition that matured in the shadow of a certain kenosis[13] of love. Origen emphasizes that it is God who joins together the two in one.[14] St John Chrysostom sees in every marriage the image of the wedding at Cana, and thus the real presence of Christ.[15] The "Lord comes there always to perform the same miracle," according to St Cyril of Alexandria.[16] "Christ has been invited in order to encompass marriage with chastity . . . and to fill future afflictions with grace," St Epiphanius declares.[17] In his *Moral Poems*, St Gregory of Nazianzus teaches that all human culture originates in the nuptial communion, "but in it there is something still higher and better. . . . Marriage is the key that opens the door to chastity and perfect love.'[18]

One may also mention the Franciscan tradition of St Bonaventure in the West, of Richard of Middleton, or of Duns Scotus.[19] Here the finalistic doctrine of the Scholastics no longer applies; the primary aim is the good of the sacrament (*bonum sacramenti*). The *sacramentum* is matrimony properly speaking; fidelity (*fides*) and procreation (*proles*) belong to the conjugal ministry (*officium conjugii*). For Hugh of St Victor, the root of marriage lies in the bond of charity, in the union of hearts.[20] "Conjugal love is the sacrament of realized communion between Christ and the Church by the effect of the Incarnation."[21] At the end of the Middle Ages certain preachers (in reaction to the Albigenses) raised the value of marriage even to placing it before the religious profession. Married people were considered as forming an order. According to Robert de Sorbon it is a holy order (*sacerordo*); for the Dominican Peregrinus, the order of spouses has God as its abbot.

Thus in the East as in the West one notes an unbroken tradition. In full agreement with Biblical teaching it strongly supports the personal meaning by showing the lovers being one for the other, one toward the other. Conjugal life does not have to be "pardoned," it is a value in itself. The East, always faithful to the personalistic conception, can only rejoice at seeing in the West a team of modern theologians whose thought is applied to the same personalistic aspect of marriage. The following may be cited: *Le sens et but du marriage*, by Herbert Doms (1935); the Dutch Hoegen; *Die Zweckfrage der Ehe in neuer Beleuchtung*, by the Swiss Bernadin Krempel (1945); N. Rocholl's *Die Ehe als geweihtes Leben* (1936). These works establish love as the primary reason for the existence of marriage. Beside the classical concept, it is also this meaning that one finds set forth in the Encyclical Letter of Pius XI, *On Christian Marriage* (1930): "[love] must have as its primary purpose that man and wife help each other in forming and perfecting themselves in the interior life, so that through their partnership in life they may advance ever more and more in virtue; . . . this mutual inward molding of husband and wife . . . can in a very real sense . . . be said to be the chief reason and purpose of matrimony."[22]

Man and woman move toward one another by "mutually getting to know each other," by revealing themselves to each other for a shared ascent; nothing comes to ennoble or legitimize, still less to "pardon" this meaning that royally imposes itself before, or even independent of, procreation.

It is from this overflowing fullness that the child can come as fruit, but it is not procreation that determines and establishes the value of marriage. St John Chrysostom says: "When there is no child, will they not be two? Most certainly, for their coming together has this effect, it diffuses and commingles the bodies of both. And as one who has cast ointment into oil, who has made the whole one, so in truth it is also here."[23] "Two souls so united have nothing to fear. With harmony, peace and mutual love, man and woman own all possessions. They can live in peace behind the impregnable wall that protects them, which is love according to God. By love's grace, they are harder than diamond and stronger than iron, they sail in abundance, steer a course toward eternal glory and attract more and more grace from God."[24] "Marriage is the intimate union of two lives,"[25] "the sacrament of love."[26]

[. . .]

Marriage and the Monastic State

The one absolute

A prayer of the sacrament of marriage asks, "Grant to these, Thy servants, chastity and mutual love in the bond of peace." Conjugal chastity and monastic virginity are contrasts that echo one another in their seeming antinomy. But the words of Christ, "Let the one who understands understand," apply to each of the two states; the one and the other are thereby situated on the level of the same ascesis of the Absolute.

There is no reason, except a pedagogic one for the masses, to call one path or the other the preeminent Christianity, since what is valid for all of Christendom is thereby valid for each of the two states. The East has never made the distinction between the "precepts" and the "evangelical counsels." The Gospel in its totality is addressed to each person; everyone in his own situation is called to the *absolute* of the Gospel. Trying to prove the superiority of one state over the other is therefore useless: it is an abstract, because impersonal, process. The renunciation at work in both cases is as good as the positive content that the human being brings to it: the intensity of the love of God.

St Paul's pastoral sense seeks the fulfilment of an "undivided service." The nuptial community, which is the "domestic church," and the monastic community shed light upon each other and help one another in this same service. Church doctrine has never lost sight of this balance. Councils and synods have defended it against the assaults of Manichaeism and extreme spirituality. About 340, the Council of Gangra[27] condemned the Eustathians who said that no one living in a state of marriage had any hope toward God. By imposing severe penalties, even excommunication, upon the heretical disdain of the marriage bond, the Council reaffirmed the equilibrium between the various aspects of the same "mystery": "We have regard for continence, . . . [but at the same time] we honor the *holy companionship* of marriage." Yet, an entire literature of an ingratiating naivety still contrives to speak, for example, of the marital "omnibus" and the monastic "express" directly linking heaven to earth . . . And if holiness appears miraculously, it is evidently "in spite of marriage." The impressive argument mentions Revelation (14:1–5), a cryptic allusion to those who have "not been defiled with women." There is no decisive reason to state that it is a matter of physiological virginity. The Church absolutely forbids viewing the marriage union as a defilement. It is therefore not at all a question of the married state but of bodily prostitution in extramarital affairs or simply of the reality of concupiscence. The chastity of the virgins in this text is a gift of God and a spiritual way of being. Every other interpretation contradicts Church doctrine on the chastity of the married life. Suffice it to ask whether the Apostle Peter should be considered "defiled."

Upon discovering the splendor of love, how many do not believe that they should flee from the Church, confounding it with a bad apology and a simplistic theology. Belittling one estate in order to praise the other offers no profit. Patristic wisdom states it clearly: What merit would there be for an ascetic to renounce matrimony if marriage were an inferior state? The true comparison only renders more luster to one of the estates, illumined by the full light of the other.

John Chrysostom insists that the requirements of the Gospel are the same. Perfection in the image of the Father in heaven, the new commandment of love, and the beatitudes are addressed equally to every human being: "When Christ orders us to follow the narrow path, He addresses Himself not only to monks but to all men. Likewise He orders everyone to hate his own life in the world. It follows from this that the monk and the layperson must attain the same heights, and if they fall they inflict the same wounds upon themselves." And further, "You are entirely mistaken if you think that there are certain things required of seculars, and others for monks . . . they will have the same account to render. . . . And if any have been hindered by the marriage state, let them know that marriage is not the hindrance, but their purpose which made ill use of marriage. Use marriage *chastely*, and you shall be the first in the Kingdom of heaven, and you shall enjoy all good things."[28]

Interiorized chastity depends on the structure of the spirit. And thus, numerous women sinners became "wise virgins" (St Mary of Egypt, St Pelagia). By contrast, while commenting on the parable of the ten virgins, the synaxarion of Great and Holy Tuesday treats the foolish virgins as sinners: it teaches us *not to rest as though safe in virginity*. Likewise, according to the *Philokalia*, numerous monks who sin in their heart "lose their virginity." The married as well as the monastic state are two forms of chastity, each one appropriate to its own mode of being.

Coventry Patmore, one of the few poets to deal with married love, says, "Those whose hearts are pure are virgins before God; marriage does not extinguish the vestal fire but makes its flame burn all the brighter; its praise is warm and living; and married lives faithful to the honor lying at the heart of love are fountains of virginity."[29]

Chastity signifies that one belongs totally to Christ, undividedly. For monks, it is an engagement of the soul in unmediated relationship, and for the spouses, engagement through the *hypostasis* of matrimony. This mediate character does not in the least diminish the value of the nuptial union. The spouses who comprehend this truth pray, "Grant, O God, that by loving one another we may love you."[30] If according to Nietzsche, "in true love, the soul encloses the body,"[31] then in the charismatic love of marriage it is God who enshrines the one nuptial being. John Chrysostom explains this by saying that when love unites the spouses to unite them more fully to God, it "does not have its principle in nature, but in God," and "they are exactly like Jesus Christ who, united to his bride the Church, was not less one with the Father."[32]

Inspired by St John Chrysostom, Boukharev applies the monastic vows to marriage: "The essence of obedience, of chastity, and of poverty consists in the promise made before God and the Church to seek only that which is due to God, to His will, His grace, His truth. Poverty does not reside in total deprivation understood in a tangible sense (the physiological view), but in the spiritual use of all goods, according to grace; likewise, chastity requires devotion and undivided faithfulness to God, to His grace and His truth. One becomes a spouse to belong in nuptial love only to the Lord (vow of chastity), to be led only by the Lord (vow of obedience), and to have recourse only to God (vow of poverty)."

In marriage, the nature of man is changed sacramentally, as it is, though in another mode, in the one who becomes a monk. The deepest inner relationship unites the two. The promises exchanged by the betrothed introduce them in a certain manner into a special monasticism, because here too there is a dying to the past and a rebirth into a new life. Moreover, the rite of entrance into the monastic order makes use of nuptial symbolism (the terms "betrothed" and "spouse"), while the ancient marriage rite included the monastic tonsure, signifying the common surrender of the two wills to God. Thus, marriage includes within itself the monastic state, and that is why the latter is not a sacrament. The two converge as complementary aspects of the same virginal reality of the human spirit. The ancient Russian tradition viewed the time of engagement as a monastic novitiate. After the marriage ceremony, a retreat in a monastery was prescribed for the newly married to prepare for entrance into their "nuptial priesthood." The monastic atmosphere, so profoundly linked to marriage in its very symbolism, only served to enhance the limpid joy of the wedding feast.

The calling

All of mankind's depravities weigh heavily upon matrimony. Commonplaces or betrayals have transformed it into a grotesque caricature, summarizing all that is most trivial and odious in society. In public places and on the stage, a crowd hungry for unhealthy spectacles has torn away the nuptial veils. It is not easy to write an apology of marriage; it is easier to scorn it and to praise solitude or celibacy. A certain romanticism will always seek striking heroism and poeticized images. Looked at from the outside, the married life seems lacking in beauty and loftiness, and is basically prosaic. The faraway star of the hermits has always seemed bright in the eyes of those who are in need of a beacon. It was dangerous to praise love before regenerating fallen man. But the slothful servant, simply out of reaction, has allowed such a distance to establish itself that pagan eroticism has led directly to the legalistic disdain of marriage.

Thousand-year-old institutions, ancient habits of mentality, are crumbling nowadays at an astonishing speed. An all too masculine civilization leads the world to the brink of the abyss. The machismo myth, that of the stud, and the counter-myth of the liberated Amazon woman are dead-end streets. The "Godless" world is above all a world without the Virgin and without the maternal priesthood of the woman. In this emptiness, Nietzsche's words addressed to women take on a prophetic ring: "It is in your love that your honor is found; to always love more than you are loved, to always be first in love." In the struggle between spirituality and Soviet materialism, the scales of the religious victory leaned toward the side where woman had put the weight of her frail womanhood. The true feminine ingenuity was found in the spiritual. The veil, symbolic of mystery, hides the "little way" of the servants of God; consumed by their fiat, they are "God's smile" that saves the world.

The time has come to assert the fullness of matrimony, its state of grace, and to free the married conscience from the complexes imposed upon it. The true monk will rejoice in this, for he, more than anyone else, is able to discern the real value of marriage. Its path is narrow, perhaps the most narrow of all, since there are two that walk upon it.

The Martha type in the Gospel is usually understood as that of matrimony. However, neither this type nor that of Mary offers a solution to the conflicts of life. There is something stilted about both, in the manner of a thesis and an antithesis. The Mary type, in so far as it is absolute, cannot be lived in the world. The Martha type is not even desirable. Through this diptych (where Martha has been sacrificed somewhat) one can understand how well both types complement one another in a single face, Martha-Mary.

Being in the world, breathing its foul air, and "gaining Christ" at every moment of one's life; remaining at the feet of Christ without leaving the world; standing simultaneously before God but also before the world.

Marriage begins in joy, but as at the wedding of Cana, "the hour has not yet come." The wedding rite symbolically summarizes the entire married life. The betrothed have already exchanged rings; they have already been crowned and they partake of the one cup of life. It is only in the evening of life that this cup, symbolic of fullness, will be taken, when the shadow of the crowns will fall upon it. It is a slow and progressive birth. Léon Bloy would speak here of the spaces of the heart that do not exist as of yet but are created by suffering. In order to be loved by the other, one must renounce oneself completely. It is a deep and unceasing ascetic practice. The crowns of the betrothed refer to martyrdom. According to Tauler, then, "certain ones undergo martyrdom once by the sword; others know the martyrdom of love that crowns them interiorly." This is the *kenosis* (emptying, humbleness) proper to married life, the heroism of which is hidden under the garment of the day-by-day. At the time of their maturity, there are nuptial unions that evoke trees whose branches are "roots that drink from heaven" – to use Rilke's image; the common cup of tenderness, of the evening sacrifice (*sacrificium vespertinum*), allows one to see, far off, "that nuptial contrasts are the poles on which the heavenly spheres revolve" (Coventry Patmore). Stripped of the attire with which the crowd had covered him, Eros lets the face of the Shulamite appear, crying with the Spirit, "Come, my Beloved!"

[. . .]

The ascetic monasticism of every believer

Since its advent, monasticism has been an integral part of the Church, because it expresses a spiritual norm that is *universal*, a normative value for *every* believer. The monks "lead the apostolic life according to the Gospel"; they are none other than "those who desire to be saved," who take seriously the call to the "one thing needful," of which the Gospel speaks, and therefore "do themselves violence in everything" (Nilus of Sinai). The one thing that remains is to make this fundamental aim suit the conditions of all and everyone.

According to *Novella* 133 of Justinian, "the monastic life is a sacred thing." Asceticism is not a system of merely moral rules, but a system of exercises implying spiritual gifts that is offered to every Christian life, as Cyril of Jerusalem explains. In his Rules,[33] St Basil compares the monks to the "violent ones" of the Gospel who "lay hold of the Kingdom," and thereby give expression to the maximalism of the Christian way of life.

However, it is in its total, natural powerlessness, recognized and lived as a free and joyful oblation, that asceticism seeks and encounters God. The entire technique of the ascetic struggle centers on this receptiveness: "Behold, I stand at the door and knock; if anyone hears my voice and opens the door, I will come in to him and eat with him, and be with me" (Rv 3:20). This passage of a clearly eucharistic nature is easily applied to the Liturgy or to the internalized Eucharist, to unceasing communion. According to the great mystics, a Christian is a miserable person, a beggar of grace, who discovers the One who is still more miserable, more of a beggar, God Himself, begging for love at the door of man's heart. A Christian, then, is someone who listens and opens the door; from the meal of shared poverty the banquet of the Kingdom springs forth.

The soul only reaches full maturity by ceaselessly transcending itself toward the Other, when it no longer belongs to self. Humility–obedience creates in us the configuration of Christ crucified: it is the radical laying aside of each appropriation of grace and the Spirit. The anticontemplative tendency contrasts Eros to Agape[34] and confuses inwardness with being self-centered. For Gregory of Nyssa, however, Eros flowers into Agape and into love of neighbor: Eros is "the intensity of Agape."[35] "God is the Father of Agape and Eros." The two are complementary: Eros, moved by the Spirit, goes out to meet divine Agape. This allows Maximus the Confessor[36] to institute the equivalent of the monastic life for lay-people living in the world – for the monks contemplation, for the active laity the unceasing feeling of an unseen closeness. Moreover, to the question about action or contemplation, St Seraphim of Sarov replies: "Acquire inner peace, and a multitude of men will find their salvation near you." The great merit of universalizing and popularizing the monastic method so that everyone could discover its equivalent belongs to Nicholas Cabasilas, layman and great liturgist of the fourteenth century. His treatise on the sacraments bears the telling title *The Life in Christ*. In this sacramental and liturgical aspect of the Church, he shows the heart of the mystical experience for all, the secret of living in God that the Church offers to all and everyone.

Notes

1 The Gnostic sect of the "Encratites," that is the "abstinent," rejected marriage as adultery. This group substituted water for wine in the eucharistic service and was called the sect of the "Aquarians." (They flourished in the East around 170 AD.)

2 For example, "Woman is the gate of Hell," "The Lord Himself opens 'the Kingdoms of the Heavens' to 'eunuchs' " (Tertullian, *On the Dress of Woman; Monogamy* III. 8). St Ambrose states that "married people ought to be ashamed of the state in which they live" (PL 16:346). To Clement of Alexandria, "for woman even to reflect on her nature results in opprobrium" (*Paedogogus*, II. 2, PG 8:429).

3 In his article titled "L'idée du mariage," in *Etudes Carmélitaines* (1938), B. M. Lavaud writes, "Suffice it to peruse a work like that of P. Browe, S. J., *Beiträge zur Sexualethik des Mittelalters* (Breslau, 1932), to have a notion of the persistence and the diffusion, during the Middle Ages, of rules and practices that can only be explained by an inadequate discernment of the moral and the 'legal' in the Old Testament (temporary removal from the Church, from the divine service, and from the sacraments, removal of the woman after menstruation, of the mother after childbirth, of the spouses after sexual relations, and so forth)," p. 169, note 2. See the study by Dominikus Linder, *Der Usus Matrimonii* (Munich, 1929).

4 From the Greek *monos*, "one," and *physis*, "nature." The heresy hearing this name confesses that in Christ there is but a single (Divine) nature, which tact thereby suppresses His human nature.

5 PL 15:1632B, note 52.

6 *The Good of Marriage*, chap. 24, PL 34:396. [The text may be read in *The Fathers of the*

Church, vol. 27 (1955), p. 47ff.]

7 Origen draws attention to this fact (see his *Commentary on Matthew*, Book XIV, chap. 16, PG 13:1229). In the Book of Genesis (1:27–28) the distinction of the sexes is a common animal function of the transmission of life. This perspective applies the term "male and female" (Gn 6:19; 7:16) to man and animals indiscriminately.

8 It speaks of the "solitude" of the nuptial communion (Gn 2:18–24). Likewise, the teaching of the Lord (Mt 19:5; Mk 10:4), and that of St Paul (Eph 5:31).

9 *The Rule of Saint Benedict*, trans. Oswald H. Blair, in *The Way to God* by Emmanuel Heufelder (Kalamazoo: Cistercian Publications, 1983), p. 237.

10 PG 3:1184.

11 *De sancto Amore*.

12 PG 51:30; *Homily II on Thessalonians*, PG 62:406.

13 *Kenosis*: self-emptying, humbling, the veil of humility hiding the Divinity of the Word in His Incarnation (cf. Ph 2:7).

14 Origen, *Commentary on Matthew*, Book XIV, PG 13:1230.

15 *In illud, propter fornicationes uxorem*, PG 51:210.

16 *In Joannis Evangelium*, Liber II, PG 73:224.

17 *Adversus haereses*, Liber II, tomus I, PG 41:942. One is far removed from the idea of "pleasure" as well as from all excessive concern with procreation. What is crucial is the integrity of the spirit, its fullness.

18 *Poemata moralia, sectio* II, PG 37:541–2.

19 See Binkowski, "Die Ehegüter nach Duns Scot," in *Wissenschaft und Weisheit* (1940).

20 See C. Schahl, *La doctrina des fins du mariage dans la théologic scolastique* (1946).

21 [Ed. I am unable to find the line Evdokimov quotes, but cf. Hugh of St. Victor, *De Sacr.* II, xi, 3 at PL 176:482.]

22 *Seven Great Encyclicals*, ed. William J. Gibbon, ST (New York: Paulist Press, 1963), p. 84. By contrast, the Decree of the Holy Office of March 29, 1944, reverts to the old concept and subordinates the communion of love to the service of procreation. It does not dispute the community of love but makes it instrumental to the interest of the species and of the common good. See R. Boigelot, "Du sens de la fin du marriage," in *Nouvelle Revue théologique* (1939), pp. 5–33; and E. Boissard, *Question théologique sur le mariage* (1948).

23 *Homily XII on Colossians*, 5–6; trans. Nicene and Post-Nicene Fathers, series 1, vol. XIII (Rept. 1979), p. 319.

24 *Homily XXXVIII on Genesis* 7.

25 *Peri gamon, On Marriage*, III. 5.

26 *Homily III on I Corinthians, Quales ducendae sint uxores*, PG 51:230.

27 Canons I, IX, X, and XIV. Likewise, V and L of the *Apostolic Canons*.

28 *Adversus oppugnatores vitae monasticae* III. 14.

29 Trans. C. du Bos, in *Etudes Carmélitaines* (1935), p. 185.

30 *Etudes Carmélitaines* (1939), p. 32.

31 *Beyond Good and Evil*. For Swedenborg, "everyone becomes the image of his own love, even in external appearance," *Heaven and its Wonders*, trans. Samuel Noble (New York, 1885), p. 481.

32 *Homily III on Marriage*, 3.

33 *Sermo de renunciatione saesuli*, PG 31:632.

34 Anders Nygren, *Eros et Agape* (Gütersloh, 1937). [English trans. by Philip S. Watson, *Agape and Eros* (New York: Harper & Row, 1969).]

35 *Epitetamene agape eros legetai*, St Gregory of Nyssa, *Homilia XIII in Cant. cant.*, PG 44:1048C. Agape alone would repress all loving return, every encounter between two subjects.

For the Fathers, Agape and Eros are two correlative expressions of divine love. Eros expresses the trensrational, ecstatic aspect of Agape. For St Maximus the Confessor, Christ is Eros crucified.

36 *Capitum de charitate centuria* II, III, PG 90:985AB, and 1041D.

Faithfulness

Robert W. Jenson

Lutheran theologian Robert Jenson here interprets faithfulness as a human participation in God's own activity of keeping faith among the trinitarian Persons. Thus the essay contributes to nuptial hermeneutics, to making meaning of marriage. Specifically, faithfulness takes advantage of a permission granted in the gospel, that "you may commit yourself." And it uses as sign and instrument the very feature of human existence that usually limits promises – the body – in order to make them.

Some Formalistic Remarks

To be cheering news to us, the gospel must be news about and for the concerns that antecedently animate our lives. If I, who am now to hear the gospel, am now taken up with politics – with concern for the future of my community and with labor to fulfill that concern – then if what I hear makes no promise about these matters, I cannot hear it as gospel. If my spouse and I are trying to work out what our fidelity to one another involves, and the church's message does not speak of the body and its communications, then the church's message is no gospel to us. Etc. As such concerns are the moral substance of life, so a word addressed to them is a piece of moral discourse. Insofar, Karl Barth was right: the gospel puts on moral direction, "torah," as its form – though by also calling this "law," he doubtless raised more issues than he settled.

In this moral self-explication, the gospel occurs as *permission*, opened by *vision*. It has the form "You may . . ., for . . .," where what follows the "may" is some free act, and what follows the "for" is some evocation of Christ's

Triumph. To those burdened by their property, the gospel says, "You may be recklessly generous, for the poor will in any case inherit the earth." To the members of the House Armed Services Committee, the gospel says, "You may withdraw America from the struggle for weapons-parity with the Soviets, for only peace-makers will be finally supported by reality." Etc. The paranetic section of one of Paul's letters is just such gospel-as-moral permission; the vision which opens it is the whole proclamation of the letter.

The gospel is simultaneously about one thing – the Lord Jesus – and about everything. Therefore theology is "systematic:" the attempt to grasp this comprehensive unity. Every theology thus tends to give some one slogan-formulation of "*the* gospel" (if it is a wise theology, it will also warn against ever preaching this slogan as such). A theology concerned for the moral reality of the gospel will give a gospel-slogan that comprehends also the gospel-as-permission. Thus Rudolf Bultmann notoriously sloganized the gospel with "You may decide" – or even merely "Decide."

My own theology gives as slogan for the gospel's permissions: "You may commit yourself." The correlated evocation of vision would perhaps be: ". . . for all human mutuality will yet be centered by one utterly committed to you." If the gospel is rightly understood when it is called God's "promise," then the freedom of the believer is rightly understood as freedom to make and keep human promises.

In their compression, both Bultmann's slogan and mine show something about the gospel – if, of course, either is well taken. They show its unity with "the law," and something of the nature of that unity. In the compression that brings all the gospel's permisions into one, that one slogan becomes purely formal; neither of our samples mentions any actual matters of "decision" or "promise." And just so, each can easily be transformed into a sort of categorical imperative: Bultmann's would be, "So decide that the possibility of future decision is enhanced;" and mine, "Keep promises." Correlated to every understanding of the gospel is a whole ethic. If the understanding of the gospel is right (*and*, of course, if the gospel itself is true!), the ethic will be right, it will state what is indeed the good of our life. If my theology is right, *faithfulness* is the good of our life.

A good case can be made, that the root '*mn* is the theological heart of the Bible. To be God is somehow to transcend time, to be eternal. The God of the Bible is not eternal in that he is immune to time – as with most other candidates to be ``God'' – but in that he *has* time, in that he is able to be faithful, in that he makes promises and keeps them. The stupendous disputes between Jahve and other would-be Gods, that occupy so much of the prophetic literature, especially of Isaiah II, all establish Jahve's deity by the same argument; Jahve has given his word and proved able to fulfill it. When at the last all his promise is fulfilled, then all nations will know that this God is indeed God.

God is God, if the Bible be true, in that he is universally and perfectly faithful. "You be perfect, as your heavenly Father is perfect."

A Case in Point

This section is about marriage. Marriage is the paradigm case of an ethic of faithfulness; and, as we will immediately see, this paradigmatic status is not happenstance.

The promises we make to one another halt by their conditionality. "Because I love you," I say to my daughter, "I will support your ambition." No conditions are stated, but she knows they are there. What if her ambition is to become the world's best thief? And in any case, my death is a condition; all my promises silently include ". . . if I live long enough." Thus our promises turn into "law" just when most needed, when the hidden conditions are called. ". . . I will support your ambition, if you choose one of which I can approve." The "if" is the essence of the law. This is why we need the gospel, the one promise actually going on in the world which, if true at all, is unconditional – but that is not now our theme.

The body is the locus of our promises' conditionality. By every promise, I commit my future in some way. But my possession of the future – so as to commit it – is tightly hedged about, by the consequences of the past. The body is the hedge, the present and limiting reality of what I have done and suffered. When a criminal wishes to escape the restrictions arising from his past, he does not repent and alter his soul, he has plastic surgery. And a disembodied spirit would indeed be immortal, and so free of all compulsion to make conditions.

Before the churches abandoned their responsibility, marriage promises used always to run something like this: "For richer and poorer, in sickness and in health . . ." Such formulations list circumstances which are the matter of the conditions normally supposed by our other promises in order to disavow them. They add up to ". . . no matter what."

The mutual commitment of marriage strains thus toward unconditionality, because it is a commitment made not only about or in spite of the body, but *by* the body, with audible *and* "visible" words, and as the profoundest of all such. Just because the body is the impediment of our promises, it is the reality-principle of commitment; and its gestures are therefore our strictest commitments. A lying promise is bad, but one sealed with an embrace is a profanation. Betrayal is bad, but what of betrayal with a kiss? Strictly mechanically, coitus is the body's deepest (the double entendre intended) gesture of mutuality; there is no way for one to turn his/her body more toward the other. Coitus just does say: "I am yours and you are mine, to the extreme limit of such mutuality among creatures."

It would be, of course, possible to decree that the body's moves say no such thing, that coitus is no gesture of promise, but purely a technique to generate pleasure. This decree, like all decrees about language, would have to be societal. And it would be different from other changes of vocabulary or syntax, for it would change the very nature of communication. Such a decree would radically sunder the mutuality of the body from the mutuality of address and response. Just so, the society that acted thus would abandon the effort to make promise with and by the body, which is the limit to promise. That is, such a society would abandon the reality-principle of promise, and so abandon the attempt to make promise effective upon reality. Such a society would be *faithless* on principle. The business about "the family" being "the foundation of society" is trite; but it also happens to be true, even analytically true – at least if by "society" we mean anything resembling those the western world has known.

We may choose a faithless society. There are many signs that we are so choosing. But as we choose, we should know that, whatever other glories such a society might have, it could not be an egalitarian or democratic society. For all such do indeed live by "social contract," that is, by the attempt to impress faithfulness on social reality. It may now seem farfetched, to assert that a society which deprived coitus of its promise-meaning would have to become illiberal. But I think the assertion manifestly true – and historical fascism is in fact libertine. The dancers on the beaches of Goa would have joined Hitler's youth groups in a flash; and the point of the Don Juan legend is that true philandering is precisely a mode of spiritual existence. Believers in the gospel, in any case, necessarily assert that as faithfulness is humanity's good, a faithless society would be evil.

Until this hell is realized, coitus says what it says. It may sometimes be a lie, and the lie may even sometimes be more or less white, or society may have to treat it as white. But it says what it says; and *therefore* the verbal promises of which it is the visible word, strain toward unconditionality.

O course, also a couple is not God, and so the vows conclude: "Till death parts us." I do not absolutely have my future, and so cannot absolutely promise it.

But in marriage I do reject all the stings and weapons of death, as conditions of my promise. Poverty may mean that staying with my spouse will kill me, but I declare that this makes no difference. Sickness may mean that staying with my spouse will kill me, but I declare that this makes no difference. Etc. Yet, though I seek to make my promise unconditional, I am not God and so may never claim that I have actually made an absolute commitment; and so I conclude "Till death parts us."

Søren Kierkegaard knew more about marriage than most, partly because of his inability to enter it. He wrote a wedding sermon on the theme: " 'Love Conquers All,' as the *Resolution* that Constitutes Marriage." It may be the best wedding sermon ever; and its theme is the theme of any possible Christian marriage counselling. It is not a *fact* that love conquers all; but we can together *choose* love's victory as our truth, and just so wed. The couple who determine to stay together so long as their "love" survives, have thereby left the question of how long love will survive to happenstance, and so made no actual commitment at all. Whether they are legally, or even ecclesiastically, "married," or just "living together," makes on this basis no great difference. Rather, precisely in that we choose to stay together *in any case*, we create the possibility that love will last – or rather, we create the possibility of the endless beginning of what the Bible calls "love."

Therefore Christian judgment can never call divorce good, no matter what the circumstances. We must, of course, admit that a broken promise has been broken; and never persecute failure, also not in ourselves. But to reckon in advance with the breaking of promise, is in all human mutuality the very deepest betrayal. Faith will never abet such reckoning. To "Should we divorce?" in the future tense, Christian judgment must always answer "No." To "Must we divorce?" Christian judgment will answer "Surely not – but let us examine the circumstances." To "We have divorced – what now?" Christian judgment must answer "Now a beginning, with us, of promise and faithfulness."

Concluding Generalizations

This is, of course, a very different ethic than we commonly encounter, in or out of the churches. This does not seem to me a shortcoming, in an ethic. And the alternatives currently urged against it, are not even *prima facie* plausible. "My duty is to fulfill myself," says the suburban cosmoite, "and I must not be bound to promises I have outgrown!" But what *is* this "self" to be fulfilled, if it is not determined precisely by the promises I have made? And just how does one outgrow a promise? Or a human being? Of course faithfulness often means pain or loss of pleasure, and very often also for those to whom someone is faithful. But the demand that this must not happen can hardly be given stature in ethics. Very often it is transparently an application merely of the consumer-ethic. It is a symptom of our situation that so many who acutely and passionately denounce the consumer ethic in all its other hiding places, propose to bring it into the very center of their humanity; but it is only a symptom, and not a seriously entertainable ethical proposal.

As finding a spouse is art, luck, and blessing, while cleaving to her/him is virtue, so we may generalize: making and not making promises is wisdom, evading the risk is cowardice, knowing to what we are and are not committed is moral judgment, and faithfulness where committed is good works. The ethic of faithfulness is perhaps not a complete statement of man's good; as no one theology can, perhaps, be a complete understanding of the gospel. But I claim that no ethic which relativizes the value of faithfulness can be right, and that much ethical confusion is simply and perspicuously sorted out, once one sees that.

The Relationship of Bodies:
A Nuptial Hermeneutics of
Same-sex Unions

David Matzko McCarthy

The two essays on theology and sexuality that I find myself quoting most often are Rowan Williams's "The Body's Grace," and this one, by David McCarthy. Both tackle the question, what is the body for? McCarthy addresses the question in terms of how bodies become meaningful in distinctively Christian relationships, or "nuptial hermeneutics."

Human bodies are open to meaning and can become charged, to put it crudely, with more or less significance. The most significant body in Christianity is of course the body of Christ. It is both the body of God in the flesh and the body of Christians in the Church. The body of Christ signifies – because it enacts – the reconciliation between God and humanity. Human bodies take on a distinctively Christian meaning from their participation in the body of Christ in the Church, because the Church carries forward the redemption of our bodies, by our bodies – by our bodies given new meaning by sacraments and christlike acts.

Marriage is a donation of Christians' specifically sexual bodies to the community of reconciliation enacted by the Church. Christians give their bodies over to the Church so that they might mean more, so that the partners might manifest, by the work of the Spirit, the reconciliation wrought in Christ. Marriage is both a school for faith, hope, and charity, and a cell of the Church in which those virtues can stretch forward in hospitality to others, including children. McCarthy argues that same-sex couples might also manifest those works of the Spirit, incorporating them into Christ's ongoing reconciliation.

McCarthy's approach also generates distinctively Christian arguments for what sexual orientation means and why gay and lesbian people ought to come out. "A homosexual orientation, properly understood, is this: gay men and lesbians are persons who encounter the other (and thus discover themselves) in relation to persons of the same sex."

Staying in the closet can be an attempt to keep the meaning of one's body to oneself; coming out can be a gift of one's body to a larger society, by which it can communicate more. In a Christian context, that "more" will participate in God's desire for love and constancy with human beings. Like marriage, and preparatory to it, "coming out represents the desire to make one's sexuality a sign, a sign that is given over to others and to a common interpretive activity. Within the framework of heterosexual marriage and similar same-sex unions, coming out is a set of actions that gives us a sense of . . . one who desires constancy, . . . the simultaneous binding and liberating of covenant love."

I also recommend another of McCarthy's articles, "Homosexuality and the Practices of Marriage," Modern Theology *13 (1997): 371–97.*

When Christian theologians make a case for same-sex unions, they usually sidestep a consideration of the body, dealing instead with general norms for moral relationships. This essay will argue that the agency of the body is fundamental. Overlooking the body is an effective means to justify homosexual unions on the same grounds as heterosexual marriage – according to the psychological character of the relationship – but doing so yields only a superficial account of marriage and same-sex unions. In each, it is the body that communicates the bond. The body is the conveyance and the substantial form of common life.

The widest possible consideration of common life (and the beginning for Christian theology) is God's reconciliation with the world, which, in the gathering of the church, constitutes a body. This body, the body of Christ, is generative of a relationship of bodies, and within this network of common life, marriage is understood as an 'embodied' theological hermeneutics, a synecdoche of God's redemptive activity. Marriage is mimesis. It is an enactment of God's faithfulness and the unity of Christ and the church, and it is a means through which the agency of a particular person's body is taken into redemption. It is a pathway of desire, to be fulfilled in semantic excess as a communicative body is given over to the language of the church.

Such is the extravagant theological landscape of Christian marriage. If homosexual men and women desire to give their bodies over to another and to fulfillment in God's reconciliation, any theological account of same-sex unions ought to identify the way in which the unions are cultivated on the same terrain. A theology of same-sex unions ought to identify the manner through which the intercourse of bodies articulates the redemptive meaning of the body's agency.

A Theological Framework

A theological rationale for same-sex unions has attained a degree of consensus among Christians who advocate gay and lesbian relationships.[1] The rationale focuses on God's steadfast fidelity and frames same-sex unions in the image of God's enduring love, insofar as they are faithful, permanent, and contribute to the continuing life of the church. An essay by Princeton Professor Andrew K. M. Adam, 'Disciples Together, Constantly', gives a cogent account of this theological proposal.[2]

Adam sets up his account by asking the question, 'Why does God care about our sexual lives?' The question leads to another, more concrete ecclesiological question, 'Why do we, as Christian brothers and sisters, care about each other's sexual lives?' The two questions are inextricably connected, inasmuch as God's relationship with the world is undertaken through the gathering of a people and as Adam notes, 'the character of our relationships with one another is inseparable from the character of our relationship with God.'[3]

Adam's treatment of sex will inevitably lead to a consideration of marriage, but he is not satisfied with simply restating the view that marriage legitimates sexual intercourse ('since marriage can in some cases simply provide a facade of legitimacy for a superficial or even malignant relationship'[4]). Adam critically examines marriage in order to identify its normative features. His conclusion: 'the central theological importance of marriage – as the church's institution for the blessing and support of human intimacy – lies in *constancy*'.[5]

'Constancy' points to abiding fidelity and hospitality. It is Adam's summary term for the rich character of God's relationship with the world. 'God makes a vow of covenanted constancy to *all* who are willing to receive that covenant',[6] and this constancy sets a pattern for a faithful imitation of God. The theological significance of marriage depends on the fact that it is 'a commitment that binds two people together for life.'[7] It 'involves the spouses in the creation of a new relational identity that is given, sustained, and sealed by God.' Adam avers that 'Scripture repeatedly makes the theological point that the relations of utmost human intimacy ought to communicate something about God's relationship to humanity.' Marriage is 'an icon of the covenant of grace'.[8]

Adam makes clear that heterosexual marriage is normative in the biblical witness and the church's theological tradition. Heterosexual marriage is set within a network of practices that order social life and provide for procreation and the nurture of children. It sustains inherent theological goods and, by bearing and nurturing life, contributes in an undeniably concrete and sacramental way to the ongoing life of human community. Procreation becomes a visible sign of the graces conveyed through marriage. Theologically, the nuptial covenant is multivalent insofar as constancy and fidelity are woven together not only with the procreative good but with accounts of self-giving to the 'other' – signified by the sexual difference of male and female.

Adam argues that, amid this complex of goods; constancy is the linchpin, that is, constancy is mimesis of God's creative reconciliation in a way that childbearing and other goods are not. Same-sex unions are not equivalent to heterosexual marriage and the network of goods that it makes concrete, but they are able to sustain the fundamental good of constancy. In fact, Adam suggests that constancy among gay and lesbian couples may provide a more striking image of God's love than many heterosexual unions.[9] Through his theological framework of constancy and covenant, same-sex unions are not merely justified but are considered an efficacious sign of God's covenant-making and gracious self-giving to the world.

Coming Out

Adam outlines a theological framework for fitting gay and lesbian unions within the church's sense of purposefulness for sexually intimate relationships. In this section, I will turn to a basic shortcoming of his presentation. Before I begin, though, I want to emphasize that I have used his account not because it is unconvincing but because it is sound and because it represents what is becoming a widely accepted theological view. My critique is not a counter-argument but a further articulation of his proposal.

The difficulty with his account is this: Adam begins with a question about the theological meaning of sex, but as his essay unfolds, he tends to minimize the relevance of sexuality, along with the agency of our bodies and the direction of our desires. He introduces the question of sex, but he justifies same-sex unions by avoiding the question. Avoidance, in fact, is an effective strategy. By minimizing the *sexual*, Adam is able to circumvent the hetero*sexual* canons that pervade the tradition. He frames sexuality in the broader context of God's love for the world, but he does not attend to sexuality and the sexual communication of the body. As a result, the type of relationships he describes are intimate but not distinctively sexual and not significantly enfleshed.

As I noted in my introduction, the larger theological issue at stake is the agency of our bodies. The body is the subject of the life of the church, living in the imitation of God, in a community set in the pattern of Christ's self-giving to the world. The church is called to be a sacrament of God's promises to the world, and that promise is a gift of the body: God's incarnation, a crucified body, a bodily resurrection, and the Spirit's enfleshment of the church as Christ's body. The language of the body is not merely symbolic. The body is the means of our reconciliation. The redemption of the body is the matrix (or we could say the womb) of a new set of social relationships inaugurated by Christ's gathering of Israel.

Adam's theological proposal does not attend to the body in the way I have suggested, but his basic question, 'Why does God care?', does set the topic of same-sex unions in a network of social relations. It is appropriate to say that a sexual relationship between two people is social in the sense that it is a matter of common significance and its meaning is made possible by a language of common life. We tend not to 'have' sex in public, and in this limited sense, sex is undertaken in private. But we certainly do find ways to communicate to others what we are up to. Sexual intimacy is 'public', insofar as sexual relationships are made intelligible within a wider set of social relations. Sex is a social utterance; it speaks of power and pleasure, common bonds, status and identity. Sex is personal because 'we' are making the social wager on 'our' identity, status and power. Sex, then, is not private if private means that I create my own meaning of what I do.

Adam's approach to same-sex unions crosses the divide between what are commonly considered public and private realms. A better way to conceptualize his account of sexual relationships in the church is to recognize that the embodied interaction between two people communicates something to others about their bond – not only the bond of the two, but how all are bound together in community and with God. In effect, the church expects the body to be theologically communicative. For this reason, marriage has held a firm place as a sign and sacrament of grace. The body gives utterance to the whole.

With that said, there are still good reasons to stay with Adam's strategy. He does indicate that same-sex unions have a positive role to play in imaging God's covenant fidelity. He asks why sexual relationships should be a concern for the church, and he answers that the church ought to be concerned with their constancy. Adam is able to avoid difficult questions about gay and lesbian embodiment which, in the tradition of the church, would be set aside easily and quickly in terms of sexual difference and the procreative end of intercourse. Procreation has functioned as the basic sign (the vocabulary) of the body's sexual agency, and recently, the differentiation of humanity as male and female has come to the fore. Adam circumvents these discursive obstacles to the significance of same-sex unions.

Despite Adam's success, his strategy is used at a high price. By minimizing issues of the body, he gives us no way of asking or answering the inverse of his question, that is, 'Why would we desire that God and the church care about our sexual lives?' The moral perspective that Adam represents seems to treat sexuality from an external point of view: Why do God and the church care about what we do? How can sexuality be reined in and set within a moral or theological framework? These questions are incomplete. We ought to ask the question from the standpoint of the agent: What do Christians, in their bodily desires for unity and constancy, indicate about the theological significance of sexuality?

This question about agency refers to communicative acts of the body – to coming out. Coming out articulates the agency of the body, as it is always already open for social signification. The act of coming out is impelled by the desire to make the body a sign that communicates one's identity. Coming out is confessing a common identity and seeking a common purposefulness for one's sexual acts. Coming out represents the desire to make one's sexuality a sign, a sign that is given over to others and to a common interpretive activity. Within the framework of heterosexual marriage and similar same-sex unions, coming out is a set of actions that gives us a sense of what it means to come out as one who desires constancy, as one who desires the simultaneous binding and liberating of covenant love.

Adam's approach, in contrast, seems to assume that the connection between God's constancy and its image in human relationships is external, something imposed. From accounts like his, it might be inferred that steadfast faithfulness provides a set of restrictions upon an otherwise misdirected desire. Such an approach does not explain the desire to be known in faithfulness. It does not appreciate the attraction of constancy as a particular movement of the body. It does not see mimesis of God's enduring love as productive of a particular form of desiring.

God's constancy is not only attractive but irresistible. Christian theology sees men and women as drawn ceaselessly to give themselves over to God's way with the world. God has given Godself in a human body, in the incarnation, crucifixion, and in the resurrected body, and we are marked by the desire to give our bodies in response. Drawn near to God, we are shaped by God's offer of reconciliation. The constant offer of God's own self-giving is God's irresistibility, and steadfast fidelity is the form of desire in the intimacy of God's relationship with the world.

Writing about coming out, Eric Marcus explains that gays and lesbians come out 'primarily because they want to be honest with those they love and trust, and because it can be difficult, exhausting, and personally destructive to pretend to be someone you're not'.[10] In its most significant occurrence, coming out is telling who we are to people who are a fundamental aspect of who we are and who we are becoming. It is a matter of self-disclosure to those who are integral to ourselves. Coming out is sometimes disturbing for those who are witnesses to the event because it is rightly received as a statement about common life. Coming out communicates a shared identity, coming out in a parade of brothers and sisters for all who are on the outside to see. This is who we are; this is where we stand, together, in the world. Those who come out ask others to rethink who they are together, to retell their own stories as they have been told through the ones who are now out.

◈ 205

The communicative acts of coming out certainly entail self-definition, but these acts of signification come through surrender to an interpretive community. Coming out is opening one's life to be told by others. This exposure is the source of dread and panic in coming out. It is also the outcome of a desire to be known, a desire for wholeness and a promise of unity of oneself and the world. Coming out articulates the sign-giving character of human, bodily life.

For the church, a similar statement of identity and desire is at stake when members of the body come out with their sexual commitments. Marriage and the celibate life write the body into the story of redemption. Both are communicative, sexual acts.[11] They are means by which the story of redemption is written through human lives, as signs of God's reconciliation – as the reconciliation of the body.[12] Coming out is a wager, opening the body to a language of redemption, opening a way for the body's agency not only in the movement of desire but in the donation of one's agency as an interpretive sign.

Any argument for or against same-sex unions in the church needs to attend to the desire of gay and lesbian Christians to make their desires known and to offer their bodies a signs of God's self-giving. For this reason, Adam's appeal to constancy only falls short. We need to push the language of common life further. An interpretation of the body cannot be circumvented through a theory about relationships. In same-sex unions, it is desire that moves us, and the body that is given.

The Body

If the body is communicative, it will be instructive to note how marriage has functioned in Christianity as a theological hermeneutics of the body. This section will outline the meaning of the body as a 'nuptial body', as it is understood in the Catholic church. I treat the Catholic view because the Catholic tradition makes a sacrament (a sign) of the body, in union with the body of Christ. Although the Catholic understanding of body and desire might appear negative, as though the body is to be denied, the contrary is actually the case. The body is the centre-piece of human reconciliation; thus, the body is defined by its essential unity with another – in nuptial union. A discussion of the Catholic view of the body will bring the issues of coming out and signification to the fore. After this brief sketch, questions of the body will be considered, in the following section, from the vantage point of same-sex unions.

A good point of departure for our treatment of marriage is a presentation by Bernard Cooke in his *Sacraments and Sacramentality*.[13] Cooke proposes that marriage is the basic sacrament among the seven sacraments in the Catholic church. His argument is twofold. First, he holds that the sacraments are a 'hermeneutics of experience' insofar as they not only convey grace but also provide a way to see our lives and the reality of God truthfully.[14] Second, he suggests that human love and friendship form a basic sacramental activity because the self-giving of persons in community embodies God's fundamental act of grace – in God's own self-giving to the world. Cooke considers marriage a paradigm of human friendship as well as a foundation of human community. Marriage is an enactment of God's faithfulness and love.

Cooke's view comes together in an interpretation of Eph. 5:21–33. The text is a standard for those who develop the theological imagery of marriage. Ephesians 5 models the relationship of husband and wife in terms of Christ's relationship to the church.

> Be subject to one another out of reverence for Christ . . . For the husband is the head of the wife as Christ is the head of the church, his body, and is himself its Savior. As the church is subject to Christ so let wives also be subject in everything to their husbands. Husbands, love your wives as Christ loved the church and gave himself up for her . . . 'For this reason a man shall leave his father and mother and be joined to his wife, and the two shall become one flesh.' This mystery is a profound one, and I am saying that it refers to Christ and the church (vv. 21, 24–5, 31–2, RSV).

When identifying the sacramental imagery of the text, Cooke focuses on the unity that is established between husband and wife. He is troubled by the hierarchy of male over female, but the believes that the essential meaning of the text does not depend upon sustaining the patriarchal structure that the Pauline text assumes as a given.[15] Cooke's interpretive setting is eucharistic: 'Jesus' death and consequent resurrection was the continuation of what was done at the supper when Jesus took bread and said, "This is my body (myself) given for you." '[16] According to Cooke, the body of Christ gives the nuptial body its character, and the nuptial body, in turn, signifies Christ's body. 'Ephesians 5 tells us that we are to understand this self-giving of Jesus in terms of the bodily self-giving in love of a husband and wife, and vice versa, we are to understand what this marital self-gift is meant to be in terms of Jesus' loving gift of self in death and resurrection.'[17]

This relationship of bodies, among husband, wife, Christ, and the church, is consistent in the church's theology of marriage, but a few additional points about this tradition ought to be noted. For instance, Ephesians 5 makes reference to Gen. 2:24 ('the two shall become one'), and this allusion to creation gives marriage another level of meaning. Marriage not only furnishes an image of God's self-giving and Christ's presence to the church, but also represents the fullness of humanity as created in the image of God.[18] The bodily relation shows the human being to be fundamentally social, differentiated as male or female, and completed in the other. In effect, the body is a sign of God's creative activity and an image of God's own 'rationality'.

Ephesians 5 has also been used, much to Cooke's chagrin, to sustain a specific 'order of love'. The order of love is a hierarchical arrangement of the husband, wife and children, which points to a functional, albeit not an essential, inequity among the sexes.[19] This division of roles has its source not merely in texts like Ephesians 5. The procreative end of marriage, in the traditional view, entails an 'order of love' insofar as fatherhood and especially motherhood are vocations that involve a specific relationship to each other as well as to children. The union of husband and wife attains its fullness in procreation. Through bearing and raising children, marriage and family attain their essential form.

I mention these points in order to indicate the thorough consistency through which the church's theological anthropology is determined by a hermeneutics of the body. Whatever criticisms may be levied against its conceptualization of gender or sexual intercourse, the church's view of creation, Christ, the church and procreation does sustain a coherent basis in the agency of the body. The human body is the concrete sign of God's image in creation. The unity of male and female bodies represents both humanity's social constitution and the reconciliation founded in Christ's relationship to the church. The relationship of bodies is the context for a calling, not only a vocation of the Christian life in general, called into the body of Christ, but also the particular calling of the married life and parenthood. A hermeneutics of the body, differentiated as male and female, holds these themes together. The body leads the way. The body's agency is understood to have an essential purposefulness, on a biological as well as on personal, interpersonal, ecclesiological, and theological levels.

In order to underline this point, I will cite a few passages from papal addresses that have been collected together as John Paul II's 'Theology of the Body'.[20] The first address is titled 'Realization of the Value of the Body According to the Plan of Creation.' The title, perhaps, says enough. In the address, John Paul asserts that 'the body, in its masculinity and femininity, is called "from the beginning" to become the manifestation of the spirit.' He argues against naturalistic and deterministic understandings of the body or gender and proposes, instead, that the agency of the body is a matter of the knowing self. As the self is known to itself, it is known as embodied, as male or female; therefore, self-discovery (rather than natural determination) comes through relationship to the other. The other, in community with us, gives us knowledge of ourselves. According to John Paul II, the spirit is manifest in the body 'by means of the conjugal union of man and woman, when they unite in such a way as to form "one flesh" ... [T]he body, in its masculinity and femininity, assumes the value of a sign – in a way a sacramental sign.'[21] This signification is called the nuptial meaning of the body.

The second address to be noted is given the title 'The Mystery of Woman Revealed in Motherhood'. Again, the title says a great deal. The Pope explains that the meaning of the body is revealed in parenthood, in knowledge as mother and father. In his account of parenthood, there is an asymmetry to the degree that fatherhood implies a vocation in the family and outward in work, while the vocation of motherhood is focused in the domestic sphere only (although outside work is not precluded).[22] How this asymmetry becomes necessary is unclear. Whatever the case on this point, the nuptial meaning of the body is clear. For John Paul, sexuality is 'a further discovery of the meaning of one's own body, a common and reciprocal discovery, just as the existence of man, whom "God created male and female" is common and reciprocal from the beginning'.[23]

Among Catholics, this nuptial hermeneutics of the body is firmly in place. Often, its details are softened in relation to issues like the procreative end of marriage, the role of women and woman's ordination. But the basic structure remains intact. A few examples are in order. First, some moral theologians bring forward an analogical view of procreation, displacing the good of raising children with a notion of outward service to community. While doing so, they seem to attenuate the connection between marriage and its concrete sign – the natural, procreative consequence of bodily union. But what these moral theologians take away with one hand, they give with the other. While procreation is understood analogically, the union between the man and woman, itself, is made more concrete. The nuptial hermeneutics is reinstated by giving a primary signifying role to the complementary bond between male and female.[24]

A second example comes from the ranks of Christian feminism. The nuptial hermeneutics is criticized soundly by some. The tradition's theological investment in gender is seen as a source of clericalism and the disempowerment of women, and criticism of the nuptial meaning of the body is levied along with a total criticism of the church's structure.[25] The two criticisms are necessarily bound together – as the body speaks of the church.

The same nuptial framework, rejected by some, is used by others to assert the necessity for the leadership of women and a reform of the institution. The claim from this quarter is that the structural dominance of men in the church is inconsistent with its anthropology. The male, the church believes, is not fit to represent the church alone.[26] If this is the case, the church's male oriented leadership is inconsistent with its theological convictions. Pushing the issue further, the claim can be made that the nuptial hermeneutics requires that humanity be theologically feminized, that the otherness which has characterized the female makes possible the identity-through-difference that constitutes the creature in relation to God.[27]

These arguments, for and against, serve to show that the nuptial hermeneutics is deeply seeded in the church's theological discourse and is a common presupposition even among contending positions. I have given a good bit of detail to this interpretive framework in order to accentuate the theme of the previous section, that marriage is a means by which the body becomes a sign. Coming out is an act of the communicative body, and coming out in the church means that the body is given over to be a sacrament of God's creative activity and reconciliation.

Certainly, this account of the body can be accused of being idealistic and far removed from the reasons that two people may express in their desire for marriage. 'We want to be married because we love each other.' 'I want to be married because I am tired of being lonely.' The reasons for marriage, proposed and actual, are countless. The set of reasons provided by a nuptial theology seems to produce an interpretive excess, reaching far beyond personal intentions. Critical questions can be raised. Does a couple need to intend to be an image of God in creation? Is such an image ever achieved on an interpersonal level? In the end, these questions do not undercut the nuptial hermeneutics. The body is given more meaning than a person alone or a couple alone is able to sustain. The nuptial interpretation of the body lifts marriage beyond the design of the couple that is united. The body's agency comes to fulfilment through personal, bodily, and semiotic donation. As the body is given, the body is received. The desire of coming out is the desire of the body to enter and to be entered, to give away and to be given identity.

In the previous section, I proposed that the desire, among Christians, to enter into permanent unions emerges from a desire of the body, which is drawn to God's faithfulness and patterned in mimesis of God's enduring love. This section has intended to show that the desire is matched by a thoroughgoing hermeneutics of the body. Through marriage, the body is given an identity that does not merely bring its agency to fulfillment but also locates the communicative acts of the body at the axis of a community's whole life. The desire of the covenanted union is matched by an excess of meaning and purposefulness. As desire is patterned in the image of God's constancy, body will be completed through the enduring presence of the other.

The Body and Same-sex Unions

After my treatment of the church's theology of marriage, a few parameters for conceptualizing same-sex unions have come into view. One basic point, already proffered in detail, is that sexual unions are theologically communicative. If the desire for steadfast same-sex unions is to be recognized and honored, the actual union of bodies cannot be ignored. The body is essential in our desire for God, and the union of bodies must be understood in the abundance of its theological meaning. Likewise, if Christian communities are asked to recognize same-sex unions, gay and lesbian couples will be called to give over their bodies, not only to each other but also to the church as communicative signs. This donation of the body is the hermeneutic version of gaining one's life by losing it, the core of Christianity's understanding of giving oneself over to God's creative activity. The church's understanding of sexuality is grounded, not just in a conception of relationships and how bodies are *used* within them, but in a hermeneutics of the body's agency – how the body leads. The body's activity in same-sex unions ought to be construed in terms beyond the union of two people in order to become expressive of God's reconciliation and the church's common life.

The communicative body has been presented through the notion of coming out. On the other side of the metaphor, the muted body is concealed in the closet. The relationship between coming out and the closet is complex – not a simple dichotomy.[28] Among heterosexuals, whether married or not, the body is open for communication; meaning is exchanged, and the body speaks. In John Paul's terms, one discovers oneself in relation to the embodied other. The closet, on the other hand, closes off a reciprocal communication between the self and other. The closet might be self-imposed as a means to conceal one's own identity, but the hidden space of the closet is constructed from the outside by a dominant discourse of the body. Both the closet and coming out are used to control the language of the body's communicative agency. While gay men and lesbians may be in the closet, it is the interests of a heterosexual and homo*social* discourse that establishes the cloistered space.[29]

The closet does not conceal homosexual acts as much as it conceals a gay identity or orientation. On the one hand, a person might be in the closet although she had never engaged in homosexual intercourse. Her identity rather than her acts are hidden. If the same person reveals her same-sex orientation, her coming out may never lead to any expression in homo-erotic activity. The so-called 'homosexual act' has no necessary relation to the communication of a gay or lesbian orientation. On the other hand, heterosexuals (young men on collegiate athletic teams for instance) have been known to engage in homo-erotic activities. Genital contact, erotic and quasi-erotic play among heterosexuals are licit utterances, but if one participant were to announce that he was gay the whole sexual exchange would collapse. In an odd way, closeting a gay identity may allow for more freedom of homosexual expression.

Orientation (once again) is the critical matter. In the church, it is common parlance to accept the homosexual but to censure the 'homosexual act', to acknowledge the homosexual orientation as a personal identity and source of agency but to hold that the act that follows from the orientation is objectively immoral.[30] At first glance, it appears that the act rather than orientation is the decisive matter, that the orientation is somehow neutral in terms of one's standing in relation to others.[31] A closer look at orientation will reveal the contrary.

In the main, homosexual orientation is conceptualized as a tendency of desire and a disposition toward an act. Orientation, whether homosexual or heterosexual, is not chosen (and therefore neither a virtue nor a vice); it is understood as a given of personal identity, what 'happens' to a person rather than what one wills.[32] Nevertheless, this facet of a homosexual identity is usually conceptualized as pertaining only to the object of one's desire. A homosexual orientation is 'an exclusive or predominant sexual attraction toward persons of the same sex',[33] it 'produces a stronger emotional and sexual attraction toward individuals of the same sex.'[34] This account of orientation excludes the phenomenology of the body that we have seen is central to Catholic theology. One's body and the body of the other communicate a reciprocal discovery of self. (Recall Bernard Cooke's nuptial use of the eucharistic 'This is my body given for you.') A person comes to awareness of his or her own embodiment through the bodily presence of the other, and (to reiterate) this relationship of bodies begins to speak of our humanity, of the image of God, and of Christ and the church.

The church sets this hermeneutics of embodiment in terms of the differentiation of humanity as male and female. As I take it, the nuptial hermeneutics points to the heart of what it means to have a heterosexual orientation. Orientation is not simply a matter of attraction or tendency toward a particular object of desire. Orientation names the discursive mechanisms through which a person comes into identity and embodiment through the other. It names a confluence of physical, psychological and social movements that bring an individual into being as a person. It names a structure of interpersonal possibilities. Orientation signifies the particular form through which embodied agency communicates common life.

Orientation (yet again) is the pivotal issue. Orientation is not entirely distinct from desires or acts, but it is superficial to refer to a homosexual orientation as merely a tendency of object-attraction. An orientation can be expressed in a multiplicity of different desires and acts, some explicitly sexual and others more akin to friendship, some temperate and others undisciplined, some superficial and others deeply expressive. In any case, orientation, while having no necessary connection to a particular form of desire, is *necessarily* articulated in how persons are physically and psychologically situated in common life – and to be situated in social life is nothing other than to be a person. The nuptial hermeneutics makes this point plain: women and men discover themselves through difference. This hermeneutics gives an indication of what it means to have a heterosexual orientation. To this degree, a homosexual orientation presents an anomaly for the church's hermeneutics of the body. Orientation has been understood as necessarily heterosexual (the differentiation of male and female), so that the only language available to speak of a homosexual orientation is the vocabulary of desire and act. But, as we have seen, object-desire and act-object do not give adequate account of orientation.

A homosexual orientation, properly understood, is this: gay men and lesbians are persons who encounter the other (and thus discover themselves) in relation to persons of the same sex. This same-sex orientation is a given of their coming to be, that is, the nuptial meaning of human life emerges for a gay man in relation to other men, and in a woman when face to face with other women. The homosexual orientation may be anomalous, but the conceptual structure of the nuptial hermeneutics does not necessarily leave same-sex unions on the outside. A homosexual orientation is anomalous even within this heuristic frame because it redoubles the meaning of nuptial difference. The nuptial hermeneutics exceeds its usual limits as a gay woman finds differentiation through women in a way that straight women are not able, and she discovers her embodiment as woman in relation to men in a similar way that heterosexual women are able. The nuptial body is intensified.

When orientation is understood as a deposit of object-desire, the object of the orientation becomes the definitive vocabulary of desire. Heterosexual and homosexual desires, then, are set in opposite directions, and same-sex unions are considered self-absorbed in contrast to the otherness implied in the heterosexual embrace.[35] If, in contrast, orientation is conceptualized in terms of otherness and difference (rather than object) and therefore distinguished from a particular form of object-desire, then a common movement of the body – desiring the difference that comes to constitute the self – can be recognized in both gay and heterosexual unions. Homosexual and heterosexual desire follow along the same path insofar as both seek fulfillment through difference.

We should remember that this movement of the body is a matter of a person's engagement in common life. Whether or not a person seeks erotic contact with another, the nuptial orientation toward difference is fundamental to human embodiment, that is, basic to how persons and common life come to be. I have not made same-sex unions necessary; nor have I justified homosexual acts as they are typically understood. What I have done is more subtle but perhaps more important. I have set out a landscape where homosexual bodies have the potential to be theologically communicative. Once they are put within the framework of the church's nuptial hermeneutics, they are embedded in a grammar and vocabulary where the unions are able to speak in a particular way – through a desire that is articulated not according to object-desire but in mimesis of God's constancy and steadfast fidelity. The nuptial body is formed in the pattern of God's creative redemption, God's reconciliation, which comes to us as we come into ourselves through God.

Any essay on same-sex unions can only illuminate the linguistic possibilities, the signification must be done by men and women who communicate a desire for God and donate their bodies as a word of the common life of faith.

Notes

1 Compare the account offered here with Margaret A. Farley, 'An Ethic for Same-sex Relations', in Robert Nugent (ed.), *A Challenge to Love: Gay and Lesbian Catholics in the Church* (New York: Crossroad, 1983), pp. 93–106.

2 In Choon-Leong Seow (ed.), *Homosexuality and Christian Community* (Louisville: Westminster/John Knox, 1996), pp. 123–32.

3 Adam, 'Disciples Together, Constantly', p. 125.

4 Adam, 'Disciples Together, Constantly', p. 126.

5 Adam, 'Disciples Together, Constantly', p. 128.

6 Adam, 'Disciples Together, Constantly'.

7 Adam, 'Disciples Together, Constantly', p. 126.

8 Adam, 'Disciples Together, Constantly', p. 127.

9 'The fact that some gay and lesbian Christians have sustained committed relationships over many years, despite the active opposition that such relationships provoke in many quarters, testifies to an admirable and rare sense of constant fidelity (a constancy that is all the more striking since many partners have undertaken overwhelming responsibilities to nurse their beloved through the devastating effects of AIDS). The dignity and integrity of their discipleship are self-evident.' (Adam, 'Disciples Together, Constantly', pp. 129–30.)

10 Eric Marcus, *Is it a Choice?* (New York: Harper Collins, 1993), p. 42.

11 For an account of the vocation of chastity, see Peter Brown, *The Body and Society* (New York: Columbia University, 1988), pp. 33–64.

12 Mention of marriage and the celibate life requires some comment about those who do not make a formal commitment to either. In the New Testament, life outside of marriage has a privileged place. It is a special vocation and a sign of God's reign, a dedication of one's life to the kingdom (1 Cor. 7 is the standard text). Long since, celibacy has been sacramentalized through religious vows, and in the process remaining single, without taking vows, has become a vulnerable and misunderstood state. Singleness has been misunderstood because the church has come to have only shallow means for articulating the meaning and commitments of such a life. Singleness is informal – without ritual expression, without a coming out. As a result, singleness evokes suspicion as an uncommitted body, with no set pattern of constancy, with no clearly established communicative relationship of the body, and with no clear sign (sacrament) of embodied reconciliation. The problem is not with the single life *per se* or with the community's interests in coming out. The fact that a person must come out as 'single' is the problem. The very status, 'single' (in contrast to vows of the religious life), shows a loss of depth in the church's language of family. If the biological, nuclear family were not dominant, then those who were not to enter marriages or formal vows still would not be considered 'single'. The tenuous status of single people in the church reveals the importance of coming out, but more importantly, it shows that coming out is always set within a particular social landscape.

13 Mystic, Conn.: Twenty-Third Publications, 1983.

14 *Sacraments and Sacramentality*, pp. 27–40.

15 In *In Memory of Her*, Elisabeth Schüssler Fiorenza argues that Eph. 5 both sustains the

patriarchal structure of the ancient household and challenges it – by setting the husband's love for his wife in terms of the servant love of Christ. See *In Memory of Her* (New York: Crossroad, 1989), pp. 266–70.

16 It is appropriate to question whether or not marriage is primary among the sacraments given that Cooke uses the eucharistic narrative as an interpretive framework for marriage.

17 Cooke, *Sacraments and Sacramentality*, p. 92.

18 See *Gaudium et Spes*, Pastoral Constitution on the Church in the Modern World (Second Vatican Council, Dec. 7, 1965), §12.

19 See *Arcanum Divinae Sapientiae*, Encyclical Letter of Pope Leo XIII on Christian Marriage (10 Feb. 1880); and *Casti Connubii*, Encyclial Letter of Pope Pius XI on Christian Marriage (31 Dec. 1930)

20 Pope John Paul II in James V. Schall SJ (ed.) *Sacred in All Its Forms* (Boston: Daughters of St Paul, 1934), pp. 124–52.

21 *Sacred in All its Forms*, p. 125.

22 See 'Fatherhood and the Family', in James V. Schall, SJ, *Sacred in All its Forms*, pp. 86–94.

23 'Fatherhood and the Family', p. 137.

24 See James P. Hanigan, *Homosexuality: The Test Case far Christian Ethics* (New York: Paulist Press, 1988); and Philip Keane, *Sexual Morality: A Catholic Perspectice* (New York: Paulist Press, 1977).

25 See Rosemary Radford. Ruether, *Woman-Church: Theology and Practice of Feminist Liturgical Communities* (San Francisco: Harper & Row, 1985).

26 See Mary Douglas, 'The Gender of the Beloved', *Heythrop Journal* 36:4 (1995), pp. 397–408; and Mary Aquin O'Neill, 'The Mystery of Being Human Together', in Catherine Mowry LaCugna (ed.), *Freeing Theology: The Essentials of Theology in Feminist Perspective* (New York: HarperCollins, 1993), pp. 139–60.

27 See Graham Ward's use of Luce Irigaray's inversion of Freud in 'Divinity and Sexuality: Luce Irigaray an Christology', *Modern Theology* 12:2 (April 1996), pp. 221–38, and 'In the Name of the Father and of the Mother', *Literature and Theology* 8:3 (Sept. 1994), pp. 311–27.

28 See Eve Kosofsky Sedgwick, *Epistemology of the Closet* (Berkeley: University of California Press, 1990), pp. 67–90.

29 Eve Kosofsky Sedgwick, *Between Men: English Literature and Male Homosocial Desire* (New York: Columbia University Press, 1985). Sedgwick argues that strictures against homosexuality are prominent in homosocial contexts, where basic social exchanges are between men.

30 Catholic and mainline Protestant churches in the US say virtually the same thing about orientation and act. For my sources, see Congregation For the Doctrine of the Faith, 'Letter to the Bishops of the Catholic Church on the Pastoral Care of Homosexual, Persons', in Jeannine Gramick and Pat Furey (eds.), *The Vatican and Homosexuality* (New York: Crossroad, 1988), pp. 1–12, and National Conference of Bishops' more recent 'Pastoral Message to Parents of Homosexual Children and Suggestions for Pastoral Ministers', *Origins* 27:17 (1997), pp. 285, 287–91.

31 On no terms is a homosexual orientation supposed to inhibit Christian love (agape). Because a homosexual orientation tends to a disordered act, it is considered a disordered condition but not a psychological or social deviance. Homosexual persons are considered

as healthy and whole as anyone else. It is difficult to sort out these distinctions. See Stephen J. Rossetti and Gerald D. Coleman, 'Psychology and the Church's Teaching on Homosexuality', *American* 177:13 (1997), pp. 6–23.

32 Karol Wojtyla (John Paul II), *Love and Responsibility* trans. H. T. Willetts (New York: Farrar, Straus, Gironx, 1981), pp. 48–9.

33 *Catechism of the Catholic Church* (Liberia Editrice Vaticana/Paulist Press, 1994), §2357.

34 Pastoral Message to Parents of Homosexual Children and Suggestions for Pastoral Ministers', p. 289.

Sanctification, Homosexuality, and God's Triune Life

Eugene F. Rogers, Jr.

While Christians have always debated "practical" issues like ordination of women, freeing of slaves, and marriage-like unions for gay and lesbian people,[1] they have also always treated embodiment as one of the "highest" concerns of their intellectual discourse, from the election of Israel to the incarnation of God and the resurrection of the dead. Put another way, theology has used one set of terms – creation, election, incarnation, resurrection – while ethically charged post-modern discourse uses another – embodiment, race, gender, orientation. Theologians such as Karl Barth tell us that ethics and high theology ought to be closely related,[2] and anthropologists of religion such as Clifford Geertz tell us similar things about ethos and worldview, or social and intellectual practices.[3] Yet only too rarely do Christian ethicists connect doctrines such as incarnation, election, and resurrection with race, gender, and orientation.[4] My constructive proposals attempt to *renegotiate* ethos and worldview in Christianity by reference to the central symbols that connect them – where ethos includes the practices of marriage (or lack thereof) for straight, gay, and lesbian people; worldview includes what Christians believe about the world, signally dogmatics ("a critical native model"[5]); and the central symbol is the body of Christ enacted in the sacraments. Marriage and the Eucharist (as well as baptism and monastic vows) tell Christians what bodies are for before God, or what they mean, by incorporating them into the body of Christ.

Along the wide spectrum of views about marriage for gay and lesbian couples, the extremes sometimes meet in claims that gay and lesbian marriages are irredeemable, on the far right because they are gay, on the far left because they are marriages. I claim the opposite: they can be a means of redemption.

Moreover, they can be a means of anticipating God's catching human beings up into that wedding feast that God celebrates in the life of the Trinity, an elevation that the tradition has had the wisdom to call consummation. The question for the right is: Given that gay and lesbian people are not going to go away, what shall the church *do* with them? The question for the left is: Given that gay and lesbian people are part of the church, how much shall it allow their bodies to *mean*? In the context of baptism, Eucharist, and (yes) monastic vows, the Spirit is now moving Christian communities to see marriage as the central symbol by which to test and renegotiate the fit of gay and lesbian bodies into the body of Christ.

Rowan Williams puts it this way:

> The whole story of creation, incarnation, and our incorporation into the fellowship of Christ's body tells us that God desires us, *as if we were God*, as if we were that unconditional response to God's giving that God's self makes in the life of the Trinity. . . . The life of the Christian community has as its rationale – if not invariably its practical reality – the task of teaching us this: so ordering our relations that human beings may see themselves as desired, as the occasion of joy.[6]

The question for both sides is then this: By what sort of sacramental practices can the church best teach gay and lesbian Christians to see themselves as occasions of joy, that God desires them as if they were God?[7] Marriage is peculiarly suited to teaching God's desire for human beings because it mirrors God's choosing of human beings for God's own. As Barth puts it, "In that the election of God is real, there is such a thing as love and marriage."[8] God's election of Israel, like marriage, involves a discipline of faithfulness in which God permits human beings to become what God sees. God's election of the mostly gentile church, like marriage for gay and lesbian couples, is (in Paul's metaphor) God's overturning of nature to graft wild olives onto a domestic tree – to include them, that is, in a structure (the law of the Spirit) that allows their selves, their souls and bodies, to mean much more than they would by nature, to be caught up into the very life and love by which God loves God.

Definitions and Disclaimers

A critic has complained that Williams's essay, just quoted, makes no "argument."[9] Williams seems to take the licitness of gay and lesbian relationships of certain sorts as given, and goes on from there. The critic thought the essay begged the question, and I thought it refreshed the debate, by not starting from the shared premises but by attempting to make its own premises attractive through disciplined elaboration. That is not a bad procedure in theology. It has been said of Karl Barth, perhaps the most important Protestant theologian since the Reformation (d. 1968), that he argued aesthetically, or by thick description: "He took the classical themes of communal Christian language molded by the Bible, tradition and constant usage in worship, practice, instruction and controversy, and he restated or redescribed them, rather than evolving arguments on their behalf."[10] Such a conceptual description does argue, implicitly; it argues from and to coherence. Even a theologian as famous for formal deduction as Thomas Aquinas can agree. Considering how theology properly mounts arguments, Thomas insists that no way lies open to persuade an opponent who begins from different premises, except to start from one's own and treat the opponent's generously as *solubilia argumenta*, difficulties to be overcome.[11]

The argument I offer is less the sort Christian theologians sometimes offer with definitions and entailments, givens and therefores, the sort a scholastic would have called an argument *ex necessitate*, or from necessity, although it is that in part. It is more an attempt to retell and renarrate bits of the Christian story so as to reveal the coherence of Christian thought with a practice of marriage broad enough to include gay and lesbian couples and leaving room for vowed celibates in community. Far from a lack of argument, that procedure mounts an argument of a different sort – one the scholastics called an argument *ex convenientia*, or from fittingness, and one Geertz would call thick description. It tests the hypothesis that gay and lesbian marriage can newly suit or befit the Christian tradition. I hope to identify fresh starting places for thinking about these matters, and treat traditional ones, liberal and conservative, constructively rather than polemically, as difficulties leading to a more adequate account, as Thomas uses objections and replies. I do not argue, that is, that Christianity could not exist otherwise, but that its existence in the way I describe does make better sense of central claims about God, the community of the faithful, and their relationship. It does them greater justice.

I ask such questions as these: What is the relation of the human body to the trinitarian life of God? To the incarnate body of God's Word? To the body of the church? To the body of Christ in the Eucharist? How does human procreation relate to divine creation? How does sex relate to grace? How does nature relate to redemption and consummation? What are gay people and celibates for? What does God want with sex, anyway?

The question of Christian marriage for lesbian and gay couples is political primarily in the sense that all theology is political: theology is always concerned with the question of life with God; life with God is a life in community, both with God and with other human beings; and politics is at best a reflection on what life in community ought to be. Talk of God's people, of God's kingdom or house, of a heavenly city, or a new Jerusalem is all talk of an ideal polity. So Thomas Aquinas characterizes life with God not only as "friendship," "homeland," and "community" but also as *"res publica,"* a commonwealth or republic, or, more literally, a political matter.[12]

Christian marriage for lesbian and gay couples is political secondarily in that marriage, too, is a community, a little polity, a domestic church, a way of life under God, one of the purposes of which is to build up that larger polity under God, the community of the faithful. So Bible and tradition describe God's choosing life with the community of Israel not only in terms of polity but also in terms of (sometimes adulterous) marriage, as they describe also the relationship of Christ and the church.

That is all miles away from the marriage politics that goes on in the Senate when politicians debate a "Defense of Marriage Act" – miles away in more ways than one, and by design. Yet a theological argument that churches should recognize gay and lesbian marriages now has political consequences of the ordinary sort in election campaigns, in legislative debates, and before the courts because religious citizens articulate positions controversial not only outside but also within their traditions.

Which traditions? I have quoted Barth, a Protestant, and Thomas, a Catholic, and spoken in Eastern Orthodox ways about sharing in God's triune life. In this my approach is ecumenically Protestant. Protestantism had its theological origin and reason for existence in a proposal about church teaching on the justification of the unrighteous.[13] Now that parties to ecumenical dialogue have experienced remarkable convergence on the very issue that divided them at the Reformation,[14] the only excuse for further Protestant proposals about church teaching (about married priests, ordained women, marriages for gay and lesbian couples) must be a return to their roots as prophetic or Pauline movements of the Spirit of unity, incomplete without magisterial or Petrine response from the rest of the church. The essay is Protestant precisely in that it does not stand alone; rather, it enjoys a characteristically Protestant obligation to take from and speak to the traditions that gave it rise. It finds itself citing Thomas Aquinas as the Catholic magisterium would not; but thus it comes inevitably into conversation with Catholics, saying: Can you not use Thomas this way? Similarly, it deploys Eastern Orthodox liturgy as the Orthodox would not, asking: Can you not use the liturgy this way? – as Protestantism too exists only from and for a community of the faithful larger than itself.

Creation, Procreation, and the Trinity

It has been argued that human beings are created in God's image in that as God creates, human beings procreate. Quite aside from the fact that it makes Jesus a deficient human being and separates celibacy from marriage, that argument makes creation necessary to God. The famous sermon is wrong that has God saying "I'm lonely. I'm gonna make me a world." Such views of creation ignore the Trinity. Even before creation, God was not lonely. Because God as Father, Son, and Holy Spirit is community already *in se*, God has no need of creation, and God's love for human beings is radically contingent.

> God has no need of us, He has no need of the world and heaven and earth at all. He is rich in Himself. He has fullness of life; all glory, all beauty, all goodness and holiness reside in Him. He is sufficient unto Himself. . . . The mystery of creation on the Christian interpretation is not primarily – as the fools think in their heart – the problem whether there is a *God* as the originator of the world . . . [but] whether it can really be the case that God wishes to be not only for Himself, . . . that *we* exist alongside and outside Him. . . . Creation is *grace*.[15]

Part of that grace is that God is vulnerable not necessarily, but by self-determination. God chooses to create; God chooses creaturely children. God woos Israel (Hos. 2:14), and Israel is allowed to ravish God (Song of Solomon 4:9a). In the love of Israel and the life of Jesus God becomes vulnerable by choice. God's need is God's *wish*. As Barth says, God is the One who loves in *freedom*. Yet God's chosen vulnerability is also not out of character for God; God is not deprived even of the blessings of mutual dependence, since the life of the Trinity is itself one of grace and gratitude, so that Jesus can truly give thanks to the Father before breaking bread. God's need is God's *wish*; God's wish is grace, and God's faithfulness to that wish, grace on grace. Created space and time, and thus our bodies, precisely as finite, are structures of mutual dependence by which we may experience grace and gratitude. In loving Israel, in the life of Jesus, in the practice of the Eucharist, called the Great Thanksgiving, God makes space and takes time for exchanges of mutual gift, for grace and gratitude.

The shock and wonder of God's self-determining love in creation has a better analogy, according to biblical metaphor, in the contingency of the love of one human being for another, than in procreation. The marriage covenant itself (human or divine) adds to love time and space for exchanges of mutual gift, with procreation or without. Passages that speak of Israel as God's bride are distinct from those that speak of Israel as God's child, and do not speak of procreation. Jesus and Paul both speak of marriage without mentioning children. That they do so because they expect the imminent end of the world only heightens the point that marriage has an integral, eschatological end in the grace and gratitude of the trinitarian life, apart from childbearing. God's extention of the covenant to the gentiles, just because it comes eschatalogically at the end of the world, grows by baptism, which is a rite of adoption, not procreation, and promises a future by resurrection, not childbirth. That is clear in Paul's metaphors too, where the gentiles do not grow naturally on the Jewish tree, but by ingrafting (Rom. 11). The whole pattern of adoption, ingrafting, and resurrection, which goes to the very heart of God's extension of the covenant to the gentiles, relativizes procreation, insisting that all human beings (that is, Jew and gentile) find fulfillment in sanctification – that is, in God. The mutual self-giving of the marriage covenant, divine or human, has an integral end not in multiplication, as such, but in the mutual self-giving of the Trinity – an end to which children may contribute.

Indeed, children constitute an extraordinary case of other people generally. Other people are our neighbors, who can help in sanctification, in making us better, and in consummation, in fulfilling our lives; if they do so, that too is grace. Children, like neighbors generally, can sanctify also by delight, a delight by which the Spirit catches up human beings into the love of the Father for the Son. Procreation can be grace, as creation is grace; and since procreation is also natural, it is a good of the species – though certainly not of every sex act and not necessarily, either, of every marriage. The inability of a human pair to procreate may be a misfortune, but not one that undermines the likeness of human beings to God. On the contrary, Christians lay more weight on God's *adoption* of them as children in baptism. Furthermore, since God is creator and human beings are creatures, the fulfillment of human community *cannot* be in more creaturely children; the fulfillment of human community is in sharing the trinitarian community of God.

Indeed, talk of children as a necessary goal of marriage risks idolatry. Here Eastern Orthodoxy's critique of western Christianity is telling. So Paul Evdokimov writes, "Both the preservation of the species and selfish sexual pleasure reduce the partner to a mere tool and destroy [human] dignity."[16] Related stories of children central to Judaism and Christianity insist that children are not to be taken for granted, but as gifts of grace. In the binding of Isaac, Abraham shows that God's fulfillment of the promise to make him a father of many nations does not, somehow, depend on his only child, a pattern that Christianity takes up and repeats in the story of the crucifixion of God's Son. At the crucial moment, Abraham trusts in God to fulfill the promise, not Isaac; for Christians it is Christ's resurrection, not their progeny, that guarantees them a future. So far from holding that children sanctify marriage, some Christian thinkers have even interpreted the remarks of Paul ignoring childbearing in marriage at 1 Cor. 7:25–40 and of Jesus positively discouraging it at Mark 13:17 and parallels as indicating that biological procreation not taken up into community with God simply carries forward the body of death.[17] Barth, who elsewhere disapproves of homosexuality, turns the tables when he comes to comment on the passage in Rom. 1 usually taken to connect homosexuality with idolatry, referring idolatry instead to child, family, and (assuming the reader is a heterosexual man) woman, putting them in the disreputable company of the Fatherland:

Wherever the qualitative distinction between human beings and the final Omega is overlooked and misunderstood, that fetishism is bound to appear in which God is experienced in "birds and fourfooted things," and finally, or rather primarily, in "the likeness of the corruptible human being" – Personality, the Child, the Woman – and in the half-spiritual, half-material creations, exhibitions, and representation of the human being's creative ability – Family, Nation, State, Church, Fatherland.[18]

A nuptial sermon has had the audacity to admonish bride and groom that rings can signify not only faithful but also idolatrous commitment, so that wedding bands can make a cult of marriage much as the Israelites took rings of idolatry to make themselves a Golden Calf.[19] The goal of marriage is God, and community with God fulfills the human sexual nature for married and unmarried alike. For celibacy in community, like marriage, makes something before God precisely of the body.

Worried about the sort of idolatry that comes from too high a view of sex and marriage, a friend has complained that "all married couples need is to have a theologian telling them that they should not only expect great sex but *spiritually significant* sex, God help us."[20] A contrary view is that of the celibate Sebastian Moore: "The most dramatic, indeed comic, instance of cross-purposes between the Vatican and the married, is that the Vatican sees the problem as one of curbing desire, whereas the married know that the problem is to keep desire going, which means to keep it growing, which means deepening."[21] Both remarks are true. It is entirely beyond the power of human beings to render sex *spiritually* significant; that expectation would be idolatrous. It is entirely in character for *God*, however, to do just that; to deny it would be to despair of God's ability to make good on creation. More important is the deepening of desire that Moore talks about; in marriage, it has the opportunity to become the more reliable means of sanctification that eros may trick lovers into: acts of faith, hope, and charity. Christian life is an expansion, a straining forward (*epektasis*) into ever-greater love of God, which means that God is constantly expanding human desire for God even as God fulfills it. True desire is ever greater.[22] Marriage is a sacrament because it gives desire time and space to stretch forward (another *epektasis*) into things that are *more* desirable. Marriage allows sex to mean *more*. "Decisions about sexual lifestyle . . . are about how much we want our bodily selves to mean, rather than what emotional needs we're meeting or what laws we're satisfying."[23] "Who devalues the body? Those for whom its gestures make no commitments, or those for whom they can make irrevocable commitments? Those who find freedom in casual nàkedness, or those who reserve this most visible word for those to whom they have something extraordinary to say?"[24] "Marriage is a place where our waywardness begins to be healed and our fear of commitment overcome"[25] – that, and much more. The last remark comes from a manifesto denying gay and lesbian couples the right to marry, yet they too need that healing and overcoming of fear. No one has seriously claimed, so far as I know, that they are any less in need of sanctification than straight couples. Indeed marriage shares with celibacy the end of sanctifying the body,[26] of permitting it something *more* to be about, something *further* to mean, something *better* to desire, until finally it gets taken up into the life in which God loves God. In this process of desiring ever more, one incidentally or intentionally gives up – lets go of, gets rid of – the petty things that one used to want, and in that way the life of ever-greater desire is one of asceticism, an asceticism in which self-control serves self-abandonment. In this way, too, the end of marriage and monasticism is one. Life with others can bring the rewards of its difficulties – that is, it sanctifies, whether in the community of monks or the community of marriage (straight or gay), whether the shitty diapers one is committed to changing come from babies or AIDS patients. Sexual activity does not make sanctification any "easier" than celibacy does. As traditional marriage and childrearing are gifts of grace more than human achievements, and means of sanctification more than satisfaction, so too monogamous, committed gay and lesbian relationships are also gifts of grace, means of sanctification, upbuilding of the community of the people of God. They are means, bodily means, that God can use to catch human beings up into less and less conditioned acts of self-donation, finally into that unconditional response to God's self-donation that God's self gives in the Trinity.[27]

Someone might object that human beings are made in God's image as God wills and acts, rather than as God is *in se*. And God wills and acts to create. Therefore, human beings are in the image of God just as they procreate, after all. So Aquinas says that we are in the image of God as ones who have the power of our own reason and act, or free will.[28] And yet we are not in God's image, but depart from it, when we will evil. Procreation is therefore normative for sex, and parent–parent–child is a human vestige, or left-over image, of the Trinity.

On the contrary, Augustine considers the human being as in the image of the Trinity in terms of internal structures, in the capacities to will and act, not in their particular use, and certainly not in terms of their use for procreation. Indeed, Augustine does consider the image parent–parent–child for the Trinity, and rejects it.[29]

Furthermore, when Aquinas considers human beings in the image of God as having the power of their own acts, he could require procreation to complete that imitation of God only if he considered procreation a necessary good of every individual human being. But he does not, since celibacy does not impugn the image of God. (Indeed celibacy makes another creation precisely of the body.) Too easy, the critic will say: procreation is not required of celibates; it is only required (as in *Humanae Vitae*) that every sex act not be intentionally closed to procreation. (Gay and lesbian couples might invoke the principle of double effect to argue that the infertility of their unions is precisely not intentional, but a foreseen yet unintended side effect.) That critic would have the facts of nature, and the sense of the great majority of the Christian faithful against him: procreation is not, naturally or faithfully, the result of every sex act, and the proper use of human reason and will involves prudence about circumstances – without being closed to the possibility of children, even accidental ones. Well then, the critic will say, procreation is necessary only for couples. It is properly a good of marriage, so that as long as the marriage is open to children (but not necessarily every sex act of that marriage), then sex is licit.

But procreation is simply not a good that belongs to the couple as such, much less to every sex act. Rather, it belongs to the species. Procreation is a good of the species because the species is what procreation exists to promote. But if procreation is the good of the species, then not every human being must accomplish it (so celibacy is allowed), and not every sex act must accomplish it (so marriages of the postmenopausal or infertile, or arguably of gay and lesbian people, are licit), and not even every fertile couple need accomplish it; rather, the species as a whole must accomplish it. There need only be enough procreation to keep the species flourishing, and then procreation as the good of the species is fulfilled. And that need, fortunately or unfortunately, is in no danger of going unmet. Genesis 1:28 famously says "Be fruitful and multiply." It is not usually remembered that the command has an explicit end: "and fill the earth." The earth is now more or less full. Already in the fourth century, Chrysostom could write, "As for procreation, it is not required absolutely by marriage. . . . The proof of this lies in the numerous marriages that cannot have children. This is why the first reason of marriage is to order sexual life, especially now that the human race has filled the entire earth."[30] Speaking precisely of the good of the species leaves room for those considerations. Sex before God is for sanctification, for God's catching us up into God's triune life. Sex is for procreation to the extent that procreation promotes that end. The chief end of sex is not to make children of human beings, but to make children of God. And Christians best imitate God's relation to them as children not when they bear and beget them, but when they adopt them.

God's Acting Contrary to Nature (Rom. 11:24) and Homosexuality

God is said to act "contrary to nature," *para phusin*, in bringing the gentiles into the covenant with Israel, grafting wild branches onto a domestic olive tree (Rom. 11:24).[31] That shocking phrase, the same one Paul uses in Romans 1 to condemn homosexual behavior, governs the earlier passage theologically because it places nature in the service of salvation. It calls for a reconceptualization of "nature" in soteriological terms, in terms – that is, of God's freedom to complete what God began with human beings,[32] God's intent to elevate nature into the glory of the trinitarian communion. Better, it reminds us that in Rom. 1, as in Rom. 11, Paul is not talking about human beings *in general*; Paul is talking about human beings as Jews and gentiles, and therefore of the nature, and salvation, not of all human beings as a class but of all human beings as Jews and gentiles. In Rom. 1, acting contrary to nature characterizes idolatrous *gentiles*, and the great amazement that drives Paul's ministry is that God pours out the Spirit also on *those* people, an amazement Paul expresses in Rom. 11 by characterizing God's saving action as itself contrary to nature. It is more than a horticultural metaphor to express how God grafts gentiles regarded as wild, idolatrous, and unfruitful into the domestic trunk of Israel – close enough already, perhaps, to justify the grafting of another group sometimes regarded as promiscuous, idolatrous, and infertile into the domestic practices of marriage. It is also another of Paul's rhetorical sting operations.[33] It is a reversal of guilt by association. God becomes "guilty" of acting contrary to nature by choosing solidarity with the gentiles, whose identifying characteristic it is to act contrary to nature. "Nature" must become logically subsequent to soteriology, to God's concrete history with Jews and gentiles, which means also that we must reconceptualize nature not in terms of predetermined end, immanent to a general human nature, or *telos* (such as procreation), but in terms of a God-determined end, or eschaton,[34] such as the mutual blessing of God's own trinitarian life. In good Barthian fashion we learn about nature, such as it is, from what God does with it: if God appears to be capable of using sexual orientations too, both heterosexual and homosexual, just in their concrete, messy details, just in their complicated relations to the larger Christian community that they both upbuild and both betray, for God's saving purposes, then that is of a piece with God's surprising salvation of the gentiles. Like the claim that the Spirit of Christ is joining the gentiles to the tree in baptism, the claim that the same Spirit is building up the body of Christ by joining together gay and lesbian couples is a pneumatological one – a claim, that is, about what the Spirit is doing new in the church, one that will one day, if not soon, be empirically verifiable in the church's life.

In Galatians 3:28, Paul writes, "There is no longer Jew or Greek, there is no longer slave or free, there is no longer male and female; for all of you are one in Christ Jesus." The formula is to be taken as a warning. If the Jew/gentile distinction is read in the way of Paul's opponent, then there is no salvation for the gentiles as gentiles, but only as circumcised, as Jews. The salvation of almost all Christians, those who are not ethnically Jews and do not observe Torah, depends on taking this verse seriously. If Christians have endangered their salvation by ignoring the other members of the formula – if they took some 1900 years to overcome the pairs slave and free, male and female – that is no argument why they should continue to do so. Prohibiting gay marriages may put some Christians in the same danger of forfeiting their ingrafting into Israel – which is their very salvation – as maintaining the distinction Jew/gentile or slave/free: it disbelieves in that ingrafting. If Paul himself failed to see that consequence, he also warns explicitly that the ingrafting is precarious and subject to reversal (Rom. 11:21–2). Failing to accept faithful, monogamous gay and lesbian marriages puts gentile Christians in danger of their salvation. Marriage for gay and lesbian spouses depends upon the work of the Holy Spirit no less than baptism for the gentiles, and disbelief in either risks blasphemy against the Spirit.

A critic may hold that "male and female" is overcome only in a way that accords with "nature," or insist that while civil rights are due groups whose distinctions are natural (such as blacks and women), similar, "special" rights are not due to those whose distinctions are moral (such as thieves and homosexuals). "Differences of race are in accord with – not contrary to – our nature, and such differences do not provide justification for behavior otherwise unacceptable. . . . Certain discriminations are necessary within society; it is not too much to say that civilization itself depends on the making of such distinctions (between, finally, right and wrong)."[35]

But "nature" applies in Paul's vocabulary also to "Jew or Greek," and in that case, most important to him of all, it is overcome. "Jew or gentile" is for Paul both a natural and a moral distinction. The application shows how discrimination of the good, moral sort has in fact not rarely, but *usually* been called upon to justify a discrimination of the bad sort. Crucial to my response are cases in which the pairs Jew/Greek, male/female, and free/slave were all cited by their defenders as moral, not neutral, distinctions. Or better, in all cases there was a natural difference that led to a moral defect. So gentiles, women, and slaves were considered in the antique Jewish tradition to be *constitutionally* incapable of keeping the commandments, and especially at risk of moral fault.[36] That reasoning is structurally isomorphic with the current Vatican line on homosexuality – that it is a natural difference, innocent in itself, which nevertheless tends toward a moral defect.[37] Similarly, some Christian slaveholders during the positive defense of slavery in the 1850s and some recent Mormons have argued that the curse of Ham represents a moral fault that, like the Fall, gives the natural difference between blacks and whites a permanent moral distinction.[38] So slavery is a "divine institution . . . not to be removed until the curse pronounced on Ham shall have been removed from his descendants."[39] Or, more mildly, slaves, women, and homosexual persons have not, perhaps, a necessary subordination, but they do have a contingent vocation in the order of things: "The slave . . . is an actor on the broad theater of life – and as true merit depends not so much upon the part which is assigned, as upon the propriety and dignity with which it is sustained – so fidelity in this relation may hereafter be as conspicuously rewarded as fidelity in more exalted stations."[40]

As all are called to fidelity in their station according to pro-slavery Christians, of which the fidelity of slaves (to masters) is only a particular case, so all are called to chastity in their state of life according to certain Christians, of which the chastity of gay and lesbian Christians (in celibacy) is only a particular calling. "Christians who are homosexual are called, as all of us are, to chaste life."[41]

Indeed, the argument is so common that I think of it as "the standard argument." In some cases, it may be true that a natural distinction leads to a moral fault. But since versions and sections of this compound argument have been offered at various times about gentiles (by Jews), Jews (by Christians), women (by Aquinas), blacks (by Southern Presbyterians before the Civil War), and gay and lesbian people (by the Vatican in the 1980s),[42] prudence suggests that *the burden of proof should shift*. Since we have rejected its implications in all the other cases, we should ask for additional proof in the case of gay and lesbian people. Let me present the standard argument in its most comprehensive form.

1. In a feature of the standard argument least often appealed to in sophisticated versions, but accounting for much of its continuing power, decline or fall narratives in Scripture purportedly reveal that God has punished certain groups. God has punished the gentiles for their idolatry with the animal character of the ass, according to Genesis Rabbah on v. 22:5. God has punished the Jews for "rejecting" Christ. God has punished women on account of Eve's sin, according to Genesis 3:16. God has punished blacks as "Hamites," or descendants of Noah's son Ham, condemned to be "a slave of slaves" for uncovering his father's nakedness, according to Genesis 9:22–25. And God has punished performers of homosexual acts as a punishment on idolatrous gentiles so that they will die out, according to Romans 1:18–27.[43]

2. God's just punishment of the disfavored group for some narrated sin comes in the form of a natural disorder or weakness that is not yet itself a moral fault. Gentiles, Jews, women, blacks, or gays are not evil in themselves, but they are so constituted (or "oriented") that they are specially subject to temptation – in each case especially sexual temptation.[44]

3. As members of a naturally labile group, gentiles, Jews, women, blacks, or gays are more prone to violate natural law or commit moral fault, although they need not. Natural disorder (orientation) tends to moral fault (act).

4. Therefore, a religious objection to equality for gentiles, Jews, women, blacks, or gays in religion or society can claim not to be based on mere prejudice, but on the disfavored group's characteristic but freely chosen behavior, which *does* constitute a moral fault.

5. And specifically, sexual restrictions can therefore purport to *protect* both the religious and the labile group. Thus Jews might not marry gentiles;

Christians might not marry Jews; blacks (until 1967 in Virginia) might not marry whites – or indeed, when slaves, legally marry each other. Such marriages, between males as between slaves, are naturally unstable and morally wrong.

6. Even should one charitably find the state of the disordered a subject of pity or apparent injustice, one can still hold that the duty of those so afflicted is to do the best they can with what they have. Thus it is the contingent vocation, if not the necessary nature, of gay people or women or slaves to have a special service, even if their condition is not their fault. It is true that calls to a particular vocation usually come not by visions or voices but by an accumulation of particular circumstances, so that being female may contribute to a vocation to motherhood or being gay to a vocation to celibacy. But to make those determinations in advance and across the board does not attend to particular circumstances, but levels them out.[45] Otherwise God would elect only the first born and not second sons, or only the fertile and not the barren, or only the righteous and not the sinful, or only the Jews and not the gentiles. As Barth was fond of quoting, *Latet periculum in generalibus*: danger lurks in generalities. In the standard argument, women are called to childrearing, blacks to service, gay and lesbian people to celibacy, in each case *as a group*, whether the particulars to which God usually attends indicate that vocation or not.

The insistence on a general theory of vocation rather than particular cases of it can persist even when the author concedes generalization's apparent injustice. For example:

> The propriety of slavery, like that of the restraints and punishments of civil government, rests on the fact that man is depraved and fallen. Such is his character, that the rights of the whole, and the greatest welfare of the whole, may, in many cases, demand the subjection of one part of society to another, even as man's sinfulness demands the subjection of all to civil government. Slavery is, indeed but one form of the institution, *government*. . . . And this is the Scriptural account of the origin of slavery, as justly incurred by the sin and depravity of man.[46]

Despite a far different account of sin, and a far higher estimate of human dignity, one now hears, to similar effect, that universal homosexual celibacy is, indeed, but one form of the virtue chastity.

Not only do I propose that the standard argument has been unjustly used so often that the burden of proof must shift, but I also propose that God's providential order of salvation specifically *overturns* the standard argument. That is one meaning of God's acting *para phusin*, or against the standard. If God has not acted to overturn the standard argument on Jews and gentiles, then we gentile Christians are not saved after all. *We are not saved!* It is the wild branches that God grafts on according to Romans 11, the gentiles with whom Paul associated sexual license and on the hearts of whom the Spirit writes a new law, in this case, I argue, the law of marriage. As God grafts gentiles, the wild branches, onto the domestic covenant of God's household with Israel, structured by the Torah of the Spirit, so God grafts gay and lesbian couples (whom detractors also associate with sexual license) by a new movement of the Spirit onto the domestic, married covenants of straight women and men.

The Body's Grace?

Williams's essay bears the title, "The Body's Grace." In it he claims that grace, like some sexual love, works a change in a human being by causing her to reperceive herself as loved by Another. This passage introduces another we have seen before:

> Grace, for the Christian believer, is a transformation that depends in large part on knowing yourself to be seen in a certain way: as significant, as wanted.
>
> The whole story of creation, incarnation, and our incorporation into the fellowship of Christ's body tells us that God desires us, *as if we were God*, as if we were that unconditional response to God's giving that God's self makes in the life of the Trinity. We are created so that we may be caught up in this; so that we may grow into the wholehearted love of God by learning that God loves us as God loves God.
>
> The life of the Christian community has as its rationale – if not invariably its practical reality – the task of teaching us this: so ordering our relations that human beings may see themselves as desired, as occasions of joy.[47]

A critic might raise related objections to the concept of the body's grace – one about grace and one about the body:[48] (1) Despite the stirring trinitarian ring, the concept of the body's grace trades on too vague a concept of grace, reducing it to any kind of transforming, positive regard, of which God's grace becomes a mere example. (2) The concept of the body's grace psychologizes the body because a concept takes the body seriously as a body only if it takes account of real bodily differences.

A shorter answer to these objections has to do with how justice constructs bodies and grace. Bodies, as we have seen, are one of the ways in which Christians ought to take particulars seriously: God chose the Jews; the incarnation took place in a particular place and time; the sacraments locate Christ again in space and time; the priest represents Christ still another way in space and time; particular bodily things – this bread and this wine – do matter. And so, to sum up, it really does matter whether someone has a penis or a vagina. I don't mean to belittle this objection. There is more to the "insert tab A in slot B" argument than meets the ear of most revisionists. Christians believe other things that are just as closely tied to the body. The question is: *Which* bodily things ought Christians to believe? Are some bodily forms, like gay and lesbian relationships, irredeemable, or can God sanctify them? Which bodily forms we revere has a lot to do with what sort of society we are, what our external boundaries and internal organs are in the *social* body.[49] And here the question depends upon what vision of justice we want to uphold. Societies that distinguish sharply between men and women have justice; it is different from the justice that obtains in an individualist society. Justice among the baptized must be specified by the formula "In Christ there is no Jew or Greek, slave or free, male and female." The center of biblical embodiment is circumcision. The important thing about Jesus' birth in space and time was that his mother was Jewish, and so was he. God's covenant with the Jews is specific, and only by being grafted into it do gentiles have a leg to stand on. But one center of the bodily, circumcision, is relativized in that saying of Paul's by another center, the body of Christ. If the bodily distinction of circumcision is overcome, then gay/straight means nothing, especially if sexual license is the issue of concern about both gay and gentile Christians. Indeed, to the peril of the church, it was unbelieving Jews, not gay and lesbian people, whom Paul assimilated to Sodom and Gomorrah (Rom. 9:29). Jewish and Christian societies have constructed gentile and Jewish bodies according to better and worse notions of justice.[50] Paul overturns those patterns. Paul (at his best) causes bodies to be constructed, not according to human justice but according to God's justification, because he believes in a God who justifies *gentiles* and justifies them *uncircumcised*.

A longer answer to the question of the body's grace depends on the theological procedure of realistic analogy. According to the procedure of analogy, related realities generate related meanings.[51] So in the standard medieval example, dating to Aristotle, both food and urine can be "healthy" because food *contributes* to health and urine *indicates* health. The two relations are not the same, but they are real, and the notion of a healthy *person* stands in the center to give sense to all appropriate uses. The healthy person is the "primary analogate," the one who gives sense to the others, whom theologians call the secondary analogate. The theory of analogy offers a solution to the problem of human language about God generally. Take the statement "God is good." If the primary analogate of "good" is *human* goodness, then it is hard to see how the word can apply properly to God. Human goodness is so unreliable that applying it to God is equivocal, not appropriate. On the other hand, if *God's* goodness is the primary analogate, then "good" applies properly to God in the first place and to human beings only derivatively, deficiently, and secondarily.[52]

The procedure is often used to defend traditional language about God. For example, on this view it is not a good objection to "Father" language for God that human fathers are unfit to represent God. They are unfit. But that is not the way the analogy works. It is not relevant that we *learn* the word first from its application to human fathers. Its true, proper application is to God. God, not a human parent, is the father *par excellence*. Human beings ordained as "father" – that is, priests – are the derivative, deficient, and secondary analogates to the fatherhood of God. And that makes biological fathers only derivative, deficient, and *tertiary* analogates. It is the father in the story of the prodigal son who teaches priests and parents what true fatherhood is like, not they who specify what God is like.

But analogy also turns to nontraditional purposes. For example, the tradition has always held that God, though spoken of as Father, is nevertheless not biologically male. It follows that God's priests may also be "father," without being male.[53] Similarly, in the Middle Ages, Jesus, though biologically male, became mother *par excellence*. Secondarily, Cistercian abbots, who were biologically male, were called mothers, too.[54] Does "the body's grace" respect or reverse the proper order of analogates?

The objection to a grace of the body, then, is this: it sounds as if it takes an all-too-general category, transformative, positive regard, as the primary analogate, of which God's grace is not the defining example, but a mere illustration, if the most impressive. To be theologically adequate, grace must be defined first of all as what God does, and the grace of the body related to that. But that is just what Williams does:

> [T]he body's grace itself only makes human sense if we have a language of grace in the first place; and that depends on having a language of creation and redemption. To be formed in our humanity by the loving delight of another is an experience whose contours we can identify most clearly and hopefully if we have also learned or are learning about being the object of the causeless, loving delight of God, being the object of God's love for God through incorporation into the community of God's Spirit and the taking-on of the identity of God's Child.[55]

The references to God's Spirit and Child are crucial. For if *God* defines what grace is, then grace is simply an impersonal name for the Holy Spirit. "The gift of the Holy Spirit is nothing but the Holy Spirit."[56] That Spirit is identified in the Christian community by the biblical stories about Jesus, since the Spirit is also the Spirit of Christ. Without saying so, Williams makes the word *grace* an analogy in the strict theological sense, where the grace of God supplies the primary analogate. The grace of the body only makes sense by reference to the grace of God identified in a community that tells certain stories of God's creation and redemption. Only thus can it emerge that the body is one of God's ways of catching human beings up in God's own life, and therefore a possible means, derivative and second or third hand, of grace. The body's grace, should it occur, is not a movement of the body up to God, but a movement of the Spirit down, so that human bodies will not be left out of salvation.

The word *body* also has to work analogously because Christian theology is committed to speaking in a number of ways about that central body, the body of Christ. The body of Christ is at once the body assumed by the Second Person of the Triune God, and thus God's body. The body of Christ was also a specifically identifiable, historical human body. The body of Christ is the church, and the body of Christ is the consecrated bread of the Eucharist. Christ's body, to sum up, names a place where God locates God's own self, a place where God has chosen to become vulnerable to human touch and taste and hurt, "God with us." Technically, Christians should say that the body of Christ is the primary analogate of the word *body* in their discourse, the use from which others derive their sense.

Salvation is itself bodily. It depends, for gentile Christians, upon the crucifixion of God's body, and it depends on their human bodies' getting taken up into God's body. For Christians, bodies are no more or less than a means by which God catches hold of and sanctifies human beings. In short, bodies are made to be saved. Union with God does not take place otherwise than by incorporating physical bodies into God's. What does that mean?

At the fraction, or breaking of the bread, of the Eucharist, the Trinity also breaks open to let human beings, through their bodies, into God's triune life. The broken bread is the broken body of Christ, which is the broken body of the triune God, the body by the breaking of which on the cross the Son was forsaken by the Father and the Trinity risked its unity, the Persons threatening to come apart. Better, for humanity's sake the Persons *promise* to come apart, their unity restored in the same way that human unity with them begins, in the Holy Spirit. As Paul writes, "If the Spirit of the One who raised Christ from the dead dwells in you, the One who raised Christ from the dead will give life to your mortal bodies also through the Spirit that dwells in you" (Rom. 8:11).[57] That is the body's grace *par excellence*, the transfiguration of the body by the indwelling of the Spirit who just is grace, the Spirit trinitarianly defined as the *Spirit* of the *One* who raised *Christ*, where Christ is defined in turn as the one who was crucified. The body's grace is first of all what identifies the Trinity by the crucifixion and reunites it in the resurrection. At the Eucharist, secondarily, the fraction breaks open the Trinity to let the body in. The Trinity is entered by the body of a believer through the broken body of the Lord, and the body of the Lord is also broken to enter into the bodies of believers. This co-enveloping or interpenetration of bodies is itself the trinitarian life embodied, broken open, entered into, which could not take place with unembodied human beings.

Human bodies, like human reason, are not left out of the Spirit's work and love's communion, but taken up into it in the pattern of the assumption of flesh by the Logos. Even as older atonement theories talked about the flesh as bait and hook, so God can use eros as bait and hook for a life of commitment and care that takes eros up into agape. As Gregory of Nyssa writes, "Agape which is aroused is called eros."[58] Yet eros still belongs among what remains of God's plan not to leave human bodies out of consummation when we abstract bodies from their purpose to incorporate human beings into God's life. Sexual desire, especially as portrayed by such celibates as St. John of the Cross, prefigures the Eucharist, in which, for Christians, God desires to enter into human bodies and to be desired bodily by them. The Eucharist also begins to consummate their life in God, since in it they partake of the trinitarian communion – they pray to the Father, invoke the Spirit, and commune bodily (the only way they can?) with the Son. Eros, for Christians, ought to be a remainder concept left over from the Eucharist; sex, like the Eucharist, is a participation, analogous and derivative, in a marriage of sacrifice for others and therefore a thanksgiving for involving us in their involvements (among them children or care of the sick). Taken up into the Eucharistic community in a marriage that upbuilds it, eros returns home, performing its task of pointing to the trinitarian community when it issues in fruits of the Spirit that satisfy only as they sanctify. It does so particularly in a wedding centered on the Eucharist, since the kingdom of heaven is like a wedding feast;[59] in a wedding feast the Spirit catches the people up in its own proper work of witnessing, blessing, sanctifying, celebrating, and enjoying the love between the Father and the Son, using the people like the couple as a means to the ascesis of living with others. A wedding feast too emparables, enacts, and furthers the unity of God as it catches human beings up in the love by which God loves God, seducing them into agape for the other even after they leave the feast, a movement prepared by the Son's commitment to the Father – the Father to whom the Son draws near precisely by going out into the far country of God-forsakenness.

Thus gay and lesbian marriages can, like straight marriages, take bodies seriously in a handful of ways:

1. Since the true body, or the primary analogate of "body" in Christian discourse, is the body of Christ, any body is taken seriously that extends and deepens the Eucharistic entry into God's body. Marriage, gay or straight, receives its sacramental character not independently but from the welcoming of the one flesh, in soteriological ways a new body, into the eucharistic community.[60]

The male–female version of the one flesh can be especially apt for representing the union of Christ with his bride the church, but not everyone need represent this union in the same way. The analogy is flexible enough already that both celibates and the married can represent it. Gay and lesbian couples also need not threaten the aptness of the relation between Christ and the church, but can be taken up into it. As the Fatherhood of God is not male, so priests need not be male to be called "Father." Similarly, the frequent identification of the human race with the figure of Mary in Roman Catholic and Eastern Orthodox traditions can lead to taking the race as a whole as ontologically female, yet not everyone must be female for the typology to work.[61] Whether male or female, priests are (as human) brides to Christ's groom and (as ordained) father to the church's children. Religious discourse works in a much richer and subtler fashion than by supposing that one has to instantiate physically what one honors or even represents figurally. What matters is mirroring the election and fidelity of God to God's people; as Barth put it, again, "in that the election of God is real, there is such a thing as love and marriage." So, too, gay and lesbian Christians need have no quarrel with the special aptness of the Genesis account of male and female and their procreation as normative for the *species*, as long as not everyone has to instantiate it to be in God's image.

To say otherwise is to limit the freedom of God in an unbiblical manner. The first chapter of Matthew picks out several stories that lead up to Mary as the supreme example – she who represents the race as a whole – of departures from "normative" marriage and childbirth: the anomalous cases of the women named in the genealogy of Jesus, Tamar, Ruth, Rahab, and "the wife of Uriah," emphasizing the adultery of David with Bathsheba. In each case God proves capable, *mirabile dictu*, of using irregular sexual unions for God's own purposes, even the purpose of human redemption. "Taking the body seriously" must leave room for the way in which the Bible shows *God* taking the body seriously in the history of salvation. Many accounts of sexual relations outside of traditional marriage do not actually leave room for the scandals God delights in using to lead up to the incarnation. They tend to rule out a category of providence or divine freedom or the blowing of the Holy Spirit that could make any more of the virgin birth than a case of unwed motherhood.

2. Any body is taken seriously in which the eucharistic community is built up. Weddings, gay or straight, build up the eucharistic community by contributing the institutional stability of marriage and because weddings represent the trinitarian life. In a wedding, third parties guarantee, celebrate, witness, bless, testify to, and delight in the love of two. When Jesus says the kingdom of heaven is like a wedding feast, and theologians say that the role of the Spirit is to guarantee, celebrate, witness, bless, testify to, and delight in the love of the Father and the Son, they are speaking of the same reality. The Spirit incorporates the wedding guests into the public of love. It bears repeating that Augustine rejects the triad father, mother, child as an analogy for the Trinity, while the analogy of the Spirit to the guests at a wedding has implicit support in the parables of Jesus (Mt. 9:15, 22:2) – the second passage issuing a dire warning about those who do not celebrate the wedding, who refuse the Spirit's work.

3. Any body is taken seriously in which the Holy Spirit dwells so as to raise it from the dead. Anticipation of that resurrection is the bodily sanctification that marriage, as a form of ascetic practice, carries out. Note well, in the Christian view marriage is not for satisfaction, but for sanctification, of which satisfaction and enjoyment will be an inalienable part of its perfection. Marriage and monasticism have exactly the same end: the sanctification of the person by means of the body, by putting the body so in the power of others that one cannot escape their love and truth.[62] Human beings imitate God when they take time and make space for each other, as God takes time and space for Israel and in Jesus; in so doing they honor the body that exists over time and in space. Sartre notoriously opined that "hell is other people"; so is holiness. Indeed, in Eastern Orthodoxy the crowns placed over the heads of bride and groom are crowns of martyrdom. This leaves room for the fading of sexual urgency in marriage (gay or straight) and its being taken up into other forms of care for the partner and the community. So it is too that "in heaven they neither marry nor are given in marriage." The pas de deux with which a romance may begin is taken up into the trinitarian circle: As the carol puts it,

> Then up to heaven I did ascend,
> Where now I dwell in sure substance
> On the right hand of God, that man
> May come unto the general dance.[63]

4. Any body is taken seriously in which a human being begins to fulfill the chief end for which she or he was made, which, according to the first answer of the Westminster catechism, is to "glorify God and enjoy him forever." Sanctification and the Eucharist and wedding feasts certainly glorify God. Properly understood, they enjoy God, too. And if human beings were so created to enjoy God, then the joy of sex, under sanctifying circumstances, cannot be unfitting. Sexual attraction is explicitly or implicitly concerned with real bodies. Gay and lesbian people care about bodies – otherwise many of them would take the easier route and settle for those of the opposite sex. There is *something* right about insert-tab-A-in-slot-B – or there is something in having tabs and slots. What is it? And why is it wrong that God should give it to some with tabs to admire the tabs of others? Or, to be less crude, the chests and shoulders? Even Augustine was able to speculate about the placement of nipples on a man's chest: "They articulate the space of the chest, and they prove that beauty is a value in itself, not tied inevitably to utility in the human body."[64] Or better, the utility is for bodies made aware of grace, the utility of joy.

Williams puts it this way:

Same-sex love annoyingly poses the question of what the meaning of desire is – in itself, not considered as instrumental to some other process, such as the peopling of the world. We are brought up against the possibility not only of pain and humiliation without any clear payoff, but, just as worryingly, of nonfunctional joy – of joy, to put it less starkly, whose material "production" is an embodied person aware of grace.[65]

Just because a body is pleasing to me I become vulnerable, and God has made us so to be vulnerable in one another's bodily presence. The embodiment of God's creation is borne in upon me and will not leave me alone.[66] Neither monogamy nor celibacy cause these interventions of God through bodily forms of the neighbor to go away.[67]

Perhaps this is the point to mention that the phenomenon of gay and lesbian desire, contrary to popular belief, can do a good job of articulating what celibacy is for in the Christian tradition. For celibacy also raises the question of nonfunctional joy. Both Jesus and Paul speak of sexual desire and fulfillment without mentioning children. If sex is for *God*, then the task of celibacy is to bear witness to that fact *directly* and *immediately*, whereas the task of people in sanctifying sexual relationships of whatever orientation is to bear witness to that *indirectly* and *mediately*.

> It is perhaps because of our need to keep that perspective clear before us [that the body's grace depends on the loving delight of God] that the community needs some who are called beyond or aside from the ordinary patterns of sexual relation to put their identities direct into the hands of God in the single life. *This is not an alternative to the discovery of the body's grace.* All those taking up the single vocation . . . must know something about desiring and being desired if their single vocation is not to be sterile and evasive. Their decision (as risky as the commitment to sexual fidelity) is to see if they can find themselves, their bodily selves, in a life dependent simply upon trust in the generous delight of God.[68]

5. Any body is taken seriously that is *ruled* by the *Spirit*. The further objection arises that if grace is properly to be described as "grace," it must occur in morally licit circumstances. The Bible and the tradition determine morally licit circumstances, and therefore it begs the question to deploy a concept of grace against received traditional morality. The body's grace, says this objection, is antinomian. But reliance on the Spirit rather than on concrete forms of the created order, or the previously revealed order (such as that of circumcision), is not antinomian. On the contrary, the Spirit's work is also and precisely that of fidelity, or of keeping faith between the Father and the Son. Fidelity is a work proper to the Spirit, particularly "the Spirit of the One Who raised Christ Jesus from the dead," the *vinculum caritatis*, the one who "restores" the bond between Father and Son and works (much less successfully?) to restore unity also among human beings, even through the witnesses of the wedding to restore unity in a couple.

The twentieth-century mystic Adrienne von Speyr suggests a name for the Spirit bridging the gap that opens between spirit and letter and makes appeals to the Spirit seem antinomian to western Christian ears. She calls the Spirit "the Rule," as in the Benedictine rule,[69] or, though she neglects to say so, the Torah – a structure that liberates us for sanctification. Similarly, Paul refers to the Spirit's law (Rom. 8:1). The Spirit loves the law enough to write it on fleshy hearts (Heb. 8:10). To rely on the Spirit is the only way not only to keep but to *"delight* in the law of the Lord" (Ps. 1:2), since it is proper to the Spirit to delight in the love of the Father for the Son. Taken up into the delight of the Spirit in witnessing, vindicating, celebrating, and furthering the fidelity of the Father and the Son, human beings also, in the community the Spirit, gather, become free to witness, vindicate, celebrate, and further analogous forms of covenant among themselves. There can be no question of antinomianism where the Spirit is rightly invoked, since the Spirit is the Rule of faith keeping.

Gay and lesbian relationships not only must exhibit the spiritual fruits of faith, hope, and charity but must also exhibit them in sacramental form. Just as marriage gives form or rule to the sanctifying possibilities of heterosexual sex, so gay and lesbian people need sacramental forms, or inspired rules. Perhaps Boswell's ceremonies provide them, perhaps not.[70] In any case they are not celebrated in the modern West. Gay and lesbian relationships must wait upon a churchly form – call it sacramental if you think of marriage as a sacrament – to give their holiness ecclesial shape, just as heterosexual relationships had to wait centuries for the church to integrate them fully into its life with heterosexual marriage forms. Conservatives are right to complain about what you might call unformed love: we must mine Scripture and tradition under the Spirit, who will rule new rules for us.

If we want to see the Rule enacted who is the Spirit, we need to look to the liturgy – especially liturgies that tell stories of lives ruled by the Spirit, or inspired by the Rule.

Sexuality as Narrated Providence in Eastern Orthodoxy

The liturgy teaches best of all that the lives of believers need inspiration by the Rule, or that nature needs reconceptualization as part of God's *oikonomia*. Consider this Orthodox prayer:

> O Lord our God, who didst grant unto us all those things necessary for salvation and didst bid us to love one another and to forgive each other our failings, bless and consecrate, kind Lord and lover of good, these thy servants who love each other with a love of the Spirit and have come into this thy holy church to be blessed and consecrated. . . . [B]estow . . . also on these, O Christ our God, . . . all those things needed for salvation and eternal life.[71]

Whatever this ceremony means, it manifests the economy of bringing *nature* to *salvation*. Similarly, in the Orthodox Order of Crowning, as the marriage proper is called, Jesus' presence at the marriage of Cana is ascribed to the "saving providence" of "the Lord our God."[72] In the order of second marriage, too, the appeal is to God's providence: "O Master, Lord our God, who showest pity upon all human beings, and whose providence is over all thy works."[73] In all those cases, the appeal to God's providence emerges from a catena of biblical and saintly examples, so that the economy of salvation of the couple before the congregation is incorporated into the economy of biblical salvation history. The Order of Betrothal is best, if few Orthodox would use it as I propose:

For thou, O Lord, hast declared that a pledge should be given and confirmed in all things. By a ring was power given unto Joseph in Egypt; by a ring was Daniel glorified in the land of Babylon; by a ring was the uprightness of Tamar revealed [!]; by a ring did our heavenly Father show forth his bounty upon his Son; for he saith: Put a ring on his hand, and bring hither the fatted calf, and kill it, and eat, and make merry.[74]

Note well: It is the prodigal – one might by application say, the gay son – that receives the ring!
And the Order of Second Marriage is wittiest:

O thou who knowest the frailty of human nature, in that thou art our Maker and Creator; who didst pardon Rahab the harlot, and accept the contrition of the Publican: remember not the sins of ignorance from our youth up. For if thou wilt consider iniquity, O Lord, Lord, who shall stand before thee? Or what flesh shall be justified in thy sight? For thou only art righteous, sinless, holy, plenteous in mercy, of great compassion, and repentest thee of the evils of human beings. Do thou, O Master, who hast brought together in wedlock thy servants, N. and N., unite them to one another in love: vouchsafe unto them the contrition of the Publican, the tears of the Harlot, the confession of the Thief; that, repenting with their whole heart, and doing thy commandments in peace and oneness of mind, they may be deemed worthy also of thy heavenly kingdom.[75]

If that can go for remarriage after divorce, how much more for almost any wedding now in our complicated society, where very few, straight or gay, save sex for marriage. What couple should *not* invoke the contrition of the Publican, the tears of the Harlot, the confession of the Thief, by the time they marry?

One might object that such narratives about God's providential rule are best understood as the way in which God acts through evil to bring about good rather than as establishing a pattern for behavioral norms. Those who put forward patterns for behavioral norms, on the other hand, tend not to take account of biblical stories in which God seems unconcerned with the ethics of the characters, or at least the editorial rescension records no moral judgment one way or the other. It would be hard to argue for divine disapproval of Tamar's subterfuge, for example; still less of Mary's bearing a child not begotten by Joseph. The "low estate" of the Magnificat refers not to barrenness, as usual, but to her apparently illegitimate pregnancy. The reason I turn to *liturgically worked* biblical texts is precisely to overcome the dichotomy between behavioral norms and providential action, between letter and spirit. In the liturgy the Spirit who rules is invoked and present. In the liturgy the church *does* take up biblical narratives and put them to moral use, integrating divine providence and behavioral norms, holding together spirit and letter. Thus the liturgies quoted neither overlook nor prettify Rahab the harlot, but invoke her for a particular purpose. In that way they serve as the proper model for the *integration* of behavioral norms and providential narratives. They invoke the latter to qualify and inculcate the former. Better, the liturgy casts the people *inside* the providential narratives as the context where alone their behavior can begin to make sense before God. It is in such a context that gay and lesbian couples must also place their lives, to make room for going on when they inevitably fail to measure up to their models and vows. It is that context that Eastern Orthodoxy calls, in a delightfully delicate word, the *economy* of salvation. It is the economy of salvation that allows the Holy Spirit to be itself a Rule or Law that gives life.

The pattern to be recovered from the liturgies is this: *everything* is given to human beings for use in God's economy of salvation, or less starkly, nothing is left out; and the economy of salvation is identified by incorporating the community into the biblical narratives. This pattern goes for *nature itself*, as we have seen, in that God conforms nature itself to the economy of salvation in grafting the gentiles onto the Jewish trunk. Not only that: the original nature, which Paul has God contravening for the salvation of the gentiles, is not so much natural in any general, metaphysical sense of the term, as covenantal. What is natural is that God should love the Jews especially. What is unnatural is that God should incorporate the gentiles into that love. The same reasoning might well go for straight and gay. What is natural is that God should love bearers of children, especially bearers of Jewish children: Abraham and Sarah. But God also incorporates into that love gentiles such as Zipporah and Ruth, the childless such as the eunuchs, and delights in irregular pregnancies, such as the ones Matthew singles out as leading to the birth of Jesus, for God's providential purposes.

Gay and lesbian unions can build up the church as well as straight marriages do, with or without children in both cases. Certainly lesbian and gay relationships can exhibit an egoism *à deux*, but they need not, any more than straight ones do. Still, marriage forms that include gay and lesbian couples would make clear that their unions too are from and for the larger community – indeed, if the kingdom of God is like a wedding feast, then it is thus that they represent the Trinity. That leads to my final offering – the charge for a wedding.[76]

Charge for a Wedding

Dearly beloved: We have come together in the presence of God to witness and bless the joining together of these God's human creatures, [N. and N.], in Holy Matrimony. Marriage signifies the mystery of the love that God bears to human beings, in that God desires, befriends, and keeps faith with us. That love is mysterious to us in that unlike us God *just is* love,[77] an interior community, never lonely, already rich. That love is open to us in that God desires, befriends, and keeps faith in God's very self, as these two desire, befriend, and keep faith with each other. And God's Spirit internally witnesses and blesses and keeps faith with the love in God[78] as today we externally witness and bless the love of these two human creatures in God's image. Today the celebration, blessing, and witnessing of this wedding catches us up into a parable of the inner love and life of God.[79]

In desire God says to us, "You have ravished my heart."[80] God declares of Israel, "I will allure her."[81] As Jacob worked twice seven years for Rachel;[82] as Ruth seduced Boaz upon the threshing floor;[83] as the soul of Jonathan was knit to the soul of David;[84] as these two of God's human creatures desire each other, so God desires us. Grace like desire transforms us by showing us to be perceived in a certain way: as significant, as desired.[85]

In the friendship of the best sort, says Aristotle, the friends make each other better.[86] As Naomi became to Ruth a teacher, and Ruth became to Naomi more than seven sons;[87] as Jonathan prepared David for kingship;[88] as these two befriend each other; so too God says, "No longer do I call you servants . . . but I have called you friends."[89] In friendship God does not merely condescend to be God with us, but God elevates us to be with God. Marriage's friendship too may elevate you so that your "love is patient and kind."[90]

In faith we grant time to desire's risk and friendship's work. Faith sustains the will to let ourselves be formed by the perceptions of another.[91] As Jonathan promised David that "the Lord shall be between you and me, between your posterity and mine forever";[92] as Ruth pledged to follow Naomi till death did them part;[93] so God, too, counts the cost of love for Israel and declares: "I will betroth you to me forever . . . I will betroth you to me in faithfulness; and you shall know [who I am]."[94]

"Beloved, let us love one another; for love is of God, and whoever loves is born of God and knows God."[95] We are created – and we marry – so that the desire of a spouse, divine or human, may show us to ourselves as occasions of joy.[96] We are created – and we marry – so that the friendship of a spouse, divine or human, may make us worthy of that showing. We are created – and we marry – so that the faithfulness of a spouse, divine or human, may teach us who we are. We are created – and we marry – so that on this wedding day we may be caught up into those things, so that we may grow into the wholehearted love of God by seeing how God loves us as God loves God.[97]

Notes

For constructive comments and fruitful objections on earlier versions of this paper, I wish to thank the Department of Religious Studies at Yale University, especially Marilyn Adams, Gene Outka, David Kelsey, and Wayne Meeks; students and faculty at Duke Divinity School, especially Stanley Hauerwas; the Department of Religious Studies at the University of North Carolina at Greensboro, especially Henry Levinson, Ben Ramsey, and Derek Krueger; other writers in this volume, especially Saul Olyan, Kathryn Tanner, Keith Green, and David Novak; David Yeago; Robert Jenson; and anonymous reviewers for the National Endowment for the Humanities and the National Humanities Center. Thanks also to Rowan Williams for delivering me a copy of "The Body's Grace" before it was easily available in the United States. Errors remain my own.

1 For more detail on "marriage-like unions for gay and lesbian people" compatible with the views of this essay, see David McCarthy Matzko, "Homosexuality and the Practices of Marriage," *Modern Theology* 13 (1997): 391–7, and Rowan Williams, "The Body's Grace," 10th Michael Harding Memorial Address (pamphlet) (London: Institute for the Study of Christianity and Sexuality, 1989), now reprinted in (and cited from) Charles Hefling, ed., *Our Selves, Our Souls and Bodies: Sexuality and the Household of God* (Boston: Cowley Press, 1996), pp. 58–68. [Reprinted in this volume.] For a political argument that deals with religious views, see Andrew Sullivan, *Virtually Normal: An Argument About Homosexuality* (New York: Alfred A. Knopf, 1995).

2 "What is called ethics I regard as the doctrine of the command of God. Hence I do not think it right to treat it otherwise than as an integral part of dogmatics." Karl Barth, *Church Dogmatics*, 4 vols. in 13 bks., trans. G. W. Bromiley et al. (Edinburgh: T. & T. Clark, 1956–75), I, 1 xvi.

3 "[R]eligious symbols, dramatized in rituals or related in myths, are felt somehow to sum up, for those for whom they are resonant, what is known about the way the world is, the quality of the emotional life it supports, and the way one ought to behave while in it." Clifford Geertz, "Ethos, World View, and the Analysis of Sacred Symbols," in his *The Interpretation of Cultures* (New York: Basic Books, 1973), p. 127.

4 Karl Barth is, as noted, an exception. For reflections on the general case of how issues of social ethics and dogmatic theology relate in Christian discourse, see Kathryn Tanner, *The Politics of God: Christian Theologies and Social Justice* (Minneapolis: Fortress Press, 1992).

5 Geertz, "Ethos," pp. 14 n. 1, 15 n. 2.

6 Williams, "The Body's Grace," 1989, p. 3, almost identical in Hefling, *Our Selves*, p. 59.

7 Even the Vatican now insists that there is such a thing as a constitutionally "homosexual

person," made in the image of God. Congregation for the Doctrine of the Faith, "Letter to the Bishops of the Catholic Church on the Pastoral Care of Homosexual Persons," reprinted in *The Vatican and Homosexuality*, eds. Jeannine Gramick and Pat Furey (New York: Crossroad, 1988), pp. 1–10, *passim*. The best commentary is Andrew Sullivan, "Alone Again, Naturally: The Catholic Church and the Homosexual," *New Republic*, 28 Nov. 1994, pp. 47, 50, 52, 54–5. [Both reprinted in this volume.]

8 Karl Barth, *Church Domatics*, III/1, 318. The comment refers in context only to heterosexual marriage.

9 Personal correspondence.

10 Hans W. Frei, "Eberhard Busch's Biography of Karl Barth," in Frei, *Types of Christian Theology*, eds. George Hunsinger and William C. Placher (New Haven and London: Yale University Press, 1992), pp. 147–63; here, p. 158.

11 Thomas Aquinas, *Summa Theologiae*, part I, question 1, article 8. Hereafter cited as: *ST* I.1.8.

12 *ST* I–II.99.2 and 100.2, 5. In saying that life with God is a political matter, I am not recommending theocracy, but simply observing that the human participation in the divine life (II Peter 1:4) is described in political terms.

13 This thesis is defended in Robert W. Jenson and Eric Gritsch, *Lutheranism: The Theological Movement and Its Confessional Writings* (Philadelphia: Fortress, 1976).

14 See, for example, H. George Anderson, T. Austin Murphy, and Joseph A. Burgess, eds., *Justification by Faith: Lutherans and Catholics in Dialogue VII* (Minneapolis: Augsburg, 1985).

15 Karl Barth, *Dogmatics in Outline*, trans. G. T. Thompson (London: SCM, 1949), pp. 53–4, italics added and sentences transposed.

16 Paul Evdokimov, *The Sacrament of Love: The Nuptial Mystery in the Light of the Orthodox Tradition*, trans. Anthony Gythiel and Victoria Steadman (Crestwood, New York: St. Vladimir's Seminary Press, 1985), p. 43. [Selections reprinted in this volume.]

17 For a recent argument along those lines, with references to Maximus the Confessor and Gregory of Nyssa, see John D. Zizioulas, *Being as Communion: Studies in Personhood and the Church* (Crestwood, New York: St. Vladimir's Seminary Press, 1985), pp. 50–65.

18 Karl Barth, *The Epistle to the Romans*, 6th ed., trans. Edwyn C. Hoskyns (New York: Oxford, 1980), pp. 50–1, reading "human being" for *Mensch*.

19 Charles Hawes, unpublished typescript. Exod. 32:1–6 mentions earrings of both men and women; Gen. 35:4 and Judg. 8:24 connect them with idol worship. [Reprinted here.]

20 Personal correspondence.

21 Sebastian Moore, "The Crisis of an Ethic Without Desire," in his *Jesus the Liberator of Desire* (New York: Crossroad, 1989), p. 104. [Reprinted here.]

22 Cf. ibid., pp. 89–93.

23 Williams, "The Body's Grace," in Hefling, *Our Selves*, p. 64. [Reprinted here.]

24 Robert W. Jenson, *Visible Words: The Interpretation and Practice of the Christian Sacraments* (Philadelphia: Fortress, 1978), pp. 24–5.

25 "The Homosexual Movement: A Response by the Ramsey Colloquium," *First Things* (March 1994): 15–20; here, p. 17.

26 This is the thesis of "Marriage and the Monastic State," in Evdokimov, *The Sacrament of Love*, pp. 65–84. For another call for holiness as the standard for committed, monogamous relationships, gay or straight, see Luke Timothy Johnson, "Debate and

Discernment: Scripture and the Spirit," *Commonweal* (28 Jan. 1994): 11–13. [Reprinted here.]

27 Williams, "The Body's Grace," in Hefling, *Our Selves*, p. 59.

28 *ST*, prologue to I–II.

29 Augustine, *De Trinitate*, bk. 12, chaps. 6–7, nos. 8–9.

30 Quoted in Evdokimov, *The Sacrament of Love*, p. 120, citing simply Chrysostom, *On Marriage*.

31 As I have learned from Richard Hays's article, "Relations Natural and Unnatural: A Response to John Boswell's Exegesis of Romans 1," *Journal of Religious Ethics* 14 (1986): 184–215, which uses it quite differently. For a reply to Hays, see Dale B. Martin, "Heterosexism and the Interpretation of Romans 1:18–32," *Biblical Interpretation* 3 (1995): 332–55.

32 A chapter title in Anselm's *Cur Deus homo*.

33 I owe the phrase, but not its application, to Richard Hays.

34 As I have learned from David Novak.

35 "The Homosexual Movement," p. 19.

36 Michael Satlow, " 'Try To Be a Man': The Rabbinic Construction of Masculinity," *Harvard Theological Review* 89 (1996): 19–41.

37 "Although the particular inclination of the homosexual person is not a sin, it is a more or less strong tendency ordered toward an intrinsic moral evil; and thus the inclination itself must be seen as an objective disorder. Therefore special concern and pastoral attention should be directed toward those who have this condition, lest they be led to believe that the living out of this orientation in homosexual activity is a morally acceptable option. It is not." Congregation for the Doctrine of the Faith, "Pastoral Care of Homosexual Persons," no. 3, paragraph boundary elided.

38 See, for example, Robert Gottlieb and Peter Wiley, "The Priesthood and the Black," in *America's Saints* (New York: G. P. Putnam's Sons, 1984), pp. 177–86. See also authoritatively Bruce McConkie, *Mormon Doctrine*, 2d edn. (Salt Lake City, Utah: Bookcraft, 1966; reprint, 1979), s.v. "Negroes." This view was overturned by special revelation to Spencer Kimball in 1978.

39 Quoted from Brigham Young, in Gottlieb and Wiley, "The Priesthood and the Black," p. 178.

40 James Henley Thornwell, *The Rights and Duties of Masters: A Sermon* (Charleston, 1850), p. 44, cited in Robert M. Calhoun, *Evangelicals and Conservatives in the Early South, 1740–1861* (Columbia, SC: University of South Carolina Press, 1988), p. 163.

41 Congregation for the Doctrine of the Faith, "Pastoral Care of Homosexual Persons," nos. 3, 12.

42 For the cases of gentiles and women, see Satlow, cited above. For the case of Presbyterians (for example), see Earnest Trice Thompson, *Presbyterians in the South, 3* vols., Presbyterian Historical Society Publication Series, no. 13 (Richmond: John Knox Press, 1963–73), 1: 1607–1861, especially the speeches indexed under Thornwell. See also Larry E. Tise, *Proslavery: A History of the Defense of Slavery in America, 1701–1840* (Athens, GA: University of Georgia Press, 1987). For the Vatican, see Congregation for the Doctrine of the Faith, "Pastoral Care of Homosexual Persons," esp. nos. 3, 6. Note that although antiquity lacked a modern-style race theory of slavery, slaves were still constitutionally incapable of keeping the law, so that a male Jew could give thanks that

God had not "made" him a woman, a gentile, or a slave.

43 On the last, see most recently, Stanley K. Stowers, *A Rereading of Romans* (New Haven: Yale University Press, 1995).

44 On the purported lability of blacks, for example, see George M. Frederickson, *The Black Image in the White Mind: The Debate on Afro-American Character and Destiny 1817–1914* (New York: Harper and Row, 1971), pp. 250–4, 273–88.

45 For detail, see M. Basil Pennington, "Vocation Discernment and the Homosexual," in *A Challenge to Love: Gay and Lesbian Catholics in the Church*, ed. Robert Nugent, with an introduction by Bishop Walter F. Sullivan (New York: Crossroad, 1984), pp. 235–44.

46 Robert Lewis Dabney, quoted in Calhoun, *Evangelicals and Conservatives*, p. 186.

47 Williams, "The Body's Grace," 1989, p. 3, almost identical in Hefling, *Our Selves*, 59.

48 I have developed these objections from personal correspondence.

49 See Mary Douglas, *Purity and Danger* (London: Routledge, 1966), chs. 2, 10. For a use of Douglas to address the homosexuality issue, see Jeffrey Stout, "Moral Abominations," ch. 7 in *Ethics After Babel: The Languages of Morals and Their Discontents* (Boston: Beacon Press, 1988), pp. 145–62. [Reprinted here.] Most recently, see Dale B. Martin, *The Corinthian Body* (New Haven: Yale University Press, 1995).

50 See Howard Eilberg-Schwartz, ed., *People of the Body: Jews and Judaism from an Embodied Perspective* (Albany, NY: State University of New York Press, 1992).

51 To readers disturbed to see references to social construction in one paragraph and reality in the next, suffice it to say that Christian theologians have seen that debate before: it is realists versus nominalists all over again. For application, see John Boswell, "Revolutions, Universals, and Sexual Categories," in *Hidden From History: Reclaiming the Gay and Lesbian Past*, eds. Martin Duberman, Martha Vicinus, and George Chauncey (New York: New American Library, 1989), pp. 17–36.

52 E.g., *ST* I.13.3, 5–6. For a recent defense, see Janet Martin Soskice, *Metaphor and Religious Language* (Oxford: Clarendon, 1985), esp. the final chapter.

53 For a defense of "Father" language for priests as not only compatible with but *requiring* the ordination of women, see Stanley Hauerwas, "Priesthood and Power: What It Means To Be a Father" (unpublished typescript).

54 Caroline Walker Bynum, "Jesus as Mother and Abbot as Mother: Some Themes in Twelfth-Century Cistercian Writing," in *Jesus as Mother: Studies in the Spirituality of the High Middle Ages* (Berkeley: University of California Press, 1982), pp. 110–69.

55 Williams, "The Body's Grace," in Hefling, *Our Selves*, p. 65.

56 Augustine, *De Trinitate* 15.19.

57 I owe my attention to this verse to David Yeago.

58 Gregory of Nyssa, *Commentary on the Song of Songs*, homily 13, trans. Casimir McCambley (Brookline, MA: Hellenic College Press, 1987), p. 234; for commentary, see Evdokimov, *The Sacrament of Love*, p. 82.

59 E.g., Matt. 9:15, 22:2.

60 Note for sacrament-counters: This statement does not make marriage an *independent* sacrament, but one that depends upon the Eucharist.

61 Human beings are ontologically female by identification with Mary in Evdokimov, *The Sacrament of Love*, pp. 34–5. For an even more recent example, see Hans Urs von Balthasar, *Theo-drama*, vol. III (San Francisco: Ignatius, 1992), p. 287. For a critique of such notions, see Marilyn Chapin Massey, *Feminine Soul: The Fate of an Ideal* (Boston:

Beacon, 1985).

62 Cf. Williams, "The Body's Grace," in Hefling, *Our Selves*, p. 62.

63 "Tomorrow Shall Be My Dancing Day," English traditional carol, in *The Shorter New Oxford Book of Carols*, eds. Hugh Keyte and Andrew Parrott (New York: Oxford, 1993), no. 76. [Reprinted here.]

64 Gary Wills, *Under God* (New York: Simon and Schuster, 1990), p. 293, citing Augustine, *City of God*, 22.24.

65 Williams, "The Body's Grace," in Hefling, *Our Selves*, p. 66.

66 See Thomas E. Breidenthal, "Sanctifying Nearness," in Hefling, *Our Selves*, pp. 46–57. [Reprinted here.]

67 Cf. Williams, "The Body's Grace," in Hefling, *Our Selves*, p. 65.

68 Ibid. Emphasis added.

69 Adrienne von Speyr, *The Word Becomes Flesh*, trans. Wiedenhoever and Dru (San Francisco: Ignatius, 1994).

70 John Boswell, *Same-Sex Unions in Premodern Europe* (New York: Vilard Books, 1994).

71 "Grottaferrata gamma," B, 2, trans. in Boswell, *Same-Sex Unions*, p. 296. [Reprinted here.]

72 *Service Book of the Holy Orthodox-Catholic Apostolic Church*, 6th rev. edn, trans. Isabel Florence Hapgood (Englewood, NJ: Antiochene Orthodox Christian Archdiocese of North America, 1983), p. 299. [Reprinted here.]

73 Ibid., p. 304.

74 Ibid., pp. 292–3.

75 Ibid., p. 304.

76 In fact, I read it at a heterosexual wedding but wrote it with both that couple and these considerations in mind.

77 1 John 4:8b.

78 Matt. 3:17, Mark 1:9–11, Luke 3:21–2, John 1:31–4.

79 Matt. 9:15, 22:2.

80 Song of Sol. 4:9a.

81 Hos. 2:14.

82 Gen. 29.

83 Ruth 3.

84 1 Sam. 18:1.

85 Williams, "The Body's Grace," in Hefling, *Our Selves*, pp. 59, 65, near quotation.

86 Aristotle *Nichomachean Ethics*, bk. 9, ch. 12, 1172a11–14.

87 Ruth 2:2, 22; 3:1–4; 4:15.

88 1 Sam. 18–23, esp. 23:17.

89 John 15:15.

90 1 Cor. 13:4ff.

91 Williams, "The Body's Grace," in Hefling, *Our Selves*, p. 62, near quotation.

92 I Sam. 20:42.

93 Ruth 1:16–17.

94 Hos. 2:19a, 20.

95 1 John 4:7.

96 Williams, "The Body's Grace," in Hefling, *Our Selves*, p. 59, near quotation.

97 Ibid.

PART

Catholic Controversies

Letter to the Catholic Bishops on the Pastoral Care of Homosexual Persons

Congregation for the Doctrine of the Faith

Observers disagree about how to interpret this statement. Andrew Sullivan, in an essay reprinted below, argues that Vatican statements on homosexuality in the twentieth century show a rising tension. Along with increasingly vehement prohibitions come increasingly confident assertions that homosexuality pertains to "persons" as well as acts, in a technical, theological sense of person: that is, to a creature in the image of God and therefore of special dignity. Mark Jordan, in his book The Silence of Sodom: Homosexuality in Modern Catholicism, *proposes that it is a mistake to look for the knowledge of the Catholic Church about homosexuality in magisterial documents.* The documents, he holds, are not intended to teach so much as to silence. According to Jordan, they distract the student of Catholicism from the real site of the Church's knowledge of homosexuality, which is the lived homosexuality (celibate or not) of numerous Catholic priests, monks, and nuns. It is this knowledge that the condemnations of magisterial documents attempt to repress. But what if the stress on homosexual persons so prized by Sullivan has actually emerged from Jordan's lived knowledge?*

[* Mark D. Jordan, "Teaching by Threatening," in The Silence of Sodom: Homosexuality in Modern Catholicism *(Chicago: University of Chicago Press, 2000).]*

1. The issue of homosexuality and the moral evaluation of homosexual acts have increasingly become a matter of public debate, even in Catholic circles. Since

this debate often advances arguments and makes assertions inconsistent with the teaching of the Catholic Church, it is quite rightly a cause for concern to all engaged in the pastoral ministry, and this Congregation has judged it to be of sufficiently grave and widespread importance to address to the Bishops of the Catholic Church this Letter on the Pastoral Care of Homosexual Persons.

2. Naturally, an exhaustive treatment of this complex issue cannot be attempted here, but we will focus our reflection within the distinctive context of the Catholic moral perspective. It is a perspective which finds support in the more secure findings of the natural sciences, which have their own legitimate and proper methodology and field of inquiry.

However, the Catholic moral viewpoint is founded on human reason illumined by faith and is consciously motivated by the desire to do the will of God our Father. The Church is thus in a position to learn from scientific discovery but also to transcend the horizons of science and to be confident that her more global vision does greater justice to the rich reality of the human person in his spiritual and physical dimensions, created by God and heir, by grace, to eternal life.

It is within this context, then, that it can be clearly seen that the phenomenon of homosexuality, complex as it is, and with its many consequences for society and ecclesial life, is a proper focus for the Church's pastoral care. It thus requires of her ministers attentive study, active concern and honest, theologically well-balanced counsel.

3. Explicit treatment of the problem was given in this Congregation's "Declaration on Certain Questions Concerning Sexual Ethics" of December 29, 1975. That document stressed the duty of trying to understand the homosexual condition and noted that culpability for homosexual acts should only be judged with prudence. At the same time the Congregation took note of the distinction commonly drawn between the homosexual condition or tendency and individual homosexual actions. These were described as deprived of their essential and indispensable finality, as being "intrinsically disordered," and able in no case to be approved of (cf. n. 8, §4).

In the discussion which followed the publication of the Declaration, however, an overly benign interpretation was given to the homosexual condition itself, some going so far as to call it neutral, or even good. Although the particular inclination of the homosexual person is not a sin, it is a more or less strong tendency ordered toward an intrinsic moral evil; and thus the inclination itself must be seen as an objective disorder.

Therefore special concern and pastoral attention should be directed toward those who have this condition, lest they be led to believe that the living out of this orientation in homosexual activity is a morally acceptable option. It is not.

4. An essential dimension of authentic pastoral care is the identification of causes of confusion regarding the Church's teaching. One is a new exegesis of Sacred Scripture which claims variously that Scripture has nothing to say on the subject of homosexuality, or that it somehow tacitly approves of it, or that all of its moral injunctions are so culture-bound that they are no longer applicable to contemporary life. These views are gravely erroneous and call for particular attention here.

5. It is quite true that the Biblical literature owes to the different epochs in which it was written a good deal of its varied patterns of thought and expression (*Dei Verbum* 12). The Church today addresses the Gospel to a world which differs in many ways from ancient days. But the world in which the New Testament was written was already quite diverse from the situation in which the Sacred Scriptures of the Hebrew People had been written or compiled, for example.

What should be noticed is that, in the presence of such remarkable diversity, there is nevertheless a clear consistency within the Scriptures themselves on the moral issue of homosexual behaviour. The Church's doctrine regarding this issue is thus based, not on isolated phrases for facile theological argument, but on the solid foundation of a constant Biblical testimony. The community of faith today, in unbroken continuity with the Jewish and Christian communities within which the ancient Scriptures were written, continues to be nourished by those same Scriptures and by the Spirit of Truth whose Word they are. It is likewise essential to recognize that the Scriptures are not properly understood when they are interpreted in a way which contradicts the Church's living Tradition. To be correct, the interpretation of Scripture must be in substantial accord with that Tradition.

The Vatican Council II in *Dei Verbum* 10, put it this way: "It is clear, therefore, that in the supremely wise arrangement of God, sacred Tradition, sacred Scripture, and the Magisterium of the Church are so connected and associated that one of them cannot stand without the others. Working together, each in its own way under the action of the one Holy Spirit, they all contribute effectively to the salvation of souls." In that spirit we wish to outline briefly the Biblical teaching here.

6. Providing a basic plan for understanding this entire discussion of homosexuality is the theology of creation we find in Genesis. God, in his infinite wisdom and love, brings into existence all of reality as a reflection of his goodness. He fashions mankind, male and female, in his own image and likeness. Human beings, therefore, are nothing less than the work of God himself; and in the complementarity of the sexes, they are called to reflect the inner unity of the Creator. They do this in a striking way in their cooperation with him in the transmission of life by a mutual donation of the self to the other.

In Genesis 3, we find that this truth about persons being an image of God has been obscured by original sin. There inevitably follows a loss of awareness of the covenantal character of the union these persons had with God and with each other. The human body retains its "spousal significance" but this is now clouded by sin. Thus, in Genesis 19:1–11, the deterioration due to sin continues in the story of the men of Sodom. There can be no doubt of the moral judgement made there against homosexual relations. In Leviticus 18:22 and 20:13, in the course of describing the conditions necessary for belonging to the Chosen People, the author excludes from the People of God those who behave in a homosexual fashion.

Against the background of this exposition of theocratic law, an eschatological perspective is developed by St. Paul when, in 1 Cor. 6:9, he proposes the same doctrine and lists those who behave in a homosexual fashion among those who shall not enter the Kingdom of God.

In Romans 1:18–32, still building on the moral traditions of his forebears, but in the new context of the confrontation between Christianity and the pagan society of his day, Paul uses homosexual behaviour as an example of the blindness which has overcome humankind. Instead of the original harmony between Creator and creatures, the acute distortion of idolatry has led to all kinds of moral excess. Paul is at a loss to find a clearer example of this disharmony than homosexual relations. Finally, 1 Tim. 1, in full continuity with the Biblical position, singles out those who spread wrong doctrine and in v. 10 explicitly names as sinners those who engage in homosexual acts.

7. The Church, obedient to the Lord who founded her and gave to her the sacramental life, celebrates the divine plan of the loving and live-giving union of men and women in the sacrament of marriage. It is only in the marital relationship that the use of the sexual faculty can be morally good. A person engaging in homosexual behaviour therefore acts immorally.

To chose someone of the same sex for one's sexual activity is to annul the rich symbolism and meaning, not to mention the goals, of the Creator's sexual design. Homosexual activity is not a complementary union, able to transmit life; and so it thwarts the call to a life of that form of self-giving which the Gospel says is the essence of Christian living. This does not mean that homosexual persons are not often generous and giving of themselves; but when they engage in homosexual activity they confirm within themselves a disordered sexual inclination which is essentially self-indulgent.

As in every moral disorder, homosexual activity prevents one's own fulfillment and happiness by acting contrary to the creative wisdom of God. The Church, in rejecting erroneous opinions regarding homosexuality, does not limit but rather defends personal freedom and dignity realistically and authentically understood.

8. Thus, the Church's teaching today is in organic continuity with the Scriptural perspective and with her own constant Tradition. Though today's world is in many ways quite new, the Christian community senses the profound and lasting bonds which join us to those generations who have gone before us, "marked with the sign of faith."

Nevertheless, increasing numbers of people today, even within the Church, are bringing enormous pressure to bear on the Church to accept the homosexual condition as though it were not disordered and to condone homosexual activity. Those within the Church who argue in this fashion often have close ties with those with similar views outside it. These latter groups are guided by a vision opposed to the truth about the human person, which is fully disclosed in the mystery of Christ. They reflect, even if not entirely consciously, a materialistic ideology which denies the transcendent nature of the human person as well as the supernatural vocation of every individual.

The Church's ministers must ensure that homosexual persons in their care will not be misled by this point of view, so profoundly opposed to the teaching of the Church. But the risk is great and there are many who seek to create confusion regarding the Church's position, and then to use that confusion to their own advantage.

9. The movement within the Church, which takes the form of pressure groups of various names and sizes, attempts to give the impression that it represents all homosexual persons who are Catholics. As a matter of fact, its membership is by and large restricted to those who either ignore the teaching of the Church or seek somehow to undermine it. It brings together under the aegis of Catholicism homosexual persons who have no intention of abandoning their homosexual behaviour. One tactic used is to protest that any and all criticism of or reservations about homosexual people, their activity and lifestyle, are simply diverse forms of unjust discrimination.

There is an effort in some countries to manipulate the Church by gaining the often well-intentioned support of her pastors with a view to changing civil-statutes and laws. This is done in order to conform to these pressure groups' concept that homosexuality is at least a completely harmless, if not an entirely good, thing. Even when the practice of homosexuality may seriously threaten the lives and well-being of a large number of people, its advocates remain undeterred and refuse to consider the magnitude of the risks involved.

The Church can never be so callous. It is true that her clear position cannot be revised by pressure from civil legislation or the trend of the moment. But she is really concerned about the many who are not represented by the pro-homosexual movement and about those who may have been tempted to believe its deceitful propaganda. She is also aware that the view that homosexual activity is equivalent to, or as acceptable as, the sexual expression of conjugal love has a direct impact on society's understanding of the nature and rights of the family and puts them in jeopardy.

10. It is deplorable that homosexual persons have been and are the object of violent malice in speech or in action. Such treatment deserves condemnation from the Church's pastors wherever it occurs. It reveals a kind of disregard for others which endangers the most fundamental principles of a healthy society. The intrinsic dignity of each person must always be respected in word, in action and in law.

But the proper reaction to crimes committed against homosexual persons should not be to claim that the homosexual condition is not disordered. When such a claim is made and when homosexual activity is consequently condoned, or when civil legislation is introduced to protect behavior to which no one has any conceivable right, neither the Church nor society at large should be surprised when other distorted notions and practices gain ground, and irrational and violent reactions increase.

11. It has been argued that the homosexual orientation in certain cases is not the result of deliberate choice; and so the homosexual person would then have no choice but to behave in a homosexual fashion. Lacking freedom, such a person, even if engaged in homosexual activity, would not be culpable.

Here, the Church's wise moral tradition is necessary since it warns against generalizations in judging individual cases. In fact, circumstances may exist, or may have existed in the past, which would reduce or remove the culpability of the individual in a given instance; or other circumstances may increase it. What is at all costs to be avoided is the unfounded and demeaning assumption that the sexual behaviour of homosexual persons is always and totally compulsive and therefore inculpable. What is essential is that the fundamental liberty which characterizes the human person and gives him his dignity be recognized as belonging to the homosexual person as well. As in every conversion from evil, the abandonment of homosexual activity will require a profound collaboration of the individual with God's liberating grace.

12. What, then, are homosexual persons to do who seek to follow the Lord? Fundamentally, they are called to enact the will of God in their life by joining whatever sufferings and difficulties they experience in virtue of their condition to the sacrifice of the Lord's Cross. That Cross, for the believer, is a fruitful sacrifice since from that death come life and redemption. While any call to carry the cross or to understand a Christian's suffering in this way will predictably be met with bitter ridicule by some, it should be remembered that this is the way to eternal life for *all* who follow Christ.

It is, in effect, none other than the teaching of Paul the Apostle to the

Galatians when he says that the Spirit produces in the lives of the faithful "love, joy, peace, patience, kindness, goodness, trustfulness, gentleness and self-control" (5:22) and further (v. 24), "You cannot belong to Christ unless you crucify all self-indulgent passions and desires."

It is easily misunderstood, however, if it is merely seen as a pointless effort at self-denial. The Cross *is* a denial of self, but in service to the will of God himself who makes life come from death and empowers those who trust in him to practice virtue in place of vice.

To celebrate the Paschal Mystery, it is necessary to let that Mystery become imprinted in the fabric of daily life. To refuse to sacrifice one's own will in obedience to the will of the Lord is effectively to prevent salvation. Just as the Cross was central to the expression of God's redemptive love for us in Jesus, so the conformity of the self-denial of homosexual men and women with the sacrifice of the Lord will constitute for them a source of self-giving which will save them from a way of life which constantly threatens to destroy them.

Christians who are homosexual are called, as all of us are, to a chaste life. As they dedicate their lives to understanding the nature of God's personal call to them, they will be able to celebrate the Sacrament of Penance more faithfully and receive the Lord's grace so freely offered there in order to convert their lives more fully to his Way.

13. We recognize, of course, that in great measure the clear and successful communication of the Church's teaching to all the faithful, and to society at large, depends on the correct instruction and fidelity of her pastoral ministers. The Bishops have the particularly grave responsibility to see to it that their assistants in the ministry, above all the priests, are rightly informed and personally disposed to bring the teaching of the Church in its integrity to everyone.

The characteristic concern and good will exhibited by many clergy and religious in their pastoral care for homosexual persons is admirable, and, we hope, will not diminish. Such devoted ministers should have the confidence that they are faithfully following the will of the Lord by encouraging the homosexual person to lead a chaste life and by affirming that person's God-given dignity and worth.

14. With this in mind, this Congregation wishes to ask the Bishops to be especially cautious of any programmes which may seek to pressure the Church to change her teaching, even while claiming not to do so. A careful examination of their public statements and the activities they promote reveals a studied ambiguity by which they attempt to mislead the pastors and the faithful. For example, they may present the teaching of the Magisterium, but only as if it were an optional source for the formation of one's conscience. Its specific

authority is not recognized. Some of these groups will use the word "Catholic" to describe either the organization or its intended members, yet they do not defend and promote the teaching of the Magisterium; indeed, they even openly attack it. While their members may claim a desire to conform their lives to the teaching of Jesus, in fact they abandon the teaching of his Church. This contradictory action should not have the support of the Bishops in any way.

15. We encourage the Bishops, then, to provide pastoral care in full accord with the teaching of the Church for homosexual persons of their dioceses. No authentic pastoral programme will include organizations in which homosexual persons associate with each other without clearly stating that homosexual activity is immoral. A truly pastoral approach will appreciate the need for homosexual persons to avoid the near occasions of sin.

We would heartily encourage programmes where these dangers are avoided. But we wish to make it clear that departure from the Church's teaching, or silence about it, in an effort to provide pastoral care is neither caring nor pastoral. Only what is true can ultimately be pastoral. The neglect of the Church's position prevents homosexual men and women from receiving the care they need and deserve.

An authentic pastoral programme will assist homosexual persons at all levels of the spiritual life: through the sacraments, and in particular through the frequent and sincere use of the sacrament of Reconciliation, through prayer, witness, counsel and individual care. In such a way, the entire Christian community can come to recognize its own call to assist its brothers and sisters, without deluding them or isolating them.

16. From this multi-faceted approach there are numerous advantages to be gained, not the least of which is the realization that a homosexual person, as every human being, deeply needs to be nourished at many different levels simultaneously.

The human person, made in the image and likeness of God, can hardly be adequately described by a reductionist reference to his or her sexual orientation. Every one living on the face of the earth has personal problems and difficulties, but challenges to growth, strengths, talents and gifts as well. Today, the Church provides a badly needed context for the care of the human person when she refuses to consider the person as a "heterosexual" or a "homosexual" and insists that every person has a fundamental identity: the creature of God, and by grace, his child and heir to eternal life.

17. In bringing this entire matter to the Bishops' attention, this Congregation wishes to support their efforts to assure that the teaching of the Lord and his Church on this important question be communicated fully to all the faithful.

In light of the points made above, they should decide for their own dioceses the extent to which an intervention on their part is indicated. In addition, should they consider it helpful, further coordinated action at the level of their National Bishops' Conference may be envisioned.

In a particular way, we would ask the Bishops to support, with the means at their disposal, the development of appropriate forms of pastoral care for homosexual persons. These would include the assistance of the psychological, sociological and medical sciences, in full accord with the teaching of the Church.

They are encouraged to call on the assistance of all Catholic theologians who, by teaching what the Church teaches, and by deepening their reflections on the true meaning of human sexuality and Christian marriage with the virtues it engenders, will make an important contribution in this particular area of pastoral care.

The Bishops are asked to exercise special care in the selection of pastoral ministers so that by their own high degree of spiritual and personal maturity and by their fidelity to the Magisterium, they may be of real service to homosexual persons, promoting their health and well-being in the fullest sense. Such ministers will reject theological opinions which dissent from the teaching of the Church and which, therefore, cannot be used as guidelines for pastoral care.

We encourage the Bishops to promote appropriate catechetical programmes based on the truth about human sexuality in its relationship to the family as taught by the Church. Such programmes should provide a good context within which to deal with the question of homosexuality.

This catechesis would also assist those families of homosexual persons to deal with this problem which affects them so deeply.

All support should be withdrawn from any organizations which seek to undermine the teaching of the Church, which are ambiguous about it, or which neglect it entirely. Such support, or even the semblance of such support, can be gravely misinterpreted. Special attention should be given to the practice of scheduling religious services and to the use of Church buildings by these groups, including the facilities of Catholic schools and colleges. To some, such permission to use Church property may seem only just and charitable; but in reality it is contradictory to the purpose for which these institutions were founded, it is misleading and often scandalous.

In assessing proposed legislation, the Bishops should keep as their uppermost concern the responsibility to defend and promote family life.

18. The Lord Jesus promised, "You shall know the truth and the truth shall set you free" (Jn. 8:32). Scripture bids us speak the truth in love (cf. Eph. 4:15). The God who is at once truth and love calls the Church to minister to every man, woman and child with the pastoral solicitude of our compassionate Lord.

257

It is in this spirit that we have addressed this Letter to the Bishops of the Church, with the hope that it will be of some help as they care for those whose suffering can only be intensified by error and lightened by truth.

During an audience granted to the undersigned Prefect, His Holiness, Pope John Paul II, approved this Letter, adopted in an ordinary session of the Congregation for the Doctrine of the Faith, and ordered it to be published.

Given at Rome, 1 October 1986.

JOSEPH CARDINAL RATZINGER
Prefect

ALBERTO BOVONE
Titular Archbishop of Caesarea in Numidia
Secretary

The Pope Converts:
Imagination, Bureaucracy,
Silence

Mark D. Jordan

This chapter poses a pneumatological question. What would it take for God to tell the Pope to change his mind? It would take an intervention of the Holy Spirit. Suppose the Holy Spirit is already so intervening? What opennesses and obstacles does it encounter? Jordan proposes that the knowledge of the Catholic Church concerning homosexuality is properly located not in documents, but in the lived lives of gay and lesbian Catholics, especially gay priests. That is the site of both the openness and the obstacles to any intervention of the Holy Spirit in magisterial teaching.

Imagine this. Overnight, God changes the hearts of a majority of officials in the Vatican. They awake in the morning convinced that the Roman Catholic church's condemnations of "homosexual acts" are both untrue and unjust. They resolve to revoke them. What would they have to revise in church doctrine or practice in order to correct the teachings about gays and lesbians?[1]

To give this question any force, we have to picture the Holy Spirit bestowing courage as well as insight. Imagine, for example, that particular morning-after at the Congregation for the Doctrine of the Faith (CDF), the Vatican's principal bureau for doctrinal surveillance. Each ecclesiastical bureaucrat is aware of a profound change of heart in himself (the masculine pronoun is appropriate). Who will be the first to broach the topic? Who will take the risk? Imagine that it is a morning toward the end of May, say the Monday after Pentecost, the commemoration of the outpouring of the Holy Spirit on the first Christian community. Outside, the signs of early summer: the sky is "almost black with its excess of blue, and the new grass already deep, but still vivid, and the white roses tumble. . . ."[2] Inside, dry mouths and palpitations over coffee.

———

So we must imagine a divine infusion of courage – not to say of independence, that rarest of virtues in any bureaucracy. Let us suppose that God has worked a change in the pope himself (here the masculine pronoun is obligatory). It would take at least a thorough conversion in the pope to make the doctrinal change possible, and it would take a pope not enchained by his handlers to make it plausible. So let us imagine that the pope's heart has been converted and then comforted with courage. He has decided to right a wrong done to homosexuals over centuries. His advisers have persuaded him at least to go slowly – to "study" the problem before acting on it. Rumor rushes down the clerical layers: The moral teachings about homosexuality are to be corrected by papal command in obedience to God's will, in faithfulness to the message of Christ. The Holy Father asks, What is required for the thorough correction of the teachings?

———

No serious answer to the question can be simple. In fact, to change Catholic teachings about homosexual acts would require changes under many other headings of Catholic theology. "Conservatives" are right to suspect this, though they are wrong to think that this is a reason for *not* correcting the teachings. The moral teachings on this topic are just the most visible sign of a larger failure. If the church could be so violently wrong about this for so many centuries, there must be some deep deformity in church governance. Any correction of teachings about homosexuality will have to begin by considering topics as different as the structures of church power and the styles of moral theology, the hypocrisies of confessional practice and the screening of seminary candidates. The correction would end . . . but that is a question.

———

What is required for a thorough correction of the teachings? No one knows. Homosexuality has been silenced so successfully in the Catholic church that we do not have the kinds of evidence required for a convincing answer. A subject that Catholic theologians cannot discuss during centuries except with thunder, derision, or disgust is not a subject on which Catholic theology is ready to speak.

Some theologians have indeed begun to speak about it more freely in the last thirty years, and they have made some helpful and even bold beginnings. We now have notable first essays in lesbian and gay theology, not least because we have lesbian and gay appropriations of liberation theology, feminist theory, the writing of church history, and so on. But three decades cannot undo two millennia. Catholic theologians will have to be able to speak freely about homosexuality for many years before they can write serious moral assessments of it.

In order for them to "speak freely," many changes will be required. It is not enough for the CDF to promise that it will no longer prosecute moral theologians who dissent from its diagnosis of homosexual orientation (though just that now seems utopian fantasy). The church, in some broader sense, will have to encourage homosexual Catholics to live openly and proudly. Serious moral theology cannot be principally the framing and manipulation of quasi-legal propositions. It must begin and end in the discovery of particular lives under grace. Lesbian and gay lives will have to become audible to the church, readable within it, before their graces can be discerned and described.

Indeed, the church will need to recognize homosexual saints in order to learn God's will in same-sex love, since it is typically and properly saints that instruct Catholic communities about how to live. By "homosexual saints" I do not mean lesbians or gays who feel obligated to martyr themselves in celibacy. I mean saints with lovers. The icons that show "Harvey Milk of San Francisco" are not just jokes, in good taste or bad. They are reminders that Catholic theology needs to watch how saints live a way of life before it can say much about it.

————

Correcting Catholic teachings on homosexuality is not only or mainly a matter of proposing amendments to specific documents. The official doctrine is more deeply embedded than that. It is more intimately connected to old arrangements of institutional power. Changing the language without reforming institutional arrangements would be useless, even if it were possible. The most important relations between Catholicism and homosexuality are not embodied in official propositions about homosexuality, nor even in official regulations for homo-sexual behavior. The forces at work here are not only the forces of words.

————

Imagine morning again. The Holy Spirit has indeed worked overnight in the Vatican, but microscopically. Conceive a middle-aged staff "theologian" who has spent an entire career being cautious. He awakes to find that his convictions have changed about – about *this*, of all things – living as a homosexual. Disturbed and yet compelled, he might try to broach the topic with colleagues in a roundabout way. Perhaps he would raise it more directly with a particular confidant. Or perhaps he would simply delay, hoping that his peculiar mood would pass.

On this May morning, his behavior would resemble that of many closeted gay men in the Catholic clergy. They feel compelled to play a sad game of concealed solicitation, of saying and not saying, of showing what they want only to those who surely want the same thing. Our staff theologian will be just like someone cruising from inside the closet. He may well have had that guilty experience, too.

―――

Behind the fixed rhetoric of the Vatican's bureaucratic speech are comprehensive structures for creating and enforcing clerical "discipline." For centuries now, these structures have been much preoccupied with controlling the appearance and the reality of clerical sexuality, especially homosexuality. The official words about homosexual activity are anchored in an apparatus for disciplining the facts of homosexual activity in the clergy.[3] Whatever the original causal relations between official teachings and clerical discipline might have been, it is now certainly true that clerical discipline keeps many clergymen from speaking candidly about the possibility of changing the official teachings. It keeps some of them from even thinking about that possibility.

―――

Clerical discipline shows itself as well in the very bureaucratic style of the modern Catholic church's moral "teachings," which is to say, its moral regulation. Whenever the Vatican does change moral teachings on a controversial point, as it did 150 years ago in the case of slavery, it insists all the more loudly that nothing has changed. Bureaucratic speech strives to maintain the illusion of unchanging control. So Vatican pronouncements work hard to convince us that nothing important ever changes in church teachings – or could change.

―――

Imagine a final version of that Monday after Pentecost. A staff theologian awakens after a night of cruising in the city – perhaps Monte Caprino on foot, for old time's sake, or the "Capolinea" and the "Colosseo quadrato." Or perhaps he has just returned from a vacation in lay clothing on the shores of the Aegean or at a gay enclave beyond the Alps. Over the years he has enjoyed regular sexual encounters – some negotiated in gay bars, some bought on the streets, some solicited within the concealing walls of church institutions. He has always been careful to hide his employment and usually his priestly status when consorting with laypeople. Not from guilt, which he claims not to feel, but from prudence. He will narrate his encounters, deliciously, to one or another friend in an informal club of similarly active clergymen, but he professes to find the very idea of "coming out" tasteless. Yet he discovers this morning that hearts have been changed around him. What has seemed so long a tidy arrangement of his private pleasures is now being called an injustice. How enthusiastically do you think he will respond to proposals for correction in official teachings?

―――

The premise of my Pentecost fantasy is not entirely hypothetical. Since gay Catholics believe that God does try to guide even the Vatican bureaucracy, and since most of them also believe that the Vatican's present teachings on homosexuality are not inspired by God, they must trust God to offer during each night and during each day the grace to change the Vatican. Every morning in Rome is a morning on which the pope or his curia could be converted. If they don't convert today, that need not imply some lack in divine will. It may imply something about human stubbornness. It may also suggest the magnitude of the changes required.

―――

The most important theological facts about Catholicism and homosexuality are not the bureaucratic words that Catholic authorities speak. The truly significant facts concern the homosexuality of the Catholic church itself – of members of its priesthood and its clerical culture, of its rituals and spiritual traditions. If the pope had succeeded in miraculously changing all the official words this morning, he still would not have touched the deepest connections between homosexuality and Catholicism. He would not have admitted the church's richest knowledge of the homoerotic.

―――

The facts or the effects of homosexual clergy are hardly unique to the Catholic church. The current controversies over ordaining "practicing" homosexuals in the major denominations suggest how ecumenical the situation is. Nor are closeted clergymen confined to Christianity. In Apuleius's *Golden Ass*, one of the best-known ancient Latin novels, the priests of Cybele purchase a donkey, who happens to be our unlucky hero Lucius in animal form.[4] There is some suggestion that they mean to enjoy his sex immediately, but their interest turns to a "built" farmer whom they invite to their private banquet in a small town. Their well-plotted orgy is prevented by the braying of Lucius, who summons the locals. The priests are driven out of town by mockery. (Do note that these pagan priests are neither exiled to permanent silence nor burned at the stake.)

This kind of story – there are others like it in Greco-Roman antiquity – raises interesting questions about the links between sexual identity and holiness. The stories can be multiplied many times over by evidence from other cultures.[5] Is it that holy figures need somehow to be set aside from the worldly game of marrying and child-rearing, which is to say, of alliance and inheritance? Are members of sexual minorities, of a "third sex," freaky or uncanny in a way that associates them with the divine? These questions direct us to analogies for what could otherwise seem particularly Catholic arrangements. But they can also distract us from looking at the evidence right in front of us. It is often easier to think about the priests of Cybele than the priests at the parish just down the block.

———

Within any society that universally persecutes same-sex desires, those desires will be kept silent. When members of that society's religious institutions feel them, they will treat them as secrets. When they act on their desires, they will do so secretly. More elaborate priestly or clerical secrecies will be constructed when the religion itself reinforces or initiates persecution of same-sex desires. The most elaborate secrecies will be found in religious institutions that condemn same-sex desires fiercely while creating conditions under which they can flourish: the situation of modern Catholicism.

———

In what follows, I consider the multiple forms or places of male homosexuality within modern Catholicism. (The restriction to men I will explain in a moment.) It is worth doing so for a number of reasons, whatever one's views about the truth of Catholic dogma.

Throughout much of the world, first, the Catholic church remains the most powerful of Christian organizations. Even in the United States, which has never been a "Catholic country," Catholic bishops enter aggressively into public debates over homosexuality and other matters of sexual morality. They are able to do so because religious condemnation remains the most potent homophobic rhetoric. So the features of Catholic homosexuality are particularly consequential outside the church.

Second, Catholic homoeroticism has a distinguished and varied history. Catholic clerical arrangements, for example, are very old by Christian standards. They produce rich articulations of male–male desire, both because of centuries of compulsory priestly celibacy and because of the enormous development of all-male religious orders.

Third, and most importantly, the Catholic management of same-sex desire has been decisive in European and American histories of what we now call "homosexuality." This is not just a matter of moral teachings, national legislation, or international bureaucracies for enforcement and punishment. In ways that I will analyze further on, Catholicism has been one of the most homoerotic of widely available modern cultures, offering encouragement, instruction, and relatively safe haven to many homosexuals. You will not understand modern homosexuality unless you understand Catholic homosexuality, and you cannot understand Catholic homosexuality unless you begin with the clergy.

———

Other general arguments could be made for the importance of paying particular attention to homosexuality in the Catholic church. But the most telling argument for me is very particular. The Catholic tradition is my Christian tradition. It is not only the one in which I found Christianity or the one I know best by experience, but it is the tradition within which I have had to work out the central paradox for any gay Christian: many Christian churches are at once the most homophobic and the most homoerotic of institutions. They seem cunningly designed to condemn same-sex desire and to elicit it, to persecute it and to instruct it. I sometimes call this the paradox of the "Beloved Disciple": "Come recline beside me and put your head on my chest, but don't dare conceive of what we do as erotic." Perhaps it is more clearly seen as the paradox of the Catholic Jesus, the paradox created by an officially homophobic religion in which an all-male clergy sacrifices male flesh before images of God as an almost naked man. How could such a religion not be officially homophobic – and also intensely homoerotic?

———

I have said that my topic would be male homosexuality, and I should underscore that limitation. Because I am concerned with internal connections between Catholic homosexuality and its most official impositions of silence, I focus on the priesthood and the male religious orders. Women are still sufficiently disenfranchised in the Catholic church to make lesbianism a separate concern in analyses of the exercise of church power. I know by observation and from historical study that women's religious communities have provided important places in which to work out both lesbian desire and women's gifts for Christian ministry. But women's religious communities have yet to gain much power over the articulation of official moral theology or the fixing of church policy. So I shall concentrate on closeted men in the clergy and religious orders. They are at once more powerful in the church and more familiar to me.

In any case, we need to think of Catholic lesbianism and Catholic gayness separately. Categories that combine gay men with lesbians are categories created to persecute both. The false sameness implied by a category like "sodomy" or "homosexuality" is useful for dehumanizing condemnation, but not for careful analysis. If lesbians and gays must now band together in self-defense, that does not mean that they can be honestly conceived in a single theological category. I certainly don't propose such a category in this book. I work in the opposite direction, focusing on male–male desires and actions. I do so as much to mark the limits of my own experience as to contest a false generalization.

It can be objected that I am being inconsistent in my scruples. After all, similar difficulties afflict the categories that are supposed to cover the range of identities or behaviors in men who (sometimes, regularly, often) desire (to see, touch, love, marry) other men. "Modern gay man" is just as much a historically constructed category as "male homosexual" or "invert" or "Urning" or "sodomite." It can become just as conceptually confusing and just as personally confining. I reply to this objection not with a windy interruption on the subject of identity logics, but by saying: Read on to see how I try to reflect the diversity of "gay" lives.

In saying that I will concentrate on male–male desires and actions within official church words and hidden church lives, I don't mean to erase gay men's debt to women's political movements or to feminist "theory." Both the theories of modern gayness and the practices of gay community-building have long depended on the earlier labors of women, especially lesbian women. If the study of lesbianism in women's religious communities or parish life has sometimes seemed less newsworthy than gay priests, it has often been more candid and more intelligent.[6] When I restrict my view for the most part to Catholic gayness, it is not because I want to deny what women have done or said. Nor am I trying to repeat the misogynistic silencing of women. Rather, I am addressing only what I have seen and understood about male–male desire in its relation to Catholic power. I refuse to practice ventriloquism in lesbian voices.

––––––

Easier said than done, because modern terminology, whether Catholic or secular, has been constructed to confuse all same-sex desire or action. It has been constructed, that is, to assimilate women's experience with women to men's experience with men. Catholic moral theology, for example, now talks in general about "homosexuals" and "homosexuality," and the arguments it deploys against both are supposed to apply equally to men and women. In fact, the theological imagination of Catholicism and its institutional arrangements are preoccupied almost entirely by male–male desire.

In what follows, I will try to use more candid terminology. When I paraphrase church teachings or rehearse our everyday conceptions, I will have to talk about "homosexuals" and "homosexuality" – or "sodomites" and "sodomy." Those terms will refer to women and men. I will use "gay," by contrast, only of men, making it the strict complement of "lesbian" for women. In my usage, all gays are men, all lesbians women. When I discuss considerations or circumstances affecting both groups, I will either use both terms or else the combination "lesbigay."

I do not use a more expansive tag – like the awkward "LGBT" for lesbian, gay, bisexual, transgendered – because the desires, actions, or identities described as "bisexual" or "transgendered" do not figure in my analysis. I do not have anything to say about them. Although our political sentiments and our worshipping communities need to be inclusive, our analyses must be precise. My analysis is concerned precisely with male–male eroticism in modern Catholicism.

――――

This book [Jordan's *The Silence of Sodom*] is constructed as three steps or stages of analysis. I could say, just as accurately, that they are three acts of literary imagination to be performed in sequence. In them, the imagination attends to very particular things – the rhetorical patterns in some recent Vatican documents, the circumstances of clerical homosexuality in America, the personal and institutional motives that keep homosexuals in the Catholic church or move them out of it. The acts of imagination attend to these particular things because they are all that we can now describe. We are not ready for mature Catholic teachings about male homoeroticism. We are in no position to recount the gay Catholic's general history (if it even makes sense to wish for such a narrative). We don't know what stable forms male–male love among Catholics will take a hundred years on. The most we can hope for is to be articulate about the things in front of us and to be cunning in trying to invent ways of talking beyond them.

――――

The first section of this book is called "Church Words." It analyzes the rhetoric of the church's bureaucratic speech about sexual morality. My point is not to argue, much less demonstrate, that official Catholic documents are usually wrong when they talk about homosexuality. I don't think that the documents call for counterargument, because I don't think that they mean to authorize discussion. They demand instead a kind of media analysis, what used to be called rhetorical study. Many official texts are scripts for preventing serious speech by scrambling it. To avoid the scrambling, we must recognize some of the rhetorical devices that the documents typically use – devices of unstable terminology, incoherent principles, fallacious argument. We must then acknowledge that the documents are part of a much larger and much older program of theological rhetoric. The first part of the book isn't a history of recent moral teachings approved by the Catholic hierarchy. It is a skeptical catalog of some typical devices in those teachings and an introduction to the rhetorical program behind them.

Those who cannot bear to reread recent Vatican documents on homosexuality are welcome to skip chapter 2. And those who have already gotten beyond the rhetorical program of Catholic moral theology since Trent can spare themselves chapter 3 as well. These two chapters make for hurtful and enraging reading, but then they treat of wounding texts.

———

The book's second section is called "Church Lives." In it I try to act on the notion that the church's knowledge about male homosexuality can be found elsewhere than in its official documents. I look for that knowledge in institutional arrangements, in fragments of history, and in unspoken but widely known features of clerical culture. The failure of official Catholic teachings on homosexuality is a failure both of official speech about lives and of the official lives themselves. The failure in speech follows on the failure to admit the enormous churchly "science" of male homoeroticism, the long institutional experimentation with it. The second section looks particularly at how Catholic speech about homosexuality is blocked by the melodrama of (open) secrecy that surrounds clerical homosexuality. The effects of this melodrama are found everywhere.

———

The book's third section distinguishes two kinds of "Church Dreams." Some dreams bind us to repeat certain forms of communal suffering, while others help us find communities without that needless suffering. The first dreams are illusions; the second, hopes. The task for imagination in this section is to identify what real choices among communities are open to gay Catholics while they wait for the official church to begin articulating mature teachings about their lives. It is not just a search for a Christian community in which one can "feel comfortable." It is rather a quest for a community in which gay Catholics can speak their beliefs as creed, as prayer, as sacrament in liturgy. After all, gay Catholics are silenced most in the present church not by being asked to parrot homophobic texts or to lie about their lives. They are most of all denied adequate words and rites, truthful preaching and sacrament, to articulate their faithful lives.

These dreamy hopes provoke an obvious question. Can anyone live happily as a gay man within Christian faith? Edmund White puts the question as an exasperated accusation: "I never thought I'd live to see the day when gays would be begging to be let back in to the Christian church, which is clearly our enemy."[7] Unfortunately, we could speak the same accusation at most of our major institutions, which have *at best* been explicitly homophobic until the last decades. Why participate in the churches? Indeed, why participate in the universities or the publishing houses or the major newspapers?

The alternative to participation is not Bohemianism, but barbarism. Thinking about how one can be gay and a member of some Christian community is just a form of a question that every homosexual faces: How can I make a place for myself in what has been and mostly continues to be a homophobic culture? To say this differently: For many gay Christians, thinking about church membership is the occasion for contemplating social membership or cultural identity generally. In the third part of this book, in the section on dreams, I try to present such an occasion.

I do not mean to suggest that questions about staying in the church should be dismissed as silly. Compelling cases can be made that identifying as a Catholic (or Christian) at this moment in American life can only be a form of collaboration with homosexuality's most dangerous enemies. I try to examine some of these cases throughout the book. But as I have already hinted, we have a great deal to learn about homosexuality from modern Catholicism, even if we never were or will not long remain Catholic. So, too, we have a lot to learn from modern homosexuality about Catholicism, perhaps especially if we are interested in continuing to conceive ourselves as somehow Catholic.

Who am I to write this book? Who am I to say such things? Any Catholic has been taught to practice self-examination and even self-abasement before daring to voice criticism, especially against the church. Self-examination can be an important antidote to pride or anger or vanity. It can also be an effective means for enforcing silence about Catholic homosexuality. It can function as one of a series of constraints, of double binds, that contrive to make it impossible for anyone to speak – except for the "competent authorities" in the Vatican.

If I were a former priest or member of a religious order, my criticisms would be dismissed as the bitter fruit of a failure to live up to my vows. I am neither a former priest nor a former religious, so they can be dismissed as uninformed.

If I were an accredited moral theologian teaching at a pontifical faculty, my criticisms would be dismissed as defection. I am not such a moral theologian, so they can be dismissed as the rant of an amateur.

If I were not "out," my criticisms would be dismissed as evidence of closeted gayness. I am "out," so they can be dismissed as my agenda.

These double binds are constructed to prevent anyone from talking about Catholic homosexuality except in the approved ways. The only people who are permitted to speak about it are just those who are guaranteed never to speak about it honestly. The only people who are authorized to speak about it are the silencing authorities themselves.

———

There are similar double binds of separation and inclusion. The topic of clerical homosexuality is connected immediately to a dozen enormous topics: the church's stereotyping of gender roles, its denigration of women, its preference for "conservative" political programs and regimes, its greed, and so on. But we have to start somewhere if we are to speak at all, and we have to speak within limits if we are to make sense.

There is also a more particular reason for treating male homosexuality as a separate topic within modern Catholicism: Catholicism itself treats it that way. The separation of the topic is not so much a testimony to its theological importance as to its political charge. Disputes over homosexuality are seen to be particularly threatening to the "unity" of the church. They are certainly threatening to its present political arrangements.

———

Then there is the double bind of Catholic diversity – of the historical, geographical, and cultural differences hidden within the term "Catholic." How can anyone presume to say anything general about so many different ways of life? This question can paralyze, in just the way that historical learning often does. The more you know of the evidence, the less you can speak about it in any coherent way.

In what follows, I emphasize the diversity of Catholic homosexualities even in modern times. I show why I am suspicious of narrative histories about homosexuality in Christianity, as I resist statistically based abstractions. Indeed, I have broken the text up into short sections, some no longer than an aphorism, precisely to remind the reader of how fragmentary are the speeches now available to us. But I do persist in trying to speak.

———

How to think of these fragments? They are *not* bits of colored glass for a mosaic, because they do not belong to a single picture or pattern. They are *not* photos and clippings for a scrapbook, because they do not belong to a single, collective life. If anything, they are scraps from notebooks – from diaries, reading journals, commonplace books.

The writing model I have followed is one that Walter Benjamin imagined for his never-accomplished study of the Parisian shopping arcades – which is to say, of nineteenth-century capitalism seen through the prism of the arcades. In sheaf "N" of materials for the project, Benjamin describes the method of his projected study as the art of quotation without quotation marks, of "literary montage."[8] "The first step along this path will be to carry the montage principle over into history. In this way to build up the large constructions out of the smallest, precisely fashioned structural elements. To detect the crystal of the total event in the analysis of the small, single moment" (p. 575, frag. N2, 6). The kind of insight afforded by montage is what Benjamin describes in a series of remarks headed by the word "Waking": "It's not that the past casts its light on the present. Rather an image is that in which the Then and the Now flash together into a constellation. In other words: image is dialectics at a standstill" (pp. 556–7, frag. N2a, 3).

If you change Benjamin's visual metaphors into metaphors of speech, you have something like my ideal. I am convinced that the homosexuality of modern Catholicism can't be written about except by "constellating" moral theology, church history, queer theory, the novel of manners, and utopian reveries. By gathering scraps from these kinds of texts, I hope to demonstrate both the inadequacy of official Catholic speeches about homosexuality and how challenging it will be to create more adequate ones.

———

In no way do I imagine that what I have written is comprehensive. I will have succeeded beyond my hopes if I have gathered one or two interesting samples under each of the main topics treated. If someone approaches tomorrow with a dozen, richer examples, that will be all to the good.

Better scraps of speech than silence. If we let the diversity of the evidence frighten us away from speaking at all, we surrender speech to its abusers. There are, of course, any number of prominent Catholics who are content to speak endlessly about homosexuality. They are the broadcasters of the official teachings, and they are curiously unconstrained by historical evidence or by the diversity of present experience, as we shall see. To be bound up in silence by the fear of overgeneralizing would be to allow the most aggressive programs of generalization to go forward without dissent.

Other contradictions bind you, my reader. Many of you who have the greatest familiarity with my topics will also have the greatest stake in denying what I say. I am not thinking in the first instance of church-employed experts in history and theology. I refer instead to closeted clergymen whose hatred of their own desire has become strict "orthodoxy" – I mean, homophobic rage.

––––

This book is not a remedy for the failure of Catholic teachings on homosexuality. We are not ready for full Catholic teachings about same-sex love – or female–male love, for that matter. The book is, instead, a rudimentary vocabulary, a first dictionary, of the unexpectedly varied expressions of Catholic gayness.

––––

According to an etymology that goes back in the Latin tradition at least to St. Jerome, patron of Catholic Bible translators, the place-name "Sodom" in Genesis 18–19 means "mute" or "silent beast."[9] Various explanations of this etymology are supplied by later theologians. Sodomites are rendered animal-like by their addiction to physical pleasure. Or sodomites lose rationality by acting against nature. Or the activity of sodomites is to be shrouded in silence among Christians. Sodomy is, after all, the "nameless" sin or crime – according to another misreading of the Scriptures (Ephesians 5:3). So Catholic confessors and preachers are warned against speaking about the sin with any clarity. They are not to inquire after it or preach against it for fear of inciting the laity to deeds not yet discovered. But the deepest sodomitic silence does not gag the laity. The explanations I have just been paraphrasing come from priestly texts written for priestly audiences. The same texts insist that sodomy is typically a priestly sin.

––––

Over the last millennium, Catholic writers have exercised themselves in painting pictures of the sodomitic soul – of the soul of the sinner given over to the practice of sodomy. They always depict the soul from outside, from far away, because of course they have never seen it up close. They show it as a Sodom in miniature – a city of anguished secrecy, of perpetual exile, of deserved death, over which fiery clouds always rain cinders. They project every vice into this city. They compare its inhabitants with the worst of history's criminals.

If these garish pictures seem to be projections of fantasy, they still capture something real. Instead of depicting the souls of average Catholics who love members of their own sex, they show the hellishly intertwined lives of closeted inhabitants of church institutions and their pharisaical persecutors. There is indeed a silent Sodom. It is housed within the structures of churchly power. Its silence must be disturbed before there can be mature Catholic teachings on "homosexuality" – or mature criticisms of how "homosexuality" itself fails to describe gay Catholic lives. The silence of Sodom envelops a Catholic science of sodomy, of homosexuality, about which we must now speak.

Notes

1 I will often use "Catholic" to mean Roman Catholic and "the church" to mean one or another bureaucracy in the network of Roman Catholic institutions. I don't mean to suggest by my usage that the sum of Roman Catholic institutions is the true church or that other Christian institutions couldn't make an equal claim to being "catholic." I only intend to begin with our ordinary shorthand for talking about these things. By the book's end, there will be more than enough questions about both the meaning of "Catholic" and the Christianity of bureaucracies.

2 Henry James, "After-Season in Rome," in his *Italian Hours*, rpt. edn. (Hopewell, NJ: Ecco Press, 1987), p. 191.

3 The notion of who constitutes Catholic "clergy" has varied tremendously over time and across different church regimes. I use it here with a clear center, but without clear boundaries. The center comprises priests who are ordained either for a diocese or in one of the religious orders. Further out from the center are various groups on the way to the priesthood and the male members of religious orders who do not seek ordination. The term "religious" contrasts any members of a religious order, ordained or not, with a member of the diocesan clergy.

4 Apuleius, *The Golden Ass*, 8.26, 8.29. The "fortissimus rusticanus" makes his appearance in 8.29 (Rudolf Helm, ed., *Opera*, 2d edn., 2 vols. (Leipzig: B. G. Teubner, 1955), 1:200.16).

5 For the merest sample of anthropological studies on relations between ritual role and homosexual or transgendered identity, see the essays in Gilbert H. Herdt, *Third Sex, Third Gender: Beyond Sexual Dimorphism in Culture and History* (New York: Zone Books, 1994).

6 So, for example, Rosemary Curb and Nancy Manahan's *Lesbian Nuns: Breaking Silence* (New York: Warner Books, 1986) gives a richer, better textured representation of the

lives it describes than most of the anthologies about gay priests or religious, which tend to be rather more statistical or polemical.

7 Edmund White, "What Century Is This, Anyway?" *The Advocate*, no. 762 (June 23, 1998), p. 58.

8 Walter Benjamin, "Das *Passagenwerk*," *Gesammelte Schriften*, ed. Rolf Teidemann, vol. 5, no. 1 (Frankfurt: Suhrkamp, 1982), pp. 572–4, especially frags. N1, 10; and N1A, 8. The parenthetical citations in the rest of the paragraph are also to this work.

9 Jerome, *Liber interpretationis hebraicorum nominum*, De Genesi "S" (Paul Lagarde, ed., *Opera*, vol. I, no. 1, Corpus Christianorum Series Latina, vol. 72 (Turnhout: Brepols, 1959), p. 71, lines 18–19).

Alone Again, Naturally: The Catholic Church and the Homosexual

Andrew Sullivan

This article is the best commentary on recent Vatican statements about homosexuality. It makes unusually good use of experience as an ecclesially formed category in the service of the church. It is the experience neither of a psychological patient nor of a pious victim, but of a Catholic Christian present in his whole body at the Eucharist and seeking to participate in charity.

Just as important, it takes a careful and balanced view of church documents. It sees two contrary trends: one of greater compassion toward homosexual persons, and one of greater severity against homosexual acts. Of these two trends, however, it identifies the mention of homosexual "persons" as most significant. In Catholic theology, "person" is an important technical term, and its use here cannot be accidental. It casts gay and lesbian people in a new light. To be a person invokes an analogy – created and distant, but participant and ontological – to the divine persons of the Trinity. It is those persons – Father, Son, and Spirit – who in loving one another constitute God's triune life, and it is as persons in God's image that God brings human beings to participate in the love by which God loves God. If there are such human beings as homosexual persons, then God is committed to taking their bodies – somehow – as means rather than impediments to that communion. Christ, after all, took a body, that human beings might participate in God's personal life.

Along the way Sullivan addresses many other arguments in Catholic moral theology. For example, he argues that alcoholism and homosexuality make a contrast rather than a comparison, and he develops an aesthetic argument to answer the question of what God may have created gay and lesbian people for.

In everyone there sleeps
A sense of life lived according to love.
To some it means the difference they could make
By loving others, but across most it sweeps
As all they might have been had they been loved.
That nothing cures.

Philip Larkin, "Faith Healing"

I

I can remember the first time what, for the sake of argument, I will call my sexuality came into conflict with what, for the sake of argument, I will call my faith. It was time for Communion in my local parish church, Our Lady and St. Peter's, a small but dignified building crammed between an Indian restaurant and a stationery shop, opposite a public restroom, on the main street of a smallish town south of London called East Grinstead. I must have been around 15 or so. Every time I received Communion, I attempted, following my mother's instructions, to offer up the sacrament for some current problem or need: my mother's health, an upcoming exam, the starving in Bangladesh or whatever. Most of these requests had to do with either something abstract and distant, like a cure for cancer, or something extremely tangible like a better part in the school play. Like much else in my faith-life, they were routine and yet not completely drained of sincerity. But rarely did they address something that could unsettle the comfort of my precocious adolescence. This time, however, as I filed up to the Communion rail to face mild-mannered Father Simmons for the umpteenth time, something else intervened. Please, I remember asking almost offhandedly of God, after a quick recital of my other failings, help me with *that*.

I didn't have a name for it, since it was, to all intents and purposes, nameless. I don't think I'd ever heard it mentioned at home, except once when my mother referred to someone who had behaved inappropriately on my father's town rugby team. (He had been dealt with, she reported darkly.) At high school, the subject was everywhere and nowhere: at the root of countless jokes but never actualized as something that could affect anyone we knew. But this ubiquity and abstraction brought home the most important point: uniquely among failings, homosexuality was so abominable it could not even be mentioned. The occasions when it was actually discussed were so rare that they stand out even now in my mind: our Latin teacher's stating that homosexuality was obviously wrong since it meant "sticking your dick in the wrong hole"; the graffiti in the public restroom in Reigate High Street: "My mother made me a homosexual," followed closely by, "If I gave her the wool, would she make me one too?"

Although my friends and family never stinted in pointing out other faults on my part, this, I knew, would never be confronted. So when it emerged as an irresistible fact of my existence, and when it first seeped into my life of dutiful prayer and worship, it could be referred to only in the inarticulate void of that Sunday evening before Communion.

From the beginning, however – and this is something many outside the Church can find hard to understand – my sexuality was part of my faith-life, not a revolt against it. Looking back, I realize that that moment at the Communion rail was the first time I had actually addressed the subject of homosexuality explicitly in front of anyone; and I had brought it to God in the moments before the most intimate act of sacramental Communion. Because it was something I was deeply ashamed of, I felt obliged to confront it; but because it was also something inextricable – even then – from the core of my existence, it felt natural to enlist God's help rather than his judgment in grappling with it. There was, of course, considerable tension in this balance of alliance and rejection; but there was also something quite natural about it, an accurate reflection of anyone's compromised relationship with what he or she hazards to be the divine.

To the outsider, faith often seems a kind of cataclysmic intervention, a Damascene moment of revelation and transformation, and no doubt, for a graced few, this is indeed the experience. But this view of faith is often, it seems to me, a way to salve the unease of a faithless life by constructing the alternative as something so alien to actual experience that it is safely beyond reach. Faith for me has never been like that. The moments of genuine intervention and spiritual clarity have been minuscule in number and, when they have occurred, hard to discern and harder still to understand. In the midst of this uncertainty, the sacraments, especially that of Communion, have always been for me the only truly reliable elements of direction, concrete instantiations of another order. Which is why, perhaps, it was at Communion that the subject reared its confusing, shaming presence.

The two experiences came together in other ways, too. Like faith, one's sexuality is not simply a choice; it informs a whole way of being. But like faith, it involves choices – the choice to affirm or deny a central part of one's being, the choice to live a life that does not deny but confronts reality. It is, like faith, mysterious, emerging clearly one day, only to disappear the next, taking different forms – of passion, of lust, of intimacy, of fear. And like faith, it points toward something other and more powerful than the self. The physical communion with the other in sexual life hints at the same kind of transcendence as the physical Communion with the Other that lies at the heart of the sacramental Catholic vision.

So when I came to be asked, later in life, how I could be gay and Catholic, I could answer only that I simply was. What to others appeared a simple contradiction was, in reality, the existence of these two connected, yet sometimes parallel, experiences of the world. It was not that my sexuality was involuntary and my faith chosen and that therefore my sexuality posed a problem for my faith; nor was it that my faith was involuntary and my sexuality chosen so that my faith posed a problem for my sexuality. It was that both were chosen and unchosen continuously throughout my life, as parts of the same search for something larger. As I grew older, they became part of me, inseparable from my understanding of myself. My faith existed at the foundation of how I saw the world; my sexuality grew to be inseparable from how I felt the world.

I am aware that this formulation of the problem is theologically flawed. Faith, after all, is not a sensibility; in the Catholic sense, it is a statement about reality that cannot be negated by experience. And there is little doubt about what the authority of the Church teaches about the sexual expression of a homosexual orientation. But this was not how the problem first presented itself. The immediate difficulty was not how to make what I *did* conform with what the Church taught me (until my early 20s, I did very little that could be deemed objectively sinful with regard to sex), but how to make who I *was* conform with what the Church taught me. This was a much more difficult proposition. It did not conform to a simple contradiction between self and God, as that afternoon in the Communion line attested. It entailed trying to understand how my adolescent crushes and passions, my longings for human contact, my stumbling attempts to relate love to life, could be so inimical to the Gospel of Christ and His Church, how they could be so unmentionable among people I loved and trusted.

So I resorted to what many young homosexuals and lesbians resort to. I found a way to expunge love from life, to construct a trajectory that could somehow explain this absence, and to hope that what seemed so natural and overwhelming could somehow be dealt with. I studied hard to explain away my refusal to socialize; I developed intense intellectual friendships that bordered on the emotional, but I kept them restrained in a carapace of artificiality to prevent passion from breaking out. I adhered to a hopelessly pessimistic view of the world, which could explain my refusal to take part in life's pleasures, and to rationalize the dark and deep depressions that periodically overwhelmed me.

No doubt some of this behavior was part of any teenager's panic at the prospect of adulthood. But looking back, it seems unlikely that this pattern had nothing whatsoever to do with my being gay. It had another twist: it sparked an intense religiosity that could provide me with the spiritual resources I needed to fortify my barren emotional life. So my sexuality and my faith entered into a dialectic: my faith propelled me away from my emotional and sexual longing, and the deprivation that this created required me to resort even more dogmatically to my faith. And as my faith had to find increasing power to restrain the hormonal and emotional turbulence of adolescence, it had to take on a caricatured shape, aloof and dogmatic, ritualistic and awesome. As time passed, a theological austerity became the essential complement to an emotional emptiness. And as the emptiness deepened, the austerity sharpened.

II

In a remarkable document titled "Declaration on Certain Questions Concerning Sexual Ethics," issued by the Vatican in 1975, the Sacred Congregation for the Doctrine of the Faith made the following statement regarding the vexed issue of homosexuality: "A distinction is drawn, and it seems with some reason, between homosexuals whose tendency comes from a false education, from a lack of normal sexual development, from habit, from bad example; or from other similar causes, and is transitory or at least not incurable; and homosexuals who are definitively such because of some kind of innate instinct or a pathological constitution judged to be incurable."

The Church was responding, it seems, to the growing sociological and psychological evidence that, for a small minority of people, homosexuality is unchosen and unalterable. In the context of a broad declaration on a whole range of sexual ethics, this statement was something of a minor digression (twice as much space was devoted to the "grave moral disorder" of masturbation); and it certainly didn't mean a liberalization of doctrine about the morality of homosexual acts, which were "intrinsically disordered and can in no case be approved of."

Still, the concession complicated things. Before 1975 the modern Church, when it didn't ignore the matter, had held a coherent view of the morality of homosexual acts. It maintained that homosexuals, as the modern world had come to define them, didn't really exist; rather, everyone was essentially a heterosexual and homosexual acts were acts chosen by heterosexuals, out of depravity, curiosity, impulse, predisposition or bad moral guidance. Such acts were an abuse of the essential heterosexual orientation of all humanity; they were condemned because they failed to link sexual activity with a binding commitment between a man and a woman in a marriage, a marriage that was permanently open to the possibility of begetting children. Homosexual sex was condemned in exactly the same way and for exactly the same reasons as premarital heterosexual sex, adultery or contracepted sex: it failed to provide the essential conjugal and procreative context for sexual relations.

The reasoning behind this argument rested on natural law. Natural law teaching, drawing on Aristotelian and Thomist tradition, argued that the sexual nature of man was naturally linked to both emotional fidelity and procreation so that, outside of this context, sex was essentially destructive of the potential for human flourishing: "the full sense of mutual self-giving and human procreation in the context of true love," as the encyclical *Gaudium et Spes* put it.

But suddenly, a new twist had been made to this argument. There was, it seems, *in nature*, a group of people who were "definitively" predisposed to violation of this natural law; their condition was "innate" and "incurable." Insofar as it was innate – literally *innatus* or "inborn" – this condition was morally neutral, since anything involuntary could not be moral or immoral; it simply was. But always and everywhere, the activity to which this condition led was "intrinsically disordered and [could] in no case be approved of." In other words, something fundamentally in nature always and everywhere violated a vital part of the nature of human beings; something essentially blameless was always and everywhere blameworthy if acted upon.

The paradox of this doctrine was evident even within its first, brief articulation. Immediately before stating the intrinsic disorder of homosexuality, the text averred that in "the pastoral field, these homosexuals must certainly be treated with understanding and sustained in the hope of overcoming their personal difficulties. . . . Their culpability will be judged with prudence." This compassion for the peculiar plight of the homosexual was then elaborated: "This judgment of Scripture does not of course permit us to conclude that all those who suffer from this anomaly are personally responsible for it. . . ." Throughout, there are alternating moments of alarm and quiescence; tolerance and panic; categorical statement and prudential doubt.

It was therefore perhaps unsurprising that, within a decade, the Church felt it necessary to take up the matter again. The problem could have been resolved by a simple reversion to the old position, the position maintained by fundamentalist Protestant churches: that homosexuality was a hideous, yet curable, affliction of heterosexuals. But the Church doggedly refused to budge from its assertion of the natural occurrence of constitutive homosexuals – or from its compassion for and sensitivity to their plight. In Cardinal Joseph Ratzinger's 1986 letter, "On the Pastoral Care of Homosexual Persons," this theme is actually deepened, beginning with the title.

To non-Catholics, the use of the term "homosexual person" might seem a banality. But the term "person" constitutes in Catholic moral teaching a profound statement about the individual's humanity, dignity and worth; it invokes a whole range of rights and needs; it reflects the recognition by the Church that a homosexual person deserves exactly the same concern and compassion as a heterosexual person, having all the rights of a human being, and all the value, in the eyes of God. This idea was implicit in the 1975 declaration, but was never advocated. Then there it was, eleven years later, embedded in Ratzinger's very title. Throughout his text, homosexuality, far from being something unmentionable or disgusting, is discussed with candor and subtlety. It is worthy of close attention: "[T]he phenomenon of homosexuality, complex as it is and with its many consequences for society and ecclesial life, is a proper focus for the Church's pastoral care. It thus requires of her ministers attentive study, active concern and honest, theologically well-balanced counsel." And here is Ratzinger on the moral dimensions of the unchosen nature of homosexuality: "[T]he particular inclination of the homosexual person is not a sin." Moreover, homosexual persons, he asserts, are "often generous and giving of themselves." Then, in a stunning passage of concession, he marshals the Church's usual arguments in defense of human dignity in order to defend homosexual dignity:

> It is deplorable that homosexual persons have been and are the object of violent malice in speech or in action. Such treatment deserves condemnation from the Church's pastors wherever it occurs. It reveals a kind of disregard for others which endangers the most fundamental principles of a healthy society. The intrinsic dignity of each person must always be respected in word, in action and in law.

Elsewhere, Ratzinger refers to the homosexual's "God-given dignity and worth"; condemns the view that homosexuals are totally compulsive as a "demeaning assumption"; and argues that "the human person, made in the image and likeness of God, can hardly be adequately described by a reductionist reference to his or her sexual orientation."

Why are these statements stunning? Because they reveal how far the Church had, by the mid-1980s, absorbed the common sense of the earlier document's teaching on the involuntariness of homosexuality, and had had the courage to reach its logical conclusion. In Ratzinger's lether, the Church stood foursquare against bigotry, against demeaning homosexuals either by anti-gay attempts to reduce human beings to one aspect of their personhood. By denying that homosexual activity was totally compulsive, the Church could open the door to an entire world of moral discussion about ethical and unethical homosexual behavior, rather than simply dismissing it all as pathological. What in 1975 had been "a pathological constitution judged to be incurable" was, eleven years later, a "homosexual person," "made in the image and likeness of God."

But this defense of the homosexual person was only half the story. The other half was that, *at the same time*, the Church strengthened its condemnation of any and all homosexual activity. By 1986 the teachings condemning homosexual acts were far more categorical than they had been before. Ratzinger had guided the Church into two simultaneous and opposite directions: a deeper respect for homosexuals, and a sterner rejection of almost anything they might do.

At the beginning of the 1986 document, Ratzinger bravely confronted the central paradox: "In the discussion which followed the publication of the [1975] declaration . . . an overly benign interpretation was given to the homosexual condition itself, some going so far as to call it neutral or even good. Although the particular inclination of the homosexual person is not a sin, it is a more or less strong tendency ordered toward an intrinsic moral evil and thus the inclination itself must be seen as an objective disorder." Elsewhere, he reiterated the biblical and natural law arguments against homosexual relations. Avoiding the problematic nature of the Old Testament's disavowal of homosexual acts (since these are treated in the context of such "abominations" as eating pork and having intercourse during menstruation, which the Church today regards with equanimity), Ratzinger focused on St. Paul's admonitions against homosexuality: "Instead of the original harmony between Creator and creatures, the acute distortion of idolatry has led to all kinds of moral excess. Paul is at a loss to find a clearer example of this disharmony than homosexual relations." There was also the simple natural-law argument: "It is only in the marital relationship that the use of the sexual faculty can be morally good. A person engaging in homosexual behavior therefore acts immorally." The point about procreation was strengthened by an argument about the natural, "complementary union able to transmit life," which is heterosexual marriage. The fact that homosexual sex cannot be a part of this union means that it "thwarts the call to a life of that form of self-giving which the Gospel says is the essence of Christian living." Thus "homosexual activity" is inherently "self-indulgent." "Homosexual activity," Ratzinger's document claimed in a veiled and ugly reference to HIV, is a "form of life which constantly threatens to destroy" homosexual persons.

This is some armory of argument. The barrage of statements directed against "homosexual activity," which Ratzinger associates in this document exclusively with genital sex, is all the more remarkable because it occurs in a document that has otherwise gone further than might have been thought imaginable in accepting homosexuals into the heart of the Church and of humanity. Ratzinger's letter was asking us, it seems, to love the sinner more deeply than ever before, but to hate the sin even more passionately. This is a demand with which most Catholic homosexuals have at some time or other engaged in anguished combat.

III

It is also a demand that raises the central question of the two documents and, indeed, of any Catholic homosexual life: How intelligible is the Church's theological and moral position on the blamelessness of homosexuality and the moral depravity of homosexual acts? This question is the one I wrestled with in my early 20s, as the increasing aridity of my emotional life began to conflict with the possibility of my living a moral life. The distinction made some kind of sense in theory; but in practice, the command to love oneself as a person of human dignity yet hate the core longings that could make one emotionally whole demanded a sense of detachment or a sense of cynicism that seemed inimical to the Christian life. To deny lust was one thing; to deny love was another. And to deny love in the context of *Christian* doctrine seemed particularly perverse. Which begged a prior question: Could the paradoxes of the Church's position reflect a deeper incoherence at their core?

One way of tackling the question is to look for useful analogies to the moral paradox of the homosexual. Greed, for example, might be said to be an innate characteristic of human beings, which, in practice, is always bad. But the analogy falls apart immediately. Greed is itself evil; it is prideful, a part of Original Sin. It is not, like homosexuality, a blameless natural condition that inevitably leads to what are understood as immoral acts. Moreover, there is no subgroup of innately greedy people, nor a majority of people in which greed never occurs. Nor are the greedy to be treated with respect. There is no paradox here, and no particular moral conundrum.

Aquinas suggests a way around this problem. He posits that some things that occur in nature may be in accordance with an individual's nature, but somehow against human nature in general: "for it sometimes happens that one of the principles which is natural to the species as a whole has broken down in one of its individual members; the result can be that something which runs counter to the nature of the species as a whole, happens to be in harmony with nature for a particular individual: as it becomes natural for a vessel of water which has been heated to give out heat." Forget, for a moment, the odd view that somehow it is more "natural" for a vessel to exist at one temperature than another. The fundamental point here is that there are natural urges in a particular person that may run counter to the nature of the species as a whole. The context of this argument is a discussion of pleasure: How is it, if we are to trust nature (as Aquinas and the Church say we must), that some natural pleasures in some people are still counter to human nature as a whole? Aquinas's only response is to call such events functions of sickness, what the modern Church calls "objective disorder." But here, too, the analogies he provides are revealing: they are bestiality and cannibalism. Aquinas understands each of these activities as an emanation of a predilection that seems to occur more naturally in some than in others. But this only reveals some of the special problems of lumping homosexuality in with other "disorders." Even Aquinas's modern disciples (and, as we've seen, the Church) concede that involuntary orientation to the same gender does not spring from the same impulses as cannibalism or bestiality. Or indeed that cannibalism is ever a "natural" pleasure in the first place, in the way that, for some bizarre reason, homosexuality is.

What, though, of Aquinas's better argument – that a predisposition to homosexual acts is a mental or physical *illness* that is itself morally neutral, but always predisposes people to inherently culpable acts? Here, again, it is hard to think of a precise analogy. Down syndrome, for example, occurs in a minority and is itself morally neutral; but when it leads to an immoral act, such as, say, a temper tantrum directed at a loving parent, the Church is loath to judge that person as guilty of choosing to break a commandment. The condition excuses the action. Or, take epilepsy: if an epileptic person has a seizure that injures another human being, she is not regarded as morally responsible for her actions, insofar as they were caused by epilepsy. There is no paradox here either, but for a different reason: with greed, the condition itself is blameworthy; with epilepsy, the injurious act is blameless.

Another analogy can be drawn. What of something like alcoholism? This is a blameless condition, as science and psychology have shown. Some people have a predisposition to it; others do not. Moreover, this predisposition is linked, as homosexuality is, to a particular act. For those with a predisposition to alcoholism, having a drink might be morally disordered, destructive to the human body and spirit. So, alcoholics, like homosexuals, should be welcomed into the Church, but only if they renounce the activity their condition implies.

Unfortunately, even this analogy will not hold. For one thing, drinking is immoral only for alcoholics. Moderate drinking is perfectly acceptable, according to the Church, for non-alcoholics. On the issue of homosexuality, to follow the analogy, the Church would have to say that sex between people of the same gender would be – in moderation – fine for heterosexuals but not for homosexuals. In fact, of course, the Church teaches the opposite, arguing that the culpability of homosexuals engaged in sexual acts should be judged with prudence – and *less* harshly – than the culpability of heterosexuals who engage in "perversion."

But the analogy to alcoholism points to a deeper problem. Alcoholism does not ultimately work as an analogy because it does not reach to the core of the human condition in the way that homosexuality, following the logic of the Church's arguments, does. If alcoholism is overcome by a renunciation of alcoholic acts, then recovery allows the human being to realize his or her full potential, a part of which, according to the Church, is the supreme act of self-giving in a life of matrimonial love. But if homosexuality is overcome by a renunciation of homosexual emotional and sexual union, the opposite is achieved: the human being is liberated into sacrifice and pain, barred from the matrimonial love that the Church holds to be intrinsic, for most people, to the state of human flourishing. Homosexuality is a structural condition that restricts the human being, even if homosexual acts are renounced, to a less than fully realized life. In other words, the gay or lesbian person is deemed disordered at a far deeper level than the alcoholic: at the level of the human capacity to love and be loved by another human being, in a union based on fidelity and self-giving. Their renunciation of such love also is not guided toward some ulterior or greater goal – as the celibacy of the religious orders is designed to intensify their devotion to God. Rather, the loveless homosexual destiny is precisely toward nothing, a negation of human fulfillment, which is why the Church understands that such persons, even in the act of obedient self-renunciation, are called "to enact the will of God in their life by joining whatever sufferings and difficulties they experience in virtue of their condition to the sacrifice of the Lord's cross."

This suggests another analogy: the sterile person. Here, too, the person is structurally barred by an innate or incurable condition from the full realization of procreative union with another person. One might expect that such people would be regarded in exactly the same light as homosexuals. They would be asked to commit themselves to a life of complete celibacy and to offer up their pain toward a realization of Christ's sufferings on the cross. But that, of course, is not the Church's position. Marriage is available to sterile couples or to those past child-bearing age; these couples are not prohibited from having sexual relations.

One is forced to ask: What rational distinction can be made, on the Church's own terms, between the position of sterile people and that of homosexual people with regard to sexual relations and sacred union? If there is nothing morally wrong, per se, with the homosexual condition or with homosexual love and self-giving, then homosexuals are indeed analogous to those who, by blameless fate, cannot reproduce. With the sterile couple, it could be argued, miracles might happen. But miracles, by definition, can happen to anyone. What the analogy to sterility suggests, of course, is that the injunction against homosexual union does not rest, at heart, on the arguments about openness to procreation, but on the Church's failure to fully absorb its own teachings about the dignity and worth of homosexual persons. It cannot yet see them as it sees sterile heterosexuals: people who, with respect to procreation, suffer from a clear, limiting condition, but who nevertheless have a potential for real emotional and spiritual self-realization, in the heart of the Church, through the transfiguring power of the matrimonial sacrament. It cannot yet see them as truly made in the image of God.

But this, maybe, is to be blind in the face of the obvious. Even with sterile people, there is a symbolism in the union of male and female that speaks to the core nature of sexual congress and its ideal instantiation. There is no such symbolism in the union of male with male or female with female. For some

Catholics, this "symbology" goes so far as to bar even heterosexual intercourse from positions apart from the missionary – face to face, male to female, in a symbolic act of love devoid of all non-procreative temptation. For others, the symbology is simply about the notion of "complementarity," the way in which each sex is invited in the act of sexual congress – even when they are sterile – to perceive the mystery of the other; when the two sexes are the same, in contrast, the act becomes one of mere narcissism and self-indulgence, a higher form of masturbation. For others still, the symbolism is simply about Genesis, the story of Adam and Eve, and the essentially dual, male–female center of the natural world. Denying this is to offend the complementary dualism of the universe.

But all these arguments are arguments for the centrality of heterosexual sexual acts in nature, not their exclusiveness. It is surely possible to concur with these sentiments, even to laud their beauty and truth, while also conceding that it is nevertheless also true that nature seems to have provided a spontaneous and mysterious contrast that could conceivably be understood to complement – even dramatize – the central male-female order. In many species and almost all human cultures, there are some who seem to find their destiny in a similar but different sexual and emotional union. They do this not by subverting their own nature, or indeed human nature, but by fulfilling it in a way that doesn't deny heterosexual primacy, but rather honors it by its rare and distinct otherness. As albinos remind us of the brilliance of color; as redheads offer a startling contrast to the blandness of their peers; as genius teaches us, by contrast, the virtue of moderation; as the disabled person reveals to us in negative form the beauty of the fully functioning human body; so the homosexual person might be seen as a natural foil to the heterosexual norm, a variation that does not eclipse the theme, but resonates with it. Extinguishing – or prohibiting – homosexuality is, from this point of view, not a virtuous necessity, but the real crime against nature, a refusal to accept the pied beauty of God's creation, a denial of the way in which the other need not threaten, but may actually give depth and contrast to the self.

This is the alternative argument embedded in the Church's recent grappling with natural law, that is just as consonant with the spirit of natural law as the Church's current position. It is more consonant with what actually occurs in nature; seeks an end to every form of natural life; and upholds the dignity of each human person. It is so obvious an alternative to the Church's current stance that it is hard to imagine the forces of avoidance that have kept it so firmly at bay for so long.

IV

For many homosexual Catholics, life within the Church is a difficult endeavor. In my 20s, as I attempted to unite the possibilities of sexual longing and emotional commitment, I discovered what many heterosexuals and homosexuals had discovered before me: that it is a troubling and troublesome mission. There's a disingenuous tendency, when discussing both homosexual and heterosexual emotional life, to glamorize and idealize the entire venture. To posit the possibility of a loving union, after all, is not to guarantee its achievement. There is also a lamentable inclination to believe that all conflicts can finally be resolved; that the homosexual Catholic's struggle can be removed by a simple theological *coup de main*; that the conflict is somehow deeper than many other struggles in the Church – of women, say, or of the divorced. The truth is that pain, as Christ taught, is not a reason to question truth; it may indeed be a reason to embrace it.

But it must also be true that to dismiss the possibility of a loving union for homosexuals at all – to banish from the minds and hearts of countless gay men and women the idea that they, too, can find solace and love in one another – is to create the conditions for a human etiolation that no Christian community can contemplate without remorse. What finally convinced me of the wrongness of the Church's teachings was not that they were intellectually so confused, but that in the circumstances of my own life – and of the lives I discovered around me – they seemed so destructive of the possibilities of human love and self-realization. By crippling the potential for connection and growth, the Church's teachings created a dynamic that in practice led not to virtue but to pathology; by requiring the first lie in a human life, which would lead to an entire battery of others, they contorted human beings into caricatures of solitary eccentricity, frustrated bitterness, incapacitating anxiety – and helped perpetuate all the human wickedness and cruelty and insensitivity that such lives inevitably carry in their wake. These doctrines could not in practice do what they wanted to do: they could not both affirm human dignity and deny human love.

This truth is not an argument; it is merely an observation. But observations are at the heart not simply of the Church's traditional Thomist philosophy, but also of the phenomenological vision of the current pope. To observe these things, to affirm their truth, is not to oppose the Church, but to hope in it, to believe in it as a human institution that is yet the eternal vessel of God's love. It is to say that such lives as those of countless gay men and lesbians must ultimately affect the Church not because our lives are perfect, or without contradiction, or without sin, but because our lives are in some sense also the life of the Church.

I remember, in my own life, the sense of lung-filling exhilaration I felt as my sexuality began to be incorporated into my life, a sense that was not synonymous with recklessness or self-indulgence – although I was not immune from those things either – but a sense of being suffused at last with the possibility of being fully myself before those I loved and before God. I remember the hopefulness of parents regained and friendships restored in a life that, for all its vanities, was at least no longer premised on a lie covered over by a career. I remember the sense a few months ago in a pew in a cathedral, as I reiterated the same pre-Communion litany of prayers that I had spoken some twenty years earlier, that, for the first time, the love the Church had always taught that God held for me was tangible and redemptive. I had never felt it fully before; and, of course, like so many spiritual glimpses, I have rarely felt it since. But I do know that it was conditioned not on the possibility of purity, but on the possibility of honesty. That honesty is not something that can be bought or won in a moment. It is a process peculiarly prone to self-delusion and self-doubt. But it is one that, if it is to remain true to itself, the Church cannot resist forever.

Gay Friendship: A Thought Experiment in Catholic Moral Theology

Stanley Hauerwas

This article performs "a thought experiment in Catholic moral theology." On Aristotelian and Thomistic grounds, Catholic moral theology seeks to know the good by consulting the wise person (or on christological grounds, the justified person). Since there seem to be Catholic gay and lesbian couples among the wise, Hauerwas proposes that Catholic moral theology might properly be done in friendship with them – precisely as part of the determination of what the moral facts of the matter are regarding gay and lesbian Christian couples.

Difficult Beginnings

'Do you believe in the virgin birth?' That was the question we were asked in Texas in order to test whether we were really 'Christian.' At least that was the way the challenge was issued during the time I was growing up in Texas. I confess I was never particularly concerned with how that question should be answered. I was not raised a fundamentalist, but I believed in the virgin birth. The problem for me was not believing in it but what difference it might make one way or the other whether I did or did not believe in it. My preoccupation was not with Mary's virginity, but with my virginity and how I could lose it. In the meantime, of course, we Texans had football to keep us from being too torn up by any anxieties that might come from questioning the virgin birth.

When I began my work as a Christian ethicist my attitude about the so-called 'homosexuality issue' was not unlike my earlier attitude about the virgin birth. I began my work in the midst of war – the Vietnam war – and in such a context sex did not seem to be *the* moral issue. Of course sex played a role in the student rebellion of the 1960s and questions about sex were at the center of debates about situation ethics. But given my concern to develop an ethics of virtue, I thought the concentration on sex, and in particular sexual acts, was a methodological mistake. Moreover the focus on sex as *the* question in ethics seemed to me an indication that any ethic so shaped was too determined by the concerns of the bourgeois. Therefore when homosexuality came along as *the* issue I resisted the presumption that this was a matter on which I had to have a 'position.'

Of course now no one, at least no one who teaches Christian ethics, is allowed to be indifferent about the status of homosexuality. It has become the equivalent to questions about the virgin birth in Texas in the 1950s. No matter where you are or with what subject you are engaged you can count on someone saying something like this: 'That is all well and good but what does what you have said have to do with homosexuality?'

The problem with such questions is not that they are unimportant, but when they are made 'the' question they have a distorting effect on the shape of Christian convictions. For example those who asked about the virgin birth were not concerned with the way questions of Mary's virginity are connected with Christological concerns, but rather were seeking to discover whether you believed the Bible is literally true. When the question of the virgin birth is raised in that context it cannot help but distort how Christian convictions should work, no matter what answer one gives to it. I have often felt the same kind of discomfort about the way the question of homosexuality is raised as 'the' moral problem today, precisely because the question seems wrongly posed.

Moreover, answers given to questions wrongly posed can have unexpected and unwelcome results. For example some of the arguments made on behalf of lessening the onus on homosexuality can also result in lessening the onus on lying and/or war. Moral descriptions are interrelated in manifold ways, not the least being whether our lives make sense. I suspect that part of the concern some have with the approval of homosexuality is how such approval may make practices such as lifelong fidelity in marriage as well as the narratives intrinsic to those practices unintelligible.

Of course many, particularly in liberal cultures, deny a connection between homosexuality and marriage. But that is not an option for Christians, since we must refuse to think of our lives as but the sum of individual decisions since that would result in alienating us from our own lives as well as isolating us from one another. We want our lives at least to make sense retrospectively, as well as to make possible a community called church that constitutes a common story.

Yet the great difficulty is even knowing how and where to begin to think about homosexuality. For example I served for a short time on the United Methodist Commission for the Study of Homosexuality. When we Methodists do not know how to think about an issue we appoint a committee to 'study' the matter, in hopes that some policy statement can be made for the whole church. The results are seldom encouraging since it does little good to pool ignorance in the hope that an outcome will be better than the process. Indeed it is usually the case that the result of a Methodist Commission turns out to be less than the sum of its parts.

I found that I had little to contribute to our deliberations since I did not think the moral status of homosexuality could be or should be determined by whether 'science' could establish the etiology of homosexuality. I had read enough Foucault to be extremely suspicious of that move. I was moreover increasingly suspicious of the very category 'homosexuality,' for the way that description was being used by both sides in the debate seemed to presume what we have come to call 'essentialism' – a position that I find philosophically problematic. I wondered even more what Christian practices would require the description 'homosexuality.'

I asked my colleagues on the commission why as Christians we needed to have a position on homosexuality. Did we not have everything we needed in descriptions like promiscuity and adultery? After all, the current ministry is not under any imminent threat from the ordination of gays, but rather is being undermined by adultery. So why do we not simply report back to the general church that we have in place all the moral language we need to deal with the problem of sexual morality? This recommendation was not only not acted on, it was not even taken seriously. It was assumed by both the anti-and pro-gay sides that the church had to have a position about homosexuality.

Of course we Methodists have to have a position about homosexuality because we do not have an adequate account of marriage. It seems we have to know how to think about homosexuality, else we might have to acknowledge we do not know how to think period. Whether you agree or disagree with Roman Catholics on this matter you at least have to acknowledge they have a consistent position. If every act of sexual intercourse is to be open to conception then it would seem the matter is fairly clear. Attempts to circumvent this 'conservative' position by describing 'sexual acts' as premoral seem to me to create as much trouble as the position they are trying to avoid.[1] Catholic conservatives and Catholic liberals seem equally to concentrate on 'acts' in the abstract.

I am going to try to provide an alternative way to think about these matters by suggesting the difference it might make if we approach the questions from the perspective of an ethic of virtue and in particular friendship. As my title suggests, I am aware that this way of beginning is 'experimental.' It is often alleged that those of us who work from the perspective of the virtues cannot deal with issues like homosexuality. I hope to show, however, that by beginning with what it means to be a virtuous friend we can better understand how Christians might think about these matters in a way to avoid some of the unhappy alternatives so present today.

Yet my approach is 'experimental' in a manner that is quite unusual for me. Early in my time at Notre Dame I was confronted by a charismatic colleague who tried to convince me I needed to have a 'personal experience of Jesus.' I told her I was raised a Methodist, which meant that by the time I was twelve I had had enough experience to last me a lifetime. Actually my unease with appeals to experience as a warrant for theological language is because I remain an unreconstructed Barthian. I do not think Christian language gains its meaning because it describes 'experiences'. Yet I cannot deny that I begin with questions of friendship because that is the way that the question of homosexuality has come home for me.

For me friendship is not merely an 'experience.' Rather friendship is at the heart of my understanding of the moral life. Indeed, given my reservations about appeals to experience, I am sure I would have never been willing to engage with the issue of homosexuality if I had not discovered that I had friends who are gay. In some of these friendships at least, I did not know in the beginning or even through much of the development of the friendship that my friends were gay. Yet they are gay, and they are among the most faithful Christians I know. It has increasingly become the case, moreover, that I have developed friendship with gays, or better they have sought friendship with me, and that has become very important for my life.

One of the interesting things I have discovered is that my friends do not try to offer 'explanations' why they are gay. They are just gay. Just as the early church had to come to terms with the reality that gentiles, who probably should not have been followers of Jesus, were in the church, so we discover that gays are also in the church. Moreover they are there in a manner that would make us less if they were not there. I take that to be a stubborn theological reality that cries out for thought. I want to try to begin thinking through what such a 'fact' might morally entail by focusing on the moral significance of virtuous friendships.

Pretending to Be a Roman Catholic Moral Theologian

Before I explore the role of friendship for how we might think about homosexuality, I need to establish the context for my reflections. To do that I am going to pretend to be a Roman Catholic moral theologian. I am aware that few contexts would seem less happy for consideration of the issue of homosexuality as well as for the approach I am taking. Yet I believe that recent discussions by Roman Catholic moral theologians, in particular the promulgation of the encyclical, *Veritatis Splendor*, and the debate it has occasioned, provide one of the richest contexts for the kind of exploration I undertake.

I realize that such a claim will strike most people, and in particular Roman Catholics, as high folly, but at the very least Roman Catholic moral theology provides a context in which argument might count. By beginning with *Veritatis Splendor* I am at least able to begin with a tradition that knows there is more involved in thinking about sex than asking whether what we do with and to one another is an act of love. The problem with 'love,' of course, is that we have no idea how it is to be specified and as a result what might count as an exemplification of loving behavior. This becomes peculiarly problematic when we live in cultures in which some now think it reasonable to think thoughts such as: 'No one has the right to tell me what I can do or not do with my body.' For all of its problems, at least Roman Catholic moral reflection on these matters provides a context in which argument counts.

I need to warn you, however, that my credentials even to pretend to be a Roman Catholic moral theologian have been questioned by some. For example Richard McCormick, SJ, criticizes a short essay I co-authored with David Burrell in which we praised the characterization in *Veritatis Splendor* of proponents of proportionalism as seeking an accommodation with the spirit of the age. McCormick says it is 'difficult to find language strong enough to condemn such motivational attribution. This is especially regrettable from authors who have played no significant role in these developments and manifest no realistic grasp of the problems, concepts, and language that surround them.'[2]

In a recent essay Joseph Selling echoes McCormick's complaint against amateurs who want to take sides in the current dispute between proportionalists and their 'conservative' opponents. Selling notes that proportionalists certainly never have doubted that there is such a thing as right and wrong, but rather are pastorally concerned to help individual persons come to terms with serious questions. He acknowledges that to the 'outside observer' such moral theology could appear as a capitulation to the 'individualistic, consumer, "anything goes" spirit of the times, but this would be a false impression.' He then clarifies what he means by 'outside observer' – they are 'anyone who did not follow the development of moral theology with a professional understanding. This would apply to theologians who were not specifically trained in that field or to non-theologians such as philosophers who knew a good deal about natural law theory or legal philosophy but relatively little about theological concepts such as grace (fundamental option), covenant (biblical theology, the meaning of sin as a theological concept) or pastoral care (diminished guilt, internal forum, material sin, or the lesser evil solution to moral dilemmas).'[3]

I know I am supposed to be intimidated by McCormick's and Selling's claims of insider expertise and knowledge, but I am going to 'damn the torpedoes' and try to provide an alternative to the debate as they understand it. I should say in some ways I am quite sympathetic to their claims of expertise. That is, I am sympathetic in the sense that I think part of their problem is they have been encouraged to think of themselves as 'experts.' At least one of the lessons we need to learn from recent debates in Catholic moral theology is that it is a dangerously over-determined tradition. For example, when you identify grace with a 'fundamental option,' and specify 'biblical theology' by a concept like 'covenant,' you have an indication that moral theology has become so specialized it is by no means clear what it means for it to be called theology.

Yet it is certainly true that I am an 'outsider' since I am a Protestant. I am also an outsider because I have not tried to participate in the proportionalist controversy, even though over the years I have tried to read the books and articles by proportionalists and their opponents. I have not taken sides mainly because I did not like the way the sides were constituted. I remember years ago that when I first read Louis Janssens, I was quite sympathetic with his concern to avoid a law-like account of morality, but quite unsympathetic with the way he was trying to provide an alternative. 'Fundamental option' seemed to be neither an option nor fundamental. In particular, I was suspicious of the lingering neo-Kantian presumptions about the self that were shaping the way Aquinas was being read. From my perspective, notions like 'fundamental option' could only seem attractive or necessary if one had forgotten how Aquinas understood the nature of practical reason, character, and the virtues.

In other words, what has bothered me about the proportionalists is not their attempt to provide an alternative to the 'old legalistic moral theology,' but that even in their attempt to provide an alternative to the legalist framework they continued to presuppose a law-like framework. Actions continued to be treated in abstraction from the virtues, but now in the name of pastoral sensitivities such actions are assumed to be infinitely re-describable. No doubt some of the ways the proportionalists put their case made them appear to be consequentialist, but that never seemed to me to be the crucial problem. Rather I have not been able to understand where they think descriptions come or what controls their use. Part of the difficulty, of course, is that those who have resorted to devices such as 'pre-moral' seem to have no sense that this is a problem.

The great achievement of *Veritatis Splendor* is to make the virtues central for the way the moral life is understood, as well as to suggest the interrelation between actions and virtues. This encyclical is often criticized for its failure explicitly to draw out the interconnections between Parts I and III and Part II. To be sure, one could have wished for a clearer display of the way the Christology in the first part should make a difference for the critique of the proportionalist in the second, but this encyclical is a remarkable achievement precisely in the manner in which it repositions the issues. Certainly the intent of the encyclical is conservative, but more important are the avenues it opens for fresh considerations of the Christian moral life including even matters such as homosexuality.

Martin Rhonheimer, in his article called ' "Intrinsically Evil Acts" and the Moral Viewpoint: Clarifying a Central Teaching of *Veritatis Splendor*,' has come as close as anyone I know to getting the issue right.[4] He emphasizes the centrality in *Veritatis* of paragraph 78, where we get the characteristic Thomistic claim that the morality of an act depends on the 'object' which has been chosen by a deliberate will. This claim is elaborated in the following manner: 'In order to be able to grasp the object of an act which specifies that act morally, it is therefore necessary to place oneself *in the perspective of the acting person.*' The Encyclical goes on to argue that the object of a moral act cannot be a process or an event of the 'merely physical order' assessed by the power to bring about a state of affairs in the 'outside world,' but rather the 'object is the proximate end of a deliberate decision which determines the act of willing on the part of the acting person.' Thomas is then quoted to the effect that someone who robs to feed the poor has not acted uprightly since 'no evil done with a good intention can be excused.'

This argument immediately precedes the claim that there are 'intrinsically evil' actions, that is, actions that irrespective of the good intentions of the agent are incapable of being ordered to God. I confess I have always found the phrase 'intrinsically evil' mystifying. In a conversation with David Burrell some years ago I asked him if he thought a certain belief was 'absolutely true.' He challenged my use of the phrase 'absolutely true' by asking what 'absolutely' added if in fact the belief is true. In the same vein I continue to wonder what the qualifier 'intrinsic' adds to an action's being evil.

I realize this seems like a small matter, but I suspect the language of 'intrinsic evil' has led to some of the confusions concerning the character of practical reason – something that it is crucial to understand properly if we are to get these matters right. For 'intrinsic evil' makes it sound like certain actions are 'out there,' abstracted from agents, and they are to be evaluated either by their intrinsic nature or in terms of the consequences they produce. But that is exactly what Rhonheimer is suggesting cannot be done if we are to rightly understand *Veritatis*. That certain actions are evil makes sense only in a view of the moral life as a life shaped by the virtues in which human actions are understood from the perspective of the first person.

An ethic of the virtues requires an account of practical rationality and action in which an agent's 'action' is by its very nature intentional. If, as Aristotle maintains, we become just by acting justly, then the way we are so habituated requires that we must do that which we do in the way in which a virtuous person would do it. Rhonheimer observes that, from the viewpoint of the agent, actions are intentional not in the sense that I am aware of what I am doing, though I may be, but simply that I must be able to claim what I have done as mine. In contrast, from a third person perspective – that is, from the viewpoint of an observer – actions appear as events that are only contingently related to certain causes. Relying on this perspective, the proportionalists construe the moral life from the third person viewpoint and accordingly treat 'actions' as external bits of behavior to be judged good or bad, ironically, as if the agent did not exist.[5]

An ethics of the virtues must insist, therefore, that there are not two states of affairs when we act rationally: that is, an action-event and the resulting state of affairs, but rather that action and agency are inseparable. Accordingly the 'goods' intrinsic to our nature are not simply a set of givens nor are we the sum of our inclinations. Rather the goods sought by our desires 'constitute the proper practical self-experience of persons as a *certain kind* of being.'[6] The claim that certain actions are always wrong is but a way of specifying that they can never be consistent with a good will, that is, with what a person of virtue would choose.[7] To be morally virtuous is not to will to do 'the right thing' time after time, but rather 'moral virtue is the habitual rightness of *appetite* (sensual affections, passions, and of the will, the rational appetite related to the various spheres of human praxis). An act which is *according* to virtue is an act which is suited to cause this habitual rightness of appetite which produces "the good person." '[8]

The virtue that is central to our ability to make our actions our own Aristotle calls *phronesis*, which Thomas develops as *prudentia*. Alasdair MacIntyre notes that the acquisition of this virtue requires the recognition of the rational authority of the precepts of the natural law and most especially the negative exceptionless precepts. We discover such precepts in the institutions and projects through which we seek variety of goods such as 'enduring relationships in the family and in friendship, goods of productive work, of artistic activity and scientific inquiry, goods of leisure, goods of communal politics and religion.'[9]

MacIntyre notes that an individual will have to learn how to discern and to order specific goods in each of these projects and activities in order to make the choices necessary for the goods to be achieved. Moreover, how those goods will be understood will differ from culture to culture. What according to MacIntyre will not vary is the kind of responsiveness by one human being to others which makes it possible for each to learn from the others' questioning. Such requirements are the preconditions for the kind of rational conversations we must have to discover the goods that come from our engagements with one another in which we need not fear being victimized.[10]

Rhonheimer, whose view of practical reason is quite similar to MacIntyre's, observes that our necessary commitments to promise-keeping and truthfulness require narrative display. For our refusal to break a promise leads us to discover new lines of action, alternatives, and hitherto unseen opportunities. 'To describe this we would need to tell a story. Virtuous actions are, in this sense, rendered intelligible only in a narrative context. But the right thing to do will always be the action which is consistent with the rightness of appetite, with the rightness of our will's relation to concrete persons with whom we live together in defined relationships.'[11]

In a follow-up article, 'Intentional Actions and the Meaning of Object: A Reply to Richard McCormick,' Rhonheimer further specifies the interrelation of the virtues, descriptions of actions, and the need for a narrative display.[12] He criticizes proportionalists for assuming that a basic action can be described and redescribed 'without looking at what the acting person chooses on the level of action (or "means"); rather, they concentrate on what he or she chooses in the order of consequences and on the corresponding commensurate reasons, all of which finally constitute the "expanded object".'[13] Rhonheimer observes, however, that such an expanded notion of object is not really a notion of 'object' at all, but rather its abolition. It is so because for Aquinas 'object' means the basic intentional content of a human act that is distinguishable from further intentions. In short, to speak of the 'object' of an act means that actions are not infinitely redescribable. At least they are not infinitely redescribable if a community is to be capable of sustaining virtuous lives.

Rhonheimer shows that the same behavioral pattern alone cannot decide everything. For example, he contrasts John, a college student who drinks whisky to induce temporary loss of consciousness in order to forget his girlfriend left him, with Fred, a soldier who drinks the same amount of whisky to avoid the pain of an emergency operation. Rhonheimer notes that while the behavioral pattern is identical, without indicating an intention, it is impossible to describe *what* John and Fred are doing, that is, what they are choosing.[14] Rhonheimer denies that this allows us simply to 'shift intention to and fro' since John cannot reasonably intend his act to be an act of anaesthesia. There are given contexts (shaped by circumstances and recognizable, as a morally significant contextual unity, only by practical reason) 'that *can* have if we choose a determined "kind of behavior," *independently* from *further* intentions.'[15]

When agents choose to act they necessarily do so under a description which is according to Rhonheimer 'precisely the description of an intent formed by reason.'[16] So the intention to have intercourse with someone who is not my spouse cannot be overridden by some further description that may involve doing so for obtaining some information necessary to save the lives of others. 'One can therefore describe concrete choices of kinds of behavior as wrong or evil independently from further intentions. Such descriptions, however, always *include* a basic intention, an intention that itself presupposes a given ethically relevant context without which no intention formed by reason, could come into being. This has nothing to do with the "expanded notion of object." But it includes a certain complexity that is due to the plurality and multiplicity of virtues that in turn reflect human life and its richness in relations between persons, including the differences of ethically relevant contexts.'[17]

Thus, against McCormick Rhonheimer maintains, for example, that it is possible without being a proportionalist to maintain there is a difference in the basic intentional content in the case of the following actions: simple killing for any end whatsoever, killing in self-defense, capital punishment, and killing in battle. These action descriptions differ not only because one might have different reasons for performing them, but because their intentional structure is different in each case. Their *structure* is different. Thus there is a difference between 'self-defense' and 'the choice to kill in order to save my life.' On some abstract level they may be identical, but from the acting person's perspective there is a different choice. 'In legitimate self-defense, what engenders my action is not a will or a choice for the aggressor's death. A sign of this is that I only use violence proportionate to stop his aggression. This may lead me to kill him, but the reason for my action is not wanting him to be dead (for the sake of saving my life); rather it is wanting to stop his aggression. Thus there is a difference of intention on the level of concrete chosen behavior, and that means, on the level of the object.'[18] Rhonheimer's (and MacIntyre's) account of *Veritatis Splendor* deftly opens the door for a fresh consideration of the way moral descriptions work. If, as Rhonheimer maintains, one has to analyze intentional contents as belonging to the structure of the virtues, then one has to consider why certain descriptions are privileged. Rhonheimer quotes the *Catechism's* teaching 'that there are certain specific kinds of behavior that are always wrong to choose, because choosing them involves a disorder of the will, that is, moral evil,' which I have no reason to dispute.[19] Yet the display of such acts requires a much thicker narrative than is usually supplied.

Which finally brings me back to friendship. An ethic of the virtues like that of *Veritatis Splendor* is unintelligible without friendship. That Aristotle devoted two books of the *Ethics* to friendship is hardly accidental. For Aristotle friendship is not just a necessity for living well, but necessary if we are to be people of practical wisdom. Through character-friendships we actually acquire the wisdom necessary, and in particular the self-knowledge, to be people of virtue. We literally cannot do good without our friends, not simply because we need friends to do good for but because the self-knowledge necessary to be good comes from seeing ourselves through our friendships.[20]

As Paul Wadell observes, friendship in Aristotle names the relationship by which we become good. The activity of friendship – and it is crucial that we understand it as an activity – is what trains us to be virtuous. 'By spending time together with people who are good, by sharing and delighting with them in our mutual love for the good we are more fully impressed with the good ourselves. Friendship is not just a relationship: it is a moral enterprise. People spend their lives together doing good because that is what they see their lives to be.'[21] In short friendship is an epistemological necessity, for moral goodness is constituted through the ability of friends to name together those activities that constitute virtue as well as vice. Friendship names the practice necessary to sustain ongoing enquiry concerning the descriptions of the objects of our actions. For as MacIntyre suggests above, that which we learn to do and not do is discovered through such practices.

On Being Friends with Gay Christians

It is often said, 'Some of my best friends are gay, but that does not mean I approve of their being gay.' However, if Aristotle is right about the significance of friendship, then there surely must be something wrong with such a statement. If 'being gay' indicates a morally problematic mode of behavior then those who would be virtuous cannot afford to be friends with gay people. Of course it can be said that we all live morally ambiguous lives, so we should not expect too much of one another in such matters. But if 'being gay' names an immoral practice, then surely being a friend of gay people would not be a wise policy for those who would be moral.

Yet as I observed at the beginning, many of us find ourselves in Christian friendship with gay people. Consider an example, a fictionalized account of a real friendship. I have a friend who is a close friend of a lesbian couple who have lived faithful lives with one another for over twenty-five years. This couple have adopted and raised two children who are profoundly mentally handicapped. They are also committed Roman Catholics.[22] What should we call this relationship? Should my friend be their friend, and should I be his friend? Am I risking corruption through his friendship with gay Christians?

Of course the answer to such questions appears easy: 'It depends on the kind of people they are.' That is, it depends on the question of whether they are virtuous.[23] To be sure, that seems right, but I cannot act as if their being gay is irrelevant to their being virtuous. To distinguish between their being virtuous and being gay threatens to introduce a distinction between public and private which I take to be the destruction of any serious discussion of the virtuous life among Christians. Moreover such a distinction prevents the narrative from being truthfully told.

Of course that does not mean that my gay friends think being gay should determine all they are or do. Indeed they tell me that one of the great problems with being gay in our current context is that such an identification becomes far too consuming. Sex, after all, just is not all that interesting, particularly as a defining characteristic that colors all of our activity. Gay people, like the rest of us, have more important things to do than to be gay.

Indeed that is one of the reasons I resist the very description 'homosexuality.'

If there is something called 'homosexuality' then that must mean I have to be something called 'heterosexual.' I am not, of course, a heterosexual; I am a Texan – a philosophical joke meant to remind us that our identities are given through participation in practices that should serve the purposes of good communities. I remember when I first went to Notre Dame and was filling out the standard forms for employment, one of the forms asked me to indicate whether I was male, female, or religious. Now there is a mode of classification that could have produced a book from Foucault!

I, of course, understand that many will find this tack beside the point for consideration of the ethics of homosexuality. It is not about friendship, stupid – it is about sex and particular kinds of sex. Moreover, as I indicated at the beginning, if you believe that every sexual act must be open to conception then the game is up. I, of course, do not believe that, though I am unsympathetic with the 'spiritualization' of sex that I think informs many of the arguments made against the view that every sexual act must be open to conception. By 'spiritualization' I mean the peculiarly modern presumption that our sexual conduct has no purpose other than the meanings we give it and so are able to derive from it. Such a view seems to make us far too 'sexual.' A seminarian at Notre Dame once told me, 'We celibates can be happily sexually adjusted.' I told him I was married, had my share of sex, but I was sure I would never be happily sexually adjusted. What a terrible burden is put on sex: requiring it always to be fulfilling because it has no other purpose.[24]

Yet the purpose of sex cannot be known from sex. This, of course, locates my disagreement with the presumption that every act of sexual intercourse must be open to conception. Marriage as a practice of the church has as one of its purposes the readiness to receive children, but even that does not entail biological children. That marriage has such a purpose, moreover, I assume is part of the church's commitment to be hospitable to the stranger requiring all the baptized to consider ourselves parents whether we have biological children or not. I have always thought it quite appropriate that celibate priests be called 'Father.' It is a radical judgement on the presumption that biology constitutes fatherhood.

If every sexual act need not be open to conception, then it seems to me that *Veritatis Splendor* offers us a perspective from which to think about how we might narrate the relation between the two women I described. They are not promiscuous. The intimacy they share is oriented to upbuilding their lives for the good of their community. Just as we can discriminate between different kinds of killing through analogous comparisons, I do not see why we cannot see this kind of relationship analogous to what Christians mean by marriage.[25] The church after all does recognize the marriage of people who are beyond the age of childbearing. On what grounds are the women I described above excluded from such recognition?

The quick answer, of course, is that they are the same sex. They are homosexual. But here we see the wisdom of the Catholic tradition and why I spent so much time discussing *Veritatis Splendor*. Catholic moral theology has never thought that a *theory* about 'homosexuality' would determine these matters, but rather asked what kind of behavior is commensurate with being the virtuous person for the upbuilding of the church.[26] I am suggesting that it would at least be possible to understand the object of the relation between the women I described above as analogous to marriage. I would put the matter more strongly – if gay Christians are to have some alternative to the sexual wilderness that today grips all our lives, gay and non-gay alike, something like what I am suggesting must be found.[27]

Such a suggestion obviously involves a complex account of the interrelation of practices and their correlative virtues, the narratives that render such practices and virtues intelligible, and the institutions necessary to sustain such narratives. I cannot pretend to have done that work adequately in this paper. Rather I have tried to provide a beginning for such work – a beginning that surely begins by entering into enquiry with our gay friends in the hope that together we might discover how to live faithfully as God's people.

I need, however, to be candid. Just as marriage between those past child-bearing age may be an exception, so it may be that the recognition of faithful relations between gay people is an exception. But exceptions are not a problem for a community that is secure in its essential practices. The crucial question is how to live in a manner that the exception does not become the rule. Just as the married bear the burden of proof in the church, given the church's presumption that we do not have to be married to be Christians, so among the married those who cannot have biological children may well bear the burden of proof. Such a burden hopefully should be seen as a means for the upbuilding of the community of believers. By asking gays to help us understand how their lives contribute to our presumption as Christians that marriage is constituted by a promise of lifelong monogamous fidelity we might discover what a life-giving promise that is.

I am aware that gay Christians may think that they already have enough burdens. Why should they be asked to justify their lives in such a manner? We certainly do not ask it of those who call themselves 'heterosexuals.' I can only say, 'This can only be asked of you because you are Christian and because we are friends.'

Notes

1 The argument works this way: homosexuality is a premoral or ontic evil, and all things being equal (or outside of any context) homosexuals should avoid evil actions by being

celibate. However, if celibacy is not an option (because the person has a big sex drive), being in a committed relationship is better than being promiscuous. A committed relationship brings about the good of unitivity, so it is acceptable to do an evil thing (homosexual act) to bring about a greater good (unitivity). Therefore in such cases, although homosexuality is a premoral evil, in certain contexts it can be rendered moral. See, for example, Philip Keane's discussion of homosexuality in his *Sexual Morality: A Catholic Perspective* (New York: Paulist Press, 1977), 84–91. One cannot help but sympathize with Keane's attempt to create a space for gay people within Catholic moral theology. Yet the methodology used to create that space cannot help but create conceptual confusions – i.e., description of actions as premoral on the assumption that an action can be intelligible without an agent. I am indebted to Dr. Kathy Rudy for helping me clarify this point.

2 Richard McCormick, SJ, 'Some Early Reactions to *Veritatis Splendor,' Theological Studies* 55, 3 (Sept. 1994), 488.

3 Joseph Selling, 'The Context and the Arguments of *Veritatis Splendor*,' in Joseph Selling and Jan Jans (eds.), *The Splendor of Accuracy: An Examination of the Assertions made by Veritatis Splendor* (Grand Rapids: Eerdmans, 1994), 21.

4 *The Thomist* 58, 1 (1994), 1–39.

5 Rhonheimer rightly argues that adherents of so-called 'teleological ethics' omit in principle an *intentional* description of particular types of actions which they later qualify on the basis of their decision-making procedures as 'right' or 'wrong.' By 'intentional descriptions' Rhonheimer is indicating the necessity of seeing the actions within a narrative required by the virtues. Because the proportionalists avoid this account of action they must describe actions as mere 'event.' They thus offer their theory as a solution to the problem of determining the right or wrong of such action, a solution, Rhonheimer nicely observes, that is required by their getting the problem wrong to begin with (35–6). Yet Rhonheimer rightly notes that the approach of the proportionalist 'is not different from traditional approaches that can be found in some classical manuals of moral theology. Some of them used to look at actions as physical processes or events, relating them afterwards to the "norm moralitatis," an extrinsic rule determining whether it is licit or illicit to perform such and such an "action." What most classical manuals failed to do was precisely to render intelligible what a human action is and that its moral identity is *included* in it because it is included in the *intentional* structure of an action' (38).

6 Rhonheimer, 'Intrinsically Evil Acts,' 14. Rhonheimer provides a quite interesting account of the inclinations correlative of our nature as bodily beings for which I have deep sympathy. In doing so he is developing the contention in *Veritatis* that 'The person, by the light of reason and the support of virtue, discovers in the body the anticipatory signs, the expression and the promise of the gift of the self, in conformity with the wise plan of the Creator' (48). I think that Rhonheimer and the Encyclical are quite right to suspect an incipient gnosticism in the moral psychology of the proportionalist. I remain more agnostic than Rhonheimer, or the Encyclical, about the extent that the natural law can be known on the basis of the knowledge that comes through our body, but I have no reason in principle to deny such knowledge. For another treatment of *Veritatis* that rightly emphasizes the significance of the body for our knowledge of the goods see Alasdair MacIntyre, 'How Can We Learn What *Veritatis Splendor* Has To Teach,' *The*

Thomist, 58 (1994), 171–95. MacIntyre glosses the Encyclical this way: 'Moral direction is not something to which the body is merely subjected as something alien and external. Physical activity is intelligibly structured towards the ends of the whole person, something that is rendered invisible by any reductive physicalism. It is the whole human person as a unity of body and soul which is ordered to its ends by natural law, when the human being is in good functioning order. The truth that it is by being so ordered that the person is enabled and empowered – a bodily enabling and empowerment – is among those truths without a grasp of which an understanding of freedom cannot be achieved' (186). The crucial issue for me concerning Rhonheimer's and MacIntyre's accounts of natural law is, in the Encyclical's language, how 'the light of reason and support of virtue' is required for the so-called natural law.

7 Ibid. 18–20.

8 Ibid. 22.

9 MacIntyre, 'How Can we Learn,' 183–4.

10 Ibid. 184. MacIntyre's account of this process at once is historicist and non-relativistic. Thus he argues his account requires an understanding of truth that is more than warranted assertibility. 'In asserting that something is true we are not talking about warrant or justification, but claiming rather that this is in fact how things are, whatever our present or future standards of warrant or justification may lead us to state or imply, that this is in fact how things are, not from the point of view of this or that culture, but as such. Such assertions of course often turn out to be false, but once again what they turn out to be is not false-from-a-point-of-view, or false-by-this-or-that-set-of-standards, but simply false' (187). Yet truth is always a matter of being 'on the way' as the truth of the negative precepts of the natural law require construal through grace. Thus MacIntyre suggests, 'unless, unlike the rich young man, we respond to God's offer of grace by accepting it, we too shall be unable fully to understand and to obey the law in such a way as to achieve that ultimate good which gives to such understanding and obedience its point and purpose' (190).

11 Rhonheimer, 'Intrinsically Evil Acts,' 26.

12 Martin Rhonheimer, 'Intentional Actions and the Meaning of Object: A Reply to Richard McCormick,' *The Thomist* 59, 2 (1995), 279–311.

13 Ibid. 294.

14 Ibid. 297.

15 Ibid. 299.

16 Ibid. 283. The language of choice in Aquinas does not mean, as it does for us, decision. That is, choice is not a chronological state prior to action nor does choice describe a cognitive operation we associate with judging. For the end, for Aquinas, is the principle, not the conclusion, of practical wisdom. For Aquinas, acts shaped by virtuous habits involve judgement and choice but not as if one precedes the other. Aquinas' account of these matters in the *Summa*, I–II, Q.6–21, is descriptive and not prescriptive. Thus his circular account of the relation of 'will' and 'reason' is not vicious since neither 'will' nor 'reason' name separable faculties but rather are descriptions meant to illumine how we become virtuous through God's activity. I am indebted to Mr. Michael Hanby for a seminal report on Aquinas' account of human action for the above account of choice.

17 Ibid. 300.

18 Ibid. 302–3. One might think I would have a stake in challenging these distinctions since

I am a pacifist. No doubt the practice of non-violence and the attending virtues might produce different kinds of descriptions, but the pacifist certainly has a stake in distinguishing different kinds of killing. For example, the pacifist certainly can (and should) maintain that self-defense is not the same as killing in war even if killing in self-defense is also not something the pacifist should do.

19 Ibid. 307.

20 For my more extended reflections on Aristotle's account of friendship see my 'Happiness, the life of Virtue and Friendship: Theological Reflections on Aristotelian Themes,' *Asbury Theological Journal* 45, 1 (Spring 1990), 35–48. A revision of these essays with a much fuller account of the virtues has appeared in a book written with my friend, Professor Charles Pinches of the University of Scranton, called *Christians Among the Virtues: Theological Conversations with Ancient and Modern Ethics* (Notre Dame: University of Notre Dame Press, 1997), 3–54.

21 Paul Wadell, CP, *Friendship and the Moral Life* (Notre Dame: University of Notre Dame Press, 1989), 62.

22 I realize that this description could be contested since some might think that their claim to be Roman Catholic can only be a pose. If they were really Roman Catholic they would give up living together or at least refuse to sleep with one another. I cannot deny that their self-description as Roman Catholic must be complex, but I ask in the name of charity that their story be accepted in good faith.

23 There is a crucial theoretical issue at stake here – that is the question of the unity of the virtues. Aquinas quotes Gregory to the effect 'that a virtue cannot be perfect as a virtue if isolated from the others: for there can be no true prudence without temperance, justice, and fortitude.' (ST, I–II, Q.65, I). If these women are virtuous, even in Aquinas' sense as 'wayfarers,' then they cannot be said to be immoral in any simplistic sense.

24 Wendell Berry observes the oddness in our time of associating 'sexual freedom' with the physical. 'In fact, our "sexual revolution" is mostly an industrial phenomenon, in which the body is used as an idea of pleasure or a pleasure machine with the aim of "freeing" natural pleasure from natural consequence. Like any other industrial enterprise, industrial sexuality seeks to conquer nature by exploiting it and ignoring the consequences, by denying any connection between nature and spirit or body and soul, and by evading social responsibility. The spiritual, physical, and economic costs of this "freedom" are immense, and characteristically belittled or ignored. Industrial sex, characteristically, establishes its freeness and goodness by an industrial accounting, dutifully toting up numbers of sexual partners, orgasms, and so on, with the inevitable industrial implication that the body is somehow a limit on the idea of sex, which will be a great deal more abundant as soon as it can be done by robots.' *What Are People For?* (New York: North Points Press, 1990), 191. This is perhaps a preamble to auto commercials where the car is suggested as something elegant to have an affair with.

25 My friend Michael Quirk argues that the false assumption shared by proportionalists and their conservative critics is that, if description is a problem, it is a problem that a *theory* of moral description will solve. 'Proportionalism founders on its need for criteria to winnow out relevant from irrelevant descriptive considerations, and proper from improper weigh-ins; anti-proportionalism founders on its parallel need to come up with descriptions of moral species that are not relative to context or purposes at hand but are normative as such, and which are in some way self-applying to particular moral cases.

Fortunately, there are practices of moral description that can provide a measure of stability for the act of moral description in the absence of readily available criteria: the ability to reveal the slave owner is at odds with his linguistic community's ascription of humanity to slaves, and hence at odds with himself, is a paradigm case of how practice can accomplish the winnowing-out of poor and false moral descriptions without reliance upon a prior set of theoretically-validated rules for doing so. There are only such rules as moral practice itself demands. And the lesson for theological ethics in all this is that the substitution of moral theory for an accounting of that which religious practice demands on its adherents – that is, for a "thick description" of the elements of the Christian life, the virtues they support, and the sorts of conduct that can be intelligibly narrated within the constraints of these virtues – will only serve the ignoble end of making disagreement and disunity more pronounced and intractable than it needs to be.' 'Why the Debate on Proportionalism Is Misconceived,' *Modern Theology* 13, 4 (Oct. 1997), 520. Quirk's point is obviously at the heart of the way I have tried so argue in this paper.

26 I am, of course, aware that there are scriptural issues involved which I am ignoring. By doing so I do not mean to imply they are unimportant. Yet I do not think that the church's position on these matters can turn on any one text even one as important as Romans 1. The issue for me is not whether texts like Romans I 'mean' what we mean by homosexuality, but rather how such texts are to be read in the light of the church's practices of singleness and marriage. Here I follow the rule that the more obscure texts should be interpreted in the light of the less obscure. The truth of the matter is the New Testament does not have that much to say about sexual conduct, which I suspect is an indication that Christian thinking about sex cannot be isolated from more determinative practices such as truth-telling, sharing goods, mutual correction that make the church the church.

27 Of course, it can be said an alternative already exists – i.e., celibacy. I would not want to dismiss that alternative, for surely celibacy is a gift necessary for the church's practice. But as it is a gift, one cannot assume that everyone in the church has been given it. Simply because someone is gay does not mean they have the gift of celibacy. If they do, it is a great gift. Of course, all Christians, married and unmarried, are called to be chaste. Indeed I expect some of our current confusion about sex among Christians derives from our loss of any understanding of how chastity is intrinsic to marriage.

PART

Trinitarian Resources

The Body's Grace

Rowan D. Williams

This essay represents the best 10 pages written about sexuality in the twentieth century. It manages to say not only what sexuality is for, but what marriage is for, what celibacy is for, and what Christianity is for. It supplies many of the principles for interpreting and selecting other essays in this anthology.

Critics have objected that it offers no "argument," by which they mean that it does not argue on their terms. Rather it argues from convenientia, *or fittingness, a time-honored Christian technique of elaboration or thick description that aims to exhibit or display how one doctrine fits in well with others. Here, Williams aims to show how committed same-sex relationships fit well with what Christians have said about the purposes of marriage, celibacy, and the Christian life.*

The essay is unusual in that its argumentation is theologically "high." So, far from beginning with experience, the argument proper begins instead with an account of God's Trinitarian life, while the lives of celibates, rather than the experience of the well-sexed, provide the heuristic clue to what sex might be about.

(Although it does begin with a story that has offended some readers, the story serves a purpose of discovery rather than morality. Many biblical stories might have been deployed in a similar way. One thinks of the women in the genealogy of Jesus: Ruth, Tamar, Bathsheba, any of them might have told a story like Sarah's in the essay.)

Sexuality, like grace, involves the transformation that comes from seeing oneself as desired by another. That other is primarily God. For some the desire of God is modeled and mediated through another human being; for others it seems to come directly. Celibates teach us that it is God who desires us, without denying that most will find transformation more effectively in relationship with another person (of the same or opposite sex) from whose transformative perceptions they cannot easily escape.

The essay is very dense; every sentence counts; it repays two or three readings; and you have understood it when you get the jokes. I call your attention to two widely separated paragraphs that seem to me to hold together the main points of the essay. You understand it, too, when you see how these paragraphs fit together:

> Grace, for the Christian believer, is a transformation that depends in large part on knowing yourself to be seen in a certain way: as significant, as wanted.
>
> The whole story of creation, incarnation, and our incorporation into the fellowship of Christ's body tells us that God desires us, as if we were God, as if we were that unconditional response to God's giving that God's self makes in the life of the Trinity. We are created so that we may be caught up in this, so that we may grow into the wholehearted love of God by learning that God loves us as God loves God.
>
> The life of the Christian community has as its rationale – if not invariably its practical reality – the task of teaching us [that, to teach us] to so order our relations that human beings may see themselves as desired, as the occasion of joy.
>
> . . . [T]he body's grace itself only makes human sense if we have a language of grace in the first place; this in turn depends on having a language of creation and redemption. To be formed in our humanity by the loving delight of another is an experience whose contours we can identify most clearly and hopefully if we have also learned, or are learning, about being the object of the causeless, loving delight of God, being the object of God's love for God through incorporation into the community of God's Spirit and the taking-on of the identity of God's Child. It is because of our need to keep that perspective clear before us that the community needs some who are called beyond or aside from the ordinary patterns of sexual relation to put their identities directly into the hands of God in the single life . . .

Why does sex matter? Most people know that sexual intimacy is in some ways frightening for them, that it is quite simply the place where they began to be taught whatever maturity they have. Most of us know that the whole business is irredeemably comic, surrounded by so many odd chances and so many opportunities for making a fool of yourself. Plenty know that it is the place where they are liable to be most profoundly damaged or helpless. Culture in general and religion in particular have devoted enormous energy to the doomed task of getting it right. In this essay, I want to try and understand a little better why the task is doomed, and why the fact that it's doomed is a key to seeing more fully why and how it matters – and even seeing more fully what this mattering has to do with God.

Best to start from a particular thing, a particular story. Paul Scott's *Raj Quartet* is full of poignant and very deep analyses of the tragedies of sexuality: the theme which drives through all four novels and unites their immense rambling plots is Ronald Merrick's destruction and corruption of his own humanity and that of all who fall into his hands. That corruption effectively begins at the moment he discovers how he is aroused, how his privacy is invaded, by the desirable body of a man, and he is appalled and terrified by this.

His first attempt to punish and obliterate the object of his desire is what unleashes the forces of death and defilement that follow him everywhere thereafter. Sexual refusal is dramatized by him in enactments of master–slave relations: he humiliates what he longs for, so that his dominion is not challenged and so that the sexual disaster becomes a kind of political tragedy. Merrick is an icon of the "body politic": his terror, his refusal, and his corruption stand as a metaphor of the Raj itself, of power willfully turning away from the recognition of those wants and needs that only vulnerability to the despised and humiliated stranger can open up and satisfy.

Interwoven with Merrick's tragedy is the story of Sarah Layton, a figure constantly aware of her powerlessness before events, her inability to undo the injuries and terrors of the past, but no less constantly trying to see and respond truthfully and generously. At the end of the second novel in the sequence, Sarah is seduced, lovelessly but not casually: her yielding is prompted perhaps more than anything by her seducer's mercilessly clear perception of her. She does not belong, he tells her, however much she tries to give herself to the conventions of the Raj. Within her real generosity is a lost and empty place: "You don't know anything about joy at all, do you?"[1]

Absent from the life of the family she desperately tries to prop up, absent from the life of European society in India, Sarah is present fully to no one and nothing. Her innate truthfulness and lack of egotistical self-defense mean that she is able to recognize this once the remark is made: there is no joy for her, because she is not able to be anywhere. When she is at last coaxed into bed, as they "enact" a tenderness that is not really that of lovers, Sarah comes to herself: hours later, on the train journey back to her family, she looks in the mirror and sees that "she had entered her body's grace."[2]

What does this mean? The phrase recurs more than once in the pages of the novel that follow, but it is starkly clear that there is no lasting joy for Sarah. There is a pregnancy and an abortion; a continuing loneliness. Yet nothing in this drainingly painful novel suggests that the moment of the "body's grace" for Sarah was a deceit. Somehow she has been aware of what it was and was not: a frontier has been passed, and that has been and remains grace; a being present, even though this can mean knowing that the graced body is now more than ever a source of vulnerability. But it is still grace, a filling of the void, an entry into some different kind of identity. There may have been little love, even little generosity, in Sarah's lovemaking, but she has discovered that her body can be the cause of happiness to her and to another. It is this discovery which most clearly shows why we might want to talk about grace here. Grace, for the Christian believer, is a transformation that depends in large part on knowing yourself to be seen in a certain way: as significant, as wanted.

The whole story of creation, incarnation, and our incorporation into the fellowship of Christ's body tells us that God desires us, *as if we were God*, as if we were that unconditional response to God's giving that God's self makes in the life of the Trinity. We are created so that we may be caught up in this, so that we may grow into the wholehearted love of God by learning that God loves us as God loves God.

The life of the Christian community has as its rationale – if not invariably its practical reality – the task of teaching us to so order our relations that human beings may see themselves as desired, as the occasion of joy. It is not surprising that sexual imagery is freely used, in and out of the Bible, for this newness of perception. What is less clear is why the fact of sexual desire, the concrete stories of human sexuality rather than the generalizing metaphors it produces, are so grudgingly seen as matters of grace, or only admitted as matters of grace when fenced with conditions. Understanding this involves us in stepping back to look rather harder at the nature of sexual desire; and this is where abstractness and overambitious theory threaten.

In one of the few sensible and imaginative accounts of sexual desire by a philosopher, Thomas Nagel writes:

> Sexual desire involves a kind of perception, but not merely a single perception of its object, for in the paradigm case of mutual desire there is a complex system of superimposed mutual perceptions – not only perceptions of the sexual object, but perceptions of oneself. Moreover, sexual awareness of another involves considerable self-awareness to begin with – more than is involved in ordinary sensory perception.[3]

Initially I may be aroused by someone unaware of being perceived by me, and that arousal is significant in "identifying me with my body" in a new way, but is not yet sufficient for speaking about the full range of sexuality. I am aroused as a cultural, not just a biological being; I need, that is, to bring my body into the shared world of language and (in the widest sense!) "intercourse." My arousal is not only my business: I need its cause to know about it, to recognize it, for it to be anything more than a passing chance. So my desire, if it is going to be sustained and developed, must itself be perceived; and, if it is to develop as it naturally tends to, it must be perceived as desirable by the other – that is, my arousal and desire must become the cause of someone else's desire.

For my desire to persist and have some hope of fulfillment, it must be exposed to the risks of being seen by its object. Nagel sees the whole complex process as a special case of what's going on in any attempt to share, in language, what something means. Part of my making sense to you depends on my knowing that you can "see" that I want to make sense. And my telling you or showing you that this is what I want implies that I "see" you as wanting to understand.

"Sex has a related structure: it involves a desire that one's partner be aroused by the recognition of one's desire that he or she be aroused."[4]

All this means that in sexual relation I am no longer in charge of what I am. *Any* genuine experience of desire leaves me in this position: I cannot of myself satisfy my wants without distorting or trivializing them. But in *this* experience we have a particularly intense case of the helplessness of the ego alone. For my body to be the cause of joy, the end of homecoming, for me, it must be there for someone else, must be perceived, accepted, nurtured. And that means being given over to the creation of joy in that other, because only as directed to the enjoyment, the happiness, of the other does it become unreservedly lovable. To desire my joy is to desire the joy of the one I desire: my search for enjoyment through the bodily presence of another is a longing to be enjoyed in my body. As Blake put it, sexual partners "admire" in each other "the lineaments of gratified desire." We are pleased because we are pleasing.

It is in this perspective, Nagel says, that we can understand the need for a language of sexual failure, immaturity, even "perversion." Solitary sexual activity works at the level of release of tension and a particular localized physical pleasure; but insofar as it has nothing much to do with being perceived from beyond myself in a way that changes my self-awareness, it isn't of much interest for a discussion of sexuality as process and relation, and says little about grace. In passing, Nagel makes a number of interesting observations on sexual encounters that either allow no exposed spontaneity because they are bound to specific methods of sexual arousal – like sado-masochism – or that permit only a limited awareness of the embodiment of the other because there is an unbalance in the relation such that the desire of the other for me is irrelevant or minimal – rape, pedophilia, bestiality.[5] These "asymmetrical" sexual practices have some claim to be called perverse in that they leave one agent in effective control of the situation – one agent, that is, who doesn't have to wait upon the desire of the other. (Incidentally, if this suggests that, in a great many cultural settings, the socially licensed norm of heterosexual intercourse is a "perversion" – well, that is a perfectly serious suggestion.)

If we bracket, for the moment, the terminology of what is normative or ideal, it seems that at least we have here a picture of what sexuality might mean at its most *comprehensive*. And the moral question, I suspect, ought to be: How much do we want our sexual activity to communicate? How much do we want it to display a breadth of human possibility and a sense of the body's capacity to heal and enlarge the life of others? Nagel's reflections suggest that some kinds of sexual activity distort or confine the human resourcefulness, the depth or breadth of meaning such activity may carry: they involve assuming that sexual activity has less to do with the business of human growth and human integrity than we know it can have. Decisions about sexual lifestyle, the ability to identify certain patterns as sterile, undeveloped, or even corrupt, are, in this light, decisions about what we want our bodily life to say, how our bodies are to be brought into the whole project of "making human sense" for ourselves and each other.

To be able to make such decisions is important. A purely conventional (heterosexual) morality simply absolves us from the difficulties we might meet in doing so. The question of human meaning is not raised, nor are we helped to see what part sexuality plays in our learning to be human with one another – to enter the body's grace – because all we need to know is that sexual activity is licensed in one context and in no other. Not surprising, then, if the reaction is often either, "It doesn't matter what I do (say) with my body, because it's my inner life and emotions that matter" or, "The only criterion is what gives pleasure and does no damage." Both of those responses are really to give up on the human seriousness of all this.

They are also, like conventional ethics, attempts to get rid of risk. Nagel comes close to saying what I believe needs saying here, that sexual "perversion" is sexual activity without risk, without the dangerous acknowledgment that my joy depends on someone else's, as theirs does on mine. Distorted sexuality is the effort to bring my happiness back under my control and to refuse to let my body be recreated by another person's perception. And this is, in effect, to withdraw my body from the enterprise of human beings making sense in collaboration, in community, withdrawing my body from language, culture, and politics. Most people who have bothered to think about it have noticed a certain tendency for odd sorts of sexual activity to go together with political distortion and corruption (the *Raj Quartet*'s Merrick again – indeed, the whole pathology of the torturer). What women writers like Susan Griffin have taught us about the politics of pornography has sharpened this observation.

But how do we manage this risk, the entry into a collaborative way of making sense of our whole material selves? It is this, of course, that makes the project of "getting it right" doomed, as I suggested earlier. Nothing will stop sex being tragic and comic. It is above all the area of our lives where we can be rejected in our bodily entirety, where we can venture into the "exposed spontaneity" that Nagel talks about and find ourselves looking foolish or even repellent, so that the perception of ourselves we are offered is negating and damaging (homosexuals, I think, know rather a lot about this). And it is also where the awful incongruity of our situation can break through as comedy, even farce. I'm tempted, by the way, to say that only cultures and people that have a certain degree of moral awareness about how sex forms persons, and an awareness therefore of moral and personal risk in it all, can actually find it funny: the pornographer and the scientific investigator of how to maximize climaxes don't as a rule seem to see much of the dangerous absurdity of the whole thing.

The misfire or mismatch of sexual perception is, like any dialogue at cross-purposes, potentially farcical – no less so for being on the edge of pain.

Shakespeare (as usual) knows how to tread such a difficult edge: do we or don't we laugh at Malvolio? For he is transformed by the delusion that he is desired – and if such transformations, such conversions, were not part of our sexual experience, we should not see any joke.

And it's because this is ultimately serious that the joke breaks down. Malvolio is funny, and what makes him funny is also what makes the whole episode appallingly and irreconcilably hurtful. The man has, after all, ventured a tiny step into vulnerability, into the shared world of sexually perceived bodies, and he has been ruthlessly mocked and denied. In a play which is almost overloaded with sexual ambivalence and misfiring desires, Malvolio demonstrates brutally just why all the "serious" characters are in one or another sort of mess about sex, all holding back from sharing and exposure, in love with private fantasies of generalized love.

The discovery of sexual joy and of a pattern of living in which that joy is accessible must involve the insecurities of "exposed spontaneity" – the experience of misunderstanding or of the discovery (rapid or slow) that this relationship is not about joy. These discoveries are bearable, if at all, because at least they have changed the possibilities of our lives in a way which may still point to what joy might be. But it should be clear that the discovery of joy means something rather more than the bare facts of sexual intimacy. I can only fully discover the body's grace in taking time, the time needed for a mutual recognition that my partner and I are not simply passive instruments to each other. Such things are learned in the fabric of a whole relation of converse and cooperation; yet of course the more time taken the longer a kind of risk endures. There is more to expose, and a sustaining of the will to let oneself be formed by the perceptions of another. Properly understood, sexual faithfulness is not an avoidance of risk, but the creation of a context in which grace can abound because there is a commitment not to run away from the perception of another.

When we bless sexual unions, we give them a life, a reality not dependent on the contingent thoughts and feelings of the people involved; but we do this so that they may have a certain freedom to "take time" to mature and become as profoundly nurturing as they can. We should not do it in order to create a wholly impersonal and enforceable "bond"; if we do, we risk turning blessing into curse, grace into law, art into rule-keeping.

In other words, I believe that the promise of faithfulness, the giving of unlimited time to each other, remains central for understanding the full "resourcefulness" and grace of sexual union. I simply don't think we would grasp all that was involved in the mutual transformation of sexually linked persons without the reality of unconditional public commitments: more perilous, more demanding, more promising.

Yet the realities of our experience in looking for such possibilities suggest pretty clearly that an absolute declaration that every sexual partnership must

315

conform to the pattern of commitment or else have the nature of sin *and nothing else* is unreal and silly. People do discover – as does Sarah Layton – a grace in encounters fraught with transitoriness and without much "promising" (in any sense): it may be just this that prompts them to want the fuller, longer exploration of the body's grace that faithfulness offers. Recognizing this – which is no more than recognizing the facts of a lot of people's histories, heterosexual or homosexual, in our society – ought to be something we can do without generating anxieties about weakening or compromising the focal significance of commitment and promise in our Christian understanding and "moral imagining" of what sexual bonding can be.

Much more damage is done here by the insistence on a fantasy version of heterosexual marriage as the solitary ideal, when the facts of the situation are that an enormous number of "sanctioned" unions are a framework for violence and human destructiveness on a disturbing scale; sexual union is not delivered from moral danger and ambiguity by satisfying a formal socioreligious criterion. Decisions about sexual lifestyle, to repeat, are about how much we want our bodily selves to mean, rather than what emotional needs we're meeting or what laws we're satisfying. "Does this mean that we are using faith to undermine law? By no means: we are placing law itself on a firmer footing" (Rom. 3:31, *NEB*). Happily there is more to Paul than the (much quoted in this context) first chapter of Romans!

I have suggested that the presence or absence of the body's grace has a good deal to do with matters other than the personal. It has often been said, especially by feminist writers, that the making of my body into a distant and dangerous object that can be either subdued or placated with quick gratification is the root of sexual oppression. If my body isn't me, then the desiring perception of my body is bound up with an area of danger and foreignness, and I act toward whatever involves me in desiring and being desired with fear and hostility. Man fears and subdues woman; and – the argument continues – this licenses and grounds a whole range of processes that are about the control of the strange: "nature," the foreigner, the unknowable future. This is not to assert uncritically that sexual disorder is the cause of every human pathology, but to grant, first, that it is pervasively present in all sorts of different disorders, and second, that it constitutes a kind of paradigm case of wrongness and distortion, something that shows us what it is like to refuse the otherness of the material world and to try to keep it other and distant and controlled. It is a paradigm of how not to make sense in its retreat from the uncomfortable knowledge that I cannot make sense of myself without others, cannot speak until I've listened, cannot love myself without being the object of love or enjoy myself without being the cause of joy.

Thinking about sexuality in its fullest implications involves thinking about entering into a sense of oneself *beyond* the customary imagined barrier between the "inner" and the "outer," the private and the shared. We are led into the knowledge that our identity is being made in the relations of bodies, not by the private exercise of will or fantasy: we belong with and to each other, not to our "private" selves – as Paul said of mutual sexual commitment (1 Cor. 7:4) – and yet are not instruments for each other's gratification.

All this, moreover, is not only potentially but actually a *political* knowledge, a knowledge of what ordered human community might be. Without a basic political myth of how my welfare depends on yours and yours on mine, a myth of personal needs in common that can only be met by mutuality, we condemn ourselves to a politics of injustice and confrontation. Granted that a lot of nonsense has been talked about the politics of eroticism recently, we should still acknowledge that an understanding of our sexual needs and possibilities is a task of real political importance. Sexuality-related "issues" cannot be isolated from the broader project of social recreation and justice.

As I hinted earlier, the body's grace itself only makes human sense if we have a language of grace in the first place; this in turn depends on having a language of creation and redemption. To be formed in our humanity by the loving delight of another is an experience whose contours we can identify most clearly and hopefully if we have also learned, or are learning, about being the object of the causeless, loving delight of God, being the object of God's love for God through incorporation into the community of God's Spirit and the taking-on of the identity of God's Child. It is because of our need to keep that perspective clear before us that the community needs some who are called beyond or aside from the ordinary patterns of sexual relation to put their identities directly into the hands of God in the single life. This is not an alternative to the discovery of the body's grace. All those taking up the single vocation must know something about desiring and being desired if their single vocation is not to be sterile and evasive. Their decision (which is as risky as the commitment to sexual fidelity) is to see if they can find themselves, their bodily selves, in a life dependent simply upon trust in the generous delight of God – that Other who, by definition, cannot want us to supply deficiencies in the bliss of a divine ego, but whose whole life is a "being-for," a movement of gift.

Sebastian Moore remarks that "True celibates are rare – not in the sense of superior but in the sense that watchmakers are rare."[6] Finding a bodily/sexual identity through trying to expose yourself first and foremost to the desirous perception of God is difficult and precarious in a way not many of us realize, and it creates problems in dealing with the fact that sexual desiring and being desired do not simply go away in the single life. Turning such experience constantly toward the context of God's desire is a heavy task – time is to be given to God rather than to one human focus for sexual commitment. But this extraordinary experiment does seem to be "justified in its children," in two obvious ways. There is the great freedom of the celibate mystic in deploying the rhetoric of erotic love in speaking of God; and, even more important, there is that easy acceptance of the body, its needs and limitations, which we find in mature celibates like Teresa of Avila in her last years. Whatever the cost, this vocation stands as an essential part of the background to understanding the body's grace: paradoxical as it sounds, the celibate calling has, as one aspect of its role in the Christian community, the nourishing and enlarging of Christian sexuality.

It is worth wondering why so little of the agitation about sexual morality and the status of homosexual men and women in the church in recent years has come from members of our religious orders. I strongly suspect that a lot of celibates indeed have a keener sensitivity about these matters than some of their married fellow Christians. And anyone who knows the complexities of the true celibate vocation would be the last to have any sympathy with the extraordinary idea that homosexual orientation is an automatic pointer to the celibate life – almost as if celibacy before God is less costly, even less risky, for the homosexual than the heterosexual.

It is impossible, when we're trying to reflect on sexuality, not to ask just where the massive cultural and religious anxiety about same-sex relationships that is so prevalent at the moment comes from. In this final section I want to offer some thoughts about this problem. I wonder whether it is to do with the fact that same-sex relations oblige us to think directly about bodiliness and sexuality in a way that socially and religiously sanctioned heterosexual unions do not. When we're thinking about the latter, there are other issues involved, notably what one neo-Marxist sociologist called the ownership of the means of production of human beings. Married sex has, in principle, an openness to the more tangible goals of producing children; its "justification" is more concrete than what I've been suggesting as the inner logic and process of the sexual relation itself. If we can set the movement of sexual desire within this larger purpose, we can perhaps more easily accommodate the embarrassment and insecurity of desire: it's all for a good cause, and a good cause that can be visibly and plainly evaluated in its usefulness and success.

Same-sex love annoyingly poses the question of what the meaning of desire is – in itself, not considered as instrumental to some other process, such as the peopling of the world. We are brought up against the possibility not only of pain and humiliation without any clear payoff, but, just as worryingly, of nonfunctional joy – of joy, to put it less starkly, whose material "production" is an embodied person aware of grace. The question is the same as the one raised for some kinds of moralists by the existence of the clitoris in women: something whose function is joy. If the Creator were quite so instrumentalist in "his" attitude to sexuality, these hints of prodigality and redundancy in the way the whole thing works might cause us to worry about whether "he" was, after all, in full rational control of it. But if God made us for joy . . .?

The odd thing is that this sense of meaning for sexuality beyond biological reproduction is the one foremost in the biblical use of sexual metaphors for God's relation to humanity. God as the husband of the land is a familiar enough trope, but Hosea's projection of the husband-and-wife story onto the history of Israel deliberately subverts the God-and-the-land clichés of Near Eastern cults: God is not the potent male sower of seed but the tormented lover, and the gift of the land's fertility is conditional upon the hurts of unfaithfulness and rejection being healed.

The imagery remains strongly patriarchal, not surprisingly, but its content and direction are surprising. Hosea is commanded to love his wife "as I, the LORD, love the Israelites" (Hos. 3:1, *NEB*) – persistently, without immediate return, exposing himself to humiliation. What seems to be the prophet's own discovery of a kind of sexual tragedy enables a startling and poignant reimagining of what it means for God to be united, not with a land alone, but with a people, themselves vulnerable and changeable. God is at the mercy of the perceptions of an uncontrolled partner.

John Boswell, in his Michael Harding Address, made a closely related observation: "Love in the Old Testament is too idealised in terms of sexual attraction (rather than procreation). Samuel's father says to his wife – who is sterile and heartbroken because she does not produce children – 'Am I not more to you than ten children?' " And he goes on to note that the same holds for the New Testament, which "is notably nonbiological in its emphasis."[7] Jesus and Paul equally discuss marriage without using procreation as a rational or functional justification. Paul's strong words in 1 Corinthians 7:4 about partners in marriage surrendering the individual "ownership" of their bodies carry a more remarkable revaluation of sexuality than anything else in the Christian scriptures. And the use of marital imagery for Christ and the church in Ephesians 5, for all its blatant assumption of male authority, still insists on the relational and personally creative element in the metaphor: "In loving his wife a man loves himself. For no one ever hated his own body" (5:28–9, *NEB*).

In other words, if we are looking for a sexual ethic that can be seriously informed by our Bible, there is a good deal to steer us away from assuming that reproductive sex is a solitary norm, however important and theologically significant it may be. When looking for a language that will be resourceful enough to speak of the complex and costly faithfulness between God and God's people, what several of the biblical writers turn to is sexuality understood very much in terms of the process of "entering the body's grace." If we are afraid of facing the reality of same-sex love because it compels us to think through the processes of bodily desire and delight in their own right, perhaps we ought to be more cautious about appealing to scripture as legitimating only procreative heterosexuality.

In a church that accepts the legitimacy of contraception, the absolute condemnation of same-sex relations of intimacy must rely either on an abstract fundamentalist deployment of a number of very ambiguous biblical texts, or on a problematic and nonscriptural theory about natural complementarity, applied narrowly and crudely to physical differentiation without regard to psychological structures. I suspect that a fuller exploration of the sexual metaphors of the Bible will have more to teach us about a theology and ethics of sexual desire than will the flat citation of isolated texts; and I hope other theologians will find this worth following up more fully than I can do here.

A theology of the body's grace which can do justice to the experience of concrete sexual discovery, in all its pain and variety, is not, I believe, a marginal eccentricity in the doctrinal spectrum. It depends heavily on believing in a certain sort of God – the trinitarian Creator and Savior of the world – and it draws in a great many themes in the Christian understanding of humanity, helping us to a better critical grasp of the nature and the dangers of corporate human living.

It is surely time to give time to this, especially when so much public Christian comment on these matters is not only nontheological but positively antitheological. But for now let me close with some words from a non-Christian writer who has managed to say more about true theology than most so-called professionals like myself.

> It is perception above all which will free us from tragedy. Not the perception of illusion, or of a fantasy that would deny the power of fate and nature. But perception wedded to matter itself, a knowledge that comes to us from the sense of the body, a wisdom born of wholeness of mind and body come together in the heart. The heart dies in us. This is the self we have lost, the self we daily sacrifice.[8]

I know no better account of the body's grace, and of its precariousness.

Notes

1 Paul Scott, *The Day of the Scorpion* (London: Heinemann, 1968), 450.
2 Ibid., 454.
3 Thomas Nagel, *Mortal Questions* (Cambridge: Cambridge University Press, 1979), 44–5. [Reprinted in this volume.]
4 Ibid., 47.
5 Ibid., 49–50.

6 Sebastian Moore, *The Inner Loneliness* (New York: Crossroad, 1982), 62.
7 John Boswell, "Rediscovering Gay History" (London: Gay Christian Movement, 1982), 13.
8 Susan Griffin, *Pornography and Silence: Culture's Revenge against Nature* (New York: Harper and Row, 1981), 154.

Trinitarian Friendship: Same-gender Models of Godly Love in Richard of St. Victor and Aelred of Rievaulx

Marilyn McCord Adams

Like several authors in this volume, such as Rowan Williams, Adams thinks the Christian doctrine of the Trinity has decisive things to say about how human beings are in the image of God, how we are to relate to one another, and what love is. An analytic philosopher and Episcopal priest who works in medieval materials, Adams notices further that one of the most influential models of the Trinity depends on taking them as three lovers. The model of friendship presupposed, furthermore, is one that the medieval author, Richard of St. Victor, and his Roman source, Cicero, only think (and historically could only think) of applying to men.

I Wrestling over the Blessing!

Currently, the blessing of "same-sex unions" is hotly contested within the churches. Several times a year, newspapers feature stories of mainline denominations inhibiting homosexual clergy from practicing their ministries, because they have made their (sexually active) partnerships known. Resolutions and counter-resolutions are brought before national church assemblies, while leaders try with mixed success to shove the issue to the back burner in order to avoid denominational schism. In my own Anglican communion, one bishop has been tried for heresy, because he knowingly ordained a coupled gay man.[2]

My own conviction is that same-gender partnerships can be, and often are, icons of godly love. My purpose in this paper is to forward this point of view, and make a constructive contribution to this debate, albeit in a narrowly defined way. Polemical tasks divide into two – the positive assignment of mustering considerations in favor of one's own position, and the negative one of overturning the opponents' arguments to the contrary. Typically, the case against blessing sexually active same-sex unions relies heavily on appeals to Scripture and tradition, and often creates the impression that these speak with one voice. Yet, what the many *pro* and *contra* biblical arguments show is that partisans within the churches are agreed in their attachment to the authority of Scripture, but divided in their understandings of what it means to treat the Bible as an authority as well as over what hermeneutical methods to apply. For the present, I leave these disputes to biblical scholars, in order to shoulder a part of the task to which my own fields of expertise – historical and philosophical theology – are more germane. Because I am a medievalist, I turn to the twelfth century – to Richard of St. Victor and Aelred of Rievaulx – to counterexample my opponents' presumption that the theological tradition is homogeneous on this matter (and thereby begin to discharge the negative burden of proof). Moreover, I retrieve from these sources and commend a model of godly love that is indifferent to the gender mix-match of the lovers (and thereby sketch[3] the features of a positive case for the churches to say "yes" to blessing same-sex unions).

II   A Trinity of Lovers!

Richard of St. Victor had the courage of his convictions when – in 1148, during a period of intense cultural ferment – he proposed to *demonstrate* the tri-unity of God with bold and concise arguments. Everyone agreed: God is all powerful, of immeasurable wisdom, and goodness. Richard declared that if perfect wisdom and power could exist in solitude,[4] Divine goodness could not! For at the heart of goodness are *charity* (*caritas*) and *benevolence, happiness* (*felicitas*) and *joy*. Charity is always other-directed, indeed involves the will to love another[5] and the will that the other be loved as oneself.[6] Likewise, benevolence acts to share benefits;[7] perfect benevolence shows itself in largeness of spirit, such freedom from greed as wishes to hold nothing back.[8] Since omnipotence is able to confer infinite abundance,[9] it would be shameful for God to keep immeasurable goodness all to Himself,[10] His greatest glory would be to share it.[11] Likewise, outward-bound charity is necessary for the highest happiness, the mutuality of love shared essential to highest joy.[12] Nevertheless, "in the Highest, the flame of love burns no hotter than highest wisdom dictates."[13] Because neither Divine charity nor Divine benevolence can help being governed by Divine wisdom, God would not give the full measure of Divine riches to anyone unworthy of them. Charity should not take unlimited delight in what isn't perfectly delightful.[14] Likewise, perfect benevolence would broker no *inordinate* flow of gifts, misproportioned to the receiver's capacity.[15] Obviously, Richard concludes, no mere creature(s) could be worthy objects of, none able to contain such Divine largesse;[16] only an equal – viz., another Divine person – could![17] The Divine Lover and Beloved are thus equally worthy[18] – equally powerful, wise, good, and blessed.[19] Because there cannot be more than one Divine essence, their *"equality"* is paradigmatic, consisting in the identity of their substance nature.[20] Because the Divine Lover seeks a worthy consort eternally by the necessity of His very nature, so that the pair are equally incorruptible, immutable, and uncircumscribable.[21] Their relationship thus enjoys the paradigmatic *permanence* of eternity.

Divine Goodness "twins"[22] itself to share the riches of its greatness (*magnitudo*), to create a "communion of majesty."[23] Charity finds a worthy object of its delight, the two bestow on one another an affection of highest desire,[24] and "solitary majesty" dissolves into the sweetness of mutual love and appreciation.[25] Yet, Divine Goodness does not consummate charity unless the two produce a third, a common love-object, so that they can share in loving the very same thing.[26] Without a common love-object, happiness would lack some sweetness because sharing was restrained;[27] glory shamed by withholding possible benefit.[28] Moreover, charity and benevolence require this third to agree with the first two in that paradigmatic equality which owns one and the same Divine essence,[29] so that – as we confess – there are three co-equal persons, one God!

Persons have names. Human names for Divine persons are furnished by Scripture and rationalized by analogies with creatures. Since human persons come in genders, it is natural to pick a gendered name, even though the incorporeal Divine nature involves no sex at all.[30] Equality among persons, the "sameness of form" that arises from their sharing the very same substance, dictates a choice of same-gendered names;[31] their common unsurpassible nature narrows options to those belonging to the "worthier sex."[32] Without hesitation, Richard vindicates traditional 'Father'/'Son' labels for the first two and considers 'Grandson' for the third before preferring 'Holy Spirit' on the ground that their common love-object is produced by the intimate sighing of two lovers Who eventually breathe (*spirant*) Holy Spirit into the hearts of the saints.[33]

III Models of Friendship

"Catching" the hints

In mid-twelfth-century France, Richard's project seemed daring for its claim to prove the mystery of the Trinity by cogent arguments, within a decade after Bernard of Clairvaux had Peter Abelard's books burned a second time for mixing philosophy and logic into theology. What made Richard's treatise striking, even twelfth-century "trendy," was his appeal to Cicero's dialogue *On Friendship* (then enjoying a stirring revival) for his social model of the Trinity. For Cicero defines "friendship" as "mutual harmony in affairs human and divine, coupled with benevolence and charity,"[34] "without which life is deprived of all its joy."[35] The whole novelty of Richard's argument turns on identifying benevolence, charity, and enjoyment as central to Divine goodness, while unity of substance guarantees trinitarian harmony of thought and will. By contrast, Richard's rationalization of names for the trinitarian persons was utterly commonplace. What riles contemporary feminists would have put his twelfth-century readers rapidly to sleep!

Anglican theology recognizes that revelation is somehow progressive. True, Holy Scripture contains "all things necessary to salvation."[36] Divine self-disclosure in Christ's Incarnation and Passion, Mighty Resurrection and Glorious Ascension, is complete and sufficient. *All the same, Divinity is a difficult subject; we humans are slow learners. We would not be able to digest it, if the Holy Spirit made everything explicit at once.* Our Lord's earthly ministry raised questions, "Who is Jesus? What is He doing?" "Who must God be if Jesus is His Son?" Several centuries elapsed before the Church was able to formulate the doctrine of the Trinity – three persons, one God – or draw boundaries around the ways we may think of Jesus as both human and Divine. *Changing polemical contexts prompt fresh queries, put the Church in a position to tumble to fresh insights, explicitly notice what was there all along.* Our present predicament is one of those triggers. Struggling in the middle of our perplexities about sexuality, what could be more obvious? Way back in the twelfth century, Richard of St. Victor made centuries-old trends explicit, when he represented *the Holy Trinity as a paradigm "same-sex" friendship.* How could we have missed it? Father, Son, and Holy Spirit, an intimate community of lovers, the center of Christian worship for over 1,600 years!

Cicero is one key that makes this explicit for us. But his account of friendship was itself revisionary. What practices was he hoping to reform?

Classic varieties

In the ancient world, friendship broadly conceived was *an institution for exchanging benefits* (originally, *charis*, something that prompts joy and delight).[37] Life is too uncertain to proceed on a strict "fee for services" basis. To survive and flourish, we need alliances with people on whose general benevolence we can presume, as they can on ours, for material assistance, for advice and support, for the general promotion of our aims.[38] *Reciprocity* is obligatory. Moreover, if friendship is born out of need and for the sake of utility, nature assists with built in tendencies towards connection. Moreover, the goals of friendship are best served when partners take each other's interests to heart as if they were their own.[39] *Trustworthiness* is required, if friends are to count upon one another to protect and promote each other's interests in competitive and hostile situations or to help when misfortune places demands on the friend's resources without any immediate prospect of return. Trustworthiness is also necessary to inspire friends to believe in one another, at least give one another the benefit of the doubt in the face of accusations and real or apparent offenses.[40] Insofar as friendship is meant to increase security, there is *a presumption of stability*: the burden of proof rests on the partner who would dissolve the relationship, even in the face of offense.[41] Likewise, friendship is *transitive*: if you are my friend, your friends are my friends, your enemies my enemies, so that each partner brings a network of obligations of varying degrees.[42] The weight of such commitments is great. To the extent that friendship is voluntary, it is prudent to be cautious, not to make friends too quickly without testing their character and resourcefulness.[43]

Ancient societies recognized and enforced many levels of friendship. If self-interest is natural,[44] (i) *family members* stake the strongest claim, bound as they are presumed to be by blood ties and common interests. Natural instinct was supposed to drive parental friendship towards offspring, bestowing on the latter both life and nurture. The child's obligation to support parents in their old age was counted as reciprocal exchange.[45] Such friendship reaches out to all blood-relatives in proportion to their degree of kinship. (ii) *Civic friendship* was another such extension. When political organization shifted from clan to city-state, the new unit was likened to a family, whose citizens are kin, the fatherland a parent who must be repaid for birth and nurture, whose interests could be pressed at the expense of smaller family units.[46] (iii) *Marriage* was another distinctive kind of friendship, established by the offering and repayment of favors, in the first instance between families,[47] but subsequently between husband and wife, who among other things shared the *charis* of sexual gratification.[48] Because friendship is transitive, marriage makes families friends and presumptive kin, which is reinforced by the indirect blood ties established in the couple's children.[49] (iv) *Personal friendships* may overlap with family and city, but may also be established with foreigners. They are initiated from one side by spontaneous favor and maintained by exchange over a lifetime of varying circumstances.[50] (v) Finally, there is the category of *friendship with the gods*, at one level commercially conceived of as an exchange of sacrifices for supernatural favors.[51]

Friendship's legion opportunities for conflicting loyalties are the stuff of literature, legend, even history. Not only is self-interest curbed by the claims of family and marriage, personal friends and state; these latter are at odds with one another. What if obligations to one, require one to betray the interests of another? What if one's friends are wicked, claim one's participation for sinister designs? Does friendship override the demands of law and virtue?

The idealizing model

Against such social realities, Cicero joins the philosophical effort to burnish friendship into an inspiring ideal. In the process, he "rubs out" commercial and need-based notions as so much smudge. For – according to him – true friendships are characteristically initiated between equals who are self-sufficient, independently well-endowed.[52] True friendships can be formed only among the good, who – if not yet perfect – already possess wisdom, loyalty, integrity, equity, and liberality in a high degree.[53] Such relationships are sparked neither by desperation for the necessities of life nor by the exigencies of upward mobility, but by nature. Humans participate in a universal natural tendency towards connection with others of the same kind, are naturally endowed with inclinations to love, to benevolence with charity.[54] Such dispositions are reinforced by actual familiarity.[55] If solitude is unnatural,[56] if humans mimic the beasts in preferring blood-relatives to strangers, fellow citizens to foreigners,[57] good men are attracted to nothing so much as virtue in others.[58] The mutual appreciation of one another's character, the sharing of such excellent life fuels the fires of benevolence and charity, gives rise to an enjoyment without which life would not be worthwhile![59] If virtue is the parent and preserver of friendship,[60] friendship is its handmaid, a context in which good character thrives and grows.[61] Moreover, such interchange and affection spawns generosity that will go to any lengths for the other,[62] leads each not only to love and to cherish but also to revere the other.[63] True friendship drives towards such perfect harmony of opinions and will[64] that one could say there is "one soul in two bodies."[65] If benevolence has wide scope, Cicero estimates, such intensity of affection and harmony is possible only between two or at most among a few.[66] Surely, he insists, this type of friendship is an end in itself. Many advantages flow from it, but they are not the aim towards which friendship is the means.[67]

True friendship never asks nor consents to anything dishonorable.[68] True friendship is utterly candid, devoid of hypocrisy.[69] True friendship believes in the friend, so far from lodging accusations, refuses to credit others' charges and suspicions unless and until the evidence is decisive.[70] True friendship relaxes sobriety, lifts seriousness, is less restrained, more genial.[71]

True friendship is not governed by false laws. It does not "adopt the same feelings towards friend and self" because it is much more extravagant in promoting the friend's cause than one's own.[72] Nor does it observe "do as you're done by," minutely balancing benevolences expended and received. True friendship is too rich, too generous for petty cost accounting.[73] So far from "valuing the friend as he values himself," true friendship corrects self-estimates, cheering the depressed or underconfident, challenging when the reckoning goes wrong.[74]

True friendship is regulated by wisdom, proportions benevolence, gives the friend as much as it can, commensurate with his ability to receive.[75] True friendship puts partners on a level plane, counts them as equals. Where there are *de facto* inequalities, the dignity of the higher now elevates the lower, now condescends to the latter's station by turns.[76]

True friendship ought to be permanent. Yet, in Cicero's estimation, nothing is more difficult than for friendship to continue to the very end of life.[77] Changing tastes, emerging conflicts of interest disrupt friendships based on advantage.[78] Consensus can be disrupted by political arguments, dispositions get changed by adversity, attention narrow under the burdens of old age.[79] Morally the most serious cause of dissolution is one partner's turn to vice.[80] Still, except for treason or outrageous scandal which call for an immediate withdrawal of affection,[81] Cicero prefers that ties of friendship be "sundered by a gradual relaxation," "unravelled rather than broken,"[82] "burned out rather than stamped out."[83] Likewise, one should take care not to give the appearance of friends becoming enemies.[84] Most of these troubles could be avoided, however, if care were exercized before making commitments,[85] if potential comrades were tested for relevant virtues,[86] if wisdom were exercized to check the headlong rush of benevolence,[87] and if alliances were delayed until persons mature into relative stability.[88]

IV Theological Transformations – "Baptizing" the Ideal!

Perhaps the very same year that Richard of St. Victor produced *On the Trinity*, Aelred of Rievaulx wrote a highly complementary treatise, *Spiritual Friendship*, the avowed intention of which was to "baptize" Cicero, to sketch a Christian theology of friendship, pouring down from God through Christ and raising us up to fellowship with God.

Utopic beginnings!

Aelred begins with Divine self-sufficiency: God is supremely powerful, Divine goodness Itself enough for God's joy, happiness, and glory. God has no need of creatures, so far as Divine being or well-being is concerned.[89] Yet, since wealth breeds liberality, Divine decision to create is unsurprising. God is the self-sufficient source of everything else: God is the cause of all being, the life of all sensation, and the wisdom of all intelligence.[90] Aelred attributes the alleged natural tendency towards connection among all creatures[91] – whether inanimate, nonrational, human, or angelic – to the unity and integrity of God's cosmic providential plan.[92] Angels were created for society among pleasant and harmonious companions, whose wills and desires agree.[93] Humans, too, were made for society among equals. Following Paul in correcting Hellenistic models, Aelred explains that God created Eve from Adam's rib to show that they are both of the same substance and so equals as true friendship requires.[94] For humans, a solitary life without the giving and receiving of love in friendship would be bestial[95] and devoid of happiness.[96] Aelred's view is that where friends are concerned, the more the merrier![97]

Unity, perverse and shattered – the consequences of Adam's fall

Cicero has taught us: nature plants charity, a desire for friendship, in the human heart; experience increases it.[98] By contrast, Adam's fall corrupts human social inclinations, results in a cooling of charity, a rise in concupiscence, self-centeredness, and a preference for private advantage over the common good.[99] Such psycho-spiritual disorganization explains why we constantly find ourselves in situations with conflicting loyalties. This accounts for the prevalence of false sorts of friendship,[100] and makes it practically wise to have a divided policy of charity towards all but friendship only for the tried and true.

Among the false, Aelred numbers "carnal" friendships which spring from mutual harmony in the vice of inordinate attachment to sensory beauty and pleasure. While they last, the law of *idem velle, idem nolle* drives them to reinforce one another's passions, each urging the other on.[101] Because affection here refuses to be governed by reason, Aelred denounces such friendships as "puerile," finds them unstable, dying down as quickly as they flared.[102]

Second is the traditional "worldly" friendship "born of a desire for temporal advantage or possessions."[103] Reason *appears* to commend these for their *ante-mortem* practical advantages (see section II above).[104] Often, the duty of reciprocal exchange engenders special affection,[105] and sometimes relationships begun this way can evolve into something better.[106] Nevertheless, Aelred is adamantly opposed to this economic conception of friendship as a "trade" "bought with money."[107] Because both its currency and emphasis are wrong, "worldly" friendships often degenerate into deceit and intrigue or vanish in the winds of changing fortune.[108]

Spiritual harmony

By contrast, true friendship is spiritual friendship, which is principally to be desired for its own sake, its completion or perfection as its own reward.[109] Psycho-spiritual goods are its medium of exchange – e.g., counsel in perplexity, consolation in adversity,[110] prayer without ceasing,[111] empathetic identification in grief and shame as much as in honor and joy.[112] Spiritual friendship is a virtue, bought with love and won by competition in generosity.[113]

For Aelred, true friendship is grounded in Christ as source, medium, and end. Christ is its beginning, Who inspires friends' love for each other.[114] Christ is friendship's pattern, Who laid down His life for His friends.[115] True friendship ascends by degrees to Christ, Who gives Himself as our Friend to love, in an endless cascade of charm, sweetness, and affection.[116] True friendship is perfected in Christ, so that friend clinging to friend in the Spirit of Christ is made one with Christ in heart and soul.[117] Thus suspended in Christ, true friendship can never conflict with legitimate norms.

On the contrary, true friendship is a safe haven in a fallen world, an ark within which the fall is being reversed! Aiming as it does at spiritual advance, it begins among the good, progresses among the better, and is consummated among the perfect.[118] The wicked cannot enter upon it, but only those who already lead a sober, just, and godly life.[119] Friends covenant to be companions in schooling the passions to the cardinal virtues (prudence, temperance, justice, fortitude), agree together to undertake the regimines needed for the cure of the soul.[120] For this friends must be trustworthy, since the freedom of candor is required. They must have no hesitation in opening themselves for the other's correction, no qualms about confessing their failings, no shame in recognizing progress won.[121] Likewise they need a safe place to share secrets and discuss plans.[122] True friendship is the best antidote to self-centeredness, because the sweetness of shared affection readies them to love the other more than self,[123] indeed to lay down life for friends.[124]

In Aelred's estimation, spiritual friendships have eschatological significance, as an "already" amidst the "not yet" in God's restoration of cosmic harmony. Participating in them makes us friends of one another and at the same time friends of God.[125] For, on the one hand, friends achieve harmony with one another by helping one another grow towards *idem velle, idem nolle* with Christ. On the other, because the love of Christ is both source and medium, ever-present, always midwyfing our love for one another, spiritual friendship is an ever-deepening participation in the knowledge and love of Christ.[126] In advanced stages, they cross over from mere virtue to spiritual zeal to a resurrection of the spiritual senses to intimacy with God.[127] Aelred transforms Cicero's idea of permanence into a vision of the communion of the saints, where love is literally stronger than death, and the harmonious unity of friends begun in this *ante-mortem* life lasts eternally.[128] Moreover, in the world to come, the transitivity of friendship makes friends of Christ all friends with one another, so that God will be all in all.[129]

Aelred captures the unity of friends with the symbol of a kiss. Just as a carnal kiss is made by the impression of the lips in such a way that the breaths are mingled and united, producing a sweetness that binds them together[130]; so a spiritual kiss involves contact, not of the mouth, but of the hearts' affections, which so mingle the spirits with one another and with the Spirit of God that there is one spirit in many bodies.[131]

V   Objections, Clarifications, and Revisions

Our two medieval treatises combine to yield the following picture: the Blessed Trinity is a paradigmatic "same-sex" friendship, Whose harmony is reflected before the fall in cosmic unity and after the fall in spiritual friendships both between couples and among the wider community of the Church. Unsurprisingly, this makes the Trinity our standard of blessed relationships, whose parameters among creatures Aelred tries to chart.

Gender flexibility

Notice, Aelred's portrait of spiritual friendship in no way privileges hetero-sexual intimacy. On the contrary, the classical models from which he is working make same-sex male intimacy paradigmatic. To be sure, in ancient culture, marriage functioned as one type of friendship broadly speaking. But the inherent inequalities of ancient marriage institutions led idealizing philosophers to discount it. Likewise, to the extent that they participated in the sexism of their cultures, they ignored the possibility of friendships among women, on the ground that the female of the species was too flimsy and fickle to be the stuff of virtue.[132] Such ideas remain barely below the surface in Augustine's *Confessions*, who mourns the loss by death of his one-soul-two-bodies male friendship,[133] later abandons the marriage his mother arranged to form a monastic community of male friends united in pursuing the knowledge and love of God, and rationalizes including Monica on the ground that she had the faith of a man in the body of a woman![134]

My contention is that Church Fathers and later theologians take such conventional wisdom for granted when they liken the Godhead to a Trinity of perfect male friends. Richard of St. Victor still finds it uncontroversial as he portrays the Trinity as a same-sex love affair. Aelred reintroduces a sometime Christian corrective that counts women as equal in Christ. He returns to the idea that Adam and Eve were friends, and so recognizes heterosexual relationships as potentially exemplary. What Aelred gives us is a model that recognizes that gender is no barrier to the intimacy we and all creation are called to have in Christ. So far as he is concerned, couplings of whatever mix-match, can be wombs for growth, schools of love in an as-yet cacophonous world.

Spirituality, embodied or dichotomizing?

All the same, suspicious spark at the word 'spiritual.' Does it not suggest that Aelred is gender-permissive only because he means to exclude bodily intimacy altogether. After all, his book was written for monks who had become Cistercians rather than Benedictines, in search of a "higher righteousness," shouldering the yoke of a yet more ascetical way.[135]

Historically, matters are murky. If not entirely convincing, Boswell's evidence is at least suggestive that ancient institutions of friendship did house "sexually active" same-sex unions.[136] Boswell and other scholars cull Aelred's works for confirmation of his own homoerotic orientation, even homosexual activity before entering the religious life.[137] By contrast with other abbots and novice-masters, Aelred does not altogether ban affectionate touch, bars friendly hand-holding or embrace only for the still vicious for whom it will be a source of temptation.[138] To be sure, Aelred does not recommend or countenance genital intimacy for monks. His written works, however, evidence no rigid dichotomizing of body and spirit. Following traditions of mystical spirituality, Aelred uses the bodily as an analogy of the spiritual (e.g., his analysis of the kiss). Aelred rejects "carnal" friendship, not because it involves passion and bodily attractions, but because the affections are unsteadied by reason and responsibility. Aelred *does* acknowledge the "sexually active" *friendship* of Adam and Eve, and so presumably does not find bodily intimacy incompatible with spiritual friendship. And in any event, Aelred identifies Divine purpose in creation as cosmic friendship that includes creatures of all kinds – rocks and plants and animals as much as angels.

My own claim does not require us to settle historical controversies or resolve textual ambiguities upon insufficient evidence. Rather it is the philosophical suggestion that Aelred's portrait of spiritual friendship provides a core out of which we can spin off models for Christian friendships of many different kinds. I suggest – with Aelred – that as Christians we center our *ante-mortem* lives on the project of growing in the knowledge and love of God, in becoming as individuals, in cultivating relationships that serve as sacramental signs of Divine love to a broken world. This priority becomes criterial for shaping the several dimensions of our many relationships, especially our most intimate friendships. Because intimate friends bear a special responsibility to foster one another's spiritual growth, it becomes necessary to ask, are we as persons spiritually compatible? Would we aid or obstruct one another's spiritual progress? Would (this sort of) bodily intimacy help or thwart our ability to love God and one another? Would it be compatible with our individual and joint responsibilities to others? Would cohabitation make us better or worse channels of charity and benevolence towards God's world?

In principle, where the spiritual core is sound, where personalities fit, physical intimacy could enhance the symbolic power of a relationship to image the Trinity. After all, human being is body as well as mind and spirit. The God Who works to harmonize the macrocosm of creation, must surely purpose friendship among the various aspects of the microcosm of human being. Ideally, this would mean, not divorce, but wholesome marriage of the two within individuals. Relationships in which "one soul in two bodies" finds expression in "one-flesh union" would surely be among the most potent signs of creation reharmonized, God's Reign-to-come. The bodies of hetero- and homosexual couples divide the symbolic labor: male and female bodies joined show forth Divine power to orchestrate variety, while same-sex unions signal the fundamental union and likeness of Divine Lovers.

Beginning with Aelred's spiritual criteria is not only gender-flexible, it wins the further advantage of bringing actual historical institutions of marriage under judgment. His model calls Church as well as society to account, for sanctioning the many ways marriage has (to put it mildly) "cramped the spiritual styles" of husband, wife, and children alike. At the same time, they challenge us to "remodel" heterosexual unions in more Christlike terms.

Same difference!

Highly formal as Aelred's model is, giving scope for variety of flavor and content, contemporary psychology predictably balks at the ancient ideal of *idem velle, idem nolle*, protests the need for "spaces in our togetherness." Even in same-gender loves, don't opposites attract? Isn't it good that they do? Don't we need "otherness" to evoke our own potential, variety to give spice to life.

Superficially, the image of one soul in two bodies depreciates difference. Many ancient authors really do imagine intimacy so complete that one shares the other's preference for chocolate over raspberry, Mozart over Beethoven, Van Gogh over Manet.

We need not construe Aelred's model so narrowly, however. Aelred's God is not composing monotone harmony, but conducting a large orchestra with instruments of many different types. Where friendship is concerned, Aelred's own instincts were "the more the merrier." While recognizing the limits of our *ante-mortem* capacity for intimacy, he insists we are destined for friendship with the whole zoo of creation. In any event, Aelred was a spiritual director of great subtlety, understood full well how different souls respond to a variety of spiritual means. Difference may be more important at some stages than others. What ideal friendships require is harmony of spiritual orientation. For Aelred, this meant both must be Christians. In our pluralistic culture, we recognize that commitment to Love, Charity, and Benevolence is polyglot, and we experience how life purposes may be fruitfully overlapping, despite diversity of names.

Too much permanence?

Ideals of friendship, both Christian and pagan, commend permanence on multiple grounds. The pledge of lifelong fidelity provides a framework of security that fosters trust. Longevity in friendship brings an increase in joy and delight. Bonds unbroken and unbreakable thereby imitate trinitarian love-ties. Nevertheless, human psychology is developmental. Some grow up faster than others. Some are ever restless to struggle forward, others readier to settle down on one or another contented plateau. "Best" friends naturally "outgrow" each other, often split at forks in the road. Likewise, contemporary society is highly mobile, the pace of life so hectic as to make it difficult to "stay in touch." Besides, for reasons both understandable and perverse, people often make bad choices. *Ante-mortem* compatibility is too difficult for some people. Many relationships are abusive, wrecking our capacities to love self and others, wrenching us away from our embrace with God.

Once again, Aelred was alert to these last possibilities, echoes ancient advice to choose carefully, test before making commitments that run deep. He recognizes that familiarity must sometimes be withdrawn when interactions are spiritually damaging, although he may seem overly optimistic in repeating Cicero's counsel of gradual withdrawl and encouraging the wronged party to maintain charity towards the former friend. Even if we recognize that friendships can be temporary without being superficial, we can share permanence as an ideal for special relationships, for those havens that reach to the heart of our personalities to re-form them in the image of Christ. As a Church, we may still agree not to lay on hands too hastily, not wish to bless unions (whether homo- or heterosexual) that have not been tested for compatibility at the core. Likewise, contemporary psychology would not dissent: ties that bind deep should not be too quickly dissolved!

Methodological reductiones, *blasphemous insinuations?*

In looking to the Trinity, I have appealed to a doctrine of speculative theology, sharpened by patristic debate, defined by Nicea and Constantinople, elaborated with the precisions of school theology, and evolved in relation to varying philosophical frameworks. Cicero's treatise *On Friendship* is a work of semi-popular pagan thought. When norms taken from the latter are mapped up as a sociological model of the Trinity and then mapped down to furnish ideals for sexually active human partnerships, don't we verge on the blasphemous insinuation that trinitarian love-life is paradigmatically erotic? Put this together with traditional names for the Divine persons, aren't we invited to envision the Father and the Son as committing incest? Just as bad or worse, doesn't this reduce the Trinity to a cosmic romantic triangle, which – projected downward

– might be seen to license the marriage of three? Doesn't all of this demonstrate the danger to Christians of trying to decide moral questions by looking to extrabiblical sources?

In reply, first let me note with Aelred that this mapping of ancient ideals of friendship upward to the Trinity and downward to the Jesus' followers is not unbiblical. Without attributing the full blown conceptuality of Nicea or Constantinople to the evangelist, we can recognize this procedure as explicitly prefigured in John's Gospel (chs. 14–15): Jesus and the Father abide in, mutually indwell one another; Jesus says only what the Father gives Him to say; does only what the Father wills Him to do. Likewise, Jesus counts the disciples friends; the Father, the Son, and the Holy Spirit/Counsellor will come and make their home with those who love Jesus and keep His words (*idem velle, idem nolle*). St. Paul may also have something like friendship between unequals in mind when he speaks of his agency in terms of "I-not-I-but-Christ" (Galatians 2:18–21). Cicero's treatise does not represent a conceptuality alien to the Bible, but merely furnishes an elegant formulation of shared ideals that remained "in the air" for centuries.

Second, what Bonaventure observed about Christology is apt with respect to the Trinity: viz., that all things are revealed for our edificiation, but not all for our emulation! Whether or not, in which personal dimensions and to what extent, human *ménage à trois* can be an icon of godly love, depends in part on our varying assessments of human capacity for intimacy and functional household organization. Given their swelling African constituency, Anglicans should be especially mindful that polygamy was taken for granted in the patriarchal period, and practiced well into monarchical times. According to the Bible story, the household from which God raised the twelve tribes of Israel was at least a (Jacob–Leah–Rachel) *ménage à trois*. Likewise, arguably, what makes incest pernicious for human beings is our developmental character, the initial and radical inequalities of power and maturity, which profoundly shape the child's conception of itself and its place in the world. By contrast, whatever causal relations may exist among the Divine persons, they are eternally equal in power, wisdom, and virtue, as ancient ideals of friendship require. Besides, the warrant for the traditional labels – 'Father' and 'Son' – is biblical. Chalcedonian Christians (among whom Richard of St. Victor, Aelred of Rievaulx, and I all number ourselves) can readily reason that the parental language arises naturally within, is "mete and right" for the relation of Christ's human consciousness to the Divine. Out of His human consciousness, Christ experiences Himself as counted a beloved son in relation to a heavenly father. But the names get transferred to the first and second persons of the Trinity, because – via the Chalcedonian definition – the hypostasis that this "Son" is, is the second person of the Trinity. Relations between them are then analogized to biological cases of paternity and filiation here below.

VI   Acknowledging the Blessing!

The Church has usually felt the tension between insisting that the Holy Spirit of God operate through proper channels, dispense grace through the offices of ordained clergy and authorized sacramental rites, and recognizing that the Holy Spirit of God "bloweth where It listeth" doing infinitely more than we can ask or imagine. God institutes sacraments because we are insecure, we need reassurance that God will really do something; *ex opere operato* is God's own guarantee that God will deliver. When we're honest, we have to concede that God made *all* things to fill them with Divine blessing, that each and every creature shines with the glory of distinctive Godlikeness. We have to confess that the Spirit works in secret, moving over and against our spirits, luring, coordinating, re-forming all creation with sighs too deep for words. If only we had eyes to see it, we could detect the hand of God, living and active everywhere. Because human attention-span is limited, sacramental rites must be selective, focus our gaze on especially momentous occasions of grace. There are the waters of baptism, acknowledging Holy Spirit's presence, making holy, with all of its purifying, sanctifying power. There is the manna of Holy Eucharist, showing forth Our Lord's death, transubstantiating us into members of Christ's Body given for the world He has made. There is the oil of healing, the assurance of pardon, the grace of ordination. And if God is always at work, if the kiss of Christ breathes the charity of Holy Spirit into all personal relationships, the Church still singles out some as especially worthy of commendation, because of their remarkable power to symbolize Divine love, the unusual depth and scope of participation in the trinitarian love affair. In solemnizing marriage and receiving monastic solemn vows, the Church does not so much call down as it acknowledges and proclaims the Good News of Divine blessing already at work.

My modest aim in this essay was to undermine confidence in the verdict of one Episcopal bishop who recently reassured his diocese that no "theological case" for "celebrating marriage-like unions of persons of the same sex" has been nor *can be* made.[139] In my judgment, Richard's picture of the trinitarian love affair combines with Aelred's account of Christian friendship to suggest how homosexual love can serve – as much as heterosexual couplings – as an icon of godly love, a sacramental participation in Love Divine. Many gay and lesbian couples make the thought-experiment concrete. Reflection on their experiences can furnish nuance and detail, and further instruct us about the scope and variety of Christlike possibilities. We the people of God should keep our baptismal vow to support them in their life in Christ. What God has joined together, we should have the courtesy to acknowledge and celebrate!

Notes

1 This paper takes its inspiration from my work at Trinity Episcopal Church, Los Angeles, where I learned much from many – on these topics, most especially from Luke Johnson and Steve Price. More recently, I have learned from discussions with Haywood Spangler, Eugene F. Rogers, Jr., and Bentley Layton. Earlier versions of this paper were presented at the "Beyond Inclusion" Conference held at All Saints' Episcopal Church, Pasadena, in April 1997, and to members of the Gay Christian Readings Group of Christ Church, New Haven.

2 Happily, Bishop Walter Righter was acquitted. But the ecclesiastical politics surrounding the trial would scarcely commend the purity of the Church to unbelievers!

3 More recently, Eugene F. Rogers, Jr., has published an impressive book-length case for this conclusion in his *Sexuality and the Christian Body* (Oxford: Blackwell, 1999).

4 Richard of St. Victor, *De Trinitate* III.16.204. References are to *Richard de Saint-Victor, La Trinite*. Introduction, trans. and notes by Gaston Salet, SJ (Paris: Les Editions du Cerf, 1959).

5 *De Trinitate* III.2.168.

6 *De Trinitate* III.11.190.

7 *De Trinitate* III.4.174.

8 *De Trinitate* III.4.176; III.6.178; III.14.198.

9 *De Trinitate* III.8.182.

10 *De Trinitate* III.4.174.

11 *De Trinitate* III.4.176; III.6.178; III.14.198.

12 *De Trinitate* III.3.172.

13 *De Trinitate* III.8.180.

14 *De Trinitate* III.2.168; III.7.180.

15 *De Trinitate* III.4.176.

16 *De Trinitate* III.2.168.

17 *De Trinitate* III.8.182.

18 *De Trinitate* V.22.346; V.24.362.

19 *De Trinitate* III.10.186; cf. III.21.214.

20 *De Trinitate* III.8.182, 184; III.9.186, 188; III.23–4.216, 218; VI.9.394.

21 *De Trinitate* III.10.186; cf. III.22.216.

22 Richard's own word; cf. *De Trinitate* III.17.206.

23 *De Trinitate* VI.6.388.

24 *De Trinitate* III.19.208, 210.

25 *De Trinitate* III.4.174; III.14.198,200.

26 *De Trinitate* III.11.190,192; III.14.200; III.18.208; III.19,208,210; VI.6.388.

27 *De Trinitate* III.12.194; III.17.206.

28 *De Trinitate* III.14.198,200.

29 *De Trinitate* III.21–4.212–18.

30 *De Trinitate* VI.4.382.

31 *De Trinitate* VI.4.384.

32 *De Trinitate* VI.4.382.

33 *De Trinitate* VI.10.398,400.

34 *De amicitia* VI.20; cf. V.19–20; VIII.26. Quoted by Aelred of Rievaulx, *Spiritual Friendship*, trans. Mary Eugenia Laker, SSND (Kalamazoo, Mich.: Cistercian Publications, 1977), I.53.

35 *De amicitia* XXVII.102.

36 *The Book of Common Prayer* (New York: The Church Hymnal Corporation, 1979), "The Ordination of a Priest," 526.

37 Mary Whitlock Blundell, *Helping Friends and Harming Enemies: A Study in Sophocles and Greek Ethics* (Cambridge: Cambridge University Press, 1989), ch. 2, 31–3.

38 Blundell, ch. 2, 31–3.

39 Blundell, ch. 2, 35–6.

40 Blundell, ch. 2, 37.

41 Blundell, ch. 2, 37–8.

42 Blundell, ch. 2, 48.

43 Blundell, ch. 2, 34.

44 Blundell, ch. 2, 39.

45 Blundell, ch. 2, 43.

46 Blundell, ch. 2, 43–4.

47 Blundell, ch. 2, 46.

48 Blundell, ch. 2, 46.

49 Blundell, ch. 2, 46–7.

50 Blundell, ch. 2, 45.

51 Blundell, ch. 2, 47.

52 *De amicitia* IX.31, XIV.51.

53 *De amicitia* V.18–19, VI.21.

54 *De amicitia* V.19–20; XXIII.88.

55 *De amicitia* IX.29,32.

56 *De amicitia* XXIII.87.

57 *De amicitia* VIII.27, XIV.50, XXI.81.

58 *De amicitia* VIII.28.

59 *De amicitia* VI.22, IX.29, 31–2, XIV.49, XXVII.102.

60 *De amicitia* V.20.

61 *De amicitia* XXII.83.

62 *De amicitia* XXII.82.

63 *De amicitia* XXII.82.

64 *De amicitia* IV.15, VI.20.

65 *De amicitia* XVII.61.

66 *De amicitia* V.20.

67 *De amicitia* IX.32, XIV.51.

68 *De amicitia* XII.40, XIII.44.

69 *De amicitia* XVIII.65–6, XXV.92.

70 *De amicitia* XVIII.65–6.

71 *De amicitia* XVIII.66.

72 *De amicitia* XVI.56–7.

73 *De amicitia* XVI.56, 58.

74 *De amicitia* XVI.56–7, 59.

75 *De amicitia* XX.73.

76 *De amicitia* XIX.69–70, 71–3.
77 *De amicitia* X.33.
78 *De amicitia* X.33–4, 74.
79 *De amicitia* X.33–4.
80 *De amicitia* X.35, XXI.78–9.
81 *De amicitia* XXI.76.
82 *De amicitia* XXI.76.
83 *De amicitia* XXI.78.
84 *De amicitia* XXI.77.
85 *De amicitia* XXI.78–9; XXII.85.
86 *De amicitia* XVIII.65.
87 *De amicitia* XVII.63; XXI.79.
88 *De amicitia* XVIII.74.
89 *Spiritual Friendship*, I.61.
90 *Spiritual Friendship*, I.61.
91 *Spiritual Friendship* I.61–2.
92 *Spiritual Friendship*, I.61–3.
93 *Spiritual Friendship* I.63.
94 *Spiritual Friendship* I.63.
95 *Spiritual Friendship* II.71,82.
96 *Spiritual Friendship* III.110.
97 *Spiritual Friendship* III.111.
98 *Spiritual Friendship* I.61–3.
99 *Spiritual Friendship* I.63.
100 *Spiritual Friendship* I.64.
101 *Spiritual Friendship* I.59.
102 *Spiritual Friendship* II.83.
103 *Spiritual Friendship* I.60.
104 *Spiritual Friendship* II.84.
105 *Spiritual Friendship* I.60.
106 *Spiritual Friendship* III.92.
107 *Spiritual Friendship* II.83; III.108.
108 *Spiritual Friendship* I.60.
109 *Spiritual Friendship* I.60; II.84–5.
110 *Spiritual Friendship* II.84.
111 *Spiritual Friendship* III.131.
112 *Spiritual Friendship* III.119.
113 *Spiritual Friendship* III.108.
114 *Spiritual Friendship* II.74.
115 *Spiritual Friendship* I.58; II.72.
116 *Spiritual Friendship* II.74–5.
117 *Spiritual Friendship* III.114, 132.
118 *Spiritual Friendship* II.79.
119 *Spiritual Friendship* III.93.
120 *Spiritual Friendship* I.61, 65.
121 *Spiritual Friendship* II.72.; III.111.

122 *Spiritual Friendship* II.72.
123 *Spiritual Friendship* II.72; III.111.
124 *Spiritual Friendship* I.58; II.72.
125 *Spiritual Friendship* II.73.
126 *Spiritual Friendship* II.73.
127 *Spiritual Friendship* III.114; III.131.
128 *Spiritual Friendship* II.70; III.111.
129 *Spiritual Friendship* III.132.
130 *Spiritual Friendship* II.75–6.
131 *Spiritual Friendship* II.76.
132 For example, Cicero's dialogue is among males, the pronouns and adjectives used to describe friends are entirely of masculine gender. Relations with and among women never come up. Cf. John Boswell, *Same-Sex Unions in Premodern Europe* (New York: Villard Books, 1994), ch. 3, 75.
133 *Confessions* IV.6.
134 *Confessions* IX.4.
135 For example, Aelred wrote his *Mirror of Charity* on orders from Bernard of Clairvaux, with a view to persuading recruits from leaving the order because of the harshness of Cistercian life. Bernard's letter and Aelred's acquiescence are translated in *Mirror of Charity*, trans. Elizabeth Connor, OCSO, intro. by Charles Dumont, OCSO (Kalamazoo, Mich.: Cistercian Publications, 1990), 69–75.
136 Boswell, *Same-Sex Unions in Premodern Europe*.
137 John Boswell, *Christianity, Social Tolerance, and Homosexuality* (Chicago and London: University of Chicago Press, 1980), ch. 8, 221–6. Cf. Douglass Roby in his introduction to the above-cited translation of Aelred's *Spiritual Friendship*, 21–2.
138 Cf. Aelred of Rievaulx, *The Mirror of Charity*, III.27.65.
139 The Right Reverend Paul V. Marshall, Bishop of the Episcopal Diocese of Bethlehem, in his pastoral letter of November 19, 1997, made these remarks in response to a contrary resolution passed in the Episcopal Diocese of Philadelphia.

PART

Anthropology and Christology

Sanctifying Nearness

Thomas Breidenthal

Breidenthal argues that sexuality serves as a physical reminder of our connection or availability to our neighbor, a sometimes hopeful, sometimes frightening sign that we cannot escape our fellows. Our vulnerability represents no individualist choice but a creature's condition. The trick is to grow into our vulnerability as intimacy with God and neighbor, so that we grow in sanctification and holiness. This involves a discipline, or ascesis, which consists not in the avoidance or control of vulnerability, but in its perfection.

In *Continuing the Dialogue: A Pastoral Study Document of the House of Bishops to the Church as the Church Considers Issues of Human Sexuality,*[1] the bishops have set out to define several broad areas of consensus in the Episcopal Church, as a basis for further discussion. The document succeeds admirably in this task. We as a church do agree that our sexuality is a part of God's creative intention for us and is therefore good; we agree that all forms of sexual abuse, harassment, and sexualized violence are bad; and we all agree (I hope) that no individual should be denied respect or civil rights on the basis of sexual orientation. Unfortunately, none of this agreeing has brought us a step closer to the resolution of the issues that divide us, namely, whether the church should bless covenanted same-sex unions and whether the church should ordain practicing gays and lesbians.

The reason for this stalemate is, in my view, that we have not yet begun to grapple with the question that really lies at the heart of this debate: Why is our sexuality a spiritual concern? What has our use of it to do with our salvation? I do not mean to suggest that no one is asking this question. Nor do I mean to suggest that the bishops have not raised it in their *Pastoral Study*. But they, and we, have not raised the religious question radically enough.

"Traditionalist" voices urge us (rightly) to take the will of God as the starting-point for our moral deliberation about issues like the blessing of same-sex unions. "Progressive" voices point out (also rightly) that the nontraditional lifestyles of many committed Christians may have something to teach us. Yet both choruses may leave us uneasy. Certainly, we must do more than invoke the will of God if we wish to recover a viable Christian sexual morality. It is not simply that the will of God has proven notoriously difficult to determine in this matter. Even if God's will is obvious, it cannot provide a rationale for any moral code until we are able to say, clearly and simply, how God's command speaks to us, how and why it addresses us not only as a demand but as good news. But we can learn from each other's Christian witness only if we have some notion of what we need to hear.

Before we can have a fruitful conversation about our Christian lives as sexual beings, we need to back up and consider first, how our sexuality encounters us as a spiritual problem, and second, how this problem is addressed by the Christian faith. I think the problem is *radical availability*.

To say that I am radically available is to say that anyone can become my neighbor: anyone can get under my skin. The word *neighbor*, after all, simply means someone who is *nigh* to me, close to me. This is also the literal meaning of the Hebrew and Greek words in the Bible that we translate as "neighbor." Nearness is experience of the other as neighbor, that is, as one to whom I am radically available. One might say that nearness "precipitates" or is the precipitation of radical availability. Nearness can be good news or bad. (The arrival of the good Samaritan could have been bad news instead of good news for the Israelite lying by the roadside.) At any moment and at any time the tactful and protective reserve that we maintain in our dealings with most human beings can be torn asunder, and we can find ourselves, for good or ill, at the disposal of a stranger, who is aware of us, sees us, and judges us.

We tend to view such chance encounters as exceptions to the distance which ordinarily separates us from one another. But what if the occurrence of nearness indicates our true condition – that is, our radical availability to one another? Then the distance that so often seems to divide us is mere pretense – a pretense which denies the close connection every human being shares with every other human being. Sometimes the occurrence of nearness seems to create distance rather than diminish it. This is particularly the case when we are suddenly confronted with the otherness of someone whom we have "annexed" to ourselves, or viewed as an extension of ourselves. But the abyss that opens between me and such a one is not a distance that protects or isolates me from the other. On the contrary, it is a distance through which and in which the other looms before me and I before the other. It is the distance that, like the space between an audience and an actor, makes for more visibility, not less.

The neighbor is neither reducible to being an extension of myself nor able to be dismissed because he or she is different from me. It is true that we can refuse to hear the cry or the invitation of the neighbor, just as we can deny the experience of availability into which the neighbor plunges us. It is also true that we can collude with one another to "paper over" these experiences – we can support one another in the illusion of self-sufficiency. But however much we may prefer to think of ourselves as essentially separate from and independent of one another, in charge of the relationships we make and the degrees of exposure we permit, the truth is that we are always already available to every other human being, and cannot prevent even a momentary encounter with a stranger from touching us to our very core.

Sexual desire can be an especially intense and unsettling reminder of our radical availability to the other. Like parental affection or simple compassion, sexual desire can cause our heart to "belong" to another, even if we do not want it to, even if we wish our desire were otherwise, and quite apart from the fact that we may refuse to allow our actions to be governed by our heart. That is to say, sexual desire, once roused, places us in a relation of connection to the object of our desire – a relation which we have not chosen and which, although we can resist acting upon it, we cannot wish away. Thus, this desire shatters any illusions we may have regarding our ability to choose when and if we shall be connected to others; indeed, it is itself a warrant for the claim that our fundamental relation to one another is one of connection. The experience of sexual desire is also intensely physical, and involves desire for physical contact with its object. Thus, by its very nature, sexual desire gives the lie to the conventional assumption that our bodies "hide" us and stand, as it were, as a barrier of defense between our inmost selves and the world with its other selves. Far from protecting us from the world, our bodies reveal the fact that we belong unqualifiedly to the world – and to one another.

Such a shift in how we regard our bodies is, I think, reflected in our ever-increasing concern with the danger of physical and sexual abuse. Our very reasonable fear of such abuse goes far beyond avoiding bodily harm. The real fear is that disrespect for our bodies or physical and sexual violence committed on our bodies constitutes an attack on our souls as well as our bodies, and it is this aspect of abuse that is the most horrifying to us. But we have come to recognize or admit the soul-destroying potential of sexual and physical abuse (and I include here sexual and physical stereotyping) only because we have acknowledged the extent to which our bodies, far from being a first line of defense against the world, are in fact the very field upon which the self is called daily to meet the world.

Given our propensity to harm one another, our radical availability to one another can be very frightening. We may dream of retreating from human community, from the world, even from our bodies. But we cannot escape from our availability to one another: it is a condition of our existence as human beings. Nor, it appears, can we stop hurting one another. This is why the question of nearness is fundamentally a religious question – because we cannot do anything about our radical availability to one another, and we cannot do anything to make our radical availability to one another safe. We are driven to look beyond ourselves for help. Depending on where we find that help, or how we frame that help theologically, salvation from the dangers of radical availability will be understood as an ultimate escape from nearness or as its ultimate redemption.

The dialogue about sexuality seldom gets down to the issue of nearness because at crucial points it falls prey to three ways of talking about the human condition that do not so much reject radical availability as pretend it isn't there. These may be summarized as follows:

1   Talking about the self as if it were essentially *cut off* from other selves;
2   Talking about the self as if it were *inviolable*; and
3   Talking about spiritual and moral values as if they were products of the *will*.

Such talk reflects an understanding of who and what we are that has dominated Western thinking for some centuries now. According to this view – which, for want of a better name, I shall call *radical individualism* – nearness is not inevitable, because we are not radically available to one another. We start out disconnected, and whatever connection we have is something we have chosen and *made*. On this view, sexuality does not so much reveal connection as facilitate it. Cast in this role, sexuality inevitably presents itself as something external to a self that remains isolated and untouchable. However much we may think of our sexuality as part of us, a dimension of who we are, it becomes very difficult not to speak of it as if it were something we "have" – a tool or resource, a kind of software program for networking between isolated selves.

Radical individualism as I have just characterized it is not compatible with the gospel, for two reasons. First, it denies the biblical insistence that we are all "one flesh," that the human race is a body that is being redeemed, a lump of dough that is being leavened. Were we really not available to one another, it would make no sense to say that the Word initiated the transformation of the human race by becoming a member of it. That transformation requires that each of us be at once the recipient and the conductor of the grace of God in Christ. But Jesus cannot get through to me unless (whether I like it or not) I am radically available to him as a fellow human being, and I cannot minister Jesus to others unless every person I engage with is radically available to me (and vice versa).

Second, radical individualism denies the fundamental biblical understanding of our relationship with God. It presupposes that the self is self-grounding, autonomous, the sole author of its own actions, the final arbiter of its own values. In its extreme form, radical individualism sets the self up in God's place. In its less extreme and seemingly more religious form, it imagines the self invited into a kind of reciprocal relationship with God. But there is no reciprocity between God and us. We cannot even, in the strict sense, reciprocate God's love. God's love is the act whereby we are created and preserved. This love is always ahead of ours, because God is pure act, the only true beginner. ("I chose you before you chose me.") It is true that I can respond to God's love by loving God back, but the response is not a new initiative. In this sense, as Bonhoeffer says in his *Ethics*, we are passive before God.[2]

To respond to God in thanksgiving is to acknowledge that we have no center in ourselves and no existence apart from God's power and will. This is not to say that we have no freedom, or that we are incapable of real action. But our action is always an answer to God: either we are praising God or denying God. Moreover, only when we respond to God in praise (rather than turning from God in pride) do we discover what we were made for, and the freedom that comes in the doing of it. True human action is always eucharistic in character.

The notion that our freedom is grounded in passivity with respect to God finds concise expression in the claim that we are made in the image of God. This "image" is none other than our capacity to love, that is, to affirm the existence of another, and this capacity is Godlike. But this capacity is God's imprint upon us, God's inscription upon our hearts, the divine impress with which we have been stamped. We have not chosen to be the bearers of the divine image, and we will always be just that – *bearers* of God's imprint, not little gods in our own right. There is no common ground between us and God. We praise God because God is *worthy* of praise, and God's worth is not (like the worth of the other in Aristotle's theory of friendship) a correlative or mirror of our worth. God is not "another self."

Even though loving God constitutes our highest happiness, we cannot speak properly of any "interest" we may have in a relationship with God. And this is so because the encounter with God is the undoing of all "interest" grounded in self-control or autonomy. God's love for us calls for a response that we cannot give if we seek to maintain the pretense of any agency that is not grounded in God's agency. If we cling to this pretense, God's love confronts us as a demand, perhaps even as an assault. If we do not cling to it, that love wells up within us as the ground of our own true freedom, which is the freedom to offer service and glory to God.

We late twentieth-century Christians – conservatives and liberals alike – are perhaps more attracted to the radical individualist ideology than we might care to admit. At any rate, our moral vocabulary very often plays two notional ends against the middle, leaning now on the notion of the self as disconnected and autonomous, and now on the notion of the self as available and passive. This is no less true of the moral vocabulary we use to discuss human sexuality. Three words come particularly to mind: *gift, intimacy*, and *mutuality*. I would like to reflect briefly on each of these words.

First, *gift*. The claim is frequently made in church circles that sexuality is a divine gift to be celebrated and used. This claim is intended (quite rightly) to affirm the goodness of sexuality as part of our created nature. But the likening of sexuality to a gift is problematic because, without quite intending to, it can suggest that our sexuality is something external to us, a resource that we can use or leave to one side, like the talents in the parable.

The difficulty here lies in the ambiguity of the word *gift*. On the one hand, I can claim that sexuality is a part of my nature: since my nature is the handiwork of a good God, my sexuality, along with everything else about me, is the good gift of God. Here *gift* retains its absolute sense as something *given*; it is my own existence and nature, including my sexuality, that is given. On the other hand, *gift* can refer to something outside myself, something given to me for my use. In this sense, the thing given is not a part of me; I exist quite apart from the gift, although I may benefit from it. It is very easy to slip unreflectingly from the first meaning of sexuality-as-gift to the second, especially when one tends, as we all do, to forget that the word *sexuality* does not designate a thing but a dimension of our existence.

After all, what is sexuality but the fact of sexual desire (ranging from mild interest to passion) as it is experienced by human beings? *Sexuality* refers not to a thing but an experience, and to give thanks to God for this experience is to thank God for making us precisely what we are. But when we begin to talk about sexuality as if it were a thing, abstractable from the rest of us, something we can "use" or "get a handle on," then we are in danger of glossing over the relation of sexuality to connection, and an assertion intended to anchor our discussion firmly in the doctrine of creation becomes an ensign under which the conversation, having lost its moorings in radical availability, drifts inexorably toward radical individualism.

A similar drift is occasioned by the notions of mutuality and intimacy, respectively. By *intimacy* I mean a certain understanding of closeness which has its roots in the ideology of disconnection, even if the word *intimacy* is not always intended in that sense. Intimacy means the kind of connection that is possible on radical individualist grounds. Literally, the word means the sharing of what is most inward (from the Latin *intimus*, "innermost"). From the radical individualist perspective, there is a certain deliciously oxymoronic quality to the idea of what is innermost being shared, that is, being held in common. From that perspective the inward is, after all, the domain of the unavailable self.

Not surprisingly, this notion of intimacy first gained currency in connection with the bourgeois myth of the family as a safe haven from the challenges and tumults of the public world. The frictionless togetherness of this family depended, of course, on mother, children, and servants all functioning as extensions of the father's own self; the intimacy or sacralized inwardness of the domestic scene coincided perfectly with his projected inwardness. Today, intimacy denotes the coming together of two impenetrable domains of inwardness – an almost ineffable transgression of the boundaries between two radically individual selves. This idea plays itself out in one of two ways. On the one hand, intimacy comes to mean the absorption of one self into another, or the mutual absorption of many selves to create a collective self. On the other hand, intimacy can name a brief and titillating exercise in gamesmanship in which two selves "play" at availability with one another. In neither case does intimacy overthrow the ideological assumption that connection and difference cannot go together. Intimacy stands for a connection which is either totalitarian or artificial – the collaborative project of two wills that remain essentially unconnected.

The term *mutuality* is no less problematic. Increasingly, this word designates a necessary (and sometimes sufficient) condition for the moral worth of a sexual act. But what is mutuality? Mutuality has always connoted reciprocity in the sense of a return in kind. That is, it refers to equals who can pay each other back. For this reason, mutuality has something to do with respect – the respect we have for an equal. Again, mutuality has tended to suggest something that is had in common – a "third term" which relates two otherwise disparate terms to each other. Thirdly (and this is, I believe, a new meaning, forged in the smithy of the church's dialogue about sexuality), mutuality has come to suggest tenderness as well as respect.

What does this mean when it comes to the consideration of what constitutes a morally worthy sexual act? In connection with the notion of intimacy, mutuality seems first to point to the agreement whereby two equal (that is, two equally autonomous and equally self-grounding) individuals exchange the gift of sexuality; it also seems to refer to the relation into which these two individuals are brought by virtue of sexuality, the "third term" which unites them. If we understand this relation as one of vulnerability, then we can see why mutuality, *as a moral principle*, has become practically synonymous with tenderness. It is because, on this view, we have a moral duty to treat tenderly those who have freely chosen to make themselves vulnerable to us in the sexual act, and we are owed the same tenderness in return. Obviously, I think there is more than a hint of radical individualism in the idea that we could *choose* to be vulnerable. Taken literally, vulnerability means something very like radical availability. Yet vulnerability often suggests a stance voluntarily taken rather than an unavoidable condition.[3]

Taken together, the notions of mutuality, intimacy, and sexuality-as-gift comprise the key features of an emerging sexual morality which sounds biblical but is in fact deeply rooted in radical individualism. According to this scheme, sex (or the vulnerability into which sex leads us) is a gift (that is, an instrument), possessed equally by all (mutuality), by which two or more individuals can achieve intimacy (that is, an achieved connection between otherwise disconnected souls) if and only if they agree not to take advantage of the vulnerability each has voluntarily entered into (mutuality again). Sex is then a moral practice whose object is intimacy and whose cardinal virtue is mutuality. This scheme seems to fit in with a vaguely Christian moral vision, since intimacy looks so much like communion or *koinonia*, and *koinonia* is surely the Christian goal. But in fact mutuality and intimacy have little to do with true communion. The reign of God is precisely *not* about the tender exchange of what is most private and inward. It is about something boundless, public, noisy, and unashamedly urban – our enjoyment of each others' uniqueness as praisers of God.

Mutuality and intimacy have very little to do with sex, either. The cult of intimacy and mutuality distracts us time and again from what is most obvious about sex, namely, its revelation of our connection to one another, its being, simply and familiarly, a register (not a cause or a condition) of our nearness to the other as neighbors who are always already radically available to each other. In so doing, the cult of intimacy and mutuality also distracts us from the spiritual question that our sexuality poses: "Are we happy with our radical availability, or not?" I imagine that many of us, to begin with, are not. Connection seems like a good thing if we can have it when we want it, on our own terms (if we are interested in power) or at least on equal terms (if we are interested in sharing). But to prefer connection as an option is precisely to recognize the ways in which the neighbor is *dangerous* – which is why a sexual morality rooted in radical individualism never involves an unqualified embrace of nearness, no matter how "permissive" it may be.

The difficulty comes when we consider embracing nearness (and therefore radical availability) not as an option, but as a given – still more, when we consider whether or not to include radical availability in our idea of salvation. Are we willing, first of all, to recognize nearness not as a product of our own will but as something that comes upon us, the manifestation of an already existing availability in the unsought-for event of connection? Can we, in the second place, rejoice that we are so available to one another, even when we abuse each other's availability more often than not?

The Bible's answer to the question about nearness is, I believe, unambiguously affirmative. The Bible is no stranger to the theme of the dangerous neighbor. Yet the New Testament, echoing the Hebrew scriptures, places before us a twofold command: Love God, and love your neighbor as yourself. This command engages us directly with the neighbor, maximizes our nearness to the neighbor, and acknowledges the neighbor's permanent involvement in our life. This is because the command to love the neighbor is also a command to love nearness itself. Love of neighbor is not the same thing as benevolence at a distance, but a "going out" of the heart to the neighbor which assumes our embracing of our radical availability to the neighbor.

This sounds like Buber's I–Thou relation. Yet the I–Thou relation allows for a kind of reciprocity which I do not mean to suggest is present here. I have in mind something more like Levinas's insistence (as against Buber) that the neighbor meets me not as my equal, in relation with whom I truly become an "I," but as one who undoes me, stripping me of my false "I" but not providing me with the counterpoise for a new "I."[4] There is no counterpoise here; there is only claim and vertigo. Love of the neighbor, like love of God, is a kind of death to self, the death of any pretense to disconnection-on-demand. Such love is direct and involving – it demands that I myself draw near to the one who has drawn near to me – and it concerns the neighbor as one who is not "another self," to whom I am nevertheless radically available and into whose hands I am, as it were, to deliver myself. Worse yet, unlike God, the neighbor whose claim on me I recognize and to whom I surrender myself is perhaps very far from loving *me*.

Yet if we consider almost any passage in the New Testament we see that this kind of surrender is what is enjoined, often with explicit reference to the neighbor who may be dangerous or unsympathetic. (Think of going the extra mile, giving the second tunic, loving the enemy, the patience of the slave in affliction, forgiving seventy times seven, turning the other cheek, blessing not cursing.) To be sure, the Christian gospel commends love as redemptive, not only for the lover, but for all whom it touches. Our Christian response to the neighbor must therefore be guided by the conviction that our love not only transcends but undoes the sin that vitiates every human relationship. Love of neighbor looks toward the overcoming of everything that makes radical availability a cause for fear, toward the restoration of everything that makes radical availability a cause for joy. The Bible witnesses in numerous ways to the dangers posed by our radical availability to one another under the condition of sin, but it also affirms the essential goodness of this availability as part of God's intention for us. Indeed, the Bible teaches us repeatedly to look forward to more nearness in the reign of God, not less. More specifically, Christian faith, when it insists on the full and irrevocable humanity of the incarnate Word, offers no escape from nearness and acknowledges no path to Jesus that does not begin and end in nearness. The whole point of the Incarnation is that the Word of God has become our neighbor, and has done so not in order to rescue us from nearness (that was the Gnostic error), but to set our nearness right.

I do not think it is an exaggeration to say that this "take" on nearness, in both its negative and positive aspects, provides Christian moral theology with one of its fundamental principles. Moral theology (or Christian ethics) is about holiness. We have already been justified by faith in Christ. Now how shall we be sanctified? How shall we grow into the full stature of Christ? One way is to live out our availability to one another in such a way that, encounter by encounter, relationship by relationship, Christ's redemption of the whole body of humanity finds its concrete fulfillment.

This brings us back to the beginning of the discussion. Why is our sexuality a spiritual concern? What has our use of it to do with our salvation? Indirectly, sexuality is a spiritual concern because it casts a spotlight on radical availability, which is the distinguishing feature of the human spirit as the image of God. Directly, sexuality is a spiritual concern because it names a domain of human experience in which I always find myself face-to-face with another who is near to me, delivered over to me (even if I am his or her victim), called to praise God in company with me. In my sexual dealings, as in all my dealings (all our dealings may involve sexual feelings, but sexual feelings are not the only way in which we find ourselves thrown into nearness), I must, as a Christian, both affirm the nearness of the neighbor and, acknowledging my own sinfulness, refer that nearness to Christ for sanctification. As Christians we seek to live lives that honor the connection which all human beings share, while recognizing that in a fallen world this connection is as likely to facilitate violence as to enable communion. Surely, lives so led are not ordered solely to our own individual sanctification. They embody disciplines by which our availability to one another, and the corporate nature of our common humanity which that availability presupposes, begin to be transformed and sanctified.

All Christian moral practices, including sexual practices, involve such rules and boundaries. Yet – and it is crucial that we remember this – the purpose of the rules is not to keep human beings apart from each other. Rather, it involves recognizing that when we draw close to one another in Christ we are still sinners. Our ability to avoid abusing those who are close to us is limited, as is our capacity to suffer inevitable abuse without buying into it ourselves.

Nowhere, perhaps, is this more the case than in our sexual dealings with one another. For centuries the church has tended to treat our sexuality with contempt. This contempt reflected an underlying refusal to affirm radical availability. We must be careful lest our new zeal to affirm sexuality leave the older and deeper sin undisturbed. I have no doubt that in heaven we will enjoy a measure of delight and fulfillment in every other praiser of God which we should not shrink from calling sexual delight and sexual fulfillment. But the wholehearted affirmation of our sexuality – an affirmation which, as I have argued, depends on the acknowledgment and affirmation of our radical availability – goes hand-in-hand with the acceptance of a certain *askesis*, a certain discipline, for the sake of the neighbor. As Christians we undertake to bring every part of our lives under the rule of Jesus, who is neighbor to each of us.

What should such an *askesis* look like? Here there is ample scope for disagreement among us – although I would not be surprised if renewed attention to the risk as well as the surpassing goodness of nearness yielded some new configurations of moral conviction. It is not to unusual these days to run across church people who are, for instance, at one and the same time increasingly open to the blessing of same-sex unions and increasingly disapproving of premarital sex. I confess to being one such person. At any rate, I offer three broad areas (beyond those already defined by the bishops' *Pastoral Study*) where consensus ought to be within reach.

First, *promiscuity is not consonant with a life devoted to the sanctification of nearness*. At its worst it exhibits, if not contempt for one's sexual partners (or for oneself), then contempt for nearness itself as the revelation of a real and lasting connection with the other. At its best, it exhibits a naive or prideful desire to jump the gun on the eschaton, an attempt to live out under the condition of sin the realization of a universal communion that is reserved for the saints in light.

Second, *infidelity is not consonant with the Christian way*. Infidelity clearly does exhibit contempt for neighbor and for nearness alike. This is so not primarily because infidelity involves a breach of contract (that really would be radical individualism talking), but because it demonstrates a failure to take responsibility for someone who has simply placed himself or herself in one's hands. It hardly makes a difference if one is released or permitted by some prior agreement to have sex with someone else, since (if we reject the individualist line) it is not in anyone's power to decide whether and how much one will "give" or "open oneself" to another. Sex is not a mere mode of communication or self-expression that leaves the inner self untouched. The Christian should know this, and should be faithful to the other for the other's sake, no matter what the other claims to permit.

Third, *sexual relations should not be entered into unless a lifetime together of spiritual work – that is, a lifelong and exclusive union – is intended*. Sex precipitates nearness, and nearness cannot be sanctified unless our actions and, in the end, our disposition toward one another are purged of every pretense to autonomy, every tendency toward collusion, annexation, or domination. I am not saying that Christians should not get out of violent and oppressive marriages; I am merely saying that marriages with built-in escape hatches are not likely to be engaged in the work of sanctification.

To Summarize:

1. Before we can locate sexuality as a moral challenge for Christians, we must understand how and why sexuality encounters us as a spiritual problem. I have suggested that the problem lies with a radical availability that has been vitiated by sin. Sexuality is a particularly insistent reminder of this radical availability.

2. Christian faith involves an affirmation of radical availability, and of the connection which it presupposes, and looks forward to the sanctification and perfection in Christ of all the bonds that already unite us one to another.

3. Christian faith is therefore a call to lifelong participation in this sanctification and perfection.

4. Christian faith also recognizes the ongoing dangers that we pose to one another in our sinfulness, and therefore relies on the preservation and development of a wide range of moral practices (for example, Christian marriage) which help to ensure that our relations with one another (sexual and otherwise) are, indeed, ordered to holiness.

5. This ordering to holiness, which is also an ordering to happiness, is what supplies any Christian moral practice with its "point," regardless of whether the practice happens to be viewed as something enjoined by the revealed command of God or as something arrived at in the painful crucible of Christian spiritual experience.

6. Christians can in good faith disagree about the value and necessity of various moral practices. We must, however, agree that all moral practices worthy to be called Christian will be grounded in the sanctification of our nearness to each other.

Notes

1 Cincinnati, Ohio: Forward Movement Publications, 1995.
2 "There is no love which is free or independent of the love of God. In this the love of [human beings] remains purely passive. Loving God is simply the other aspect of being loved by God." See Dietrich Bonhoeffer, *Ethics*, ed. Eberhard Bethge (New York: Macmillan, 1955), 53.
3 I do not, of course, mean to suggest that the words *mutuality* and *intimacy* are always or even usually intended to carry the freight I have assigned to them in this essay. I merely

argue that these words, which we all use frequently, signal a shift in the center of gravity of current Christian discourse about sexuality – a shift in the direction of what I have been calling radical individualism.

4 See Emmanuel Levinas, [extracts from] "Time and the Other" and "Martin Buber and the Theory of Knowledge" in *The Levinas Reader*, ed. Seán Hand (Oxford: Blackwell, 1989), 54 and 72–4 respectively.

[Logos and Biography]

John Boswell

Biography has become a standard genre in which gay and lesbian Christians seek to make a case against traditional church policies. Biography can mount detailed, often persuasive arguments from experience. John Boswell's introduction to Chris Glaser's Uncommon Calling: A Gay Man's Struggle to Serve the Church *(1988), however, takes a more theological approach. He first argues from tradition and the lives of the saints that the best Christians may find themselves in opposition to religious authorities. Then he takes a christological turn. Even* God *makes a biographical argument, in that God makes God's own argument – the Logos, God's own story – in the living out of a human life, the life of Jesus. Those who make arguments from their lives and biographies do not, Boswell implies, argue from "mere" experience. Rather, they conform themselves to the pattern of God's own argument in the person of Jesus, molding their own stories, their own* logoi, *by the pattern of the Logos. Like Jesus, they argue in the shape of a life lived to God.*

Finding oneself in conflict with the church is a hallowed Christian tradition. Suffragettes, abolitionists, pilgrims, Protestant reformers, St. Joan of Arc, St. Francis, early monastics – almost every major reformer in Christian history was condemned and opposed by other Christians for beliefs or lifestyles or both. This might have been anticipated; the founder of the religion also encountered opposition and hostility from the authorities of his day, and he explicitly warned his followers that they would not endear themselves to the establishment – religious or secular – by pursuing his teachings.

Although Christianity began as a radical alternative to existing social and religious structures, its very success eventually transformed it into the establishment itself, and then it was as often part of the problem as it was the solution. From as early as the fourth century AD Christians were confusing Christian society with the Christian religion, and assuming that the rules about behavior they learned from family, friends, teachers, laws, public discourse, and so forth, must be Christianity, because the people who taught them were Christians and part of a Christian state. "In order to be moral," Augustine wrote in *The Good of Marriage*, "an act must not violate nature, custom, or law," forgetting perhaps that Jesus had frequently violated all three.

In fact, the majority of the customs and laws of Western Christian societies have not been Christian in any meaningful sense. Many statutes and customs that would seem to be derived from "Christian morality," such as those prohibiting marriage with close relatives and determining the date and mode of celebrating Christmas, are derived from explicitly pagan traditions. Confusing such human constructs with religious principles is precisely the mistake Jesus warned his disciples against when he criticized the Pharisees. Although they were devoted to God's revelation, the Pharisees consistently elevated their cultural habits to the status of religious truth or failed to see any underlying truth that might override literal understandings of scripture or traditions.

We could all learn from Jesus' message to the Pharisees. We are all Pharisees at times, and Jesus called us all to strive to become outsiders in regard to the religious establishment, challenging it to understand morality and Christian hope at a deeper level, to separate God's message from our cultural context, to focus on the essential rather than the external in formulating a godly society.

Nowhere have the conflicts between the religious establishment and Christian reformers been more acute in the second half of the twentieth century than in the case of gay people. As early as the 1950s Quakers were comparing homosexuality to left-handedness as something irrelevant to Christian morality and important only because of cultural prejudice. But many Christian bodies are still wrangling acrimoniously over the acceptance of gay people as clergy or even as members of the church.

Other minorities have fought oppression by Christian society: Jews, black people, women. In each of these cases the establishment used religious claims to justify inequality or injustice and the churches were often among the last organizations to respond to reform. Schools in the South, for example, were integrated before most churches; women have much greater access to civil office in most of this country than to ecclesiastical positions. When we now look back we find it incredible, for the most part, that scripture or Christian teaching was used to defend such inequities, but these efforts were not simply the cynical manipulations of malicious people: they were often the result of sincere confusion of social patterns with the Christian message. The conflation occured in both directions: since black people occupied an inferior place in Christian

357

society, it seemed a "Christian" tenet that blacks were inferior, though there is no such Christian teaching. Since Paul said that women were to keep quiet in church and remain subordinate to men in the household, they obviously should occupy an inferior position in civil structures as well, although this did not follow logically even from the most literal understanding of the Pauline utterances. It is only hindsight that enables us to separate an underlying social prejudice from the fragments of religious tradition used to make it presentable.

Fragments of this sort are still used to buttress arguments against acceptance of gay people. There were objections in the early Church to homosexual acts (though not to gay people), but they were a small part of an elaborate program of moral asceticism, the other portions of which – prohibitions of remarriage after the death of a spouse, of lending at interest, of going to the theater, of intercourse during Lent or menstruation – have been discarded or reinterpreted by most Christian denominations or are simply ignored.

There are fragments in the Bible that can justify as "Christian" hostility to gay people, just as there are biblical passages used to oppose equal rights for black people or women or to oppress Jews. Many Christians with no wish to oppress anyone are naturally concerned about the meaning of such passages, but personal concern about the morality of certain acts is different from social oppression or discrimination. It is striking that Christian society, which cavalierly resists even token observance of many biblical injunctions (e.g., Matt. 5:28, 27, 40, 42; 23:9, 1 Cor. 5:11, to mention but a few) should make a fetish of rigorously enforcing the most literal and restrictive interpretation of a few biblical fragments possibly regarding homosexuality with the force of civil law. Divorce was opposed by Christ himself in three of the Gospels and unanimously opposed by theologians for the first 1,700 years of Christian history; yet the status of the divorced and remarried hardly begins to provoke the passion, bitterness, and hostility inspired by the subject of homosexuality, about which Jesus made no comment at all and which was a minor point of Christian ethics during most of Christian history.

The difference clearly results from the social prejudice against gay people so pervasive in this culture (as it is in some others, including non-Christian societies such as China and the Soviet Union). It is difficult for many people to separate moral ambiguities from personal misgivings of this sort, and many Christians mistake one for the other or conflate both. Violence against gay people in Christian societies, for example, is scarcely ever related to homosexual activity (which is not normally observable), but rather to the suspicion that the victim is a gay *person*, occasioned by his or her dress or manner. In some cases Christian leaders appear to pander deliberately to such prejudices as a means of maintaining or inspiring support for a general program of more conservative moral order. Almost no prominent churchmen of any denomination, for example, publicly campaign to bring divorce laws into conformity with strictly literal interpretations of scripture or tradition, but many lobby for laws restricting the rights of gay people. The reason for this is clearly a conscious or unconscious recognition that the latter will evoke visceral support from the general population while the former will not: hardly a sound doctrinal basis for establishing priorities.

Even within churches, although a distinction is sometimes made between "practicing" and "nonpracticing" homosexuals, the uneasiness, hostility, and discomfort focus much more on the person of the homosexual than on behavior actually under his or her control. The oft-invoked word "avowed" is evidence of this: "avowal" is merely honesty about who one is, not the performance of an act that may or may not violate an ethical code. Honesty and openness are admired in this society in all contexts other than sexuality, where a social taboo overrides other values. Clearly the "homosexual activity" most disturbing to many modern Christians is *being* a homosexual, something not condemned in scripture or Christian theology.

Since nearly all experts now regard homosexuality as an involuntary aspect of character fixed at birth or in early childhood, an exegesis that suggested gay people were condemned simply for *being* gay would be morally indefensible and would ultimately undermine the moral authority of the exegete rather than strengthen a case against homosexuality. Although it took most of a century, the claim by Southern segregationists that blackness was the curse of Ham eventually inspired more disrespect for its white supporters than for the black people they hoped to keep in servitude. It is worth remembering, however, that many of those who argued for it at the time doubtless believed that they derived their views from the Bible rather than from social prejudice.

The origins of such hostilities toward distinctive social minorities are complex and not clearly understood. Nor is it clear how best to combat them. Correcting the false assumptions underlying them is an important but limited approach. In this book, Chris [Glaser] paraphrases a favorite saying of mine: you can't use reason to argue someone out of a position he didn't get into by reason. Precisely because it is, at rock bottom, a visceral feeling rather than a rational position, antigay hostility both inside and outside the Christian church can not be overcome simply by appeal to history, theology, or logic.

There are, on the other hand, ways to communicate and enlighten not dependent on mere information that can overcome deeply embedded prejudices better than argument. A life can be an argument; being can be a reason. An idea can be embodied in a person, and in human form it may break down barriers and soften hardness of heart that words could not.

This is, at least in part, what John the Evangelist means when he refers to Christ as *logos*. Although translators often render it as "word," it is much more than that. It is Greek for "reason" and "argument": our word "logic" comes from it. Christ was God's unanswerable "argument." His people had hardened their hearts against his spoken reasons, the arguments propounded – in *words* – for centuries by the prophets and sages. So he sent an argument in the form of a human being, a life, a person. The argument became flesh and blood: so real that no one could refute or ignore it.

"If anyone says, 'I love God,' and hates his brother, he is a liar; for he who does not love his brother whom he has seen, cannot love God whom he has not seen" (1 John 4:20). God found it necessary, finally, to send his son to become a flesh-and-blood brother to humans, so they would at last "see" him and be able to love him concretely. It is hard to love something too alien, too "other," and recognizing this, God made himself less "other" to help humans love him. It is easier to hate someone, by contrast, when one makes them as "other" as possible, by denying or ignoring the human elements that would form the basis of empathy, understanding, and affection. Stereotypes emphasize the particular "otherness" of some group of people and obscure the much greater area of common humanity the labeled share with the labelers. Sensitive people discover as they grow, however, that most of the "others" they feared, condemned, or hated as invisible abstractions – Communists, Jews, Catholics, "niggers" or "faggots" – turn out to be much less alien in the flesh when they can actually be seen. How likely is it, John asks us, that someone who could *not* recognize and love the humanity he shares with another person could truly love the divine, so much more different from him?

One of the beauties of Chris Glaser's story and life is that by choosing to be open and honest about his feelings he transforms "homosexual" from an alien, despisable abstraction into a real, flesh-and-blood brother to other Christians. They can see him, as they can not see an abstraction: see that he is one of them – a struggling, loving Christian human being, with the graces and flaws and glories and failings of a fallen and redeemed people. It is much harder for most people to remain hostile to and unmoved by a living brother than it is to rail against an abstraction. This is not only John's message in his epistle, but the whole message, in many ways, of the New Testament. God had to become one of us for us to see him. By remaining within the church as a gay man, Chris and others like him make gay people part of the Christian community in a way they were not before. Though rejected, they remain cornerstones, following in the footsteps of Christ.

The chance to meet our abstractions as real human beings is a gift, and also a test. The fair-minded person, confronted with a living person who challenges traditional labels and categories, reconsiders the labels. The bigot reconsiders the person. In Chris's story there are bigots of this sort, but there are more people struggling to understand more deeply, to see with more light, to follow the trail of truth even when it means stepping outside protective walls and opening closed doors.

Chris and other gay Christians are *logoi* in this sense, arguments incarnated in persons, like all the outsiders who have remained loyal to the church in the face of its hostility, and who thereby made their commitment, their lives, their beings an unanswerable, living statement of faithfulness and love. It is hard for them, and hard for their fellow Christians. Christianity is only easy when it is not taken seriously. For the Pharisees the answers are simple; for the followers of Christ they are not. They must struggle endlessly with new challenges and difficult questions. The followers who do so are themselves the answers.

[Marriage and Idolatry]

Charles Hawes

Episcopal priest Charles Hawes offers a wedding sermon in which he proposes that marriage can become idolatrous.

Richey/Smith Wedding
Black Mtn. Presby Church
May 28, 1994

+*In the Name of God*: Who made us and saves us and will not leave us alone. Amen.

"Never use love as an excuse for anything unworthy of it," my father once told me when I was young and crazy about Gretch the Wretch of Westport.

He was talking about my sliding college grades, not about what I was doing with Gretchen.

Still, his point was right.

"Never use love as an excuse for anything unworthy of it."

Never use it, say, to build a molten calf out of gold rings.

– An idol out of wedding rings.

Jesus never was big on American families or traditional family values, you know.

He never got married, far as we can tell, and he was a pain-in-the-tail son. One story has him running away when he was a boy and telling his worried parents to get off his back, he had his own life to live. Later on, at that famous wedding in Cana we opened on here, he told his other he didn't much care what was on her mind.

Then, of course, he warned his followers that following him might start World War Three at home. "I haven't come to bring peace, but a sword. I've come to set a man against his father, a daughter against her mother, a young wife against her mother-in-law, and a man will find his enemies under his own roof."

A real "family" attitude problem Jesus had, I think.

– That finally got explained in his teaching that his *real* family, his *real* brothers and sisters and mother, aren't 'blood' at all but those who do God's will.

It isn't 'God's will' we should build a molten calf out of gold rings.

– An idol out of wedding rings.

– Which is just what we do when we set marriage up to measure what's right and what's wrong with people's best loving. It turns into a moo-faced fertility god demanding the sacrifice of all it doesn't describe.

It celebrates and sanctifies not the humanity we share as god-imaged creatures from the same Creator, as god-imaged lovers from the same Lover, as "Greek and Jew, circumcised and uncircumcised, barbarian, Scythian, slave and free," all included in the saving, reconciling plan and work of God. It celebrates and sanctifies instead division and separation, segregation and estrangement.

It celebrates and sanctifies sin.

It singles out singles and makes them suspect and lamentable and "not quite right."

It makes men and women who love their own kind "queer."

"Where you go I will go, and where you lodge I will lodge, your people shall be my people, and your God my God; where you die I will die, and there will I be buried. May the Lord do so to me and more also if even death parts me from you."

A love song for your wedding, Jeff and Kelly.

A love song sung by a Gentile to a Jew.

A love song sung by a woman to a woman.

A "queer" sort of love song sung by a woman who became mother to the line of David and Jesus.

How can it be?

Ah God, how can it not?

"– Above all, (put on Christ,) put on love *which binds everything together in perfect harmony*," Paul wrote.

And so put off everything that tears things apart, draws dumb lines in the dirt, flies stupid flags, brags "my old man can lick your old man."

– Whatever "uses love as an excuse for anything unworthy of it."

My father was right!

So then, Kelly, Jeff, let this public celebration of your love, let your lives lived together deliberately and unselfishly in plain sight of the rest of us through every kind of good and bad the rest of life can sling, let these things become here and now not an idol but an icon.

– A "sign of God's love to this broken world, that unity may overcome estrangement, forgiveness heal guilt, and joy conquer despair."

– An outward and visible 'sign' of an irresistible inward and spiritual grace.

– A pure, blessed sacrament of inspiration for us all, single, married, straight, gay, and undecided, that how you fit your lives together, we may, and all humanity may, too.

There's an old saying from the Spanish that Gabriel Garcia Marquez introduced me to: "Love is eternal for as long as it lasts."

My prayer for you, and for us who look to you today in hope for ourselves, is fifty years from now yours will still be eternal.

Amen.

PART

Ecclesial Voices

Disputed Questions: Debate and Discernment, Scripture and the Spirit

Luke Timothy Johnson

With this essay, Luke Johnson began a debate about whether God's inclusion of the Gentiles in Acts might provide a model for how the Spirit works to change the community of the faithful and include previously excluded groups. Is the Spirit doing something similar with homosexuality in the church?

Homosexuality as an issue internal to the life of the church poses a fundamental challenge not only to moral discernment and pastoral care (the two aspects touched on in the recent *Catechism of the Catholic Church*) but to the self-understanding of the church as at once inclusive ("catholic") and separate ("holy"). The question is not only how we feel or think or act concerning homosexuality, but also how those feelings, thoughts, and actions relate to the canonical texts which we take as normative for our lives together. Homosexuality in the church presents a hermeneutical problem.

The present essay has the modest goal of clearing some space for debate and discernment by setting out what seem to be appropriate boundary markers for what promises to be a long and difficult discussion. I proceed by staking out three basic premises concerning ecclesial hermeneutics, and then a number of theses pertinent to the issue of homosexuality.

I take it as a given, first, that any process of discernment within the church takes as its fundamental framework the Irenaean triad of ecclesial self-definition: the canon of Scripture, the rule of faith, and the teaching authority of bishops. To step outside this framework is to shift the debate to other grounds entirely. Conservatism in commitment to canon, creed, and council is paradoxically the necessary condition for genuine freedom in scriptural interpretation.

Second, I take it as basic that hermeneutics involves the complex task of negotiating normative texts and continuing human experiences. Within the faith community, this means an openness to the ways in which God's revelation continues in human experience as well as a deep commitment to the conviction that such revelation, while often, at first, perceived as dissonant with the symbols of Scripture, will, by God's grace directing human fidelity, be seen as consonant with those symbols and God's own fidelity. Essentially, however, the call of faith is to the living God whose revelation continues, rather than to *our previous understanding* of the texts. Faith in the living God seeks understanding; theological understanding does not define faith or the living God.

My third premise is that Scripture does not characteristically speak with a single voice. Rather, as an anthology of compositions it contains an irreducible and precious pluralism of "voices," shaped by literary genre, theme, and perspective. The *authority* of these texts, furthermore, is most properly distinguished in terms of their function. Their highest authority is found in their capacity to reliably "author" Christian identity. Almost as important is the way in which these texts "authorize" a certain freedom in interpretation, by presenting a model of how Torah was reinterpreted in the light of new experiences. A third sort of authority is important but not as fundamental. The Scripture contains a wide range of "authorities" in the sense of *auctoritates*, or "opinions," not on all the subjects we could desire, but on many of great significance. Responsible hermeneutics claims the "freedom of the children of God" authorized by the New Testament, and seeks to negotiate the various "voices/authorities" within the texts in an effort to conform to that "mind of Christ" (1 Cor. 2:16) that is the authentic form of Christian identity which those texts are, through the power of the Holy Spirit, capable of "authoring."

I would like to think that these three premises, though perhaps nontraditional in formulation, are in essence profoundly Catholic, fairly and accurately representing not only the implications of the New Testament's own origin and canonization, but also of much loyal and creative interpretation within the tradition.

Before moving to the specific case of homosexuality, it might be helpful to amplify slightly two aspects of these premises which without explication might appear careless if not cavalier. The first concerns the experience of God in human lives. Nothing could be more offensive than to challenge tradition on the basis of casual or unexamined experience, as though God's revelation were obvious or easy, or reducible to popularity polls. The call to the discernment of human experience is not a call to carelessness, but its opposite; it is a call to the rigorous asceticism of attentiveness. I repeat: an appeal to some populist claim such as "everyone does it," or "surveys indicate" is theologically meaningless. What counts is whether *God* is up to something in human lives. Discernment of experience in this sense is for the detection of good news in surprising places, not for the disguising of old sins in novel faces.

Yet it is important to assert that God *does*, on the record, act in surprising and unanticipated ways, and upsets human perceptions of God's scriptural precedents. The most fundamental instance for the very existence of Christianity is the unexpected, crucified, and raised Messiah, Jesus. A considerable amount of what we call the New Testament derives from the attempt to resolve the cognitive dissonance between the experience of Jesus as the source of God's Holy Spirit, and the text of Torah that disqualifies him from that role, since, "cursed be every one that hangs upon a tree" (Deut. 23:21; *see* Gal. 3:13).

Another example is the spread of the gospel to the Gentiles. It is easy for us at this distance, and with little understanding of the importance of the body language of table fellowship, to take for granted such a breaking of precedent that allowed Gentiles to share fully in the life of the Messianic community without being circumcised or practicing observance of Torah. Good for us, also, therefore, to read Acts 10–15 to see just how agonizing and difficult a task it was for that first generation of Christians to allow their perception of God's activity to change their perceptions, and use that new experience as the basis for reinterpreting Scripture.

The second aspect of the premises I want to amplify slightly is the requirement for responsible hermeneutics to take every voice of Scripture seriously. I spoke of the *auctoritates* as diverse and sometimes contradictory. But every ecclesial decision to live by one rather than another of these voices, to privilege one over another, to suppress one in order to live by another, must be willing to state the grounds of that decision, and demonstrate how the experience of God and the more fundamental principles of "the mind of Christ" and "freedom of the children of God" (principles also rooted in the authority of the text) legitimate the distance between ecclesial decision and a clear statement of Scripture. Do we allow divorce (even if we don't openly call it that) when Jesus forbade it? We must be willing to support our decision by an appeal, not simply to changing circumstances, but to a deeper wisdom given by the Spirit into the meaning of human covenant, and therefore a better understanding of the sayings of Jesus. This is never easy. It is sometimes – as in the case of taking oaths and vows – not even possible. But it is the task of responsible ecclesial hermeneutics.

How does this approach provide a context for the hermeneutics of homosexuality? First, it cautions us against trying to suppress biblical texts which condemn homosexual behavior (Lev. 18:22; Wisd. 14:26; Rom. 1:26–7; 1 Cor. 6:9) or to make them say something other than what they say. I think it fair to conclude that early Christianity knew about homosexuality as it was practiced in Greco-Roman culture, shared Judaism's association of it with the "abominations" of idolatry, and regarded it as incompatible with life in the Kingdom of God. These *auctoritates* emphatically define homosexuality as a vice, and they cannot simply be dismissed.

Second, however, Scripture itself "authorizes" us to exercise the freedom of the children of God in our interpretation of such passages. We are freed, for example, to evaluate the relative paucity of such condemnations. Compared to the extensive and detailed condemnation of economic oppression at virtually every level of tradition, the off-handed rejection of homosexuality appears instinctive and relatively unreflective. We are freed as well to assess the contexts of the condemnations: the rejection of homosexuality, as of other sexual sins, is connected to the incompatibility of *porneia* with life in the Kingdom. We can further observe that the flat rejection of *porneia* (any form of sexual immorality) is more frequent and general than any of its specific manifestations. We are freed, finally, to consider the grounds on which the texts seem to include homosexuality within *porneia*, namely that it is "against nature," an abomination offensive to God's created order.

Such considerations, in turn, provide an opening for a conversation between our human experience (including our religious experience) and the texts of our tradition. Does our experience now support or challenge the assumption that homosexuality is, simply and without exception, an "offense against nature"? Leviticus and Paul considered homosexuality a vice because they assumed it was a deliberate choice that "suppressed the truth about God." Is that a fair assessment of homosexuality as we have come to understand it? It is, of course grossly distorting to even talk about "homosexuality" as though one clearly definable thing were meant. But many of us who have gay and lesbian friends and relatives have arrived with them at the opposite conclusion: for many persons the acceptance of their homosexuality *is* an acceptance of creation as it applies to them. It is emphatically *not* a vice that is chosen. If this conclusion is correct, what is the hermeneutical implication?

Another order of questions concerns the connection of homosexuality to *porneia*. The church, it is clear, cannot accept *porneia*. But what is the essence of "sexual immorality"? In the moral quality of sexual behavior defined biologically in terms of the use of certain body parts, or is it defined in terms of personal commitment and attitudes? Is not *porneia* essentially sexual activity that ruptures covenant, just as *castitas* is sexual virtue within or outside marriage because it is sexuality in service to covenant?

If sexual virtue and vice are defined covenantally rather than biologically, then it is possible to place homosexual and heterosexual activity in the same context. Certainly, the church must reject the *porneia* which glorifies sex for its own sake, indulges in promiscuity, destroys the bonds of commitment, and seduces the innocent. Insofar as a "gay life style" has these connotations, the church must emphatically and always say "no" to it. But the church must say "no" with equal emphasis to the heterosexual "*Playboy/Cosmo* lifestyle" version. In both cases, also, the church can acknowledge that human sexual activity, while of real and great significance, is not wholly determinative of human existence or worth, and can perhaps begin to ask whether the church's concentration on sexual behavior corresponds proportionally to the modest emphasis placed by Scripture.

The harder question, of course, is whether the church can recognize the possibility of homosexual committed and covenantal love, in the way that it recognizes such sexual/personal love in the sacrament of marriage. This is a harder question because it pertains not simply to moral attitudes or pastoral care, but to the social symbolization of the community. The issue here is analogous to the one facing earliest Christianity after Gentiles started being converted. Granted that they had been given the Holy Spirit, could they be accepted into the people of God just as they were, or must they first "become Jewish" by being circumcised and obeying all the ritual demands of Torah? Remember, please, the stakes: the Gentiles were "by nature" unclean, and were "by practice" polluted by idolatry. We are obsessed by the sexual dimensions of the body. The first-century Mediterranean world was obsessed by the social implications of food and table-fellowship. The decision to let the Gentiles in "as is" and to establish a more inclusive form of table-fellowship, we should note, came into direct conflict with the accepted interpretation of Torah and what God wanted of humans.

The decision, furthermore, was not easy to reach. Paul's Letter to the Galatians suggests some of the conflict it generated. Even the irenic Luke devotes five full chapters of Acts (10–15) to the account of how the community caught up with God's intentions, stumbling every step of the way through confusion, doubt, challenge, disagreements, divisions, and debate. Much suffering had to be endured before the implications of Peter's question, "If then God gave the same gift to them as he gave to us when we believed in the Lord Jesus Christ, who was I that could withstand God" (Acts 11:17), could be fully answered: "We believe that we [Jews] shall be saved through the grace of the Lord Jesus, just as they [Gentiles] will" (Acts 15:11).

The grounds of the church's decision then was the work that God was doing among the Gentiles, bringing them to salvation through faith. On the basis of this experience of God's work, the church made bold to reinterpret Torah, finding there unexpected legitimation for its fidelity to God's surprising ways (Acts 15:15–18). How was that work of God made known to the church? Through the narratives of faith related by Paul and Barnabas and Peter, their personal testimony of how "signs and wonders" had been worked among the Gentiles (Acts 15:4, 6–11, 12–13).

Such witness is what the church now needs from homosexual Christians. Are homosexuality and holiness of life compatible? Is homosexual covenantal love according to "the mind of Christ," an authentic realization of that Christian identity authored by the Holy Spirit, and therefore "authored" as well by the Scripture despite the "authorities" speaking against it? The church can discern this only on the basis of faithful witness. The burden of proof required to overturn scriptural precedents is heavy, but it is a burden that has been borne before. The church cannot, should not, define itself in response to political pressure or popularity polls. But it is called to discern the work of God in human lives and adapt its self-understanding in response to the work of God. Inclusivity must follow from evidence of holiness; are there narratives of homosexual holiness to which we must begin to listen?

Homosexuality in the Church: Can there be a Fruitful Theological Debate?

Oliver O'Donovan

This piece shows so much change from earlier, more abstract accounts of homosexuality by noted conservative Oliver O'Donovan (such as the account in Resurrection and Moral Order*) that I found myself moved. I asked O'Donovan how he mustered the tremendous effort of moral imagination it must have taken. He replied that he had written it by reading paragraphs over the phone to a friend dying of AIDS. In this way it represents the sort of moral inquiry that Hauerwas recommends in "Gay Friendship" and the account of communal change commended by others. Notable is the proposal about how God may use minority communities. Advocates of same-sex marriage, however, may find that O'Donovan goes too far now in a "liberal" direction when he assumes in passing that same-sex relationships may be intrinsically more "episodic" than opposite-sex ones, and tries to find ways of approving that feature.*

The title should be understood literally. It is not my intention to explain my opinions about homosexuality, but simply to ask how a fruitful debate can proceed in the Church. Putting the question that way, of course, implies that a fruitful debate is not now taking place. Certainly there is a debate – as the bibliographies attest – and not only about homosexuality as such but about the particular questions that trouble the Church. But one must say, it is a debate 'about', not a debate 'with'. For a truly theological debate to occur, the Church must be able to speak 'with' its homosexual members who have something they wish to say to it. There must be a 'conciliar process', as Bernd

Wannenwetsch has finely described it.[1] Yet at this point we encounter much dispute, no debate.

A debate occurs when people take up the arguments that others have raised against them, and try to give serious answers. To do that they must think their opponents mistaken, certainly, but not wholly foolish or malicious. They must suppose that some misconception, or some partial truth not fully integrated into other truths, has limited their vision. They must accept the burden of showing how the partial truth fits in with other truths, or of identifying and resolving the misconception. This cannot happen while there is still a struggle for rhetorical dominance; that is to say, while each side hopes to win a monopoly for the categories in which they themselves frame the question. For while that goal is in view, it is a matter of strategy to ignore the alternative categories in which the opponent is thinking. One may not grant the opponent the courtesy of direct quotation, but can only attribute to him or her positions framed in one's own categories, which, predictably, will look ridiculous. This describes, not too unjustly I hope, the style of the disagreement heard in the British churches, and even more in the North American; and I need hardly comment on the tendency of media involvement to reinforce their stubborn and bitter character. Sorry as this situation is, we need not suppose that it arises simply from malice or ill-will. It has an epistemological source. When people find themselves moved by convictions which for them have immediate certainty, not subject to dialectical questioning, they will find it imaginatively impossible to accept that there are other certainties, other ways of construing the situation, which may be held without disingenuousness. In this position the only way forward is through debate – real debate, that is, and not mere regulation, by some means or other, of the dispute. I say a 'theological' debate, though that term should be otiose if one takes with due seriousness the fact that this debate must occur within the Church. I do not mean a debate confined to theologians, but a debate which has a theological purpose, to comprehend the truth of the homosexual phenomenon, whatever it may be, in the light of the Christian Gospel.

That this debate has not yet begun, does not mean that new pastoral initiatives, such as that taken recently by the Evangelische Kirche in Germany to authorise non-liturgical blessings for certain homosexual couples, are premature. The logical order may be to achieve a common clarity first, and only then implement it in pastoral action. But this is never actually the order of events. Our search for clarity makes its way forward through thought and action simultaneously. What it does mean, however, is that pastoral decisions made in this context can have only a provisional and experimental character. They cannot provide firm ground upon which we can build, for they do not rest upon the catholic conviction of the Church. *Lex orandi lex credendi* is, in my view, a perilous dictum; and most of all when it suggests that one may dictate *lex credendi* by the shrewd measure of gaining or retaining control over *lex orandi*. This caution applies not only to innovatory practices, such as that recently adopted by the EKD, but conservative practices too. In 1991 the Bishops of the Church of England avowed a policy of not ordaining candidates for ministry who were in homosexual partnerships. This was only a continuation of what had been undeclared practice from time immemorial; but, as those who attacked it quickly appreciated, because of the current confusion in the Church it could have only a hypothetical status. Confusion is precisely the state in which tradition is impotent to exercise its authority over us. Tradition depends for its authority on the general perception that it faithfully mediates the faith and practice of the Gospel.

Here, then, is a task for the Church, and one in which the theologians, though having no monopoly, will have their work cut out. For a long time, I must admit, I held back from engagement with this question, partly out of distaste at the sheer bad temper that it generated, partly because, although I had my own opinions – which of us does not? – I had no clear view of the contribution that a moral theologian ought to make. For the task of the theologian is not simply to engage in the debate on the side that appears to have the greater right; it is to safeguard the Gospel integrity of the debate, by clarifying what the questions are that must be at issue. This point should not be misunderstood. It does not mean that there are no right and wrong decisions, whether at the level of definite action or at the level of rules and principles. Not everything is shrouded in moral ambiguity! Nor does it mean that the theologian must assume a specious irresolution when the argument points irresistibly in one direction. (Karl Rahner's remarks on the false consciousness of moral theologians in the Vietnam War must not be forgotten at this point!) It means simply that, like Ezekiel's watchman on the walls, the theologian has a specific responsibility, which is to make things clear. Whatever decisions are taken in the city, whether in faith or in wilful disobedience, the watchman must ensure they are taken in full consciousness of what is at stake.

In 1995, as the dispute blazed hotter and more virulently within our Church, a small group of theological colleagues and I produced the short position-paper which was called, from the date of its publication, the St Andrew's Day Statement. It was not an 'agreed statement' in the ecumenical mould, composed by representatives of opposed groups. It was the work of an *ad hoc* group that shared a common mind. But its mind was not about the rights and wrongs of homosexuality as such, but about certain key theological principles that it saw implicit in the discussion and believed should be brought to the fore. It was an attempt, in other words, to describe the parameters of a debate which was lacking in the Church, by inviting protagonists to turn back from their immediate certainties and counter-certainties to the ultimate certainties which they would share with other Christian believers. Since the publication of this statement the process has entered a second stage: a series of meetings between its authors and individuals who can be identified as theological voices on either side of the dispute, to explore with them how far the parameters described in the Statement allow them room to formulate positions they wished to put before the Church. Its theological strategy, then, was, after all, ecumenical: it aimed to provide a catholic agreement in faith within which disagreements could be located and pursued constructively.

The St Andrew's Day Statement suggests an answer to one objection that I can envisage being raised against that search. 'What we need', someone might say, 'is not a debate, but a Confession. It is built into the process of debate that the outcome will be some kind of compromise. If we believe that the tradition as we have received it is good and lifegiving, then we ought simply to declare it. Anything else is a fine cloak for retreat and withdrawal.' I take this objection seriously, despite its intransigent sound, because there is plenty of evidence that what it fears will happen, does happen. Light and lazy talk about 'development' and 'new insights' may often do no more than announce a change of fashion. What intellectual historian can deny that great intellectual changes may be brought about by quite unintellectual causes, such as shifts in economic power, collapsing educational institutions and so on? We are right to fear that kind of change in the Church. For we are right to fear unfaithfulness. We should want not to lose our institutional memories, forsake our loyalties and succumb to the forces of irrational change that dictate intellectual currents without intellectual accountability. These are all forms of godlessness, of bondage to arbitrary powers.

In answer to this not negligible anxiety, however, I make two points. First, to describe the parameters of a true Church-debate is already to make a Confession. The St Andrew's Day Statement is a form of Confession as well as a proposal for debate, in that it attempts to declare no more and no less than what the Church must be able to say together if it is to debate fruitfully. Secondly, no Confession, if it is undertaken as a venture in the witness of the Spirit, could be a static affair. It must lead the Church forward. The St Andrew's Day Statement describes the enterprise as follows: 'The Spirit of Jesus Christ . . . directs us in the task of understanding all human life and experience through the Scriptures. And so, guided by the Spirit of God to interpret the times, the church proclaims the Word of God to the needs of each new age' (p. 6). If we put ourselves in the way of that ministry to us, and under that authority, then we are in the way of a true development of Christian understanding as well as being protected against pseudo-developments. It implies learning things we did not know, not randomly substituting new and untried for old and tried wisdom, but by an ordered and coherent growth of Christian testimony, as the Gospel sheds illumination on the needs of a new period of history. Our first and last duty in this sphere is to discern the light the Gospel sheds on the gay movement of our time. The Church must learn to attest its faith in the Gospel before this cultural phenomenon. The gay Christian must learn to attest the truth of the gay self-consciousness in the light of the Gospel. What we commit ourselves to, when we commit ourselves to true debate, is no more and no less than this learning. But let nobody presume to announce in advance what we are going to learn before we come to learn it! That, indeed, is the mark of a false prophet!

In asking how a debate may proceed fruitfully, I consider first how it identifies its object, then the canons of theological understanding that it brings to bear upon it.

Such a debate will not assume that we know precisely what homosexuality is. It will operate in an open theoretical field. If there is anything more disconcerting than the hesitation and uncertainty with which theologians propose their answers on this subject, it is the dogmatic certainty with which they frame their questions. Here, it seems, science and statistics allow us a security that neither faith nor pastoral experience can sustain! Yet while the theologians embrace empirically based accounts, these are more and more repudiated by the intellectuals of the gay movement itself. Inspired in part by Foucault's historical sociology of knowledge, the critique of the 'medicalisation' of homosexuality has become vigorous. The debates pursued within the gay intelligentsia – and especially the debate between the 'essentialist' and 'constructionist' accounts of homosexuality – are important for the Church to overhear, if it is to encompass the full width of the theoretical possibilities, free of pseudo-certainties which are invoked simply to settle questions quickly. Of course, some theories are better supported than others – there is no need for infinite patience with the fantastic. Some theories are more capable of bearing weight – and why should not medical ones be among those that are more worthy of confidence? The point is not to banish all theories but to keep them in play, open to supplement and qualification, to doubt and to testing against experience. 'The true homosexual has no freedom of choice in the matter'; 'the incidence of homosexuality is uniform in all societies, only the recognition of it is variable'; 'homosexuality is the expression of a deeper personality disorder'; 'homosexuality is the product of rapid social change'; 'one is born with a sexual orientation that does not change, only manifests itself'; these are all examples of claims which are often made far too strong. They belong in our discussion only when deployed hypothetically, in a self-conscious strategy of exploration.

And we must bear in mind the fact – here, surely, the word 'fact' is in place – that the homosexual phenomenon is changing before our eyes. Whatever the truth about homosexuality was, we must now reckon also with a cultural movement that has acquired its own social reality. When a group of people with

377

a common cause gains a sense of its own solidity, it develops as a cultural force, defining its aesthetic preferences, its critique of the hegemonic culture, its practices of association and communication, and, of course, its recruiting mechanisms. These, indeed, have given rise to some of the sharpest pastoral, indeed political difficulties, when they have been directed, as they naturally are, at the young. For this cultural movement I use the term 'gay' – its own self-chosen style in the English-speaking lands – while 'homosexual' refers simply to the psychosexual patterns of emotion. To be 'gay' one must have a prevailing interest in homosexuality, an identification with homosexual people, and an assertive programme which may often present itself as a series of demands for accommodation though in some forms of assertiveness, especially those of an artistic order, demand is much less significant than display. Within this description many theoretical and practical differences are accommodated. The gay consciousness is loosely knit theoretically; it has no orthodoxy; which is why a certain *orthopraxis* of aggressive protest and loyal mutual defence is important to its sense of identity. But it is equally clear that not all who think of themselves as homosexual, especially within the Church, want any part of the gay movement. Some of the hostility in the debate arises from the resentment this causes; just as some of the hostility of feminists has been directed not against men but against conservative women.

A good debate will need to be open not only to many theories but to many experiences. In the first place there is the major difference to be noticed between women's and men's experience. A special importance attaches to the female gay culture as it forms a channel by which serious philosophical reflection, largely derived from the French feminists, has influenced the movement. Then we must attend to the experience of those who have been in the gay culture and left it, while still thinking of themselves as homosexual; of those who have been homosexual and have ceased to be; of those who have married and become homosexual subsequently, sometimes in middle life; those who identify with the gay culture aesthetically and morally, though only doubtfully homosexual; literary and cultural gays; educationally low-achieving gays of deprived backgrounds, and so on. All of them demand distinct pastoral, as well as theoretical, recognition. And here I must interject a word about another category, that of the so-called 'bisexual'. The early medical theorists attempted to describe what they called 'true' homosexuality, distinguishing it from various shadow manifestations such as that which occurs in adolescence or in intense single-sex communities. This created a still-current style of psychotherapy which proposed to assist the patient by making an authoritative resolution of ambiguities, pronouncing decisively on whether he or she was a 'true' homosexual. Considering the criticism addressed to other psychotherapeutic techniques in this field, one can only be surprised at the complaisance with which this technique has been accepted. But if statistics do anything useful, they warn us of the dangers of this either – or categorisation. A larger proportion of the human race, apparently, has the capacity to respond to sexual stimuli of both same-sex and other-sex types than responds only to same-sex types. What is needed is not to sweep this considerable number of moderately sensitive human beings into one or the other of two abstract categories, but to develop a less rigid view of how sexual stimulation affects the whole personality. Here, too, the problem is that we are theory-bound.

Beside listening to theories and experiences, a debate will attend to proposals from the gay culture, and will take them the more seriously the more they rise above the level of demand and recrimination and begin to articulate what the movement stands for, its vision and its critique of society. Some gay thinkers have located themselves within the various strands of modernity-criticism; that alone must give what they say a particular interest. I mention, as an engaging example, the Canadian writer Scott Symons, who in 1965 left his marriage and his career, choosing (as he insists!) to adopt a gay lifestyle in protest against the dominance of the Liberal Party in Canadian politics, the stranglehold of Presbyterian and Methodist traditions in Ontario (he himself being an occasional Anglican worshipper), and the syllabus for teaching English literature at the University of Toronto. He said: 'there was a sense of vocation, and a sense of civic action . . . I knew that this was where one had to move, to open the doors to male sentience'.[2] What would this programme mean? How does the 'erotisation of society', to use a phrase which has gained some currency, offer liberation from sin and oppression to all of us? Could it even be a serious alternative to the *sexualisation* of society, which we experience at present without any of the beauty or the joy in creation that eros may be thought to connote? Could it mean a liberation, that is, from the legacy of Sigmund Freud? Of course, I do not know the answers to these questions; but they are questions which would certainly be asked in the course of a good debate.

Addressing now the theological content of the debate, we begin with a brief prolegomenon. The theological weight cannot rest wholly upon biblical exegesis. In theological circles where the need for debate has been felt, this, understandably, has been the first route taken, and much thought has been given to the brief and uncompromisingly negative references to homosexuality in Scripture, either explaining their tone as responses to special cultural features which were an aspect of that practice in biblical times, or insisting on the essential identity of the phenomenon despite variations. (A third type of proposal has been to dismiss the whole attempt to get insight from exegesis, a move which in my view lacks theological responsibility.) In finding the exegetical discussion inconclusive, I do not think it can be dispensed with – wearisome as some aspects of it have been. Faced with yet another attempt to get at the meaning of *arsenokoites* by philology, I cry: Enough! You have satisfied the curiosity of a generation!

It is a principle in the hermeneutics of biblical ethics, that scriptural precepts bear upon us as they are mediated through evangelical doctrine. The difficulty with the biblical references to homosexuality is that they are so incidental that they give us little help in situating them doctrinally. The famous discussion in Romans 1, however, is an exception, articulating a connection between homosexuality and idolatry, which are treated as two aspects of a cultural development. (A mirror-image, one might think of the view of Scott Symons, for whom marriage had become the emblem of the idolatrous ex-Puritanism that had dominated Canadian society.) If we could explore the relation between worship and patterns of sexual behaviour to which St Paul points us, we could, I think, achieve a more effective grip on the problems before us. We need, however, a broader doctrinal base than those texts on their own afford, yet not forgetting that they, too, demand an account.

Let us begin, then, from a systematic question, the question of *identity*. What can be meant by this term, and can there be such a thing as a homosexual identity? 'I have become a great question to myself' (Augustine, *Conf.* IV.4.9). We ask ourselves 'Who am I', 'What am I?', and the term 'identity' serves to sum up the answers we reach. But Christians believe there is a definite order to be observed in finding those answers. We may not simply consult the most immediate data of our self-consciousness; the risk of self-misunderstanding is never absent from those data and is always perilous. Our identities, the Gospel tells us, are given us in Christ risen from the dead; they are to be found within that lordly humanity which stands before God in the 'last Adam'. Other identities, whether national, class, family or whatever, are relative and secondary. But there can be no fundamental divisions within that restored human nature. Even the division between male and female is, from the point of view of Galatians 3:28, eschatologically suspended, though it is given back to us as an element of restored creation, to be reclaimed and reinterpreted. What status, then, has the identity-claim 'I am a homosexual'? In the minds of those who make this claim, is there a division between homosexual and heterosexual, fundamental to the human race, like that described, for example, in Aristophanes' speech in Plato's *Symposium*? Such a conception could have no theological standing. Even the male–female division itself is acknowledged only to the extent that it serves as an integrating factor in the redeemed human race: 'The woman is not without the man nor the man without the woman in the Lord' (1 Cor. 11:11), a remark which reaches beyond sexual attraction to encompass all the varied ways in which our awareness of our own humanity is given to us through the mediation of the opposite sex. The formal distinction between this division and a supposed hetero-/homosexual division is plain: heterosexuals are not drawn to homosexuals nor homosexuals to heterosexuals, as men are drawn to women and women to men. Where the division between the sexes functions as a polar structure that ensures relationship, the division between the sexual orientations would be a structure of apartness. The authors of the St Andrew's Day Statement, then, concluded that they must make a definite denial: 'At the deepest ontological level . . . there can be no such thing as "a" homosexual or "a" heterosexual; there are human beings, male and female, called to redeemed humanity in Christ.' I am bound to say that I think this denial essential: it marks a limit upon what the Church can, with any integrity, contemplate. If it is asked to adopt some alternative myth of creation-order to replace that in which Adam acclaims Eve as 'bone of my bone and flesh of my flesh', it can only refuse.

But short of this confessional point there may be ways in which a homosexual identity can be contemplated, just as forms of national and class-identity can be contemplated, within the Christ-given human identity that admits of no division. Not every form of apartness is a denial of that fundamental togetherness. We have been used in this century to confronting potentially or actually idolatrous forms of national apartness; perhaps this has made us too slow to recognise non-idolatrous forms, which offer service to the unity and co-ordination of the whole. Lest I be suspected here of advocating the characteristic British view of national identities, let me mention a very different example. I have a special concern for small and threatened linguistic communities, which preserve in their separate speech a special poetry and a special insight without which the world would be poorer. At Pentecost all heard the Gospel in their own language; none had to abandon their linguistic identity to hear it. But a small language needs a certain cultural apartness; it can be too easily destroyed by the erosion of a powerful lingua franca. To assist such a community to find the shelter that it needs could be a service offered in good conscience to God, and also to the wider human community which needs pluriformity of language and culture to fulfill its calling. In that case an 'identity' assumed within this community would not be a stubborn element of alien loyalty which resisted Christ's identity, but a 'vocation' to serve in a certain distinct context and manner. Could we find an analogy here? Could a homosexual 'identity' become a vocation?

The concept of vocation is a differentiated one. It arises in the first place from the passage of 1 Corinthians 7 where St Paul advises newly converted Christians to remain in the state 'in which' they were called. A vocation is here the objective social condition within which one finds oneself, so that one's first duty, though not necessarily one's last, is to occupy it as a Christian witness. But the use of the term extends further, especially in Reformed thought, to include what St Paul calls a *charisma*, something one is given in particular by God. And this again has two senses. Elsewhere in the same chapter Paul refers to the alternative states of marriage and singleness as 'gifts': 'each has his own gift from God, one this way, one that' (7:7). This is a personal fitness for one of these two forms of social existence. But in 1 Corinthians 12 the term recurs in a yet more individualised sense, as an endowment of the Holy Spirit to enable the individual to exercise a special function within the body which will complement the functions of others. This gives us three senses, then, of ascending force, in which we might ask whether there could be such a thing as a vocation to be a homosexual Christian: an objective condition 'within which' one must learn to serve Christ; a fitness for either marriage or singleness; and an equipment for a special service one may render the whole body.

But together with the notion of vocation we must explore the notion of *sin*. That these two conceptions of the gay Christian's position, apparently opposed, must be considered together, should not surprise us, if we are alert to the dynamics of the concept of vocation in Paul's thought: his example of a condition within which one is called is slavery – which he views as prima facie contrary to the liberty of a Christian ('I do not want you to be slaves of men'), and his argument for marriage as a state for which some are fitted turns upon the problem of *porneia*. The difficulty we feel in bringing together the notions of vocation and sin arises from the shrinking of our conception of sin to a voluntarist idea of particular transgression, torn out of the wider context of need and despair which are so important if we are to grapple with the relation of sin to the emotions. I take it that the Vatican was seen to be adopting this shrunken and legalistic idea when it spoke (in the SCDF's *Personae Humanae* of 1975) of 'homosexual acts' as 'intrinsically disordered and . . . never to be approved'; and that this is one reason why those words won so few friends even in churches inclined to a conservative view.

This perception may have some justice. Still, there is another reason why one might reasonably confine one's negative judgment to homosexual *acts*, and that is to leave questions about emotion, patterns of affection and, most strikingly, domestic provision, questions which the moral tradition as a whole has never been under pressure to resolve decisively, wide open. It is also to distance this judgment from judgments about the attribution of personal fault, of which it is said twice in the same paragraph that there is no straightforward correlation between the one judgment and the other. Of course, in noticing this point one should not credit the Vatican with the view – indefensible in itself as well as alien to Roman Catholic teaching – that the objective assessment of an act and the subjective obligation of an agent are quite separable and unrelated matters. It is simply that the correlation of objective and subjective is complex. And if we assume charitably that the complexity was mentioned at that point in the document not as a way of cutting the discussion short but of opening it up, then we have here, too, an encouragement to undertake the kind of debate we envisage: one which is open at once both to the question of a homosexual vocation and to the judgment, so strongly supported by Scripture, that in the sexual act performed between persons of the same sex we confront a manifestation of the fallen and sinful character of our humanity. The essential element, as I suppose, in this latter judgment is that human powers of *physical sexual* expression are tied decisively to the polar opposition of the two sexes and so to their mutual attraction. The ground for taking up the question of vocation, on the other hand, is that the *emotional and affective* expressiveness of human beings, closely intertwined with the sexual powers from a psychological point of view, are not simply bi-polar but multifaceted. To give the physical polarity its due, and at the same time to give the affective variety its due, is the demanding task which confronts any responsible description; and for this we need to deploy both the category of sin and the category of vocation.

One could imagine a minimal claim for a homosexual 'vocation' in the weakest sense of that word: someone already living in a partnership becomes a Christian, and conceives him or herself to have a primary duty of fidelity to the partner – not excluding the duty to maintain a sexual relationship on which the other is dependent. This claim could be made by someone who accepted *au pied de la lettre* the traditional assessment of homosexual acts, since it requires only a generous concept of pastoral expediency. It would be analogous to policies now not infrequently admitted by churches in polygamous cultures, of permitting a new male convert to preserve a polygamous household.

A second, stronger claim could arise from the idea of vocation as a fitness for marriage. If this fitness is discerned in terms of a lack of fitness for the celibate life, then it would seem that some people are fitted for intimate partnership but not with the opposite sex. The same emotional need, the same threatening possibility of *porneia* and the disintegration that it brings in its train, require us to acknowledge para-marital states in which the couple assist each other in their discipleship by mutual affection and faithfulness. This claim does not require the additional insistence, which on our grounds would make it inherently unacceptable, that homosexual and heterosexual marriage have equal ontological status. It is perfectly compatible with the belief that heterosexual marriage is the norm, homosexual 'marriage' the adaptation. To that extent it can retain the judgment that homosexual acts are 'intrinsically disordered'; but it cannot retain the corollary, 'never to be approved'. For the sake of remedy for sin, the argument goes, this accommodation should be approved, since it is what these disciples are fitted for and to that extent called to. The nearest analogy for such a para-marital condition, besides the polygamous one already suggested, lies in the way those who think marriage intrinsically indissoluble view the second marriages – for them, 'marriages' – of divorced people: not marriages in the full sense, but an approximation to marriage which may be the best course morally available for those involved. (This analogy, of course, carries less weight in a mainstream Protestant tradition where such marriages are viewed as ontologically real marriages, though they may be regrettable ones.)

It has been widely assumed in the Church that some form of claim for homosexual marriage is *the* challenge that the gay movement presents. This, however, has been put in question recently by two gay Christian writers, Elizabeth Stuart and Michael Vasey, who have argued independently that marriage is not the right paradigm for homosexual relations, but that 'affective friendship' is what the homosexual is fitted for. For Vasey an important reference point within the tradition is the role of single-sex monastic communities which illustrate how structures may be devised for unmarried Christians to find scope for committed relationships within the context of shared domestic life.[3] (This is the correct use to be made of Aelred of Rievaulx's *On Spiritual Friendship*, a work from which much more tendentious conclusions have sometimes been drawn.) On this account the sexual element in a homosexual friendship is neither so important to the relation itself nor so important a problem to be got over in defending it. If the marriage-model builds on the traditional concept of remedy for sin, the friendship model could be said to exploit the Augustinian idea of excess sexual energy as venial sin, unnecessary to the logic of the relationship and to that extent unhelpful, but, when accepted with patient good humour by the partner, unharmful too. This approach, though capable of accepting, perhaps, that in some sense a homosexual act was both 'intrinsically disordered' and 'not to be approved', would be inclined to protest against the opinion (again from the Vatican) that 'to judge homosexual relationships (i.e. sexual ones) indulgently . . . goes against the . . . moral sense of the Christian People'. *Indulgentia* is precisely the term used by Augustine in relation to this excess of sexuality, and, indeed, perfectly characterises the view that the whole anxiety of the Christian tradition over sexual *acts* has been overdone. This view, indeed, since it has no interest in emulating the exclusive lifelong bond of marriage, is prepared to view 'indulgently' even what the advocates of the marriage-model are inclined to deplore as 'promiscuity'. Yet at the same time it would de-emphasise the importance of a sexual element to a serious relationship.

This is one of those disagreements of gays among themselves that the Church has to listen attentively to. I welcome the alternative model, in that it seems to take seriously, and, indeed, even make a virtue of, an often-observed feature of male homosexual relationships, their episodic character, and so brings a rather wider range of homosexual experience into the discussion. Consider what happens if we think of homosexual relations as para-marriages, and perhaps introduce some kind of Church recognition of them. After some years' cohabitation, a male couple may say to each other, 'We will always be grateful and always love each other; but for each of us to pursue his life's goals at this point it is better for us to part, not from incompatibility or breakdown, but simply in pursuit of new horizons.' The marriage-model requires the Church to frown on this. But would it be right to do so? Could it be certain that the arguments which would apply to a marriage would apply here also? I, certainly, am not certain; and so I welcome the opportunity to engage with an account of the gay consciousness that treats the homosexual dynamic as simply different.

The third concept of vocation is the strongest. May we discern a special gift that the gay Christian has to offer the Church? This notion could, I think, be intelligible if we were to frame it in terms of prophecy, and ask whether there is some message that is offered for our common upbuilding – something, that is, more than a demand for accommodation, something about the authenticity and integrity of Christian living. It is easier to envisage such a message, I would think, emerging from that side of the gay movement that advocates an affective dimension of friendship, for there it is more evident how what it has to say would touch us all. One might, building on suggestions in their writings, conceive the message as follows. The Church made a mistake when it swallowed the uncompromising critique of Eros which was developed in the first half of this century out of Kierkegaard by figures such as Anders Nygren and Denis de Rougemont, riding on the anti-idealist wave that swept through Christian thought at the time. Eros, the quest for the ultimate, mediated through earthly beauty and its hold on our desires, is essential to the joy and delight of the Gospel. It liberates the energies evoked by sexual imagery for transference to the higher cultural, moral and spiritual goods, commuting the yearnings of the body into the heroism of the soul and the visionary rapture of the spirit. To be a fellowship of Agape, the Church must at the same time be a fellowship of Eros. The homosexual, with a special gift for affective friendship, serves to cultivate Eros in the Church, to renew its sensitivity and its instinctive responsiveness to beauty, and so to attest the beauty of God.

There, at any rate, is a thesis worthy of debate, the more interesting in that it has parallels with other theses that have emerged from quite different quarters. I do not know where the debate could lead us. One thinks at once, of course, of counter-theses and counter-questions. How could a Christian Eros acknowledge the critique of idolatry, such as arises from Deuteronomy or Deutero-Isaiah, with its strongly anti-iconic bias? How seriously will a gay eroticism take the ascetic disciplines which are associated with the erotic ladder of ascent? My point is not to pursue the debate here and now, but merely to point to it as the road by which we might move out from the present stalemate to discover something together. Will that happen? Well, it depends considerably upon how the Christian gay movement addresses the Church. So long as it is content to present itself in the guise of injured protest, armed with a list of rights it has been denied, then, whatever does happen, a meeting of minds will not happen. The language of rights is completely impotent to resolve this kind of issue. 'Right', it used to be said, 'flows from the spring of righteousness'. Rights are not foundational; they derive from that fabric of right (in the singular) that belongs to the network of relations that constitutes reality. Until there is agreement upon what is *real*, any discussion about what is *right* remains floating in the air. The rights that some claim to be deprived of appear to others as no more than the moral furniture of a fantastic and make-believe world. If, however, the gay movement conceives its role theologically, and assumes, not only in rhetoric but in substance, the task of speaking to the Church out of the word of God, then, whether what it says is what I have projected for it or something else, the Church will have something it must listen to. Only, one word of caution for those who speak and those who listen when God's word is abroad. The first, and surely the hardest demand that it makes on them is: patience.

Notes

1 'Das natürliche und die Moral', *Zeitschrift für Evangelische Ethik*, 38, no. 3, 1994, 168–89.
2 'The Decade of the Last Chance: An Interview with Scott Symons', *The Idler* (Toronto), 23, 1989, 21–30.
3 Michael Vasey, *Strangers and Friends* (Hodder & Stoughton, 1995). Elizabeth Stuart, *Just Good Friends* (Mowbray, 1995).

Theology amidst the Stones and Dust

James Alison

Continuing in the ecclesiological vein, this essay is remarkable and moving for proposing how disputants in the culture wars might come to forgive one another.

> *"For surely your servants take delight in its stones, and are moved to pity by its dust."*
>
> (Psalm 102:14)

A Heart-close-to-cracking

I would like to create with you something like a space in which a heart might find permission to come close to cracking. It is a space which I am discovering to be necessary for participation in theological discourse. This closeness-to-cracking comes upon us at a moment when we do not know how to speak well, when we find ourselves threatened by confusion. It is where the two principal temptations are either to bluster our way out of the moment, by speaking with too much security and arrogance so as to give the impression that the confusion is not mine, but belongs somewhere else. Or on the other hand to plunge into the shamed silence of one who knows himself uncovered, and for that reason, deprived of legitimate speech. This space of the heart-close-to-cracking, poorly as it seems to promise, and difficult though it be to remain in it once it is found and occupied, seems to me the most appropriate space from which to begin a sketch of ways forward towards the stutter of a theology for the third millennium.

I would like to take three biblical moments to help us in the creation of this space, three examples which point in the same direction. The first moment is in the text, and the other two are, rather, moments from which texts have been forged. Let us look closely, first of all, at the prophet Elijah. The altars of Yahweh are in ruins, Ahab's régime favours the followers of Baal. Elijah, the champion of Yahwism, undertakes to wage a valiant war against the prophets of Baal, organizing a competition to see which god can burn a sacrificed bull with fire from heaven. As the prayers and litanies of the prophets of Baal pile up, Elijah mocks them, suggesting, among other things, that perhaps Baal can't put in an appearance owing to being busy with a bowel movement. When it is Elijah's turn to offer his sacrifice, first he rebuilds the altar of Yahweh, then soaks his bull completely, and boom! the lightening strikes. All present fall to the ground, crying: "The Lord is the true God." Elijah immediately takes advantage of this unanimity to point his finger at the 450 prophets of Baal, ordering that they be seized and killed. His order is at once obeyed.

After this triumph, feeling somewhat depressed, Elijah goes off to the desert, where he desires death. God gives him food necessary for survival, but not even that pleases him much, and an angel has to tell him to eat up, and then to go for a 40-day and 40-night hike to Mount Horeb, like Moses to whom God had spoken at the same place. Once there, Elijah hides in a cave, where God has to come and find the disillusioned prophet. God asks him what he's doing there, and he replies:

> I have been very jealous for the LORD, the God of hosts; for the people of Israel have forsaken thy covenant, thrown down thy altars, and slain thy prophets with the sword; and I, even I only, am left; and they seek my life, to take it away.[1]

God orders him to come out of the cave and to stand before the Lord, who announces that he is going to pass by. Well, you know the story: first comes a mighty wind which rends the mountains and breaks the rocks in pieces, but the Lord was not in the wind. Then comes an earthquake, but the Lord was not in the earthquake, and then comes a fire, but the Lord was not in the fire. After the fire there comes a still small voice. At this Elijah goes and stands at the entrance to the cave, and God speaks to him, asking what he's doing there, and once again, Elijah repeats:

> I have been very jealous for the LORD, the God of hosts; for the people of Israel have forsaken thy covenant, thrown down thy altars, and slain thy prophets with the sword; and I, even I only, am left; and they seek my life, to take it away.[2]

Then, in an extraordinary anticlimax, God tells him to go to Damascus to anoint Jehu king, and to pick Elisha as his successor, adding that God will reserve for himself 7,000 men who haven't bent the knee before Baal. Elijah goes off and obeys. From then on his interventions are few until he's whisked off to heaven and Elisha's ministry begins.

So, what seems to be a story of the triumph of Yahwism is in fact presented as the story of the undeceiving of Elijah. Elijah before his undeceiving was a champion fighter without problems of self-esteem or self-confidence. God was a god like Baal, but bigger and tougher, and Elijah was his spokesman, the one who pointed out his victims. The contest of Mount Carmel was a splendid battle between rival shamans or witch-doctors. After the bloody interlude, which he had won, Elijah sinks into a depression, and doubts the value of all that:

Enough, O Lord, take away my life; for I am no better than my fathers.[3]

The sacred author presents us with something rather remarkable: not a series of praises for the Yahwist champion, but rather the story of how Elijah learnt not to identify God with all those special effects which he had known how to manipulate to such violent effect. All the commotion around Mount Horeb is presented as something rather like a deconstruction of the sacred scenario associated with Moses, for the Lord was present in the still small voice, rather than in something of more imposing majesty. Furthermore, rather than taking advantage of the zeal which Elijah bleats on about, Yahweh gives the prophet some rather modest tasks – instructions for passing on command to others. Where Elijah, thinking himself something of a heroic martyr, tells God that he's the only one who has remained loyal, Yahweh tells him that he has 7,000 men up his sleeve who haven't bent the knee before Baal. One can understand what might be meant by zeal exercised on behalf of a god who appears with hurricanes, earthquakes, and fires. But what on earth might it mean to be zealous in the service of a still, small voice? It is a somewhat humbled Elijah who sets off to carry out his appointed tasks.

Well, I'd like to suggest that this scene offers us a valuable witness to the theological process which is at work in the development of the Hebrew scriptures: the theological power of the crisis of confidence which goes along with the collapse of the sacred. At the beginning we have a sacred Yahwism, which can shine alongside another sacred religion, but whose sacrifices are more efficacious, whose God is more powerful, and whose capacity to unite people for a sacred war is greater. Then we have all that undone. The still small voice says much more than it seems to: it says that God is not a rival to Baal, that God is not to be found in the appearances of sacred violence, Elijah, when he entered into rivalry with the prophets of Baal became one of them, because God is not to be found in such circuses, nor in the murders which go along with them. At the end of his undeceiving, Elijah is more Yahwist, more atheist, less of a shaman, less of a sacrificer, because God is not like the gods, not even so as to show himself superior to them. The cave of Horeb was, for Elijah, the theological space for a cracking of heart.

Here we are face to face with the collapse of the sacred, a real demolition of personal structures and ways of speaking about God. This collapse is the crucible in which theological development is wrought. I would like to point to two key moments where just such a collapse of the sacred is combined with the boldest theological development. The first moment is the fall of Jerusalem in 587 BCE. Think what this would have meant to you if you had been a Judean of that time. Not only had your capital been sacked and your king, court, and intellectuals deported. The Temple was destroyed, there where you had thought that Yahweh would dwell forever. The monarchy was brought to an end, where you had thought that God had promised that David's line would reign in perpetuity. Now there is no worship, no sacrifice: the priesthood is in exile. The bulwarks which gave structure to the worship of the one true God have all been knocked flying. It even seemed as though the Babylonian gods, Marduc and company, must be superior to Yahweh, since they had triumphed over him, and dragged off his followers. Let us try to imagine this from within, put ourselves in the place of these our forefathers in faith. Our books of theology imagine this as a moment of decisive rupture in the intellectual history of the development of universal monotheism, but they absolve us from appreciating the process of that development. The process is likely to have been experienced as one of total annihilation. All the structures of group belonging, of personal, family and tribal belonging, in the dust. The whole imaginative world within which Yahweh was worshiped, torn to shreds. We gravely underestimate the force of what happened if we don't understand that the process of recovery, which gave rise to a religion of texts, and of interpretation of texts, with the temple, the cult and the monarchy relegated to second place or, in the case of the monarchy, treated as an utopia, this process of recuperation which undertook to rescue elements from among the ruins was, in truth, little less than a new religion, the new form of community life which we call Judaism.

The process which we see is the process of an upset which forces the gradual learning of how to become unattached from everything which seemed divine and holy, the collapse of zeal for the Lord of hosts. At the same time it leads to an apprenticeship in listening to the still, small voice, and the reinvention of a new type of zeal. This means the reinvention of a new form of Yahwist life, where Yahweh is disassociated from many of the things which had seemed immutable and indispensable elements of his worship.

The third biblical moment which shares this same structure and which I wish to examine with you is the conversion of Saul. I say the same structure, because Paul himself points it out. In his letter to the Galatians,[4] when he describes his own conversion, Paul narrates it with allusions to the story of Elijah: he used to persecute with great violence, and he advanced beyond his compatriots in having a zeal (the word is key) much greater than theirs. After his experience of conversion, he didn't consult with anybody, but immediately went off to the desert, like Elijah, and from there he returned to Damascus, where Elijah had to go, after his experience with the still small voice, to anoint Jehu. So, Paul narrates his experience within the framework provided by Elijah's collapse of zeal that we have just seen. His whole life and apostolic experience afterwards is marked by the collapse of a sacred world within which he had been an especially ferocious militant, a collapse produced by the recognition that in his zeal to serve God, it had been God whom he had been persecuting. For him the still small voice was the voice of the crucified and risen victim whose breath is the Holy Spirit.

I emphasize this for a simple reason. As a backdrop for the theological discussion which I wish to begin with you, I want to bring out a very important dimension of the experience of the resurrection which normally doesn't get its due hearing. The experience of the novelty, vitality and exuberance of God which was provoked among the apostolic witnesses by the appearances of the risen Lord, and which little by little changed their whole perspective and imagination, was not only an experience of an addition to a pre-existing good. To each step of the clearer and more complete revelation of God, that is to say, to each purification of faith, there is a corresponding and simultaneous collapse of a whole series of elements which seemed to have been indispensable bulwarks of faith. For these elements turn out to be parts of an idolatrous order of things which had previously been confused with the worship of the true God. This emphasizes something which I imagine to be obvious, though little mentioned in Catholic treatises on faith, which is that faith in the living God automatically introduces into the world a process of unbelieving. Someone who begins to believe in the living God automatically begins to lose faith in the inevitability of things. Things like fate, the sacredness of the social order, inevitable progress, horoscopes, and so on. For the moment our imagination and emotional and mental structures begin to absorb what is meant by the vivaciousness of the Creator God who brings into being and sustains all things, all those other elements start to be revealed as part of a dead sacred order, as attributions, of divinity and thus of fixity, to things which are human, which are structured socially, culturally, and economically, and are for that reason dependent on human responsibility and potentially mutable through the exercise of that same responsibility.

There is more. The resurrection, as it was received, incarnated, and understood by Paul, not only provoked a purification of the human perspective on God. That purification was shown to be absolutely inseparable from the presence of a crucified and risen human victim, whose presence inaugurates and keeps perpetually alive a process of desacralization of the religious matrix within which the crucifixion and resurrection had occurred, and within which Saul had been a certain sort of participant. All of Paul's preaching, all of his theology, is characterized by the process of the collapse of a certain sacred structure, and by the slow discovery of the perspective given by a new focus on Yahweh, the Pauline equivalent of Elijah's still small voice. Paul's whole argument about the Law is nothing other than the attempt to make it clear that, from the moment when the resurrection makes present the crucified one as a constant hermeneutical companion in our living of the religion of Yahweh, even that which had seemed sacred and untouchable in that religion, the very Torah of God, is desacralized. It has to be understood according to whether it contributes to the sacrifice of other victims within a sacred order, or whether it is interpreted in such a way as to deconstruct the world of sacrifices and sacred orders.

I would like to suggest something else. Paul understood very well that, starting from his experience, what was wanted was not the foundation of a new religion, which might forge a new sacred order more in accordance with the new perspective on Yahweh. What was wanted rather was the preaching of the constancy in our midst of the presence of God as crucified and risen victim. The very fact of that presence opens up the possibility of living in the world by means of the continuous deconstruction of the artificial sacred in all the forms of life in which we find ourselves, contributing in this way to the construction of a new form of human social life where every apparently sacred social distinction begins to be knocked down, leading to an as yet unimagined fraternity.

So this experience, the experience of the collapse of the sacred which we saw in the case of Elijah and in the Jewish exile, is not a moment of the past, but a constant part of the process of the faith which is being brought into being. We cannot understand the preaching of the resurrection if it is understood as a miraculous moment which founds a new religion. If it is taken thus, we are in fact denying the force and efficacy of the resurrection. For the resurrection brings about the definitive installation in our midst, as a constructive hermeneutical principle, of the cult of Yahweh who knows not death, and who is worshiped in a continuous apprenticeship in participating in, and not being scandalized by, the collapse of the sacred. A sacred whose secret is always the victims which it hides, and on whose sacrifice it depends.

This, then, is what I understand by making space for a heart close to cracking: the space where we learn to forge a way of talking about God in the midst of the ruins of the forms of the sacred which are in full collapse. A space where we recognize our own complicity in the sacred forms of the past, with all their violence and their victims. A space where we are coming to understand that God has nothing to do with all that, but also a space where we learn, precisely in the midst of the deconstruction of all that, new ways of speaking words of God so as to participate in the new creation. That is to say, it is the Eucharistic space *par excellence*, where Christ is present as the crucified one, and we as penitents learning to step out of solidarity with our multiple and varied modes of complicity in crucifixion; but where Christ is present as crucified and risen Lord, so not as accusation of our participation, but as fount of, and power for, a new, unimagined, and unending reconstruction.

If I've taken my time to get to this point, which is perhaps far too obvious, it is because it seems to me that we find ourselves in the midst of just such ruins. At the turn of the millennium, and at thirty-something years from the end of Vatican II, we find ourselves in the midst of a shouting match between two sorts of sacred, two types of sacred zeal. On the one hand the restoring trumpet blasts of a Catholicism nostalgic for a sacred and stable past, upholder of purity of doctrine and of customs, of sacred differences and sacrificial techniques for the maintenance of order and unity. On the other hand, a no less sacred trumpet blast, that of those who adopt the position of victims, who make of positions of authentic marginalization sure platforms for protest, for the revindication of innocence and of sacred status. Both these sacred blasts have their priesthoods capable of pointing the finger at those who do not conform, demanding the sacrifice of those who do not participate in the unanimity of the group. In one case as in the other, the question which gives away the sacrificial mentality underlying group belonging is the same: are you for us, or are you one of them? It is the question which reveals the impossibility of a cracking of heart, and thus the impossibility of Eucharist. What I would like to suggest is that both trumpet blasts are phantoms, the noise of those who do not accept the reality of being in the midst of ruins, who don't accept that Jerusalem has been razed to the ground, and who do not know how to take delight in its stones, nor are capable of being moved by pity for its dust, so as, with these unpromising remains, to take part in the building up of the new Jerusalem.

Receiving a Perspective

One of the things which is clear from the stories of Elijah, of the returning exiles, and of Paul, is that they had nowhere to start except from where they found themselves to be. There was no universal principle, all-embracing idea, or preformed discourse which they could simply adopt. They couldn't be converted to something pre-existent, learning how to adapt themselves to its rules and ways of structuring self and belonging. The only perspective which was available to them, and starting from which they might make sense of the stones and the dust, was their own. And, please note, their perspective in each case was not that of someone who has just arrived at the scene, innocent, with a *tabula rasa* for a personality, someone who starts everything anew, a heroic founder. That would be a grabbed perspective, heroic, but incapable of a cracking of heart. No, in each case, the perspective from which they had to begin was a perspective received by the process of finding themselves to have been involved in something which had been knocked to the ground. Without that knocking down, there would have been no such perspective. In each case their perspective was received by the force of the circumstances within which they had participated, and within which their participation had been, in one way or another, shaken to the core.

I would like to suggest that if there is to be Catholic theology in the third millennium, a similar process awaits us all. The space which allows us close to a cracking of heart is the space where we learn to receive our perspective, so as from there to be able to learn to speak well of, and to imitate, God. The perspective will be, in the case of each one of us, rather different. For catholicity doesn't mean a unity of perspective from which we start, but the discovery and construction of a real and surprising fraternity which begins with overcoming the tendency to forge from our own perspective a sacred which excludes. It is in this context, then, that I offer elements of the perspective within which I am finding myself, as a resource which may perhaps be useful in your own construction of catholicity. I am very conscious that I am from a culture, race, language, background, and history that is strange to most of you, and for that reason I am far from imagining that what I have to say will reach you all in the same way. However, I hope that, however foreign to your experience be the elements of this story, you will find something in it capable of arousing an echo in your own.

Some years ago, in a Latin American republic which I will not name, I found myself in a strange situation. I had arrived to take up a new job as a teacher of theology. After three days, my boss called me in and said: "Bad news, James. I've received a phone call from fourteen religious superiors who are meeting in another country to tell me that if I don't sack you immediately on the grounds that you are a militant homosexual, then those superiors will not send any pupils to our course." This threat implied the non-arrival of the money necessary for the course to function. Now please note this: the superiors made no allegation of a homosexual practice on my part, and at no time in the investigation which followed did they raise that as a question. The accusation was one of, let us say, a political or ideological militancy. My boss, an honest heterosexual, who found it difficult to understand the force of the violence unleashed by the gay question in the ecclesiastical milieu, absolutely refused to sack me, offering to resign his post rather than to accept such blackmail. A higher superior intervened, suggesting to the fourteen superiors that they had acted without the proper procedure, and that each one should put into writing and sign any accusation that he might have against me, so that the accused could answer his accusers. That is, the superior insisted on due process. However, no written charge was made. When an informal enquiry wondered whether there might be some accusation that one of them might like to mention, but not write down, again there was no accusation. One or two apparently said "Of course, I don't know the guy personally, but I have it from a very good source that . . ."

Well, this is the story of a fairly unpleasant piece of violence, and I could embellish it in such a way as to win your sympathy, presenting myself as a victim. In that case the very act of telling the story would be something like a denunciation, and there would be goodies and baddies in the story. If that were the case, I would have learnt nothing from the incident. I would have adopted one of the perspectives which our culture offers us, that of the sacred victim. And I would have adopted that perspective as a weapon with which to attack one of the stereotypical "baddies" with which our culture also supplies us, the obscurantist and violent group of ecclesiastics. Thank God, much though I would have liked to present things in this way, God did not indulge me. Some weeks later, still devastated by what had happened, I went off to make a Jesuit retreat, and in the midst of that retreat something totally unexpected reached me: a perspective which I had perhaps understood intellectually, but which had never got through to my gut. It was the absolute separation of God from all that violence. I understood something new: that God had nothing to do with what had happened, and that it was simply a mechanism of human violence, nothing more. What enabled me to reach this, and here I am talking, of course, of the human means, was the realization that, since of this group of fourteen, I had only ever met three, all that violence (and apparently they had worked themselves up over this for a couple of days, finding it difficult to get round to the agenda of their meeting) could not be taken personally. Rather it was a mechanism within which the participants had got themselves caught up in such a way that they couldn't perceive what they were doing. The moment I realized that I was dealing with a mechanism whose participants were its prisoners, at that same moment I was able to take distance from what had happened, and forgiveness started to become possible.

However, that perception was not all. For, when I understood that God had nothing to do with all that violence, I began to understand something much more painful: the degree of my own participation in the mechanism of violence, not as its victim, but as a manipulator. For the charge that I was an "Internationally known homosexual militant" did not fall like lightening from a clear sky. Rather this incident was the third time that my behavior and attitudes in different countries had provoked a similar rejection. In fact, even though I have been "out" since I was 18, I had always denied being a militant. I had answered those who had been enraged by my attempts to open the possibility of honest and open speech, that they should indicate to me a correct and nonmilitant way of speaking with honesty about a matter which affects so many people in the ecclesiastical milieu, and which leads to gossip, accusations, and frequent injustice. Of course, within the ecclesiastical milieu, there is, as yet, no such correct way. The very fact of suggesting that there is, in this field, something real in which we are involved, and about which we must try to speak if we are to have a modicum of transparency and honesty as Catholic Christians, the very suggestion is only perceived, and can only be perceived, as a threat. Where denial, mendacity, and cover-up are forces which structure a reality, the search for honest conversation is, of itself, the worst form of militancy.

Well, my reply, while formally correct, allowed me to hide from myself something which my various accusers had perceived perfectly clearly: that I was myself on a sort of crusade, that I had a zeal, and that this zeal was of a prodigiously violent force, powered by a deep resentment. In fact, I was wanting to create for myself, taking advantage of the ecclesiastical structures which sustained me, a space of security and peace, of survival. Thus I hoped to avoid what I had seen happen to gay people in country after country: social marginalization, destruction of life projects, emotional and spiritual annihilation. That is to say, my brave discourse was a mask which hid from me my absolute cowardice of soul, for I was not prepared to identify myself fully with that reality, which I knew to be mine, with all its consequences. At root, I myself believed that God was on the side of ecclesiastical violence directed at gay people, and couldn't believe that God loves us just as we are. The profound "do not *be*" which the social and ecclesiastical voice speaks to us, and which forms the soul of so many gay people, was profoundly rooted in my own being, so that, *au fond* I felt myself damned. In my violent zeal I was fighting so that the ecclesiastical structure might speak to me a "Yes," a "Flourish, son," precisely because I feared that, should I stand alone before God, God himself would be part of the "do not *be*." Thus I was absolutely dependent on the same mechanism against which I was fighting. Hiding from myself the fact of having despaired of God, I wanted to manipulate the ecclesiastical structure so that it might give me a "self," that it might speak to me a "Yes" at a level of profundity of which the ecclesiastical structure, like any human structure, is incapable. For the "Yes" which creates and recreates the "self" of a son, only God can pronounce. In this I discovered myself to be an idolater. I had been wanting to negotiate my survival in the midst of violent structures, and negotiation in the midst of violent structures can only be done by violence. The nonviolent, the blessed of the gospels, simply suffer violence and perish, either physically or morally.

I am attempting to describe for you the form taken in my life by the irruption of the extraordinary grace which I received during my Jesuit retreat. Of course, I am describing schematically something which was a nonschematic whole, and which I have taken several years to begin to understand. First there was the perception of the absolute non-involvement of God in all that violence, then the perception of my non-innocence, and of my idolatrous and violent manner of having been caught up in all that. And then, at root, what began this whole process of beginning to untie myself from the idols I had so assiduously cultivated, what I had never dared to imagine, the profound "Yes" of God, the "Yes" spoken to the little gay boy who had despaired of ever hearing it. And there, indeed, I found myself absolutely caught, because this "Yes" takes the form, not of a pretty consolation for a spoiled child. Rather, from the moment it reached me, the whole psychological and mental structure by which I had built myself up over all the previous years began to enter into a complete collapse. For the whole structure was based on the presupposition of a "No" at the center of my being, and because of that, of the need to wage a violent war so as to cover up a fathomless hole. The "I," the "self" of the child of God is born in the midst of the ruins of repented idolatry.

A further point in this narrative, if you can bear it. In the months following this incident, I had to give a course of theology. I called the course: "Fix your minds on the things that are above," taken from Paul's letter to the Colossians. Ironically, I managed to give the whole course, which has even been published in book form,[5] without tumbling to the significance of the verse which follows the one I had chosen:

for you have died, and your life is hidden with Christ in God.[6]

But it was exactly this that, at last, I was learning. The whole of my previous life had been marked by an absolute refusal to die. The absolute refusal to take on my baptismal commitment. Of course, because I was unable to imagine that my "self," the "I" who will live forever, is hidden with Christ in God. And that was why I had to fight all those battles. The "I" who was present in all those battles was the old Adam, or Cain, a "self" incapable of understanding that it is not necessary to seek to shore up for itself a place on this earth, to found a safe space, to protect itself violently against violence. The "I" of the risen one only becomes present when, at last, the old "I" is put to death. And, thank God, this was exactly what the fourteen superiors had managed to set up for me. With the force of what Paul calls the Law, that is the mechanism of violent exclusion dressed up as the word of God, they had at last managed to kill that resentful old man. In its place, being something rather like a still small voice, something which I can in no way possess, nor grasp, is the "I" from which I now start to live. The "I" that is hidden with Christ in God, little by little, and somewhat tentatively, begins to build a new life story in the midst of the ruins of the previous collapse.

Well, all of that was so as to illustrate what I have wanted to call the process of reception of a perspective from which to help forge catholic theological discourse. I will now step outside the highly risky zone of the autobiographical so as to share with you some of the hints which I am learning since I have had to start to understand theology anew, rather as someone who has had a stroke has to learn to talk again. I want to look at some themes of what used to be called fundamental moral theology. That is, rather than trying to look at a specific moral issue, I want to examine the very possibility of moral discourse starting from that theological nonplace in which I am surprised and grateful to find myself, the place of the much-loved queer.

Dead Man Talking

One of the richest and most sophisticated texts of the New Testament is the passage at the end of Luke's gospel where two demoralized disciples are walking to Emmaus. They don't recognize the traveler who joins them, nevertheless it is he who explains to them the meaning of what has just happened in Jerusalem, and he does so making use of the whole Torah and the Prophets, starting with Moses. That is to say, he makes available a new and unheard of interpretation of scripture so that they might find a new meaning in their lives and be empowered by this interpretation, until the moment when they recognize their companion in the breaking of the bread, and he vanishes. Well, you all know the story. We all know that it is a basic text for the understanding of the Eucharist: the presence of the Lord who interprets scripture, making it possible for the hearers to restructure their own imagination, and, duly fired up, go out to reconstruct the world.

Well, I'd like to draw attention to one element of this story, a story which offers not so much a key to reading scripture as an ongoing hermeneutical principle which we do not control, and which is alive independently of us and transforms us. This element is indispensable for those of us who are trying to imagine the catholic faith in the third millennium. It is the fact, little commented, that what is odd about the Emmaus story is that it is a dead man who is talking. I think it very important that we don't make the separation which we are accustomed to when talking about the risen Jesus, imagining that he is alive, and for that reason, not dead. No, what is fascinating about the doctrine of the resurrection is that it is the whole human life of Jesus, including his death, which is risen. The life of God, since it is totally outside the order of human life and human death, doesn't cancel death, as if it were a sickness which is to be cured, but takes it up, assumes it. Luke offers us a vision of a risen Jesus who has not ceased to be a dead man, and who, starting from his living-out-being-a-crucified-man, teaches and empowers his disciples by his presence.

Please indulge me as I try to suck out some juice from this apparently absurd scenario. Let us imagine a prisoner in the Louisiana state penitentiary, which, curiously enough, is called Angola, someone sentenced to die, just as in the film which many of you will have seen, *Dead Man Walking*. Well, the prisoner is led to the execution chamber, and, at the very same instant in which the doctors pronounce him dead, he becomes entirely free of the law, and of the social and police structures of the state of Louisiana, as indeed of the Federal Government of the United States. Now, follow me with your imagination. The moment he is free, not only of the law, but of social structures, life commitments like marriage, and so on, he is also absolutely free of resentment. If we imagine him a guy who had been completely opposed to the process which led him to his death, one who protested his innocence, and who considered the use of the death penalty to be an atrocity, then, up till the moment of his death he imagined himself as a victim of all that. His presence was characterized by a tremendous struggle to prevent them taking him to his death, a struggle which was, of course, ineffectual in the face of the strength and weapons of the forces of public order of the State of Louisiana.

Now, the moment he dies, he's completely free of that whole game of power and victimization of which he was part, no longer is he struggling with those powers: he doesn't have to, for they have no dominion over him, they no longer affect him in any way at all. The resentment disappears completely, because resentment only has its place within that game. Let's stretch the fantasy a little more: since the powers of the law, of social custom, and so on, no longer affect him, our dead man can begin completely to restructure his imagination with respect to his previous experience of life in the State of Louisiana. For the first time he begins to see it from the perspective of one who is no longer resentful and pushed around by it. Perhaps he's not much interested by his former life, and heads off elsewhere, no longer weighed down by what he lived. But let us imagine that he does take an interest in Louisiana, in such a way that, now that he sees things with a certain clarity, he wants to help build a better, more just, State. So he becomes present to other people, people totally caught up, as we all are, in the reigning social, political, and economic structures, in order to help them understand what they are really doing in their way of leading their lives and their social belonging. Thus, little by little, they will be enabled to undo all that is sacrificial and resentful in all that, at every level, economic, social, military, religious, and begin to be able to live with the same freedom which he now enjoys.

Well, of course, the example is at least as misleading as it is useful, and that's why I've called it a fantasy. However it's a fantasy in the service of something which is not a fantasy, but a rather important theological point. When we speak of the risen Jesus speaking to the disciples on the road to Emmaus, we are talking about a dead man, totally free from resentment. For this reason he is not present as an accusation, seeking to avenge himself on his executioners. He is present as one who begins to make of the story of his life and death a way of opening the imagination of his disciples, offering a new interpretation of texts which they already knew, so that they, not yet dead, might begin to live from then on with the same lack of resentment, free as he is from being bound in by laws and sacrificial customs, aiming for the construction of a human way of being together not marked by the powers of death.

Now, please notice a word which I have used a great deal in this explanation: it is the word resentment. Resentment, which is typically incarnate in our world as a seeking to protect oneself against death, and, because of that, in considering oneself a victim, is exactly the opposite of grace. A resentful presence is exactly the reverse of a gratuitous presence. A gratuitous presence isn't trying to protect itself against anything, isn't insisting on anything for itself, nor is there as part of the give and take of resentful reciprocity. It is not seeking to establish itself, because it does not fear disappearing, ending, or being destroyed. Well, what I'd like to do now is to suggest some hints of an imagination of a Catholic moral theology which starts from this place of the one who, as a dead man, has no need to establish himself. One capable of offering a nonsacrificial, eucharistic, constructive critique which aims at the bringing about of a fraternity not marked by death. This we can do if we attend to the Pauline verse which I quoted to you before: "Fix your minds on the things that are above . . . because you have died and your life is hid with Christ in God."

Towards a Eucharistic Morality

Let us return to the place from which I told you that I'd like to begin my approach to catholic moral theology, that of the much-loved queer. Those many of you who are not gay will discover, I hope, by means of a small imaginative leap, changing some details, that this place is not entirely alien either to your interests or your experience. The experience of many gay people is that the Church in some way or other kills us. Typically in official discourse we are a "they," dangerous people whose most notable characteristic is not a shared humanity, but a tendency to commit acts considered to be gravely objectively disordered. Typically our inclusion within the structures of Church life comes at a very high price: that of agreeing not to speak honestly, of disguising our experience with a series of euphemisms, of having to maintain, through a coded language shared with other "insiders" within the system, a double life. The message is: you're fine just so long as you don't rock the boat through talking frankly, which is the same as saying: "You're protected while you play the game our way, but the moment that something 'comes to light,' you're out. The moment you say something which causes scandal, Watch out!" And please notice that the scandal in question is not a scandal for a great part of the heterosexual population, who tend to be indifferent to all this, when not mildly amused by what they always suspected. It is a scandal for the group which fears the consequences for itself of the revelation of truths about its group composition.

In this the non-explicit message of the ecclesiastical mechanism is exactly the reverse of the explicit message of the Church. The explicit message is: God loves you just as you are, and it is from where you are that you are invited to build with us the banquet of the kingdom. The latent message is: God loves you just so long as you hide what you are and deny yourself the search for the integrity and transparency of life and of virtues which it is your task to teach to others. Here I am speaking, of course, not only of the clerical and religious world, whether masculine or feminine, but of any instance sponsored by the Church – teachers in catholic schools, doctors and nurses in catholic hospitals, young people in catholic youth groups, journalists in catholic newspapers, and so on.

It seems to me that in the face of all this, there have been two typical reactions: that of pathological loyalty, and that of pathological rejection. Pathological loyalty, we all know it: the inability, or the unwillingness, to distinguish between the violent sacred of the ecclesiastical institution and the revelation of the love of God, and the consequent suppression of the latter in favor of the former. That is to say, participation in the Church is founded on an act of sacrifice of the "other" who causes perplexity, even when that "other" includes a large part, and maybe the best part, of the "I" of many of its loyal members. All this is, no doubt, tremendously obvious. More interesting is the other reaction, that of pathological rejection. This is the entirely comprehensible reaction of those who are so scandalized by ecclesiastical violence that they either abandon the faith completely, at least in an ecclesially recognizable form, or seek to form groups of resistance. Typically the aim is the building up of the soul and the recovery of the psychological well-being of people who have been seriously traumatized, at deep levels of their being, by their experience with the moral and pastoral voice of the Church. And not only of the Church, but the voice of society mediated by parents, schools, and mass media. In the United States a great part of the voice which has been raised, demanding an attitude that is at least minimally Christian on the part of the ecclesiastical authorities, comes from people, or groups of people of this sort. Typically this protest lays hold of the sciences of the individual, brandishing the truths of psychology against ecclesiastical barbarism and ignorance.

Well, here we are faced with a dead end. The tendency of the ecclesiastical institution is to privilege the social group with its expulsive mechanisms, saying: the "we" must prevail, and the dangerous "I" must either be lost, or expelled. The tendency of the group which identifies itself by its victim status is to privilege the "I," expelling or seeking to expel the "we," considering it as a hostile and dangerous element, transforming it into a "they," an implacable enemy. Well, where the "we" transforms a possible "I" into a "one of them," and when the "I" sees a possible "we" only as a dangerous and perverse "they," then we are faced with a symmetry of enemy twins which is without possible rescue. We are back with those deaf trumpetings which characterize the moral struggle in the world of so-called postmodernity. We are without the possibility of a cracking of heart, and without the possibility of Eucharist.

However there is another possibility, not so much a theoretical possibility, as one of praxis. And it is the occupation by much-loved queers of the space of the heart-close-to-cracking. In the midst of this space the dead and risen Christ offers us the means for the edification of a victimless sacred. A sacred where the "we" creates and recreates the "I" and where the "I" receives its identity as a child of God from a "we" to which it contributes without resentment, learning to stretch out the hand to other victims, yet to be identified. Now this is, I am quite sure, immensely difficult, emotionally, intellectually, and spiritually. But the Gospel itself, considered as a program for reconstruction in the midst of the ruins, which means, read eucharistically, offers us many elements for the task.

Consider quite how extraordinary is this verse from St. Matthew:

And call no man your father on earth, for you have one Father, who is in heaven. [7]

This verse, read from amongst the ruins, suggests a rather remarkable perspective: that Jesus taught that there is on earth no analog for divine paternity, and that divine paternity can only come to be known by means of learning fraternity with him. This would be the meaning of Jesus' reply to Philip in John's Gospel when Philip asks him:

Lord, show us the Father and we shall be satisfied. [8]

Jesus replies:

He who has seen me has seen the Father. [9]

Indeed, if there is no earthly paternity capable of reflecting God, and we only accede to the paternity of God by means of learning fraternity with Jesus, who is at exactly the same level as us, that is, who is a human being, then we can begin to understand that the apparent fatherhood of this world is not fatherhood in the divine sense, but fratricidal fraternity dressed up as fatherhood. This is exactly what Jesus says to a group of his interlocutors who were denying his teaching that his Father cannot be identified with the group paternity to which they subscribed, calling themselves sons of Abraham:

You are of your father the devil, and your will is to do your father's desires. He was a murderer from the beginning, and has nothing to do with the truth, because there is no truth in him. [10]

Let me insist a little on the extraordinary anthropological rupture which this phrase produces. When we grasp on to any form of earthly paternity, seeking to establish our identity from this paternity, then we are ignoring the fact that the principle of earthly paternity, that is, the element which has structured it from within since the beginning, was the primeval murder, that of Abel by Cain. All human paternity comes internally structured by fratricide and, *as paternity*, is incapable of truth, because it will always be protecting itself against the "other."

Just in case you think I'm making this up, let's go back to Matthew, to the verse before the one I quoted to you:

> But you are not to be called Rabbi, for you have one teacher and you are all brethren.[11]

That is to say, in Matthew, Jesus inverts the order which would be natural to us. We typically imagine that biology is prior to culture, and so that first should come the phrase about paternity: "One alone is your Father who is in heaven, and you are all brethren. And don't let anyone call you Rabbi, because one alone is your Master." However, in fact Jesus doesn't share our mentality. For him, here, as in John, it is culture which comes before biology. Fraternity is the matrix of our cultural formation, and because of that we have to attend to our absolute equality in the matter of learning about things divine, so as to avoid false attributions of divinity to nonfraternal ways of presenting the divine truth. Within this matrix of the apprenticeship of fraternity we also have to learn to deconstruct the false paternity of this world, for even biological paternity is nothing other than intergenerational fraternity, and thus capable of being exercised constructively or destructively.

Well, if all human paternity comes internally structured by fratricide, this opens up for us some extraordinary possibilities for the Eucharistic construction of fraternity. For example, I suspect that I'm not the only person to have imagined and received the whole force of the social, cultural, and ecclesiastical hatred of gay people as if it were a paternal force. A crushing paternal force which demanded that I either buckle under or die, or both at the same time. And of course, against paternal force there is no right of reply, since none of us is at the same level as the paternal. And for that reason, the relation, being between unequal parties, can never truly be one of love. For love depends on equality. Nor, in the case of being crushed, can there truly be forgiveness, for forgiveness also can only really take place between equals – in fact it is what is creative of equality.

Now if, as Jesus teaches, this imagination of the paternal as a crushing and murderous force is not real, but mythical, for the paternal is only fratricidal fraternity dressed up as paternity, then, yes indeed, one can forgive, really and constructively. If the eucharistic presence of the crucified and risen Christ is the fraternal presence which returns not as accusation but as forgiveness, and as a presence which opens up the imagination so that we recognize our complicities and begin to construct forgiveness, then indeed the place of the much-loved queer is a place from which one can begin to reimagine the Church fraternally. We can begin to look at the whole institutional structure not as a paternal and devastating "they," but begin to imagine it as an occasionally fratricidal "we." The moment we begin to perceive that what seemed to be something paternal is only a bad fraternity, which exercises itself fratricidally, then we can begin to rethink every instance of how it works, how it teaches, how it treats people. And we do so not from the perspective of one who accuses it while on the way to being victimized by it, but from that of one who always forgives, and is, even if rejected and killed, on the way to offering new possibilities of life.

Let us try an example. If the teaching of the Church is, and can only be, at the fraternal level, then we have not only the right, but the duty, to undertake the task of reimagining it in such a way that what it says, and how it says it, reflects the voice of Christ. He only imagines himself as our brother, and never as our father. Here I'm not introducing a new criterion for theological discernment, but applying a distinction which Jesus himself taught:

> The scribes and the Pharisees sit on Moses' seat; so practice and observe whatever they tell you, but not what they do; for they say, but do not do.[12]

Since it is Very God of Very God, of one being with the Father, who introduces this distinction, we would do well to imitate him. Let us notice something: the instruction to "practice and observe whatever they tell you" is an unstable instruction. For, the moment Jesus introduces the distinction between "what they say and what they do," he opens up the possibility of the recognition that even "what they say" reaches us in a way that is distorted by "what they do." That is to say, the suspicion that their practice forms the framework for their teaching. Ideological suspicion is not something alien to the Gospel, but is rather close to the heart of the project of the removing of idols which characterizes Jesus' presence. However, ideological suspicion is not for the purpose of attacking, but for self-critical reconstruction. That is to say, the moment we recognize that these people are but brothers entrapped by forces which they do not understand, the same forces which tend to destroy us all, and before whose gods we have all, on many occasions, bent the knee; the moment we understand that their voice tends to reproduce at least as much the violence of those forces as it does the truth of God, then we can begin to examine the violent mechanism, bringing it into the light, because the violent mechanism is only a perversion of fraternity, and as such is capable of human analysis, and of being redirected towards a fraternity that tends to build up others.

Discourse from the position of the crushed, victimized queer can only be a voice of accusation, demanding approval. It looks at the ecclesiastical "closet" as something incurably hypocritical and violent, and so can only protest against it, rejecting the possibility that something evangelical, something emancipatory, something truthful, might come out of it. I'm suggesting that there is another possibility: the ecclesiastical "closet," since it is a reality which works at the fraternal, and not at the paternal, level, is available to rational discussion. For example, the Vatican published in 1992, during the election campaign which was won by Bill Clinton, a document directed to the US bishops. The document was an attempt to discourage catholic voters from electing candidates who were in favor of introducing legislation to protect the rights of employment, and other rights, of gay people. It says so quite explicitly. Well, this document was not well received. A number of bishops and the conference of religious superiors-general emphatically rejected not only the abusive electoral practice (evidently inspired by some republican-leaning bishops), but also the content of the document. They rejected the idea that it can be just to fight in favor of legislation which discriminates against part of the population.

Leaving this aside, some phrases in the document were very revealing of the perspective of those writing:

> As a rule, the majority of homosexually oriented persons who seek to lead chaste lives do not publicize their sexual orientation. Hence the problem of discrimination in terms of employment, housing, etc., does not usually arise. Homosexual persons who assert their homosexuality tend to be precisely those who judge homosexual behavior or lifestyle to be "either completely harmless, if not an entirely good thing," and hence worthy of public approval.[13]

So, with a certain clarity at last, the Vatican is not talking about particular sexual acts, but about strategies for survival in a recognizedly violent world. The person who remains silent within the "closet" will have no problems; the one who is "out" deserves the problems that will befall him, and no legislation should protect him.

Well, rather than treating the authors as monsters, let us question them as brothers. You are affirming something which is independent of acts committed or avoided, for it is not simply self-evident that the closeted gay man is either more or less inclined to acts held to be sinful than the one who is "out". That is, you are affirming, as part of a fraternal church teaching, that the "closet" is the most appropriate place for the human and Christian well-being and flourishing of people with a homosexual orientation. The one who "comes out," and runs the risks which may befall him, puts himself into a less propitious place for human and Christian well-being and flourishing. This is what you are affirming. We can ask: but is this true? We might ask whether, for example, chastity, a virtue which it behoves every Christian, including the married, to learn and exercise, can better be learned and exercised within the process of learning to relate honestly to a whole network of friends, and even close friends and maybe a partner, where the center of emotional and erotic gravity of those involved can be talked about? Or whether, on the contrary, chastity is best learned by detaching oneself from language, and preferring a mode of presence that is anonymous and reticent even with those closest at work, at play, in the family, and so on. The answer is not self-evident, which is why it has to be discussed.

We might ask also whether the psychological effects of remaining in the closet are more or less propitious for the process of discovering oneself a son or daughter of God than the psychological effects of "coming out" and beginning to find out what it might mean to be a child of God in the much riskier terrain of a social world where people speak quite openly about these things. We might ask: How do you reconcile the maintenance of the "closet" with the explicit teaching of the Gospel about the fact that everything hidden will be uncovered, and what is said in secret will be preached from the rooftops?[14] Perhaps there is a way of reconciling it, but you haven't made the case for the Christianity of your position, and it would be important that we understand what that position is, so as to see whether it be in continuity with Christ's teaching or not.

We might note that the, entirely correct, affirmation that the person of homosexual orientation, has, as have all Christians, to carry his cross every day, is capable of two interpretations. The interpretation of the closet suggests that the sacrifice demanded by God is that of the "I" understood as something which seeks its flourishing in a necessarily disordered manner. This would be the application to the person of same-sex orientation of the phrase:

> If any one would come after me, let him deny himself and take up his cross daily and follow me.[15]

However, there exists another interpretation, that of those who declare themselves. Here the denial of self and the taking up of the cross correspond, among other things, to an insistence on living in a worthy and honest way in a social milieu which tends to count those gay people who strive for honesty, as it counts all people who seek to live with a certain integrity, amongst the transgressors, and for this reason to despise, calumniate, and crucify them. It is not evident that the interpretation which calls for a search for the private holocaust of the "self" be necessarily a more Christian interpretation than the one where, in order to create a more fraternal life for self and for others, a person every day runs the risk of various forms of public violence. About this we can dialogue.

The moment it becomes clear that we are not dealing with a monstrous sacred block, but of strategies for survival each of which have implications about how human well-being and flourishing are understood, then the closet becomes something about which we can dialogue.

Of course, we may indeed find brothers and sisters who do not want to dialogue about this. Perhaps for such people the question of the well-being of their brothers and sisters is less important than the maintenance of doctrine, and the recommendation against "coming out" is only a manner of avoiding the further discussion of the matter. If there are people who really do think that man is made for the Sabbath rather than the Sabbath for man, then it would be very difficult to proceed. However, in fact, there will always be brethren, even in very high ecclesiastical positions, who understand that it is their task to help interpret doctrines in such a way that they don't become idols which demand sacrifice and go against the well-being of their brothers and sisters. With such people one can indeed dialogue about ways of conceiving human well-being.

However, here we tread on a very difficult terrain. For, in a dialogue, who will represent the "closet"? Cannot this only be done by someone who isn't in it? For, the moment someone undertakes to represent the closet in a dialogue, either it is a "straight" person who has to recognize a limited capacity to represent well people of whose state of life he with difficulty has deep knowledge. Or it is someone who, by the very fact of speaking, "comes out." An accusatory mentality would rejoice at this evident difficulty. But the forgiving mentality, which tries to understand the expulsive mechanism as, at root, a phenomenon at the fraternal level, rather takes it as a sign that we must proceed with extreme delicacy and gentleness towards brothers who are unable to speak for themselves. And I say unable not only in the formal sense, because speaking out would be coming out, but in the deeper sense: perhaps they are unable to start from a viable "self" capable of creating fraternity through the medium of language. Maybe their conscience is so deeply bound by the supposed paternity which is in fact a form of fratricide that they are incapable of imagining themselves as much-loved children, except by rejecting themselves completely. For such reasons many people have killed themselves, whether physically or morally, and there we do indeed need to remember the still, small voice:

> A bruised reed he will not break, and a dimly burning wick he will not quench; he will faithfully bring forth justice.[16]

Well, if we reach this point, this space close to a cracking of heart, we have creatively to imagine into existence something much more glorious, much more merciful. In the face of those who have no voice, we must, above all, avoid being strong with the weak.[17] Rather we have to rework Catholic moral theology in such a way as to make it capable of unbinding the consciences of people who fear, at a very deep level, receiving the conscience of a child of God. We have to offer, in a nonthreatening way, the possibility of being introduced into the dynamic movement which I have tried to sketch out, of becoming detached from idols so as to receive divine sonship. We have to learn how to present in a much clearer way something which I have only begun very superficially to sketch out. The lovingkindness and audacity of God who invites us just as we are to create fraternity by means of the crucified and risen brother who opens up our minds to imagine the new Jerusalem in the midst of the ruins of all our idolatries, all our acts of cowardice. No small task for the third millennium.

Notes

1 1 Kings 19:10.
2 1 Kings 19:14.
3 1 Kings 19:4.
4 Gal 1:11–17.
5 *Raising Abel* (Crossroad: New York 1996). The same book was published in 1998 in the UK by SPCK, who changed the title to *Living in the End Times*.
6 Col. 3:1–3.
7 Mat. 23:9.
8 John 14:8.
9 John 14:9.
10 John 8:44.
11 Mat. 23:8.
12 Mat. 23: 2–3.
13 "Responding to Legislative Proposals on Discrimination Against Homosexuals," para. 14, taken from *Origins*, Aug. 6, 1992, vol. 22, no. 10. The quote is from the CDF's 1986 letter concerning "The Pastoral Care of Homosexual Persons." [Reprinted here.]
14 Luke 12:3.
15 Luke 9:23.
16 Isaiah 42:3.
17 Cf. 1 Cor. 10:23–30.

Appendix: Biblical Resources

1 Creation and Categorization
  a. Two creation accounts (Genesis 1:26–31, 2:15–24)
  b. Prohibitions of category-crossing (Leviticus 11:1–19, 18:1–30, 19:1–4, 19)
2 This Was the Sin of Your Sister Sodom
  a. Hospitality of Abraham, Sodom and Gomorrah (Genesis 18:1–33, 19:1–29)
  b. The Unnamed Woman (Judges 19:1–30, 20:1–6)
  c. Characterizations of the Sin of Sodom by Deuteronomy, Ezekiel, Amos, Jesus, and Paul (Deuteronomy 29:22–7, Ezekiel 16:6–48, 53–5, Amos 4:11, Matthew 10:14–15, Romans 9:27–9)
  d. Sex with Angels (Jude 6–7)
3 The Kingdom of Heaven Is Like a Wedding Feast
  a. God the Lover of Israel in the Prophets (Song of Songs 1:1–17, 2:8–17, 5:2–8, 8:6–7, Hosea 1:1–10, 2:1–2, 11:1–4, Isaiah 62:4–5, Ezekiel. 16:1–14)
  b. Wedding Feast, Wise and Foolish Bridesmaids (Matthew 8:11, 9:15, 22:1–14, 25:1–13)
  c. The Ring and Feasting of the Prodigal (Luke 5:34–5, 15:22–3)
  d. Reciprocity (I Corinthians 7:1–7)
  e. The Nature of Love (I Corinthians 13:1–12)
  f. Mirroring the Love of God (Ephesians 5:22–33)
  g. The Wedding of the Lamb (Rev. 19:9, 21:2, 9; 22:17)

4   "It runs in the family," or Jesus's Women Ancestors
- a.   Women Named in the Genealogy of Jesus (Matthew 1:1–18)
- b.   Tamar (Genesis 38:1–30)
- c.   Rahab the Harlot (Joshua 2:1–24)
- d.   David and "the Wife of Uriah" (II Samuel 11:1–26, 12:1–24)

5   "Biblical Sexuality"
- a.   Abraham and Hagar (Genesis 16:1–15)
- b.   Rachel and Leah (Genesis 29)
- c.   Solomon's Wives (I Kings 11:1–13)

6   Same-sex Relationships?
- a.   David and Jonathan (I Samuel 18:1–30, 19:1–24, 20:1–42, II Samuel 1:1–27)
- b.   Ruth and Naomi (Ruth 1:1–22, 2:1–23, 3:1–18, 4:1–22)
- c.   The Entimos Pais (Matthew 8:5–13)

7   Sex, Gentiles, and How the Church Changes
- a.   Gentiles and God Act in Excess of Nature (Romans 1:8–32, 2:1–11, 11:13–24)
- b.   Gentiles Receive the Spirit (Acts 10:1–48, 11:1–18)

Scripture Index

Scriptural references appear in roman typeface, page numbers in italic.

General Index

Authors represented in this anthology are referenced in **bold**.